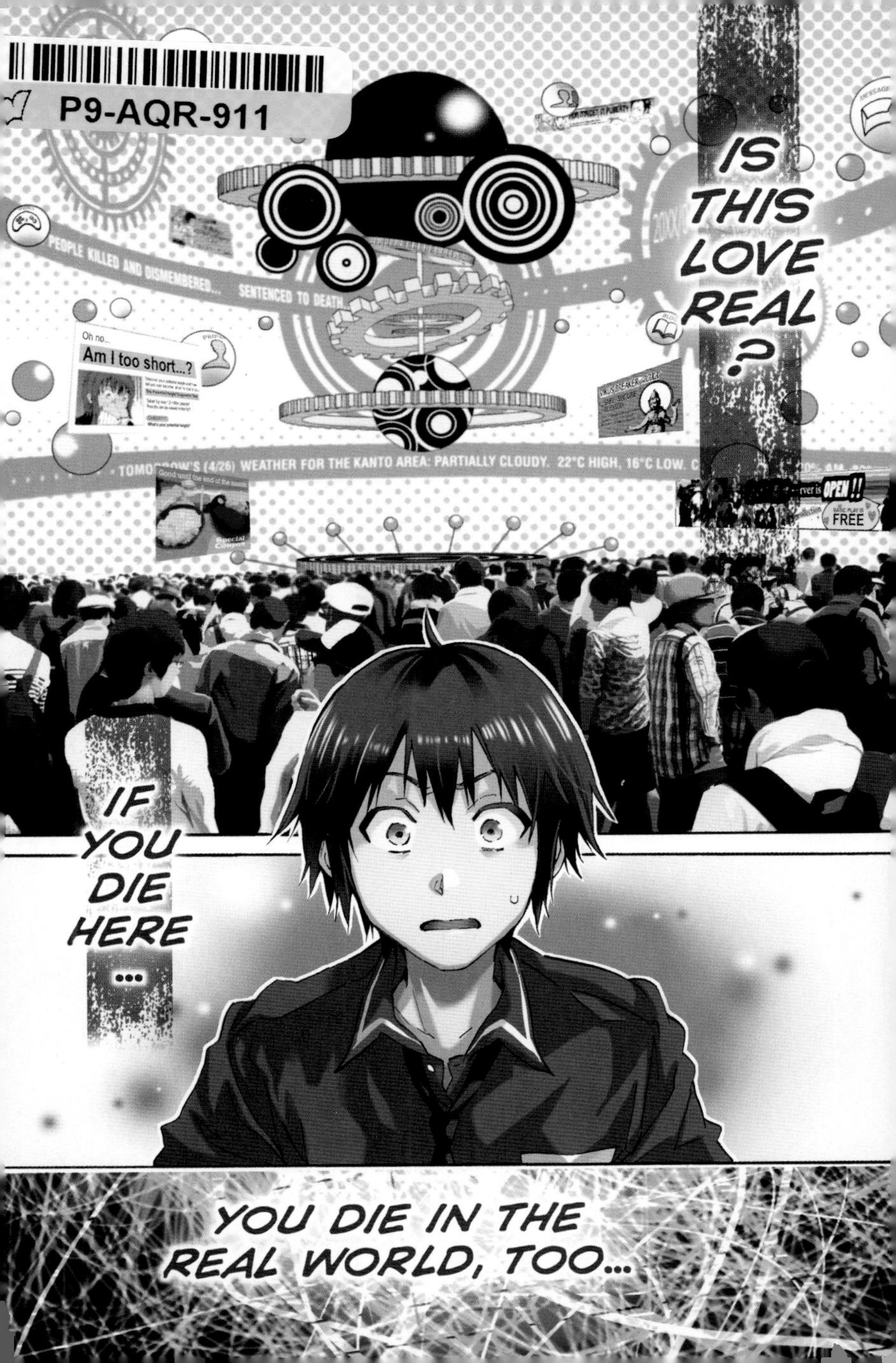
IS THIS LOVE REAL?
PEOPLE KILLED AND DISMEMBERED... SENTENCED TO DEATH
Oh no...
Am I too short...?
WEATHER FOR THE KANTO AREA: PARTIALLY CLOUDY. 22°C HIGH, 16°C LOW.
OPEN!!
BASIC PLAY IS FREE
Special Coupon
IF YOU DIE HERE...
YOU DIE IN THE REAL WORLD, TOO...

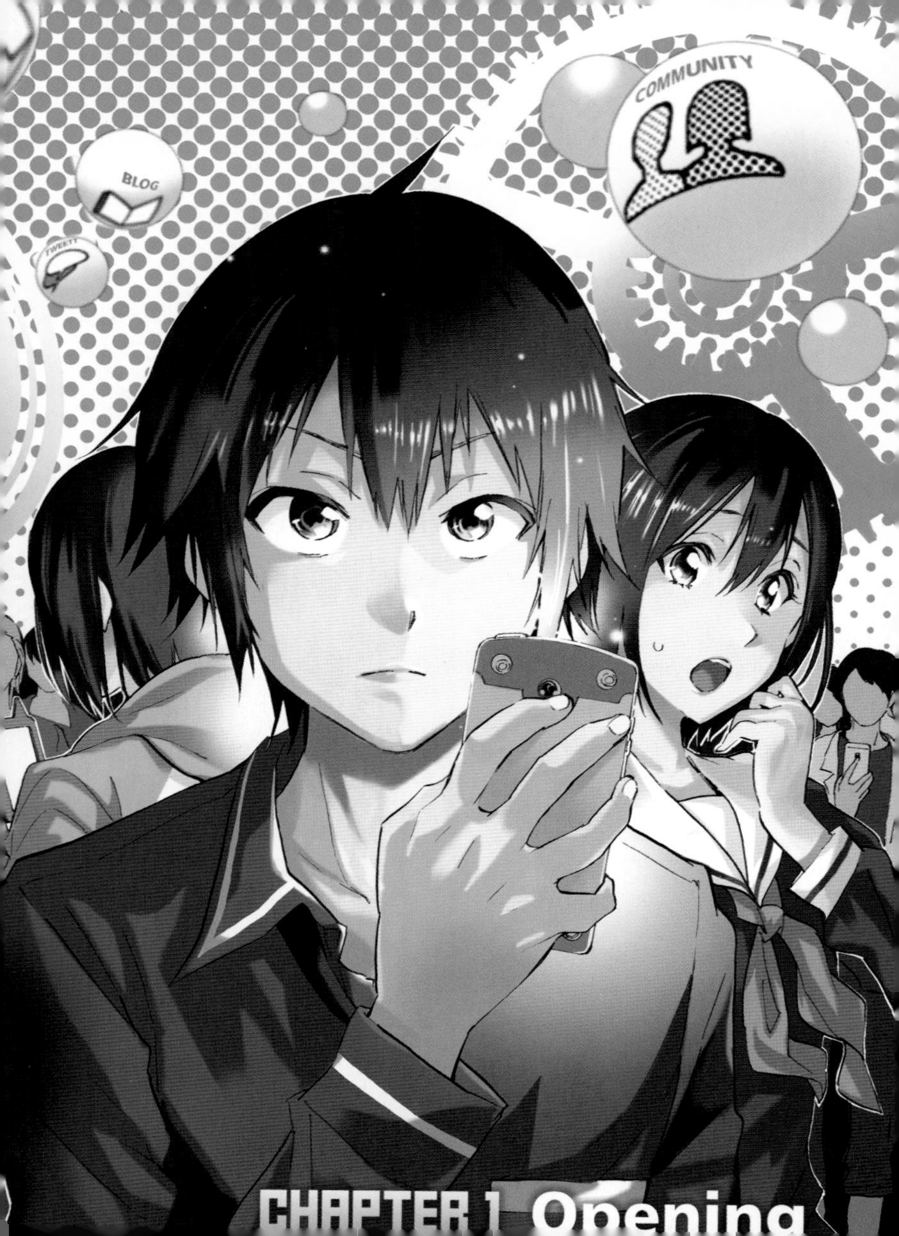
COMMUNITY
BLOG

CHAPTER 1 Opening

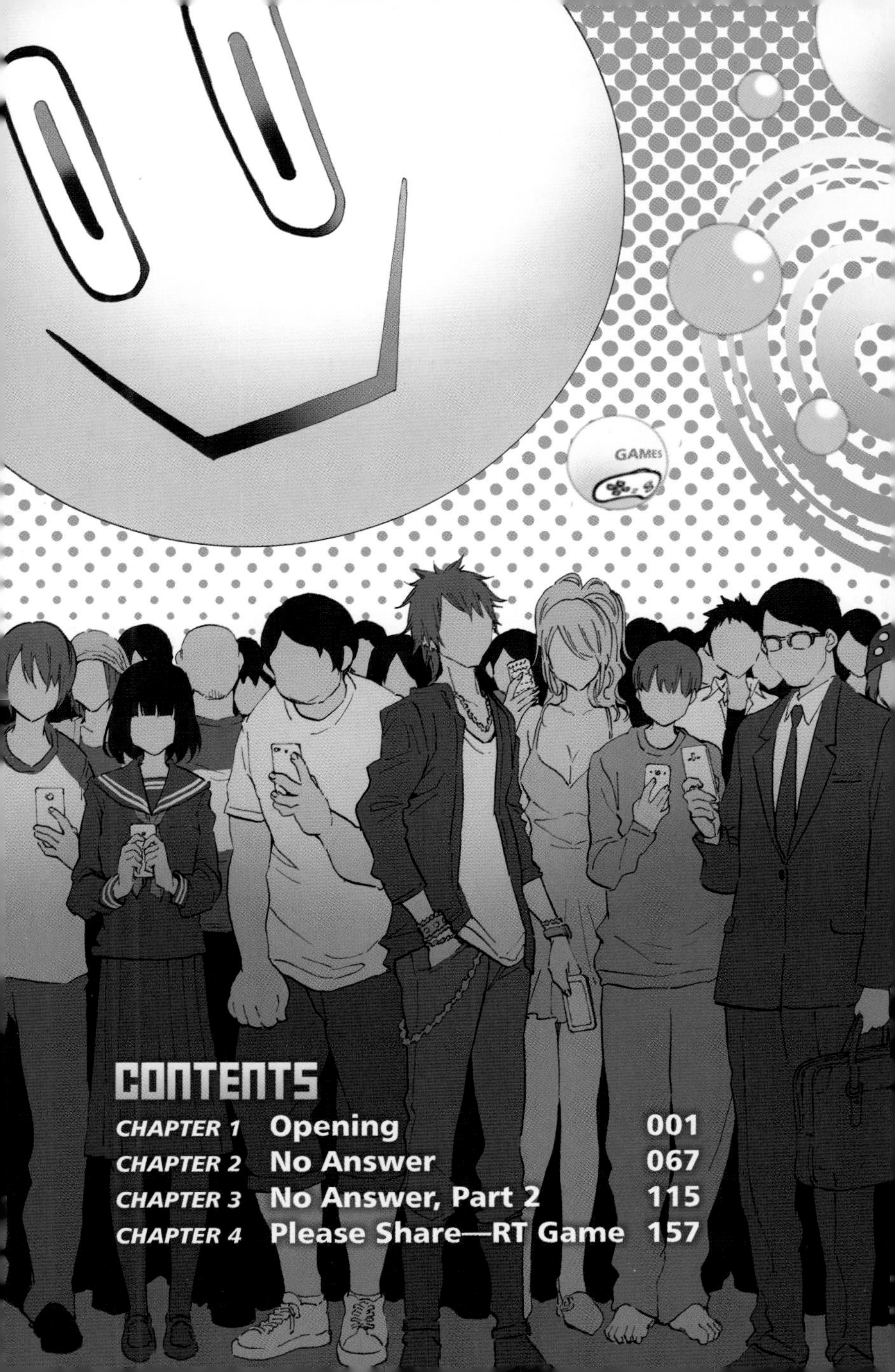
GAMES

CONTENTS

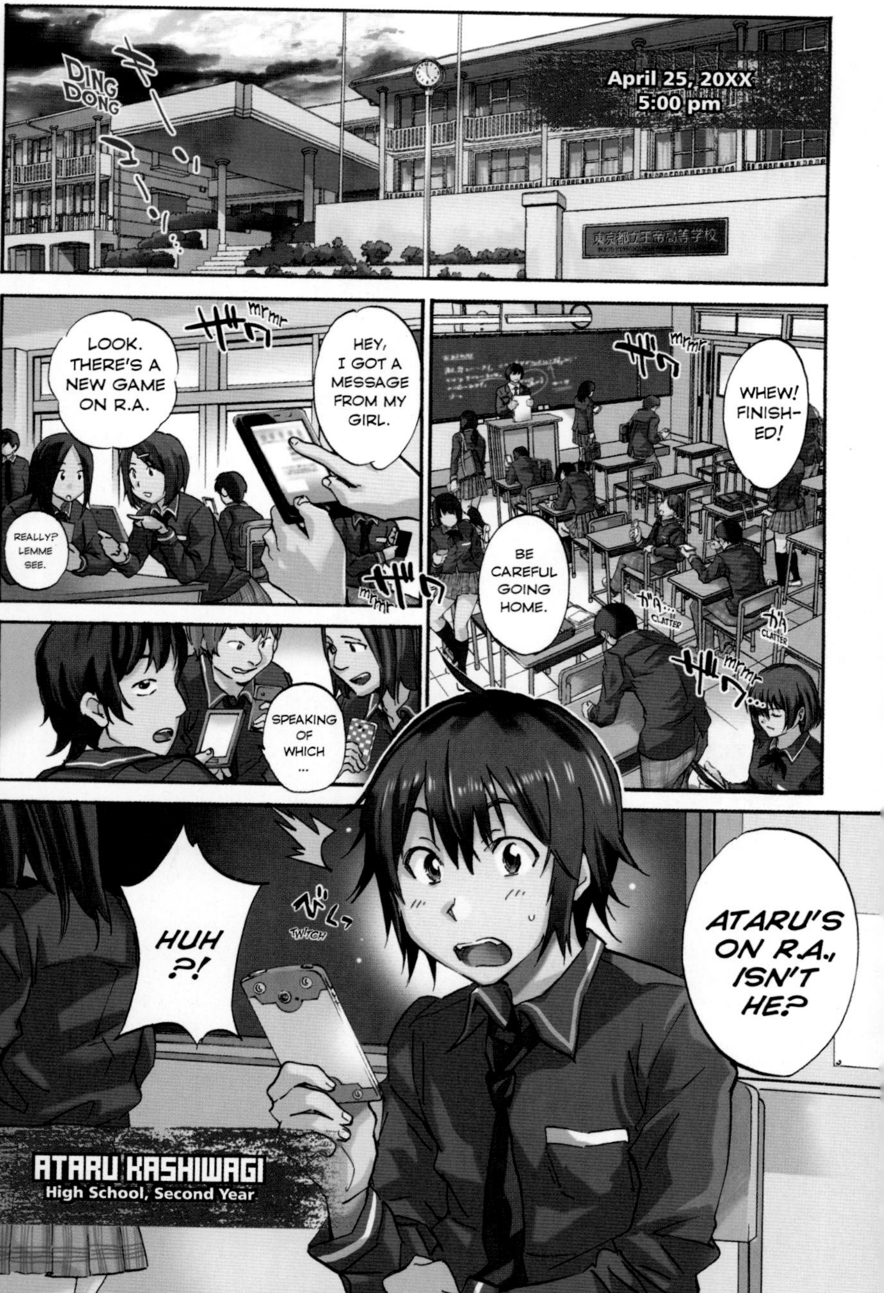
April 25, 20XX
5:00 pm
DING DONG
東京都立王帝高等学校
mrmr
WHEW! FINISHED!
BE CAREFUL GOING HOME.
CLATTER
CLATTER
mrmr
mrmr
HEY, I GOT A MESSAGE FROM MY GIRL.
LOOK. THERE'S A NEW GAME ON R.A.
REALLY? LEMME SEE.
mrmr
SPEAKING OF WHICH ...
ATARU'S ON R.A., ISN'T HE?
TWITCH
HUH ?!
ATARU KASHIWAGI
High School, Second Year

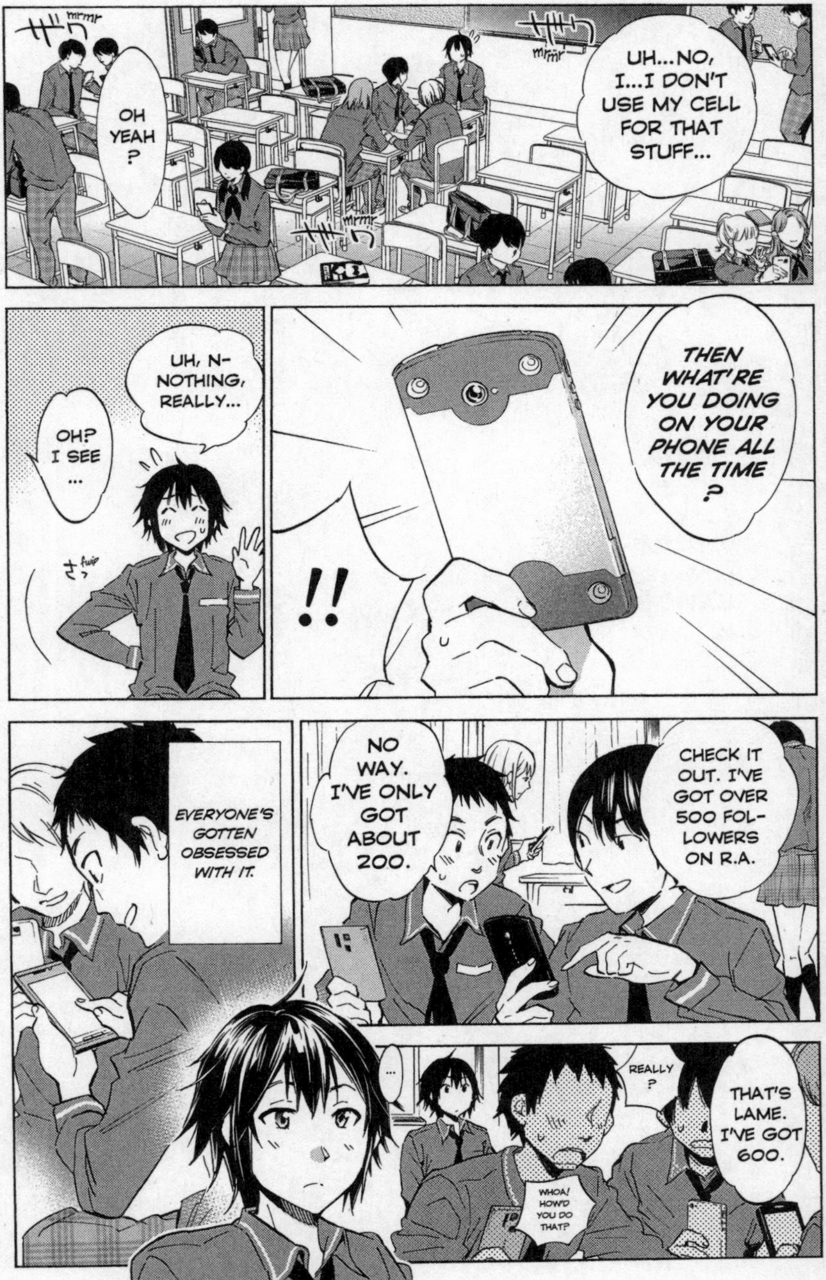
UH...NO, I...I DON'T USE MY CELL FOR THAT STUFF...
ザワ mrmr
ザワ mrmr
ザワ mrmr
OH YEAH?
THEN WHAT'RE YOU DOING ON YOUR PHONE ALL THE TIME?
!!
UH, N-NOTHING, REALLY...
OH? I SEE...
さっ fwip
CHECK IT OUT. I'VE GOT OVER 500 FOL-LOWERS ON R.A.
NO WAY. I'VE ONLY GOT ABOUT 200.
THAT'S LAME. I'VE GOT 600.
REALLY?
WHOA! HOW'D YOU DO THAT?
...
EVERYONE'S GOTTEN OBSESSED WITH IT.

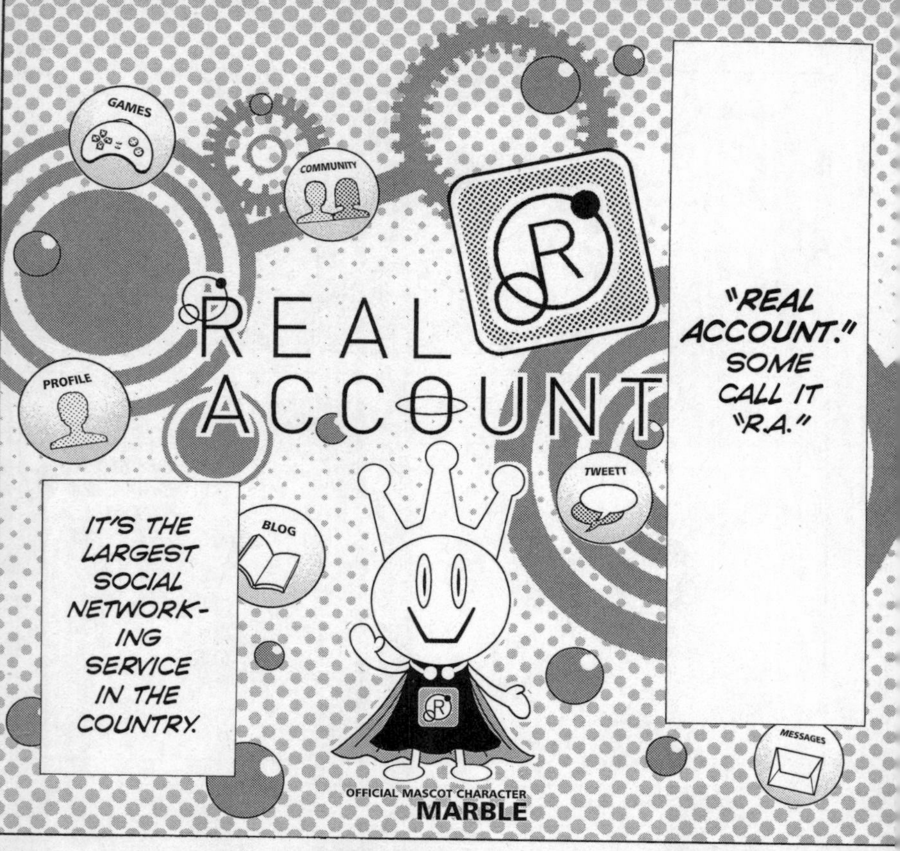
"REAL ACCOUNT." SOME CALL IT "R.A."
GAMES
COMMUNITY
REAL ACCOUNT
PROFILE
TWEETT
BLOG
MESSAGES
IT'S THE LARGEST SOCIAL NETWORKING SERVICE IN THE COUNTRY.
OFFICIAL MASCOT CHARACTER
MARBLE
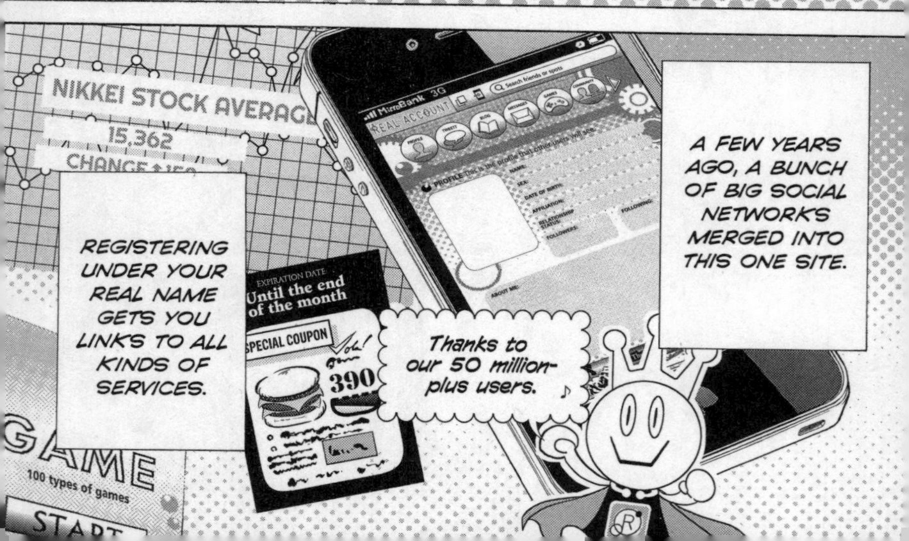
A FEW YEARS AGO, A BUNCH OF BIG SOCIAL NETWORKS MERGED INTO THIS ONE SITE.
Thanks to our 50 million-plus users. ♪
REGISTERING UNDER YOUR REAL NAME GETS YOU LINKS TO ALL KINDS OF SERVICES.
NIKKEI STOCK AVERAGE
15,362
EXPIRATION DATE
Until the end of the month
SPECIAL COUPON
390
GAME
100 types of games

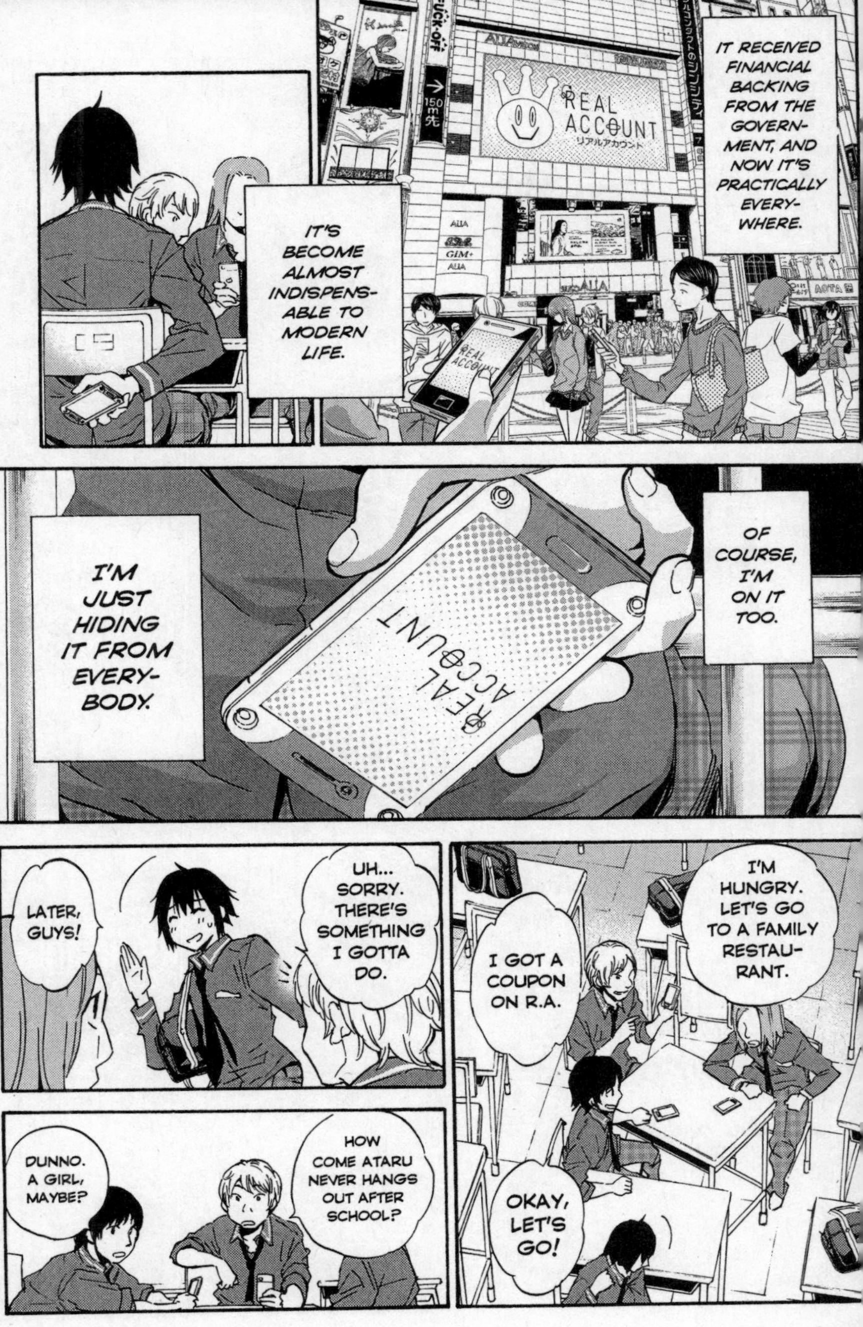
IT RECEIVED FINANCIAL BACKING FROM THE GOVERN-MENT, AND NOW IT'S PRACTICALLY EVERY-WHERE.
REAL ACCOUNT
リアルアカウント
REAL ACCOUNT
IT'S BECOME ALMOST INDISPENS-ABLE TO MODERN LIFE.
OF COURSE, I'M ON IT TOO.
REAL ACCOUNT
I'M JUST HIDING IT FROM EVERY-BODY.
I'M HUNGRY. LET'S GO TO A FAMILY RESTAU-RANT.
I GOT A COUPON ON R.A.
OKAY, LET'S GO!
UH... SORRY. THERE'S SOMETHING I GOTTA DO.
LATER, GUYS!
HOW COME ATARU NEVER HANGS OUT AFTER SCHOOL?
DUNNO. A GIRL, MAYBE?

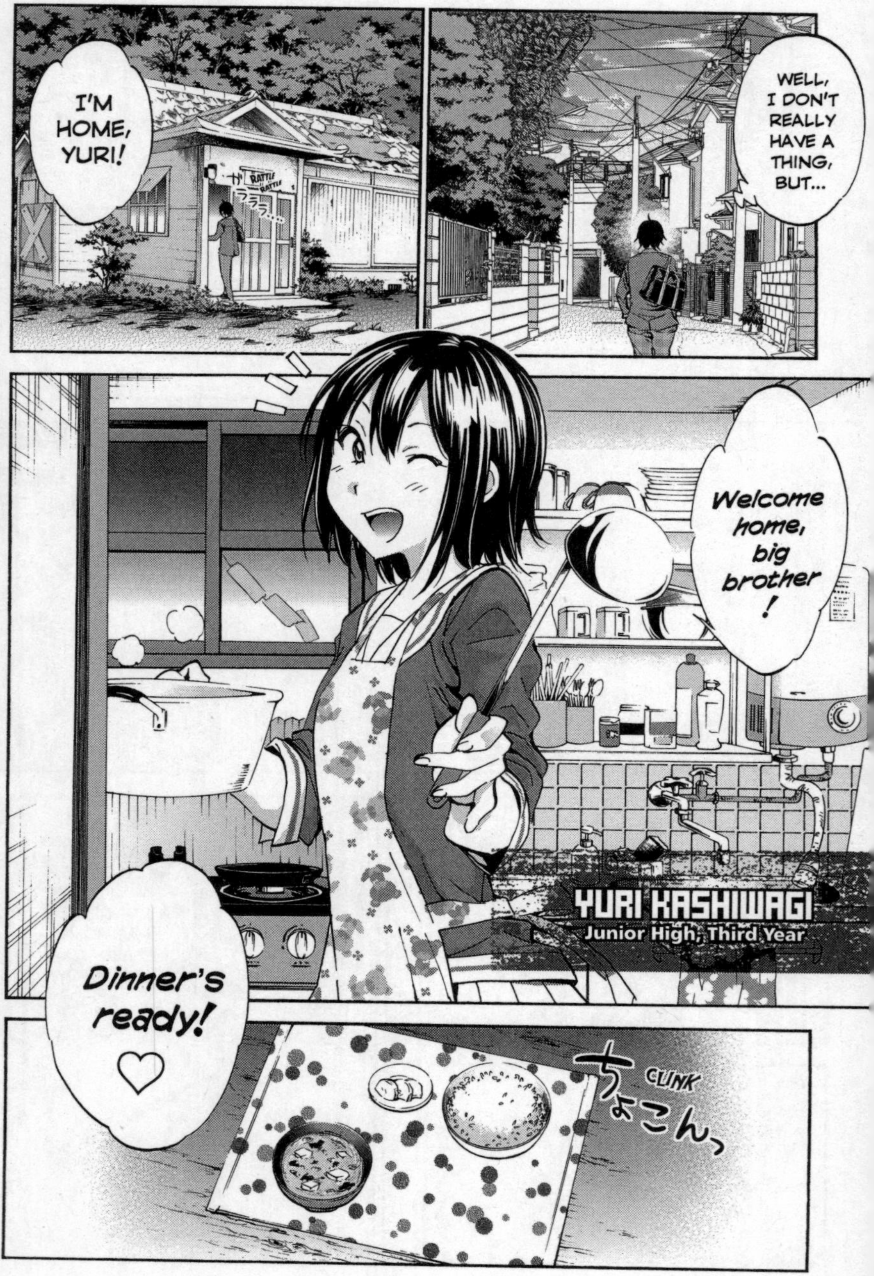
WELL, I DON'T REALLY HAVE A THING, BUT...
I'M HOME, YURI!
RATTLE RATTLE
ガラララ...
Welcome home, big brother!
YURI KASHIWAGI
Junior High, Third Year
Dinner's ready! ♡
ちょこんっ
CLINK

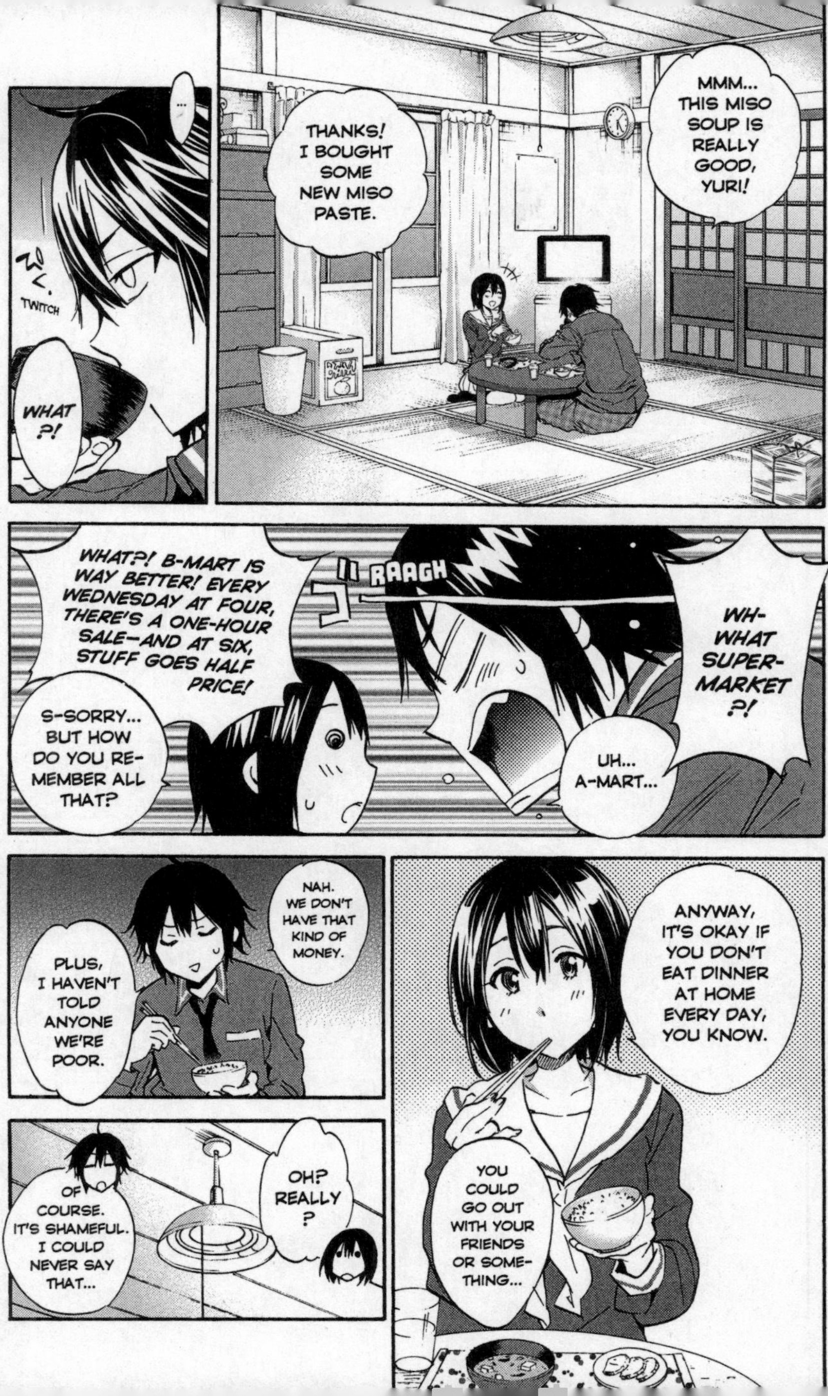

MMM... THIS MISO SOUP IS REALLY GOOD, YURI!
THANKS! I BOUGHT SOME NEW MISO PASTE.
...
TWITCH
WHAT?!
WH-WHAT SUPER-MARKET?!
UH... A-MART...
RAAGH
WHAT?! B-MART IS WAY BETTER! EVERY WEDNESDAY AT FOUR, THERE'S A ONE-HOUR SALE—AND AT SIX, STUFF GOES HALF PRICE!
S-SORRY... BUT HOW DO YOU RE-MEMBER ALL THAT?
ANYWAY, IT'S OKAY IF YOU DON'T EAT DINNER AT HOME EVERY DAY, YOU KNOW.
YOU COULD GO OUT WITH YOUR FRIENDS OR SOME-THING...
NAH. WE DON'T HAVE THAT KIND OF MONEY.
PLUS, I HAVEN'T TOLD ANYONE WE'RE POOR.
OH? REALLY?
OF COURSE. IT'S SHAMEFUL. I COULD NEVER SAY THAT...

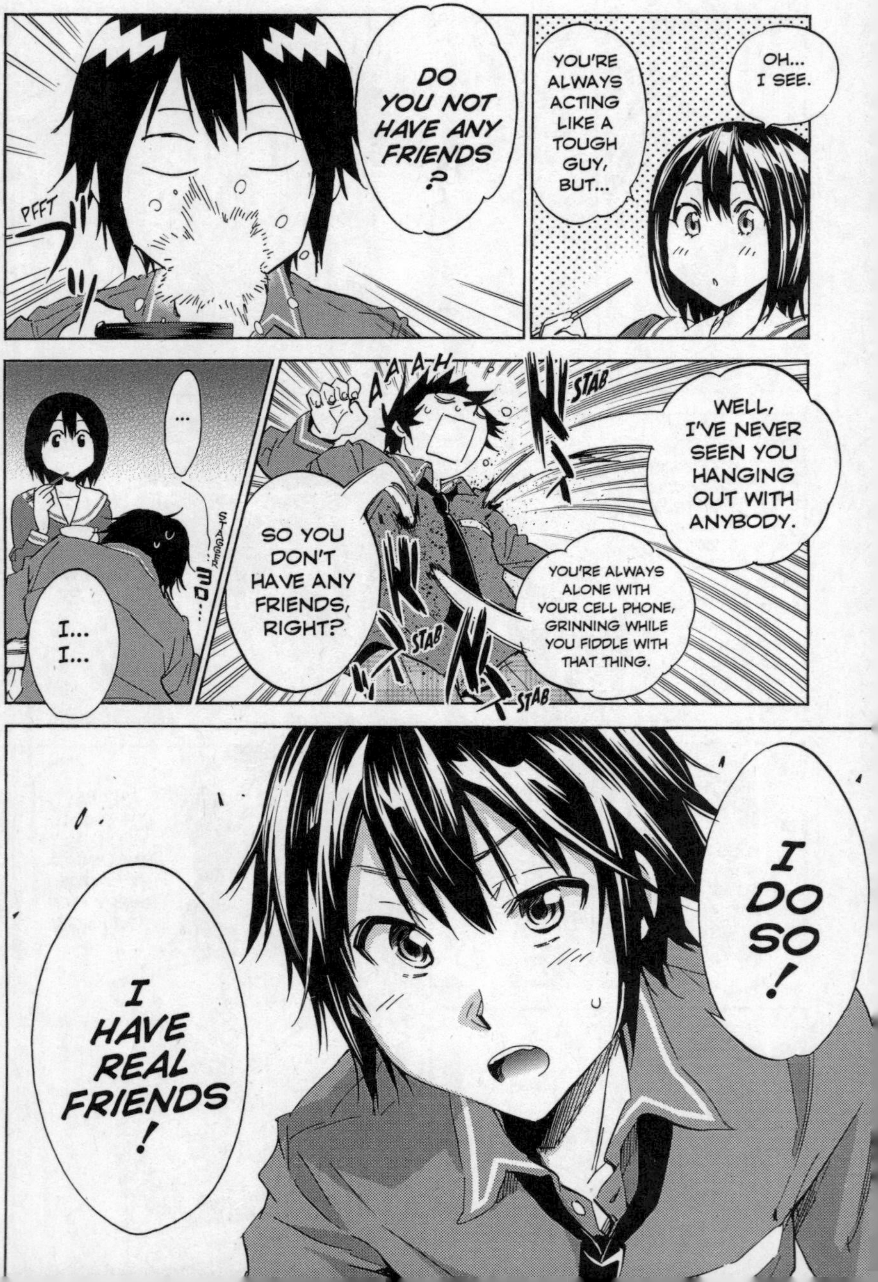
OH... I SEE.
YOU'RE ALWAYS ACTING LIKE A TOUGH GUY, BUT...
DO YOU NOT HAVE ANY FRIENDS?
PFFT
WELL, I'VE NEVER SEEN YOU HANGING OUT WITH ANYBODY.
STAB
AAAH
YOU'RE ALWAYS ALONE WITH YOUR CELL PHONE, GRINNING WHILE YOU FIDDLE WITH THAT THING.
SO YOU DON'T HAVE ANY FRIENDS, RIGHT?
STAB
STAB
...
I... I...
I DO SO!
I HAVE REAL FRIENDS!

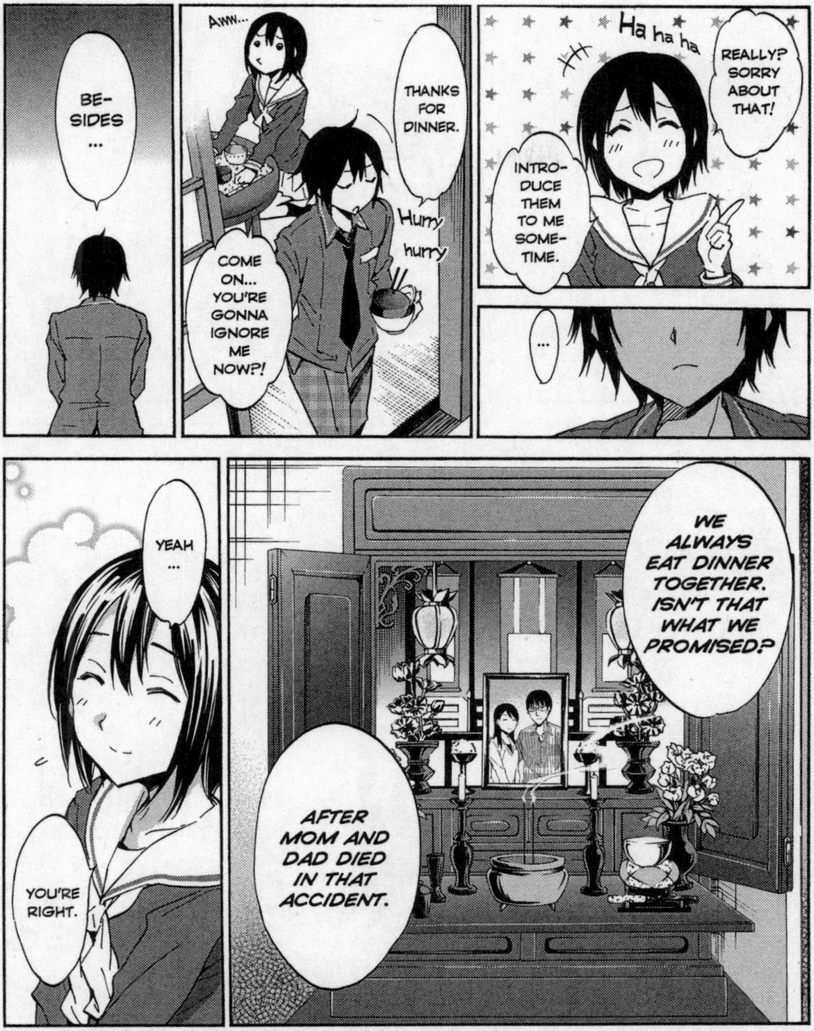
REALLY? SORRY ABOUT THAT!
Ha ha ha
INTRODUCE THEM TO ME SOMETIME.
...
THANKS FOR DINNER.
Aww...
Hurry hurry
COME ON... YOU'RE GONNA IGNORE ME NOW?!
BESIDES...
WE ALWAYS EAT DINNER TOGETHER. ISN'T THAT WHAT WE PROMISED?
AFTER MOM AND DAD DIED IN THAT ACCIDENT.
YEAH...
YOU'RE RIGHT.

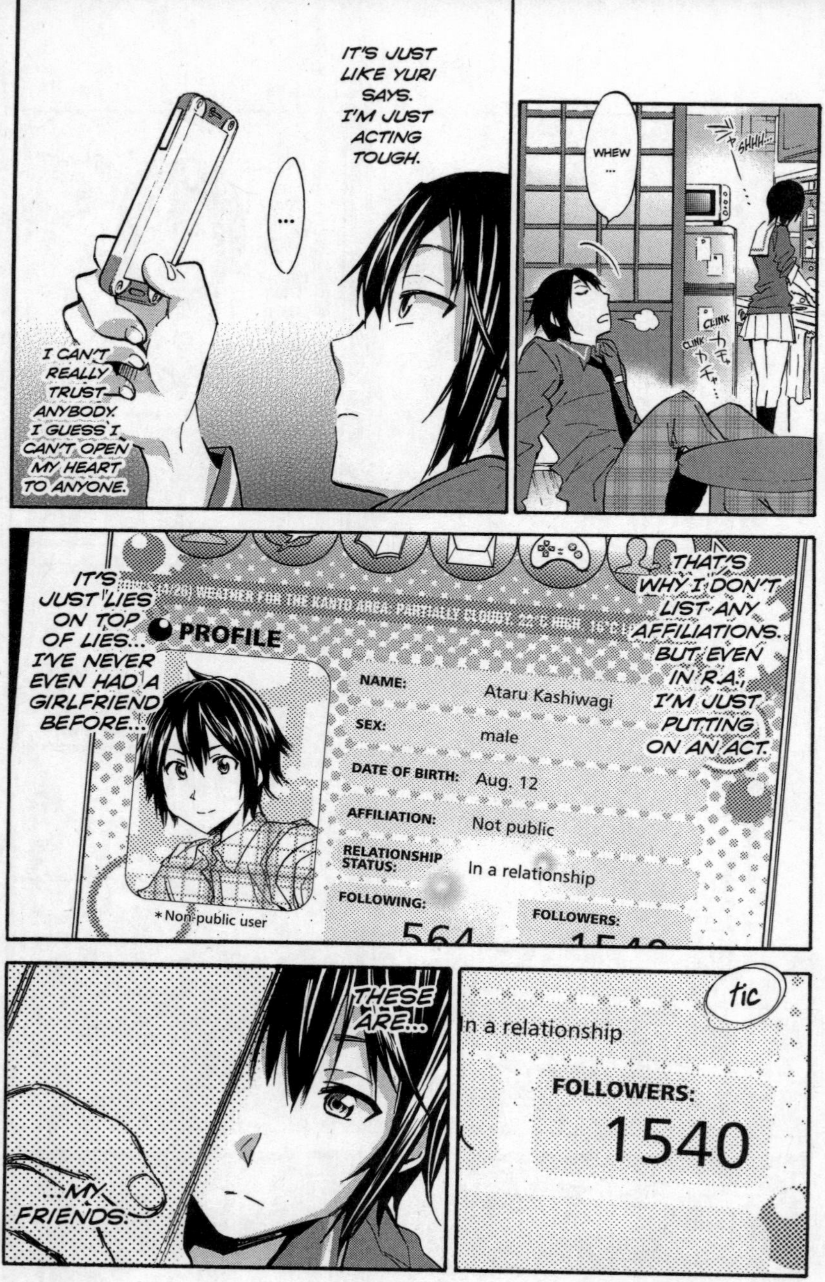
WHEW ...
SHHH...
CLINK
CLINK
IT'S JUST LIKE YURI SAYS. I'M JUST ACTING TOUGH.
...
I CAN'T REALLY TRUST ANYBODY. I GUESS I CAN'T OPEN MY HEART TO ANYONE.
THAT'S WHY I DON'T LIST ANY AFFILIATIONS. BUT EVEN IN R.A., I'M JUST PUTTING ON AN ACT.
WEATHER FOR THE KANTO AREA: PARTIALLY CLOUDY 22°C HIGH 16°C
IT'S JUST LIES ON TOP OF LIES... I'VE NEVER EVEN HAD A GIRLFRIEND BEFORE...
PROFILE
NAME: Ataru Kashiwagi
SEX: male
DATE OF BIRTH: Aug. 12
AFFILIATION: Not public
RELATIONSHIP STATUS: In a relationship
FOLLOWING:
FOLLOWERS:
*Non-public user
tic
In a relationship
FOLLOWERS:
1540
THESE ARE...
...MY FRIENDS.

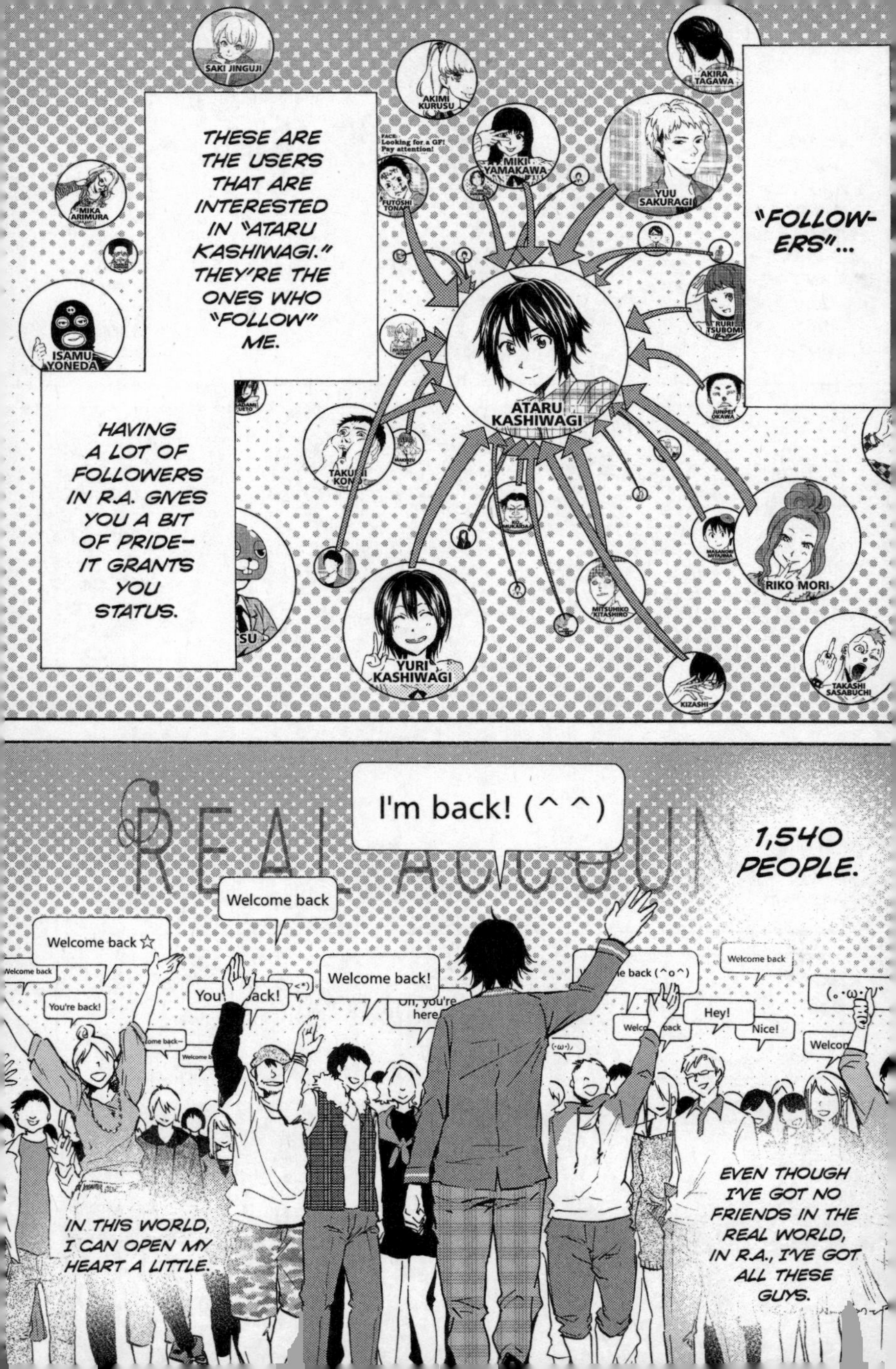
"FOLLOW-ERS"...
THESE ARE THE USERS THAT ARE INTERESTED IN "ATARU KASHIWAGI." THEY'RE THE ONES WHO "FOLLOW" ME.
HAVING A LOT OF FOLLOWERS IN R.A. GIVES YOU A BIT OF PRIDE–IT GRANTS YOU STATUS.
AKIRA TAGAWA
YUU SAKURAGI
AKIMI KURUSU
SAKI JINGUJI
MIKI YAMAKAWA
FACE: Looking for a GF! Pay attention!
MIKA ARIMURA
RURI TSUBOMI
ISAMU YONEDA
ATARU KASHIWAGI
JUNPEI OKAWA
RIKO MORI
MASANORI MIYAJIMA
MITSUHIKO KITASHIRO
YURI KASHIWAGI
KIZASHI
TAKASHI SASABUCHI
1,540 PEOPLE.
I'm back! (^ ^)
Welcome back
Welcome back ☆
Welcome back!
You're back!
Hey!
Nice!
Welcome back
EVEN THOUGH I'VE GOT NO FRIENDS IN THE REAL WORLD, IN R.A., I'VE GOT ALL THESE GUYS.
IN THIS WORLD, I CAN OPEN MY HEART A LITTLE.

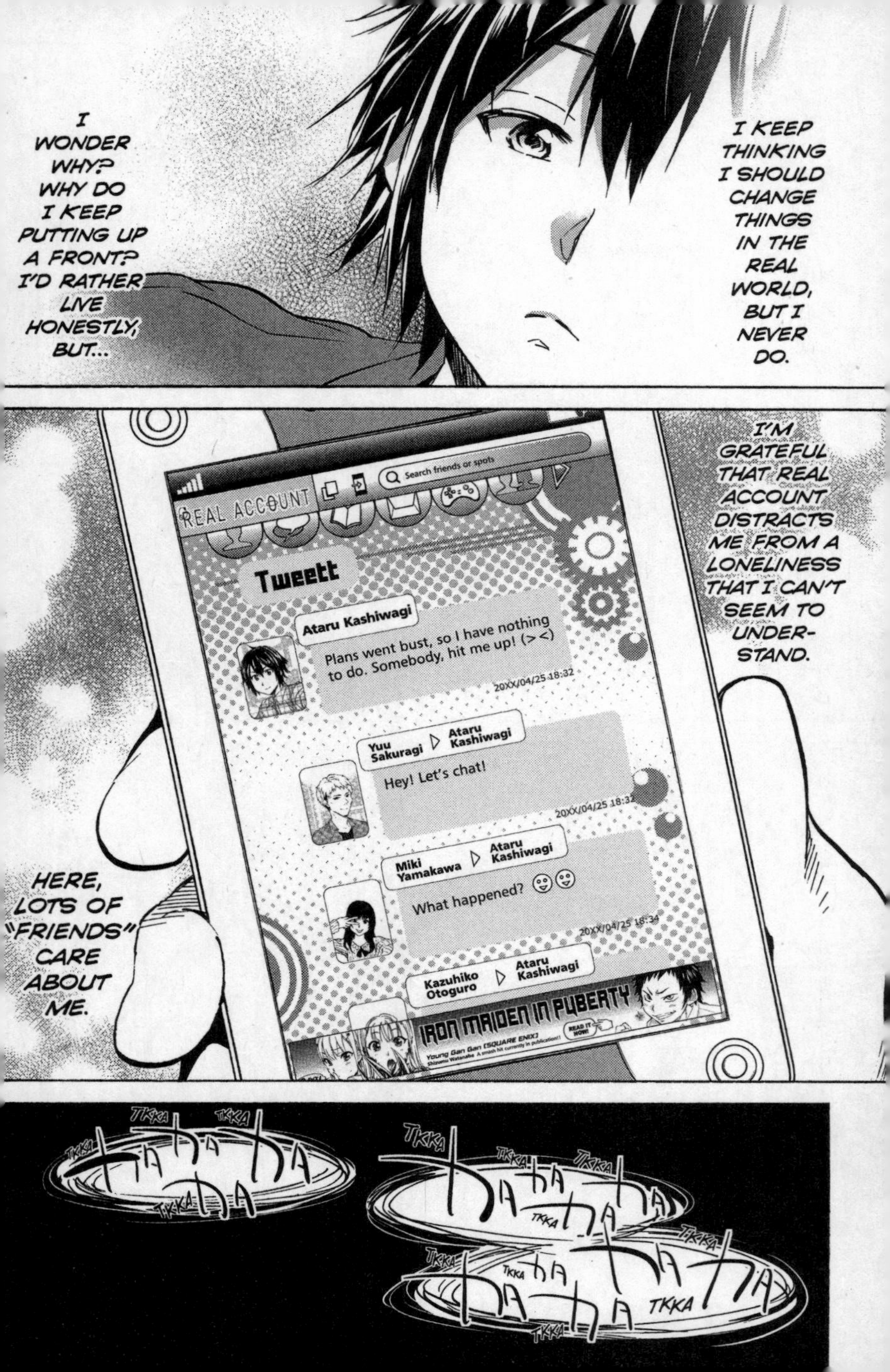
I KEEP THINKING I SHOULD CHANGE THINGS IN THE REAL WORLD, BUT I NEVER DO.
I WONDER WHY? WHY DO I KEEP PUTTING UP A FRONT? I'D RATHER LIVE HONESTLY, BUT...
I'M GRATEFUL THAT REAL ACCOUNT DISTRACTS ME FROM A LONELINESS THAT I CAN'T SEEM TO UNDER-STAND.
REAL ACCOUNT
Search friends or spots
Tweett
Ataru Kashiwagi
Plans went bust, so I have nothing to do. Somebody, hit me up! (><)
20XX/04/25 18:32
Yuu Sakuragi ▷ Ataru Kashiwagi
Hey! Let's chat!
20XX/04/25 18:32
Miki Yamakawa ▷ Ataru Kashiwagi
What happened?
20XX/04/25 18:34
Kazuhiko Otoguro ▷ Ataru Kashiwagi
IRON MAIDEN IN PUBERTY
READ IT NOW!
Young Gan Gan (SQUARE ENIX)
HERE, LOTS OF "FRIENDS" CARE ABOUT ME.
TKKA TKKA TKKA HA HA HA HA TKKA
TKKA TKKA TKKA TKKA HA HA HA HA TKKA
TKKA TKKA TKKA HA HA HA HA HA TKKA TKKA

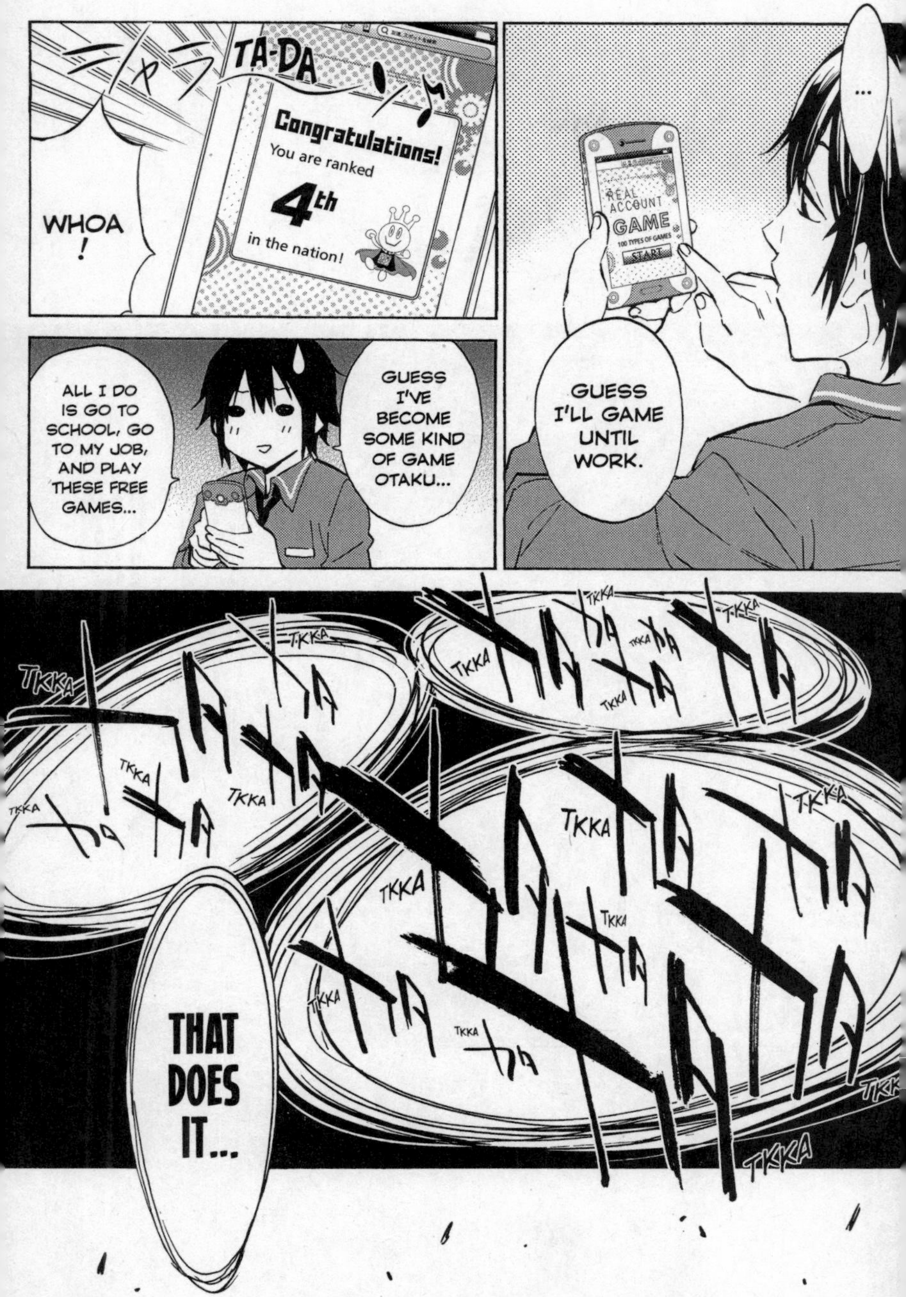
...
REAL ACCOUNT GAME
100 TYPES OF GAMES
START
GUESS I'LL GAME UNTIL WORK.
TA-DA
Congratulations!
You are ranked
4th
in the nation!
WHOA!
GUESS I'VE BECOME SOME KIND OF GAME OTAKU...
ALL I DO IS GO TO SCHOOL, GO TO MY JOB, AND PLAY THESE FREE GAMES...
TKKA
TKKA
TKKA
TKKA
TKKA
TKKA
TKKA
TKKA
TKKA
TKKA
TKKA
TKKA
TKKA
TKKA
TKKA
TKKA
THAT DOES IT...

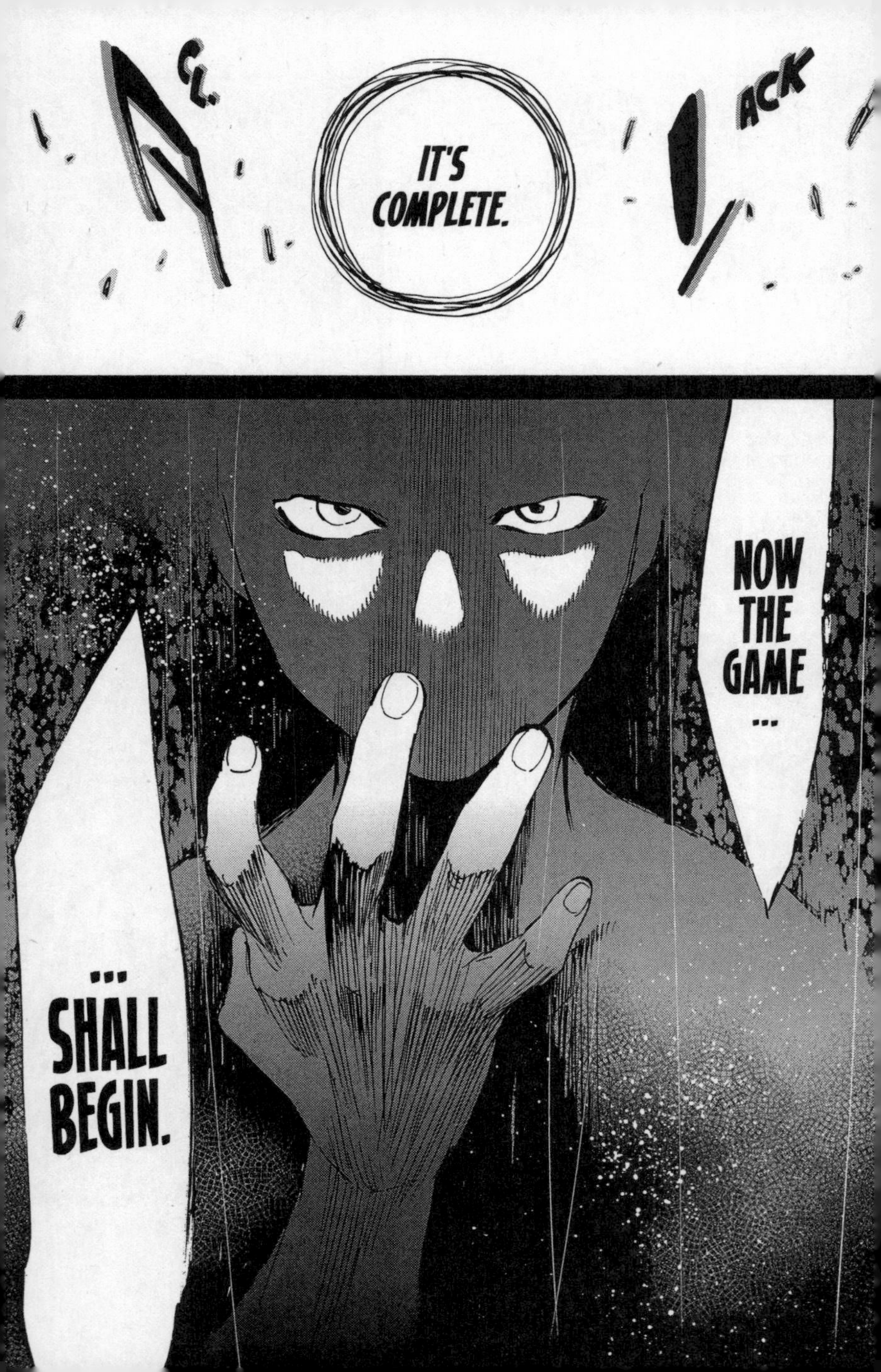
CL...ACK
IT'S COMPLETE.
NOW THE GAME ...
... SHALL BEGIN.

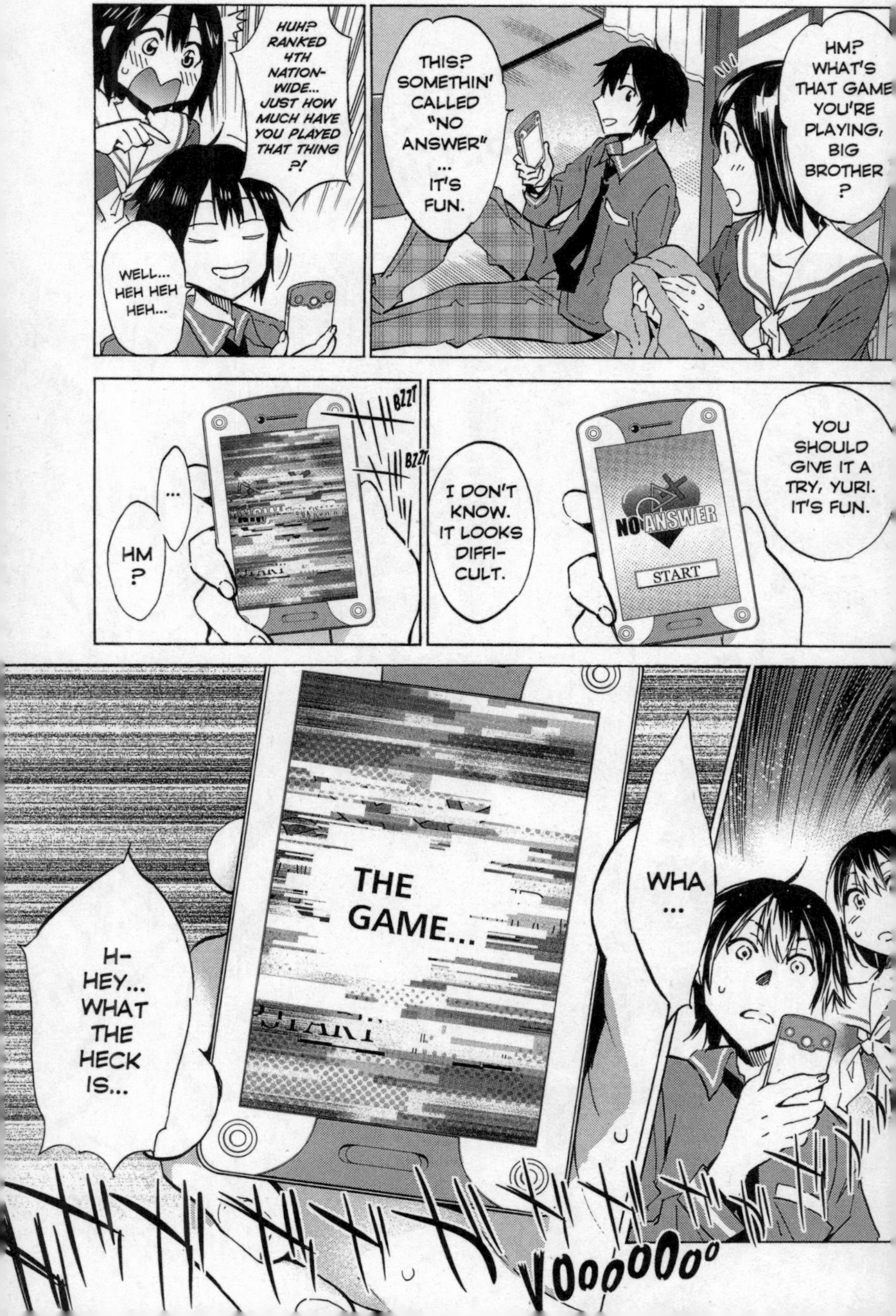
HM? WHAT'S THAT GAME YOU'RE PLAYING, BIG BROTHER?
THIS? SOMETHIN' CALLED "NO ANSWER"... IT'S FUN.
HUH? RANKED 4TH NATION-WIDE... JUST HOW MUCH HAVE YOU PLAYED THAT THING?!
WELL... HEH HEH HEH...
YOU SHOULD GIVE IT A TRY, YURI. IT'S FUN.
I DON'T KNOW. IT LOOKS DIFFI-CULT.
NO ANSWER
START
BZZT
BZZT
...
HM?
WHA...
THE GAME...
H-HEY... WHAT THE HECK IS...
VOOOOOOO

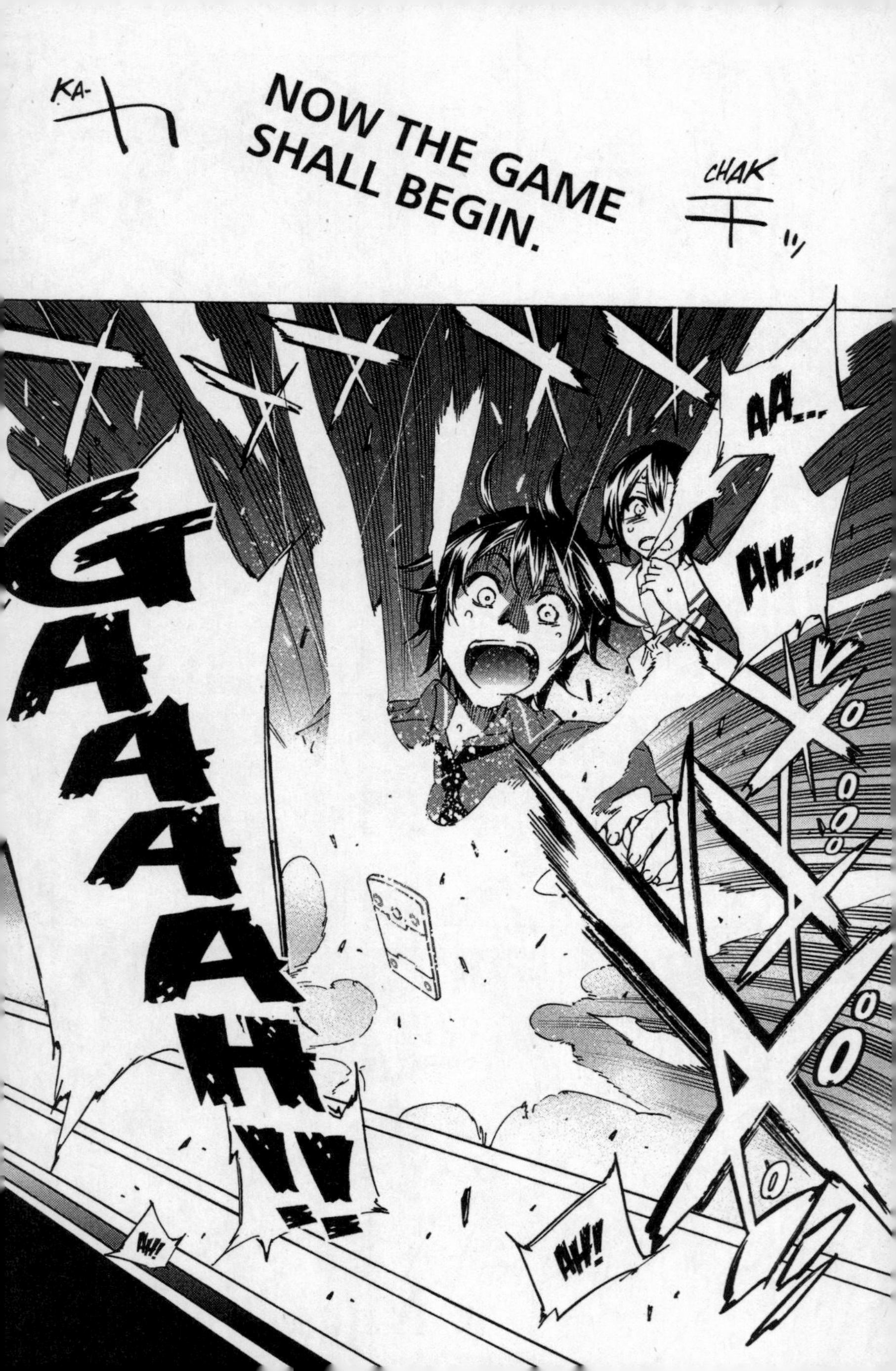
CHAK
NOW THE GAME SHALL BEGIN.
KA-
AA...
AH...
VOOOOOOO
GAAAAH!!
AH!
AH!

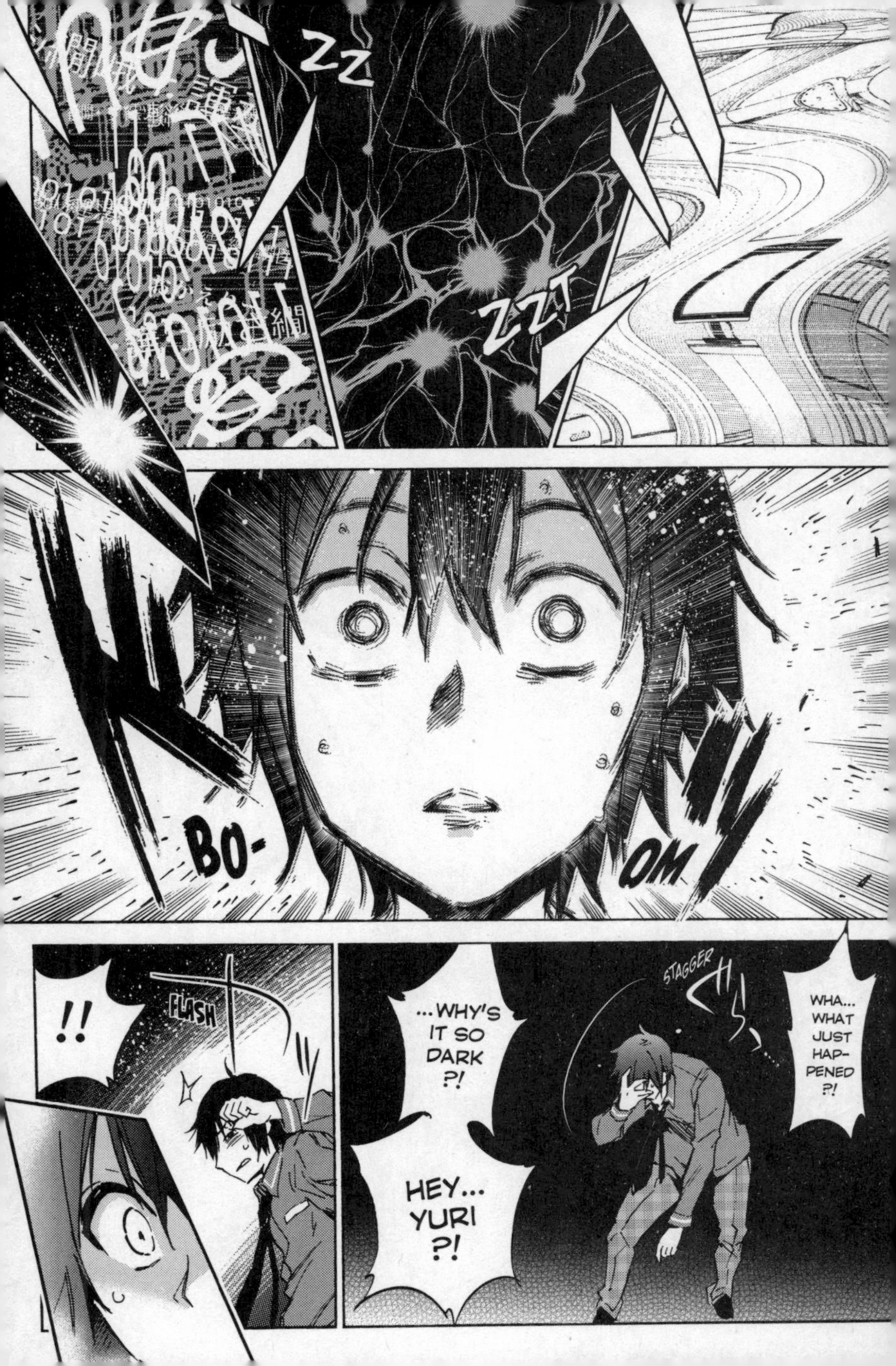
ZZ
ZZZT
BO-
OM
WHA... WHAT JUST HAPPENED?!
STAGGER
...WHY'S IT SO DARK?!
HEY... YURI?!
FLASH
!!

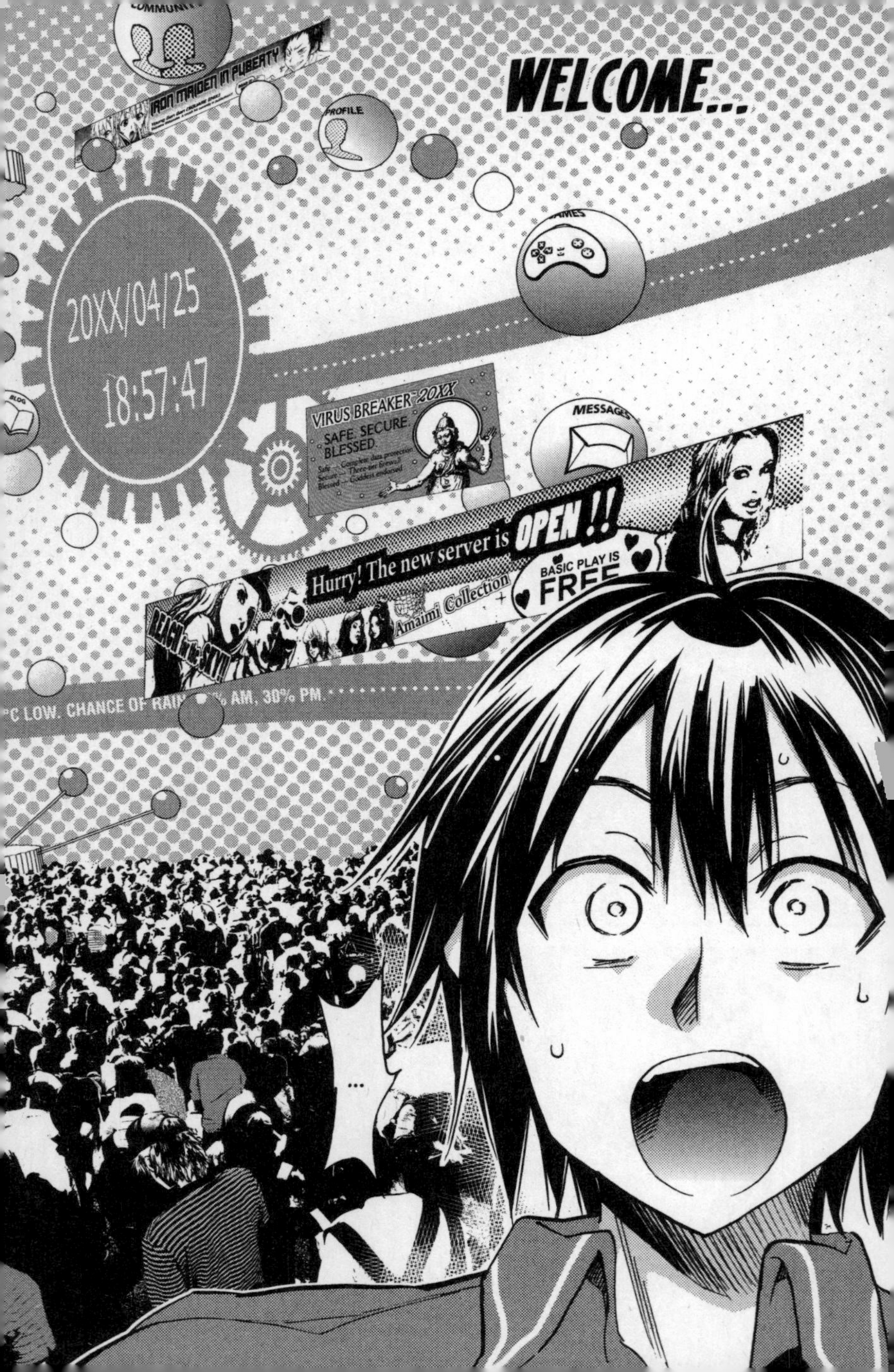
WELCOME...
IRON MAIDEN IN PUBERTY
PROFILE
20XX/04/25
18:57:47
BLOG
VIRUS BREAKER 20XX
SAFE. SECURE. BLESSED.
Safe --- Complete data protection
Secure --- Three-tier firewall
Blessed --- Goddess endorsed
MESSAGES
Hurry! The new server is OPEN!!
BASIC PLAY IS FREE
Amaimi Collection
REACH for the SKY!!
...

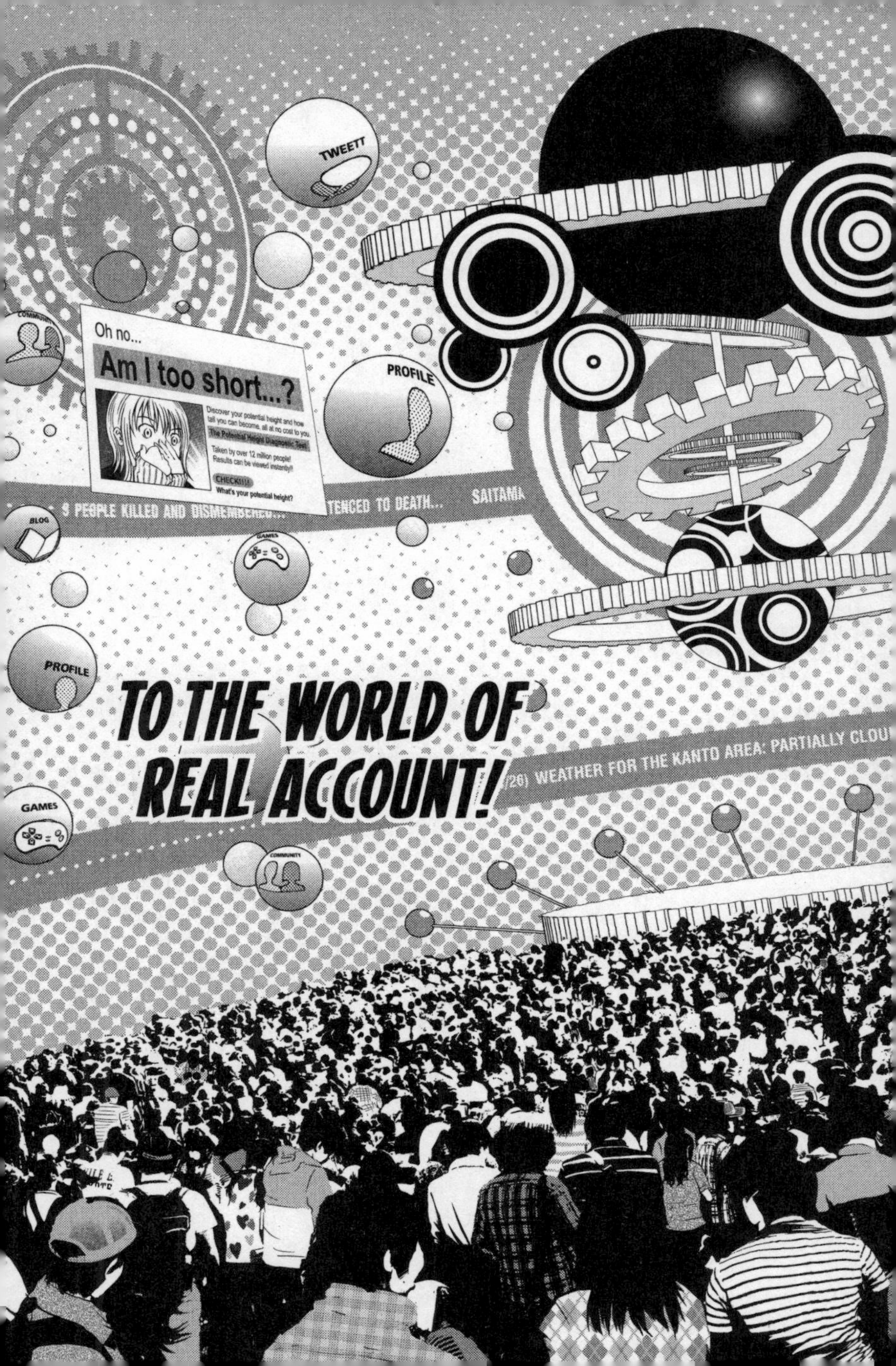

TWEETT
COMMUNITY
Oh no...
Am I too short...?
Discover your potential height and how tall you can become, all at no cost to you.
The Potential Height Diagnostic Test
Taken by over 12 million people! Results can be viewed instantly!!
CHECK!!!!
What's your potential height?
PROFILE
9 PEOPLE KILLED AND DISMEMBERED...
TENCED TO DEATH... SAITAMA
BLOG
GAMES
PROFILE
TO THE WORLD OF REAL ACCOUNT!
(26) WEATHER FOR THE KANTO AREA: PARTIALLY CLOU
GAMES
COMMUNITY

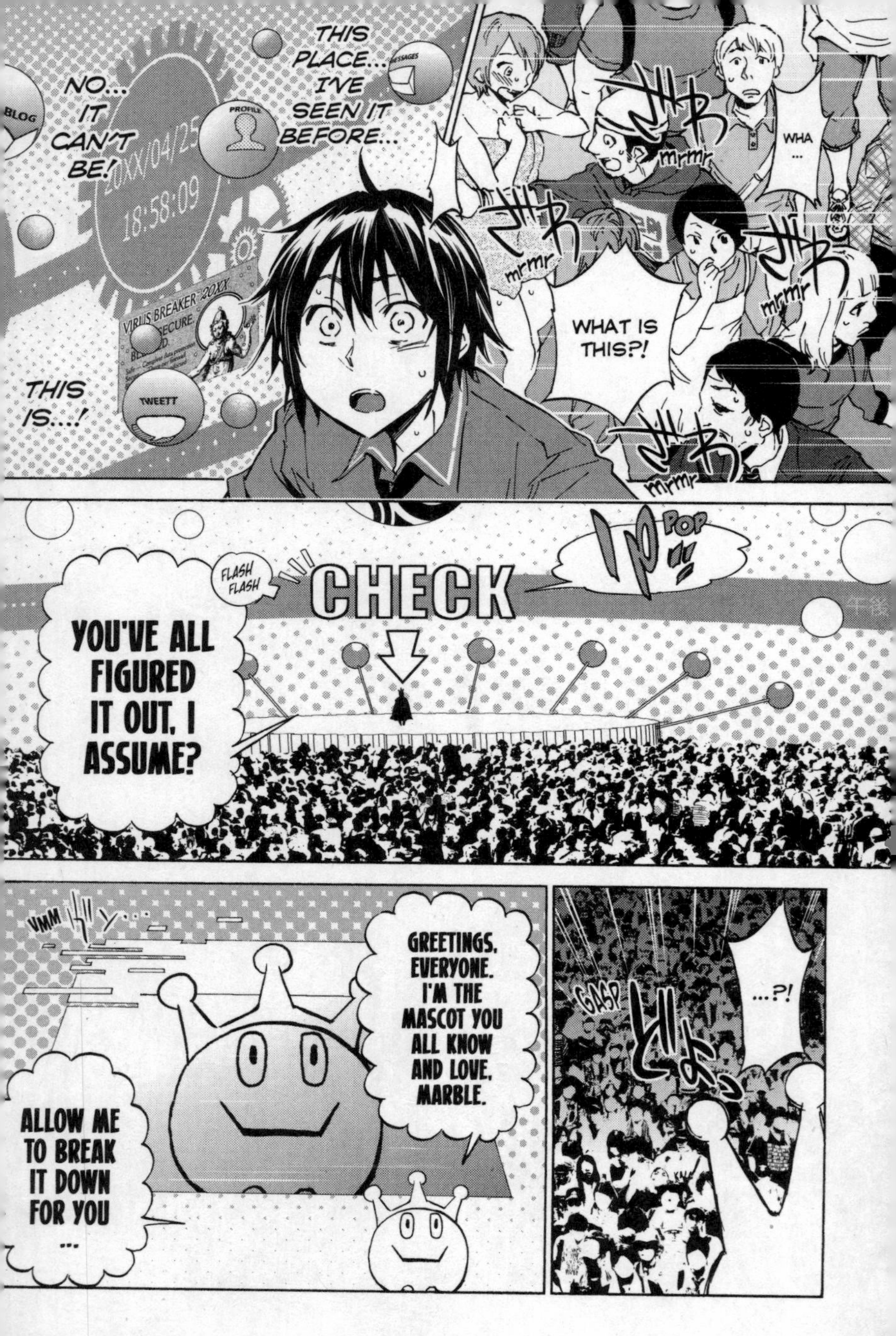
WHA ...
THIS PLACE... I'VE SEEN IT BEFORE...
MESSAGES
mrmr
PROFILE
20XX/04/25
18:58:09
NO... IT CAN'T BE!
BLOG
mrmr
mrmr
WHAT IS THIS?!
mrmr
VIRUS BREAKER 20XX
TWEETT
THIS IS...!
POP
CHECK
FLASH FLASH
YOU'VE ALL FIGURED IT OUT, I ASSUME?
...?!
GASP
GREETINGS, EVERYONE. I'M THE MASCOT YOU ALL KNOW AND LOVE, MARBLE.
VMM
ALLOW ME TO BREAK IT DOWN FOR YOU ...

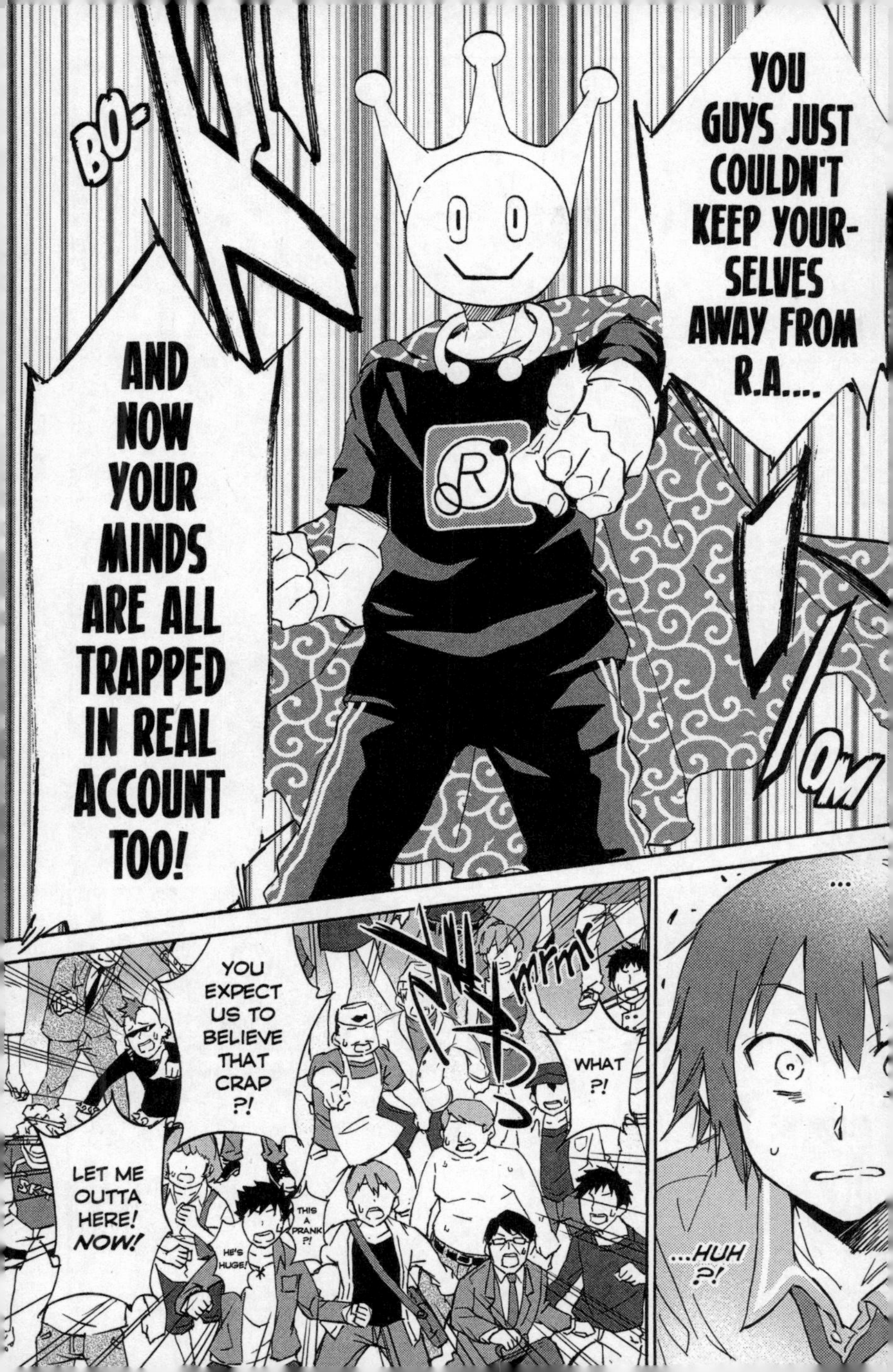
YOU GUYS JUST COULDN'T KEEP YOUR-SELVES AWAY FROM R.A....
BO-
OM
AND NOW YOUR MINDS ARE ALL TRAPPED IN REAL ACCOUNT TOO!
...
...HUH ?!
mrmr
WHAT ?!
YOU EXPECT US TO BELIEVE THAT CRAP ?!
THIS A PRANK ?!
HE'S HUGE!
LET ME OUTTA HERE! NOW!

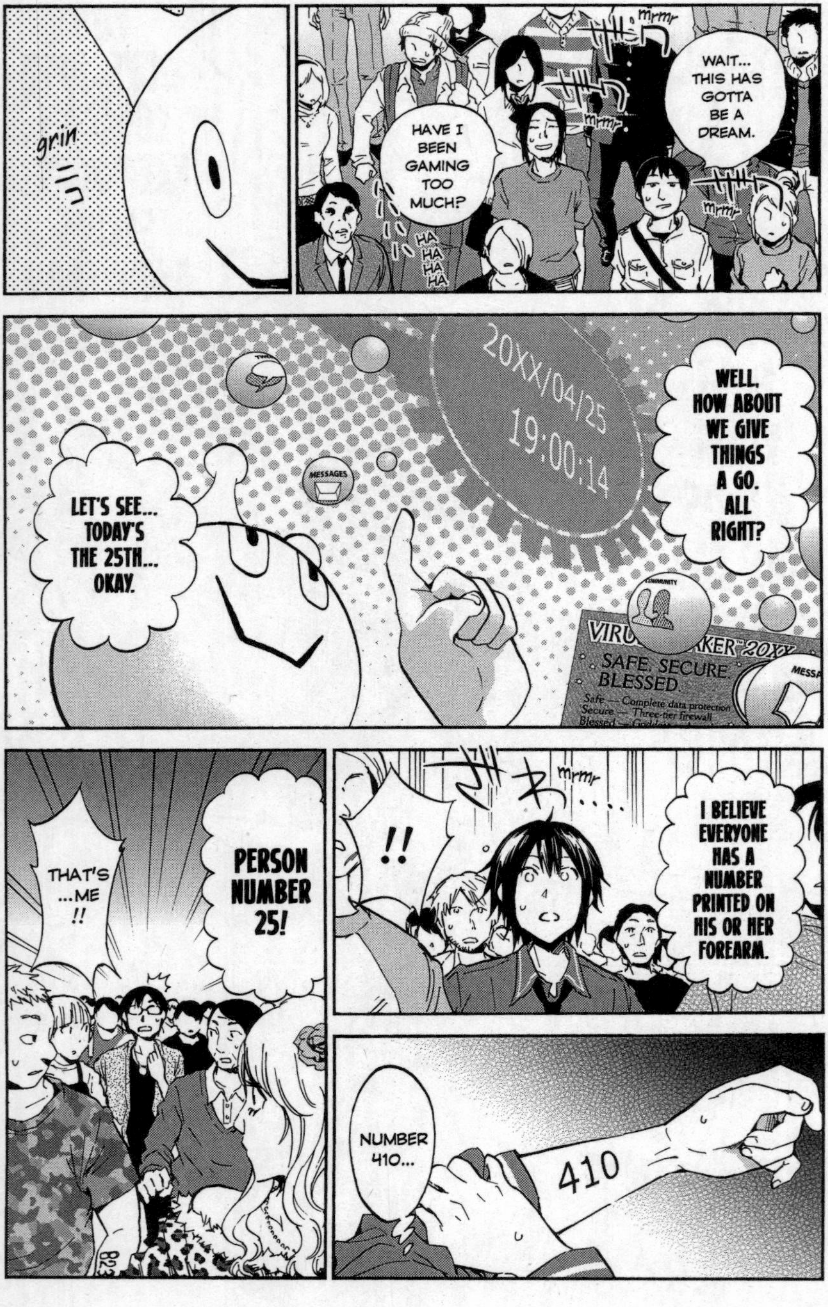
mrmr
WAIT... THIS HAS GOTTA BE A DREAM.
mrmr
mrmr
HAVE I BEEN GAMING TOO MUCH?
HA HA HA HA
grin
WELL, HOW ABOUT WE GIVE THINGS A GO. ALL RIGHT?
20XX/04/25
19:00:14
MESSAGES
LET'S SEE... TODAY'S THE 25TH... OKAY.
COMMUNITY
SAFE. SECURE. BLESSED.
Safe — Complete data protection
Secure — Three-tier firewall
mrmr
I BELIEVE EVERYONE HAS A NUMBER PRINTED ON HIS OR HER FOREARM.
!!
NUMBER 410...
410
PERSON NUMBER 25!
THAT'S ...ME !!
823

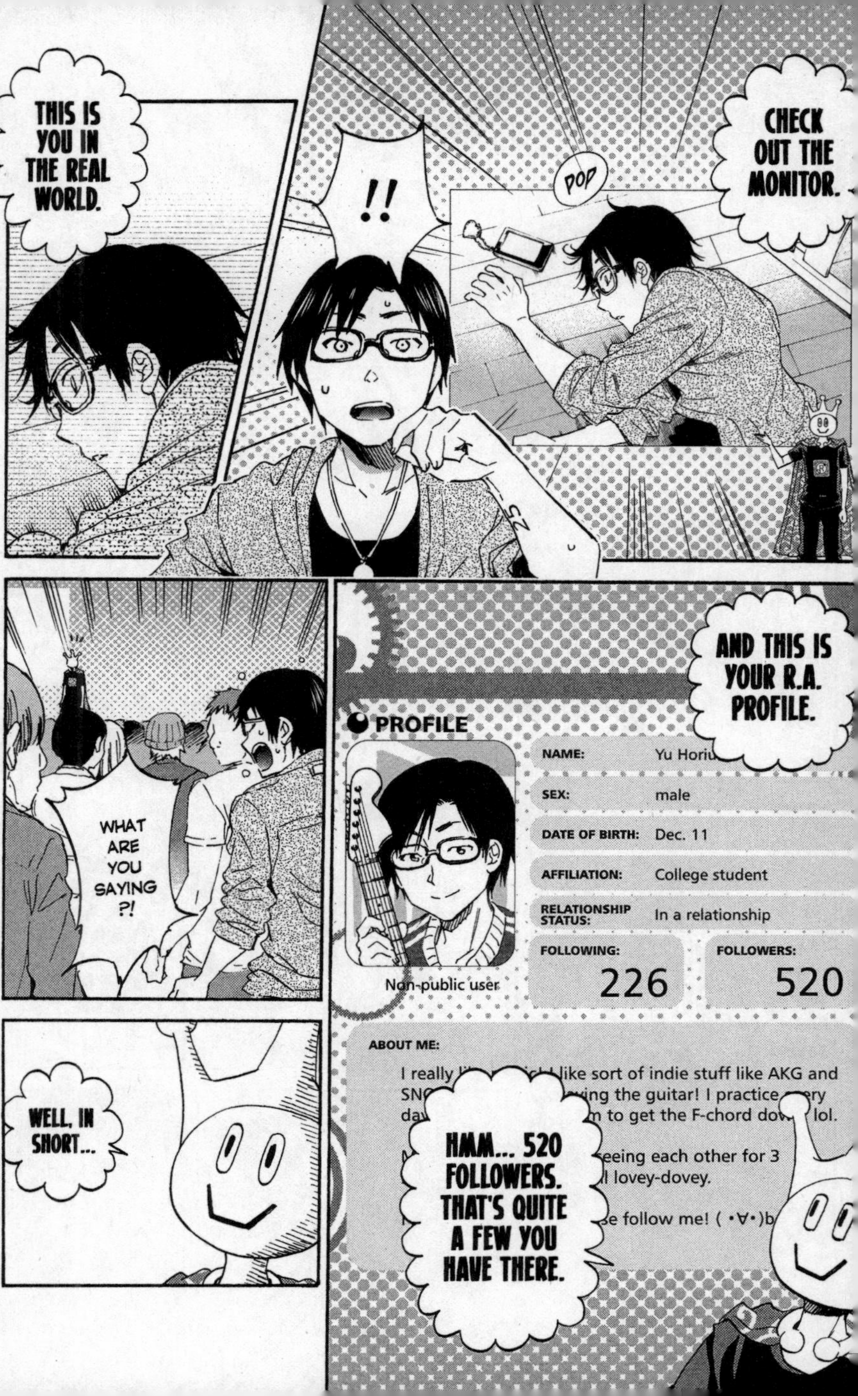

CHECK OUT THE MONITOR.
POP
!!
THIS IS YOU IN THE REAL WORLD.
AND THIS IS YOUR R.A. PROFILE.
PROFILE
NAME: Yu Horiu
SEX: male
DATE OF BIRTH: Dec. 11
AFFILIATION: College student
RELATIONSHIP STATUS: In a relationship
FOLLOWING: 226
FOLLOWERS: 520
Non-public user
ABOUT ME:
like sort of indie stuff like AKG and
ying the guitar! I practice
m to get the F-chord dow lol.
seeing each other for 3
l lovey-dovey.
se follow me! (•∀•)b
HMM... 520 FOLLOWERS. THAT'S QUITE A FEW YOU HAVE THERE.
WHAT ARE YOU SAYING?!
WELL, IN SHORT...

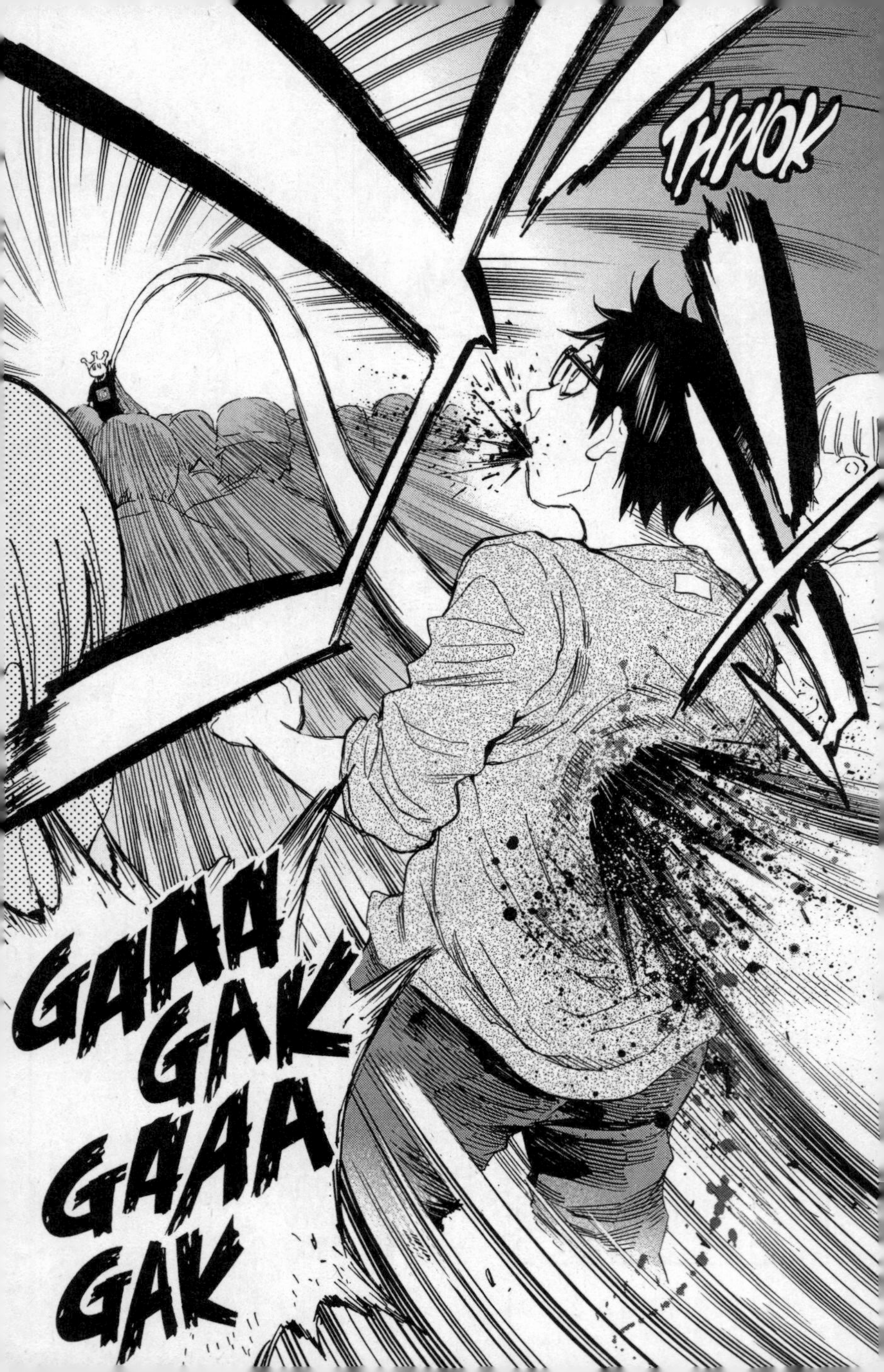
THWOK
GAAA GAK GAAA GAK

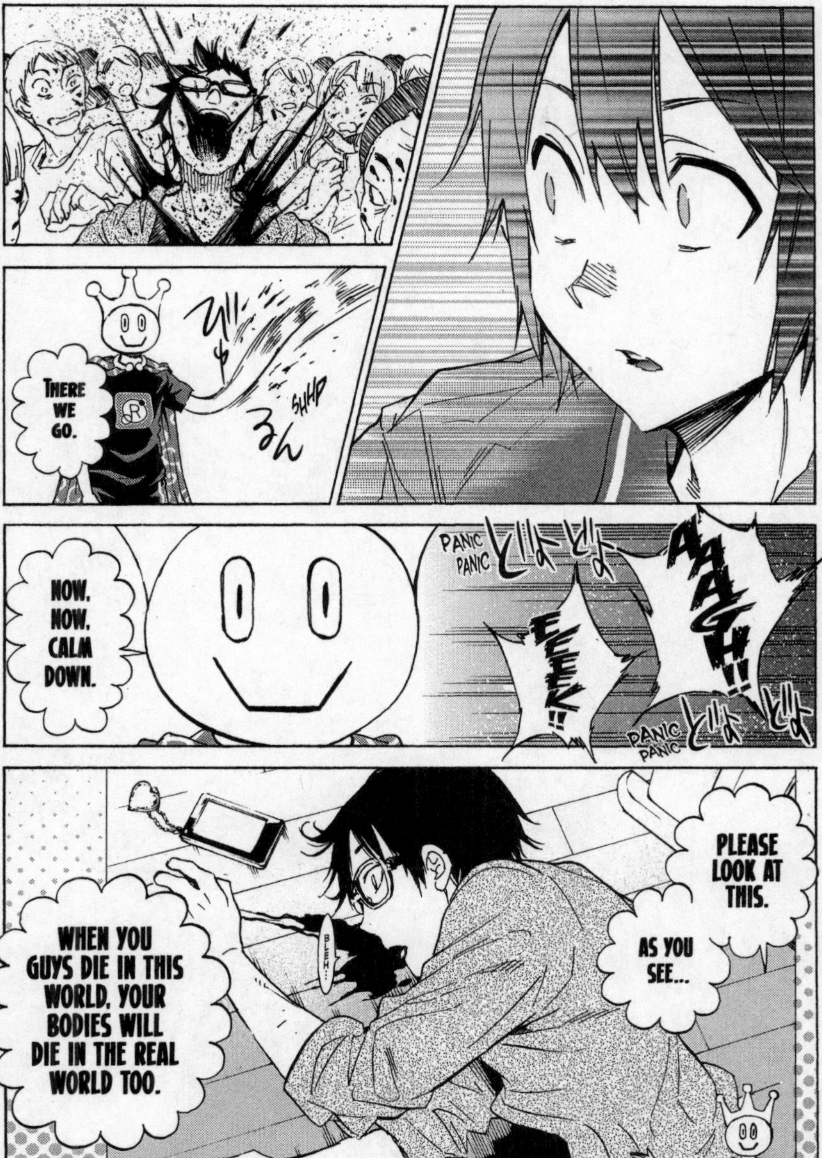
SHHP
THERE WE GO.
AAAGH!!
PANIC PANIC
EEEK!!
PANIC PANIC
NOW, NOW, CALM DOWN.
PLEASE LOOK AT THIS.
AS YOU SEE...
BLEH...
WHEN YOU GUYS DIE IN THIS WORLD, YOUR BODIES WILL DIE IN THE REAL WORLD TOO.

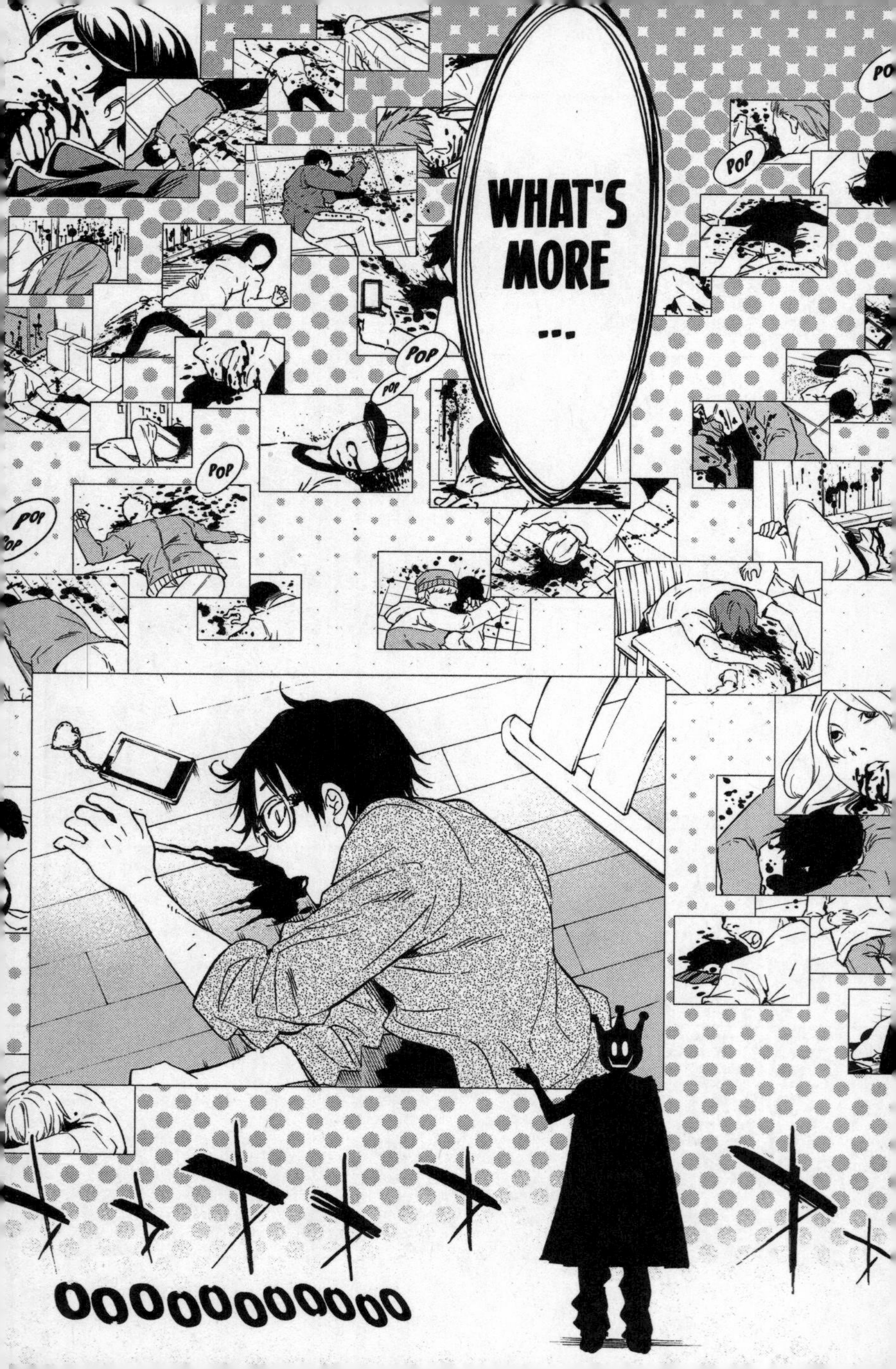

POP
WHAT'S MORE ...
POP
POP
POP
POP
OOOOOOOOOOOO

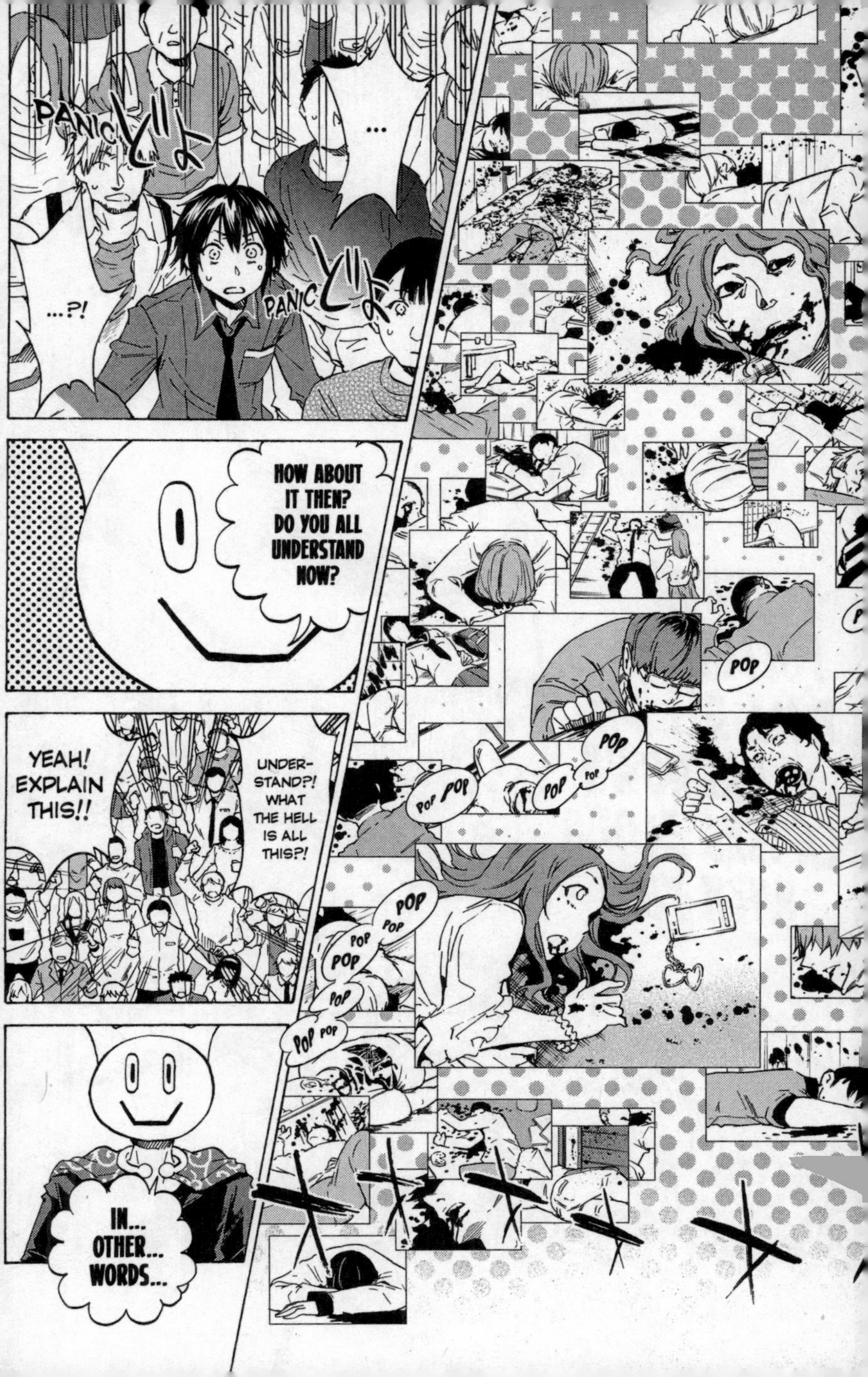

POP
POP
POP
POP
POP POP
POP
POP
POP
POP
POP
POP
POP POP
...
PANIC
PANIC
...?!
HOW ABOUT IT THEN? DO YOU ALL UNDERSTAND NOW?
UNDER-STAND?! WHAT THE HELL IS ALL THIS?!
YEAH! EXPLAIN THIS!!
IN... OTHER... WORDS...

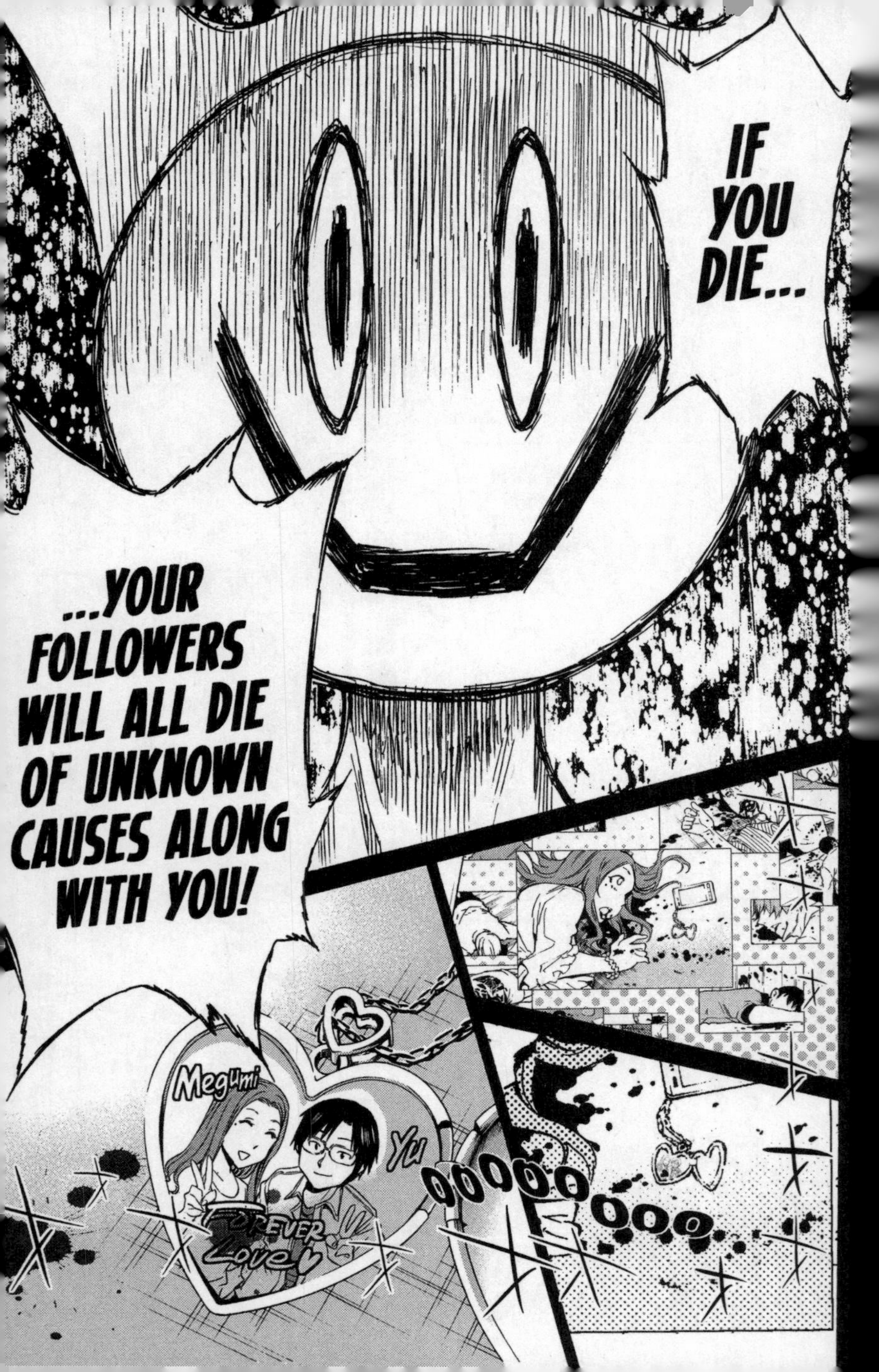
IF YOU DIE...
...YOUR FOLLOWERS WILL ALL DIE OF UNKNOWN CAUSES ALONG WITH YOU!
OOOOOOOOOOOO
Megumi
Yu
FOREVER Love

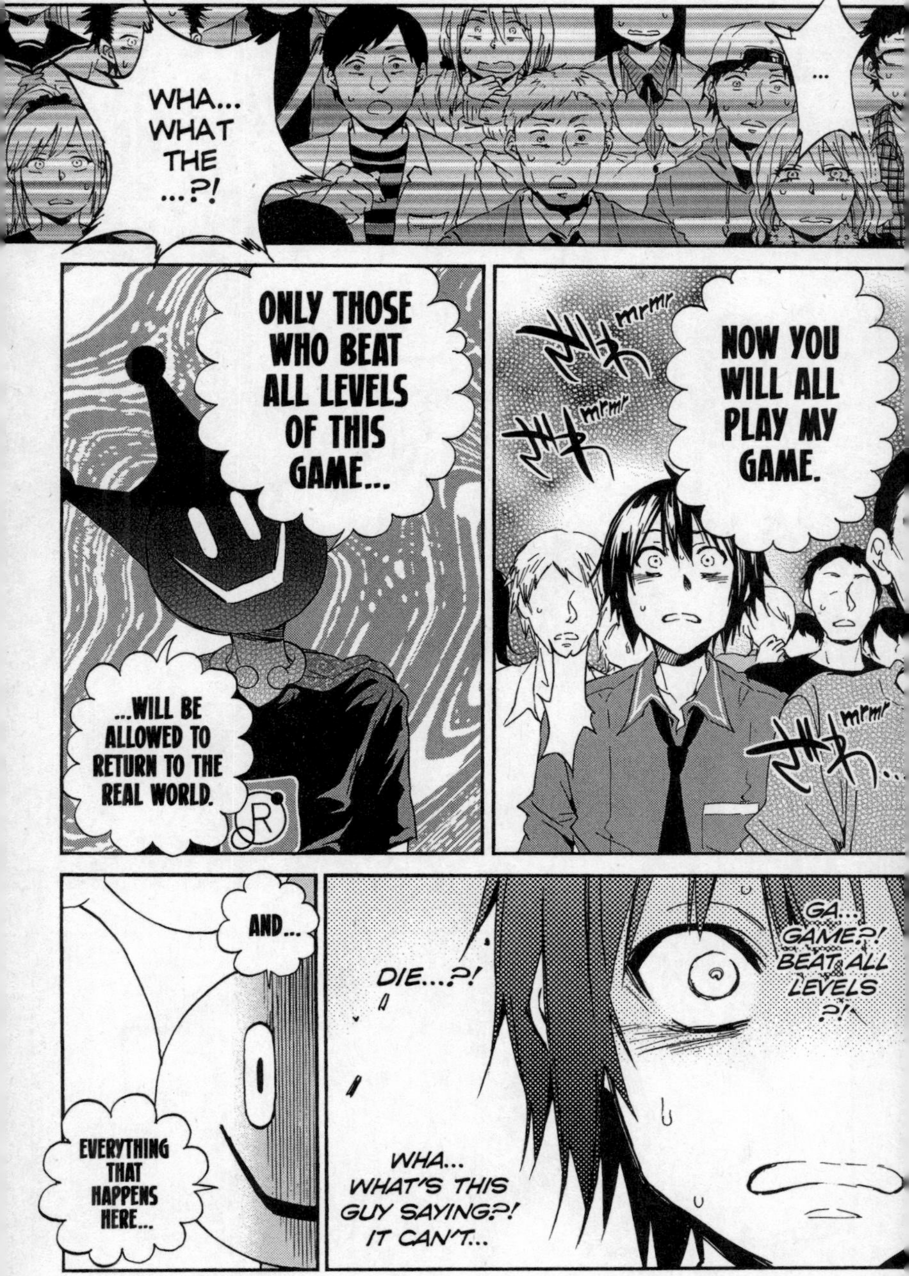
...
WHA... WHAT THE ...?!
NOW YOU WILL ALL PLAY MY GAME.
mrmr
mrmr
mrmr
ONLY THOSE WHO BEAT ALL LEVELS OF THIS GAME...
...WILL BE ALLOWED TO RETURN TO THE REAL WORLD.
GA... GAME?! BEAT ALL LEVELS ?!
DIE...?!
WHA... WHAT'S THIS GUY SAYING?! IT CAN'T...
AND...
EVERYTHING THAT HAPPENS HERE...

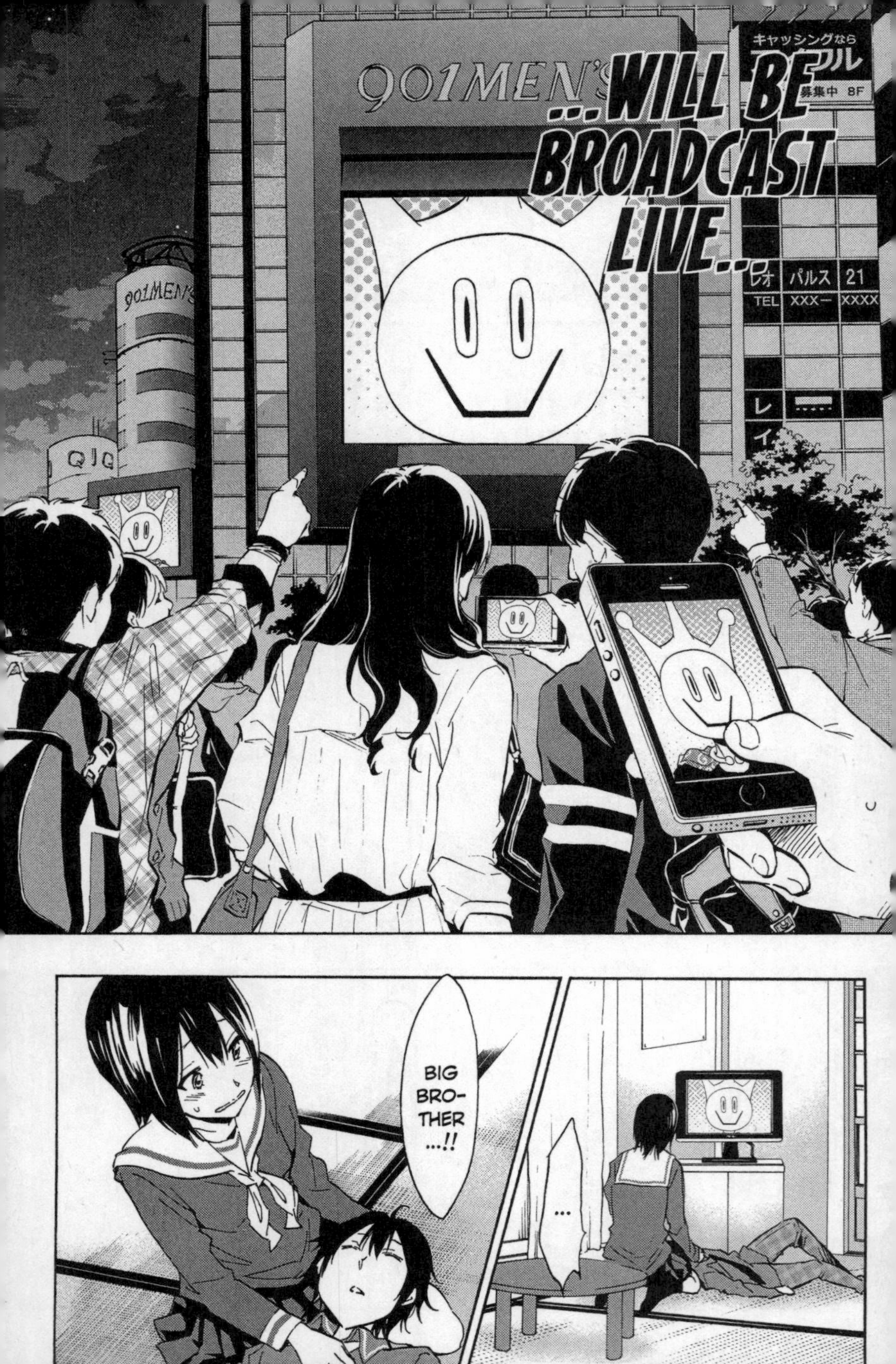
901MEN'S
キャッシングなら
募集中 8F
...WILL BE BROADCAST LIVE...
レオ パルス 21
TEL XXX－ XXXX
901MEN'S
...
BIG BRO-THER ...!!

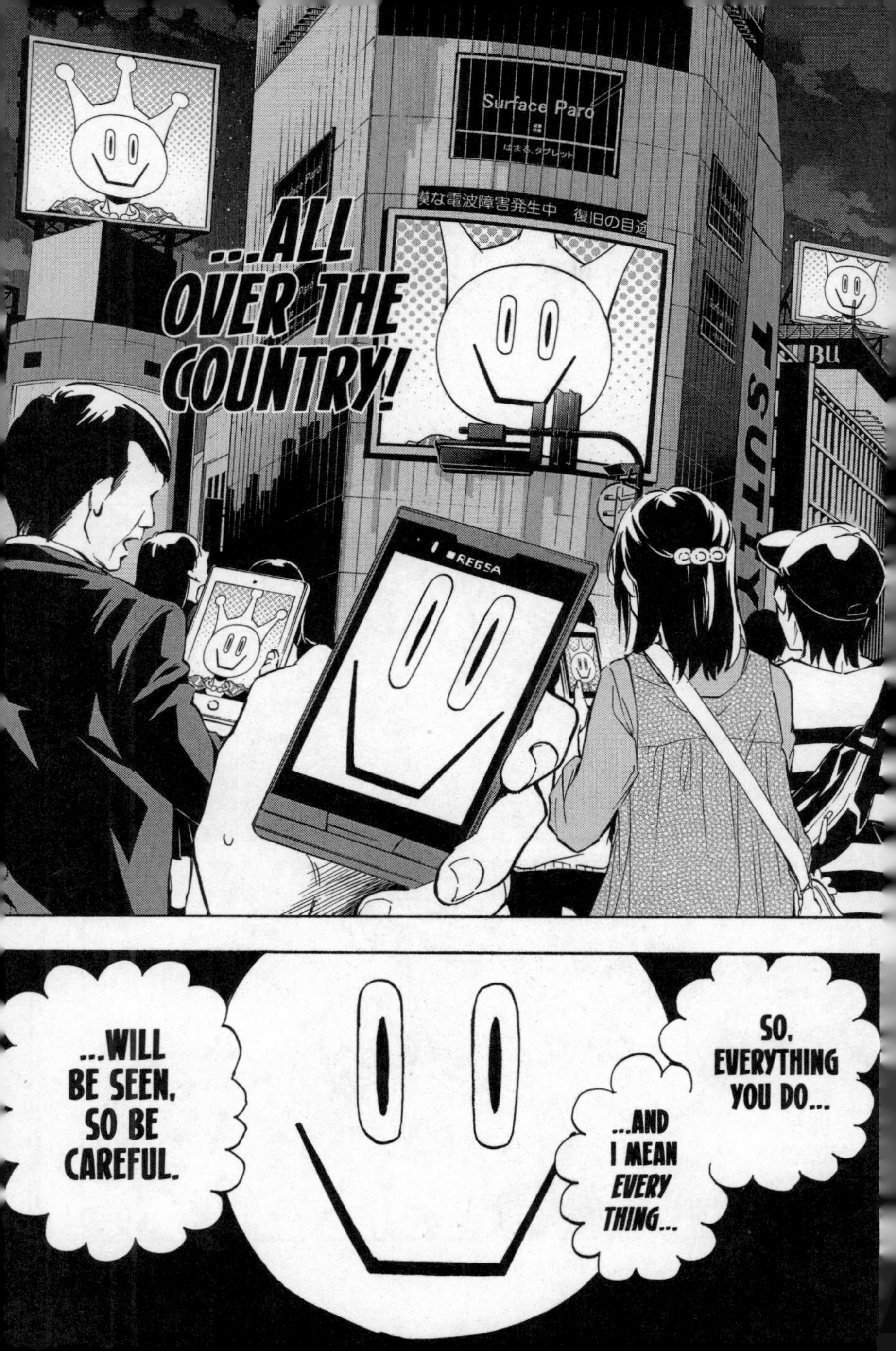
Surface Paro
模な電波障害発生中　復旧の目途
...ALL OVER THE COUNTRY!
REGSA
SO, EVERYTHING YOU DO...
...AND I MEAN *EVERY* THING...
...WILL BE SEEN, SO BE CAREFUL.

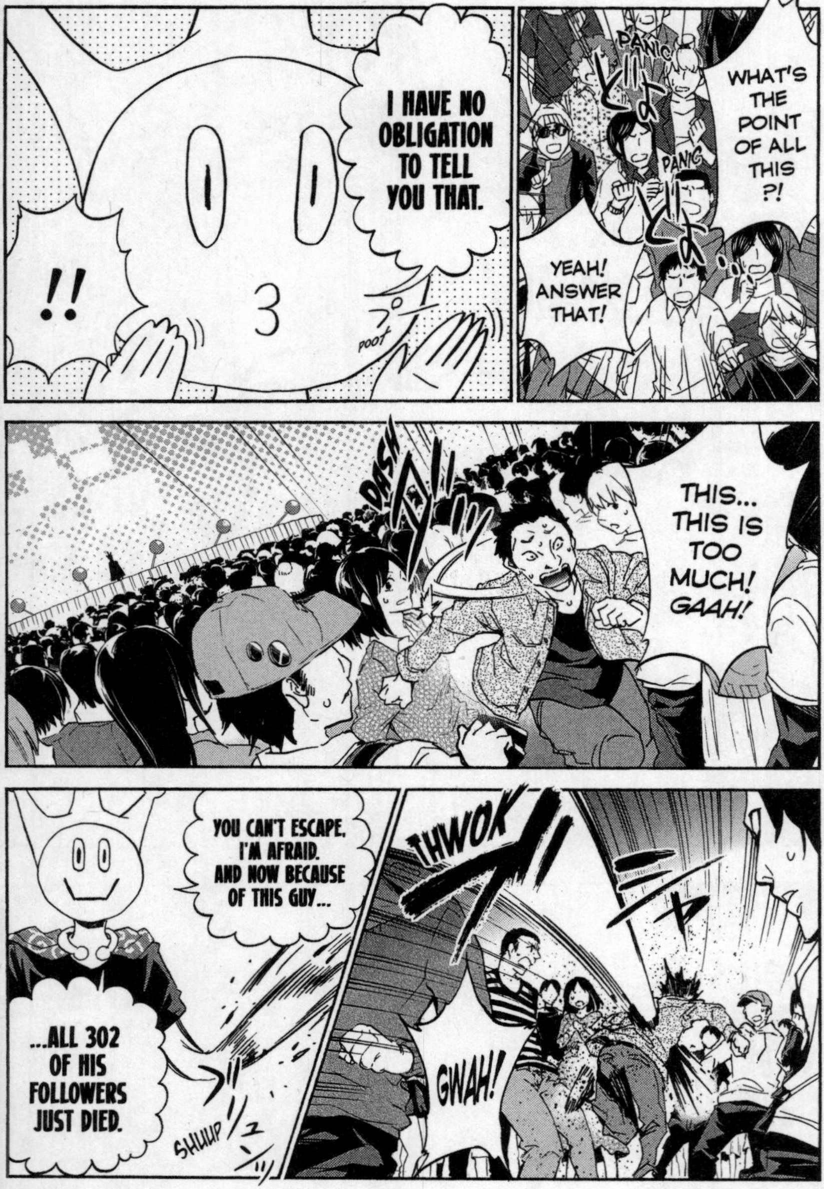
WHAT'S THE POINT OF ALL THIS ?!
PANIC
PANIC
YEAH! ANSWER THAT!
I HAVE NO OBLIGATION TO TELL YOU THAT.
!!
POOT
THIS... THIS IS TOO MUCH! GAAH!
DASH
THWOK
GWAH!
YOU CAN'T ESCAPE, I'M AFRAID. AND NOW BECAUSE OF THIS GUY...
...ALL 302 OF HIS FOLLOWERS JUST DIED.
SHUUP

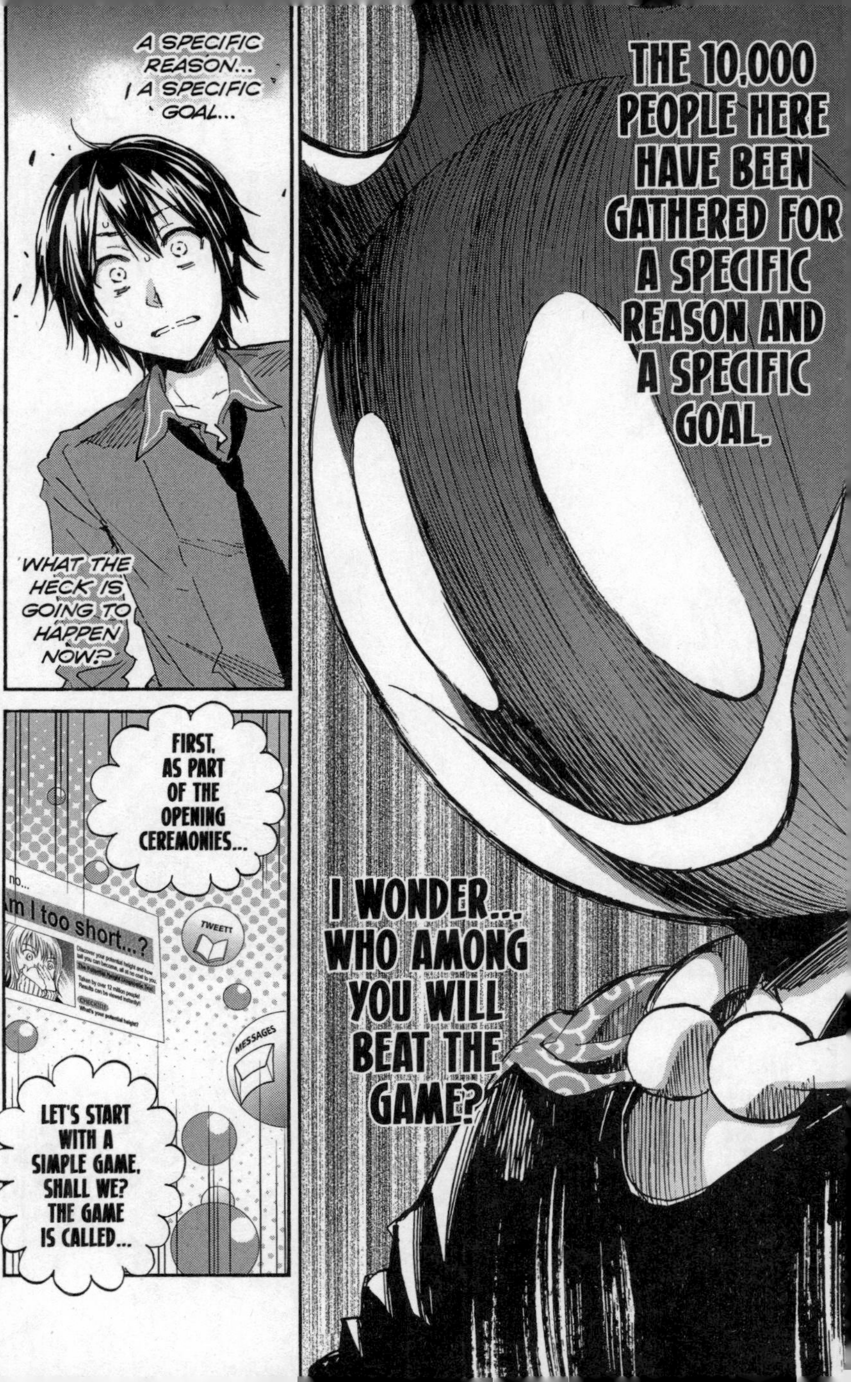
THE 10,000 PEOPLE HERE HAVE BEEN GATHERED FOR A SPECIFIC REASON AND A SPECIFIC GOAL.
I WONDER... WHO AMONG YOU WILL BEAT THE GAME?
A SPECIFIC REASON... A SPECIFIC GOAL...
WHAT THE HECK IS GOING TO HAPPEN NOW?
FIRST, AS PART OF THE OPENING CEREMONIES...
m I too short...?
TWEET
MESSAGES
LET'S START WITH A SIMPLE GAME, SHALL WE? THE GAME IS CALLED...

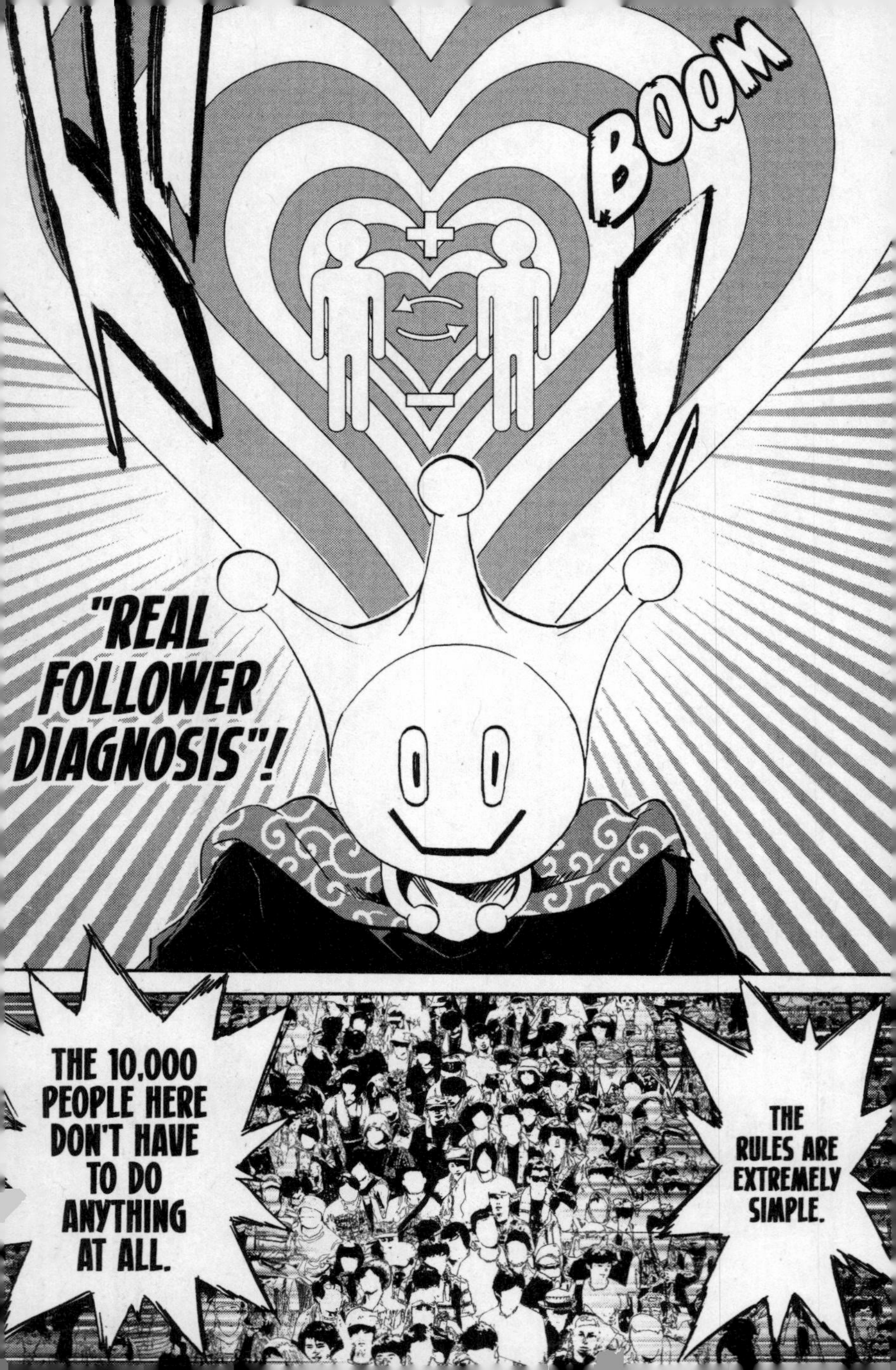
BOOM
"REAL FOLLOWER DIAGNOSIS"!
THE RULES ARE EXTREMELY SIMPLE.
THE 10,000 PEOPLE HERE DON'T HAVE TO DO ANYTHING AT ALL.

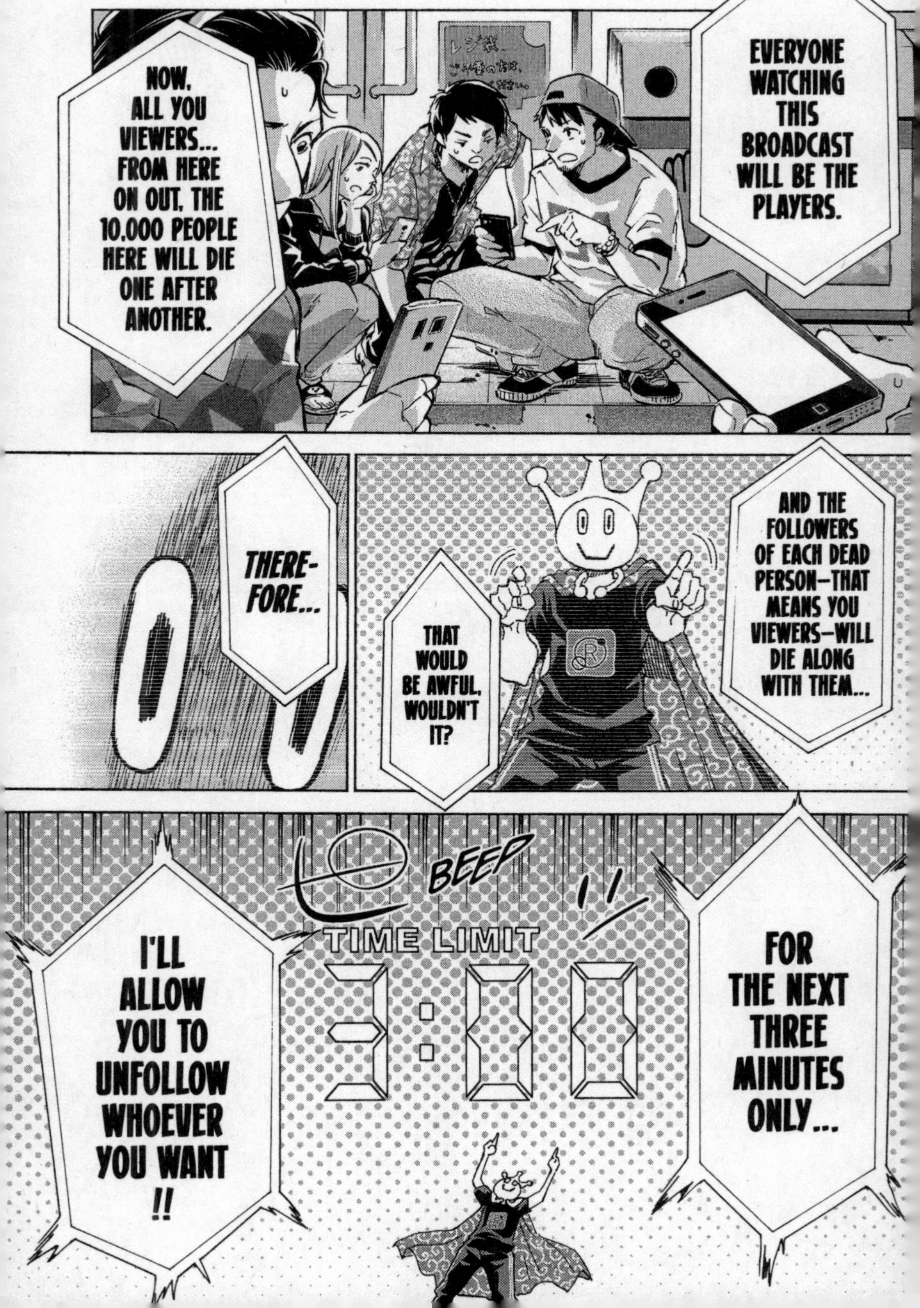
EVERYONE WATCHING THIS BROADCAST WILL BE THE PLAYERS.
NOW, ALL YOU VIEWERS... FROM HERE ON OUT, THE 10,000 PEOPLE HERE WILL DIE ONE AFTER ANOTHER.
AND THE FOLLOWERS OF EACH DEAD PERSON—THAT MEANS YOU VIEWERS—WILL DIE ALONG WITH THEM...
THAT WOULD BE AWFUL, WOULDN'T IT?
THEREFORE...
FOR THE NEXT THREE MINUTES ONLY...
BEEP
TIME LIMIT
3:00
I'LL ALLOW YOU TO UNFOLLOW WHOEVER YOU WANT!!

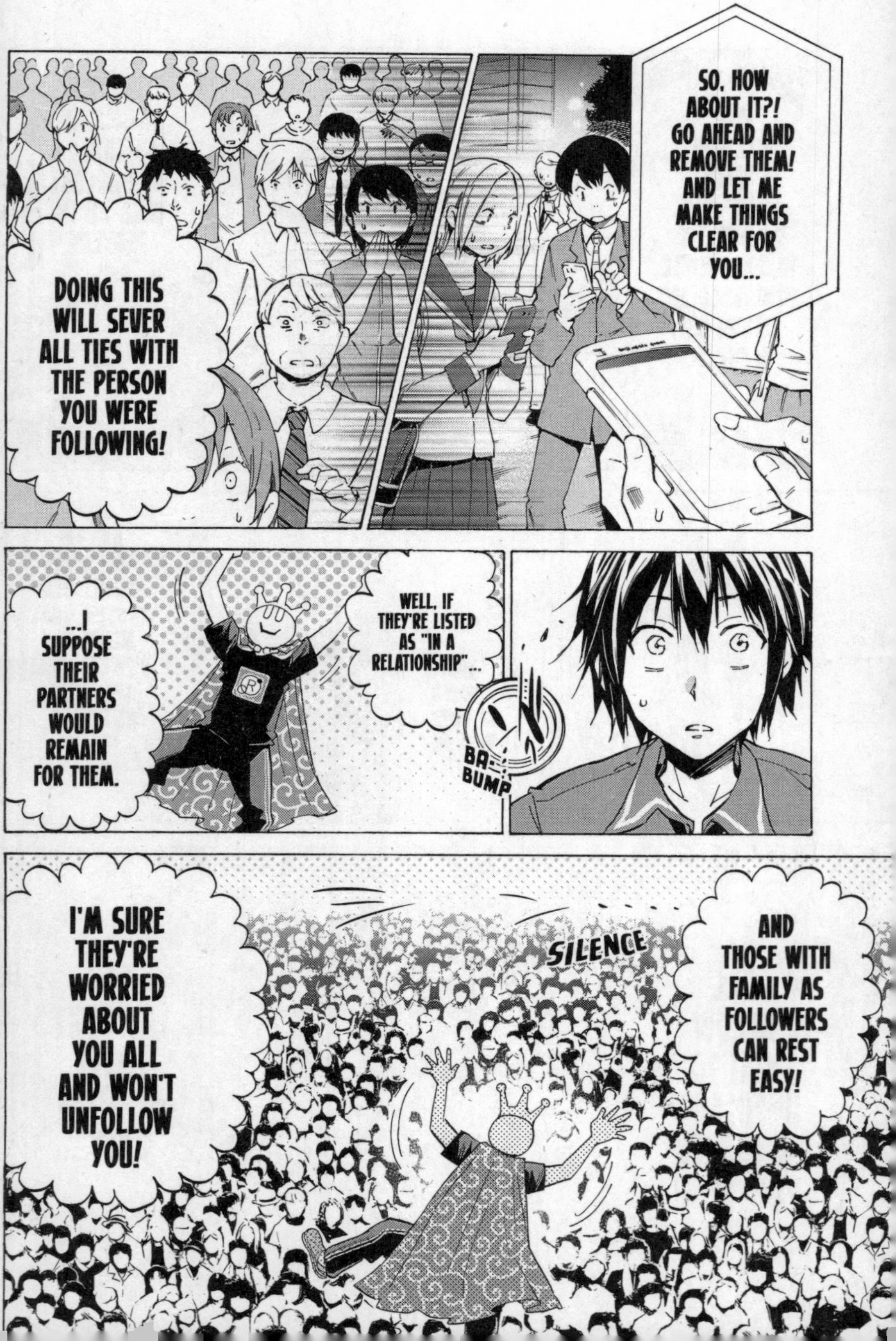
SO, HOW ABOUT IT?! GO AHEAD AND REMOVE THEM! AND LET ME MAKE THINGS CLEAR FOR YOU...
DOING THIS WILL SEVER ALL TIES WITH THE PERSON YOU WERE FOLLOWING!
BA-BUMP
WELL, IF THEY'RE LISTED AS "IN A RELATIONSHIP"...
...I SUPPOSE THEIR PARTNERS WOULD REMAIN FOR THEM.
AND THOSE WITH FAMILY AS FOLLOWERS CAN REST EASY!
SILENCE
I'M SURE THEY'RE WORRIED ABOUT YOU ALL AND WON'T UNFOLLOW YOU!

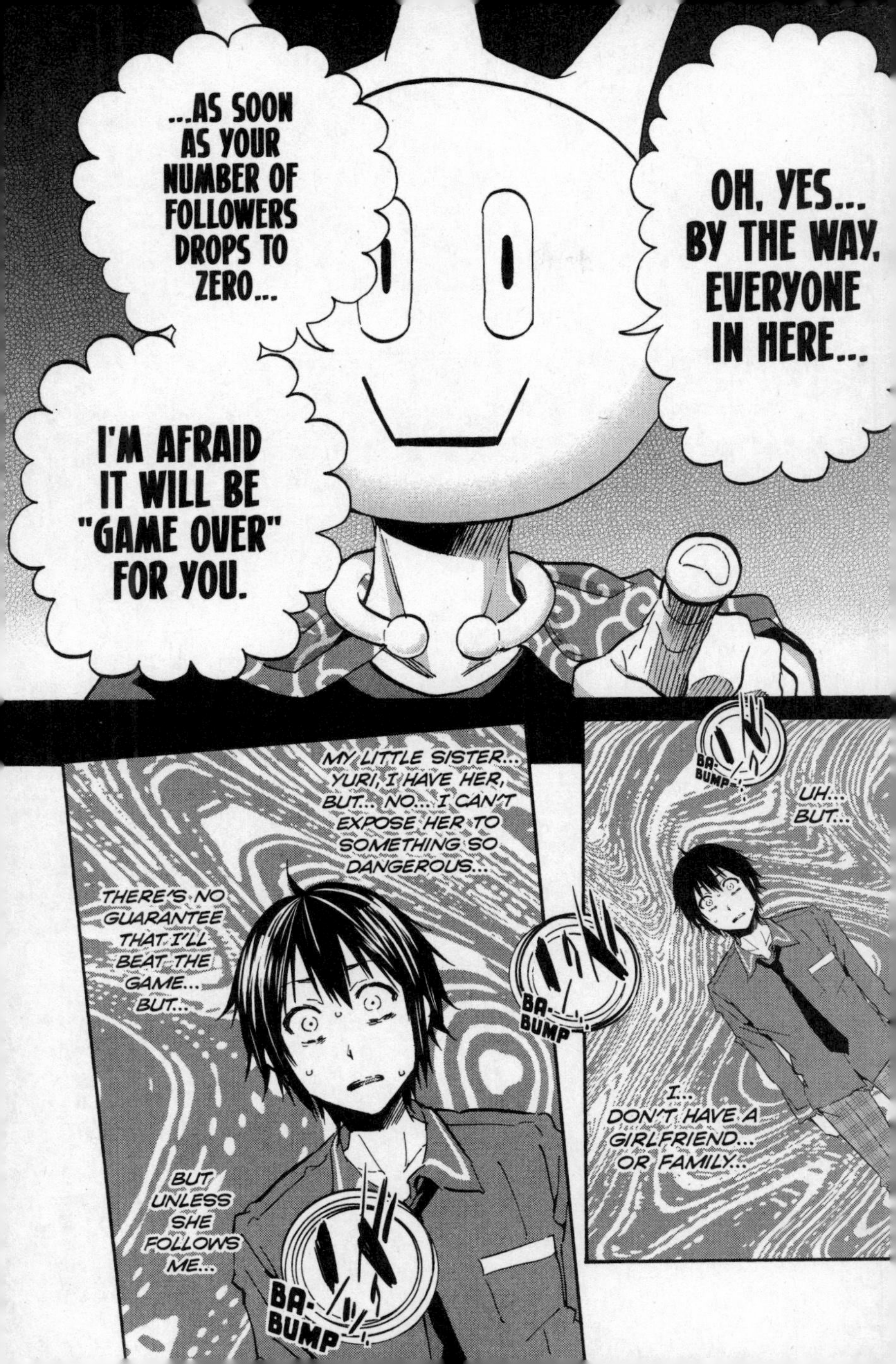
OH, YES... BY THE WAY, EVERYONE IN HERE...
...AS SOON AS YOUR NUMBER OF FOLLOWERS DROPS TO ZERO...
I'M AFRAID IT WILL BE "GAME OVER" FOR YOU.
BA-BUMP-!
UH... BUT...
I... DON'T HAVE A GIRLFRIEND... OR FAMILY...
MY LITTLE SISTER... YURI, I HAVE HER, BUT... NO... I CAN'T EXPOSE HER TO SOMETHING SO DANGEROUS...
BA-BUMP
THERE'S NO GUARANTEE THAT I'LL BEAT THE GAME... BUT...
BUT UNLESS SHE FOLLOWS ME...
BA-BUMP-!

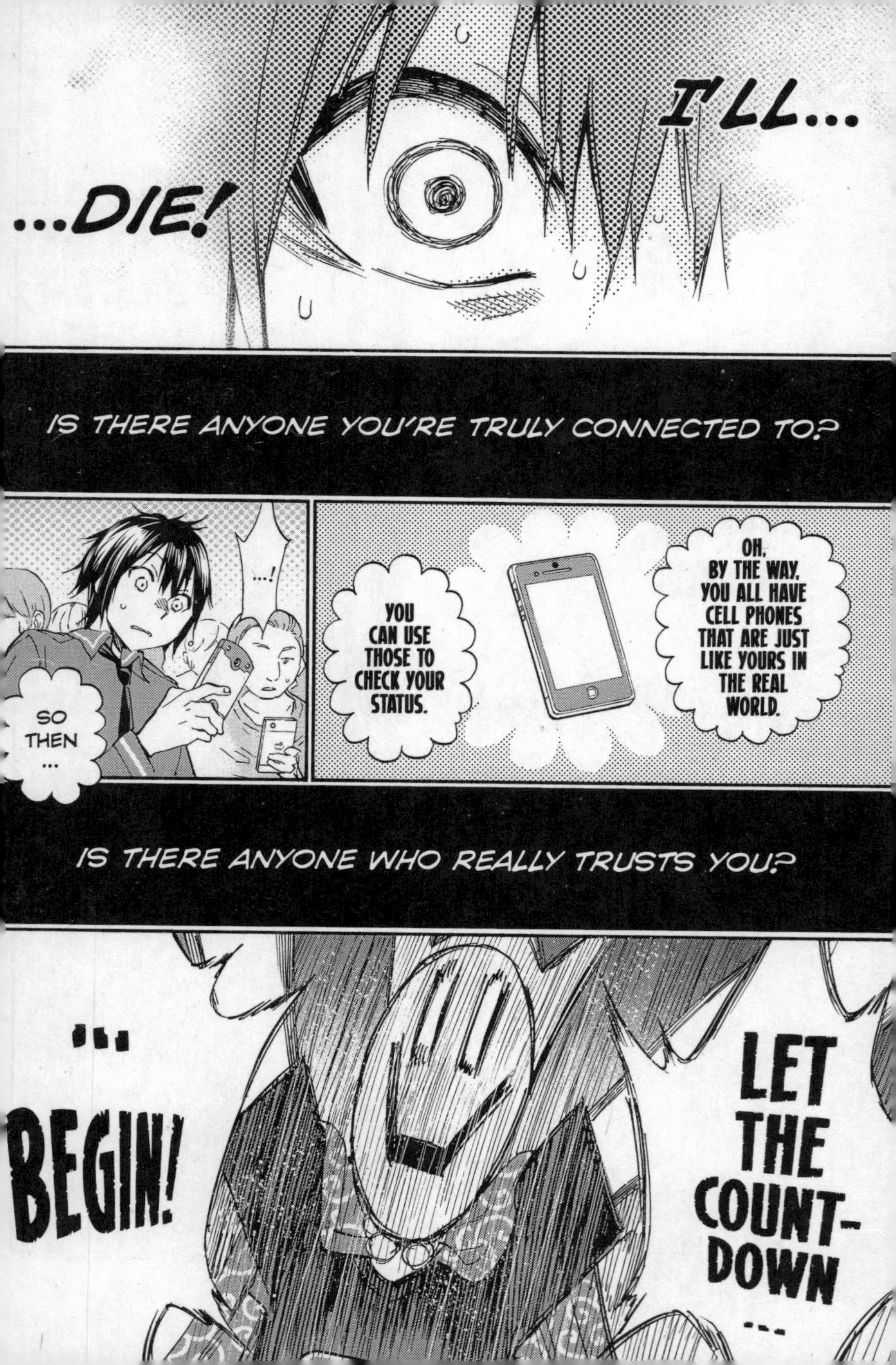
I'LL...
...DIE!
IS THERE ANYONE YOU'RE TRULY CONNECTED TO?
OH, BY THE WAY, YOU ALL HAVE CELL PHONES THAT ARE JUST LIKE YOURS IN THE REAL WORLD.
YOU CAN USE THOSE TO CHECK YOUR STATUS.
...!
SO THEN ...
IS THERE ANYONE WHO REALLY TRUSTS YOU?
LET THE COUNT-DOWN ...
... BEGIN!

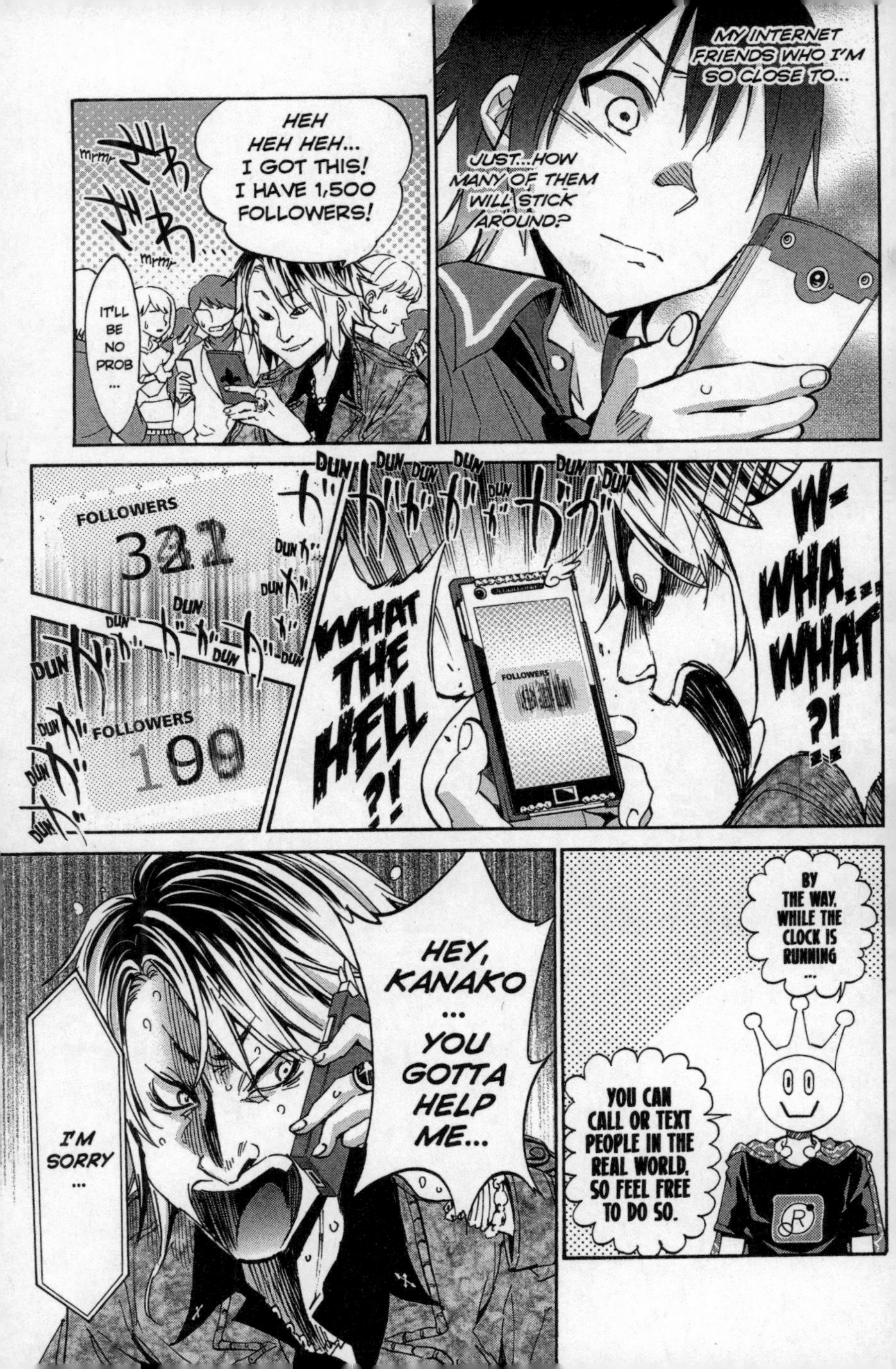
MY INTERNET FRIENDS WHO I'M SO CLOSE TO...
JUST...HOW MANY OF THEM WILL STICK AROUND?
HEH HEH HEH... I GOT THIS! I HAVE 1,500 FOLLOWERS!
mrmr
mrmr
IT'LL BE NO PROB ...
W-WHA... WHAT ?!
WHAT THE HELL ?!
DUN DUN DUN DUN DUN DUN DUN
FOLLOWERS
321
DUN DUN DUN DUN DUN DUN DUN DUN DUN DUN
FOLLOWERS
199
FOLLOWERS
BY THE WAY, WHILE THE CLOCK IS RUNNING ...
YOU CAN CALL OR TEXT PEOPLE IN THE REAL WORLD, SO FEEL FREE TO DO SO.
HEY, KANAKO ... YOU GOTTA HELP ME...
I'M SORRY ...

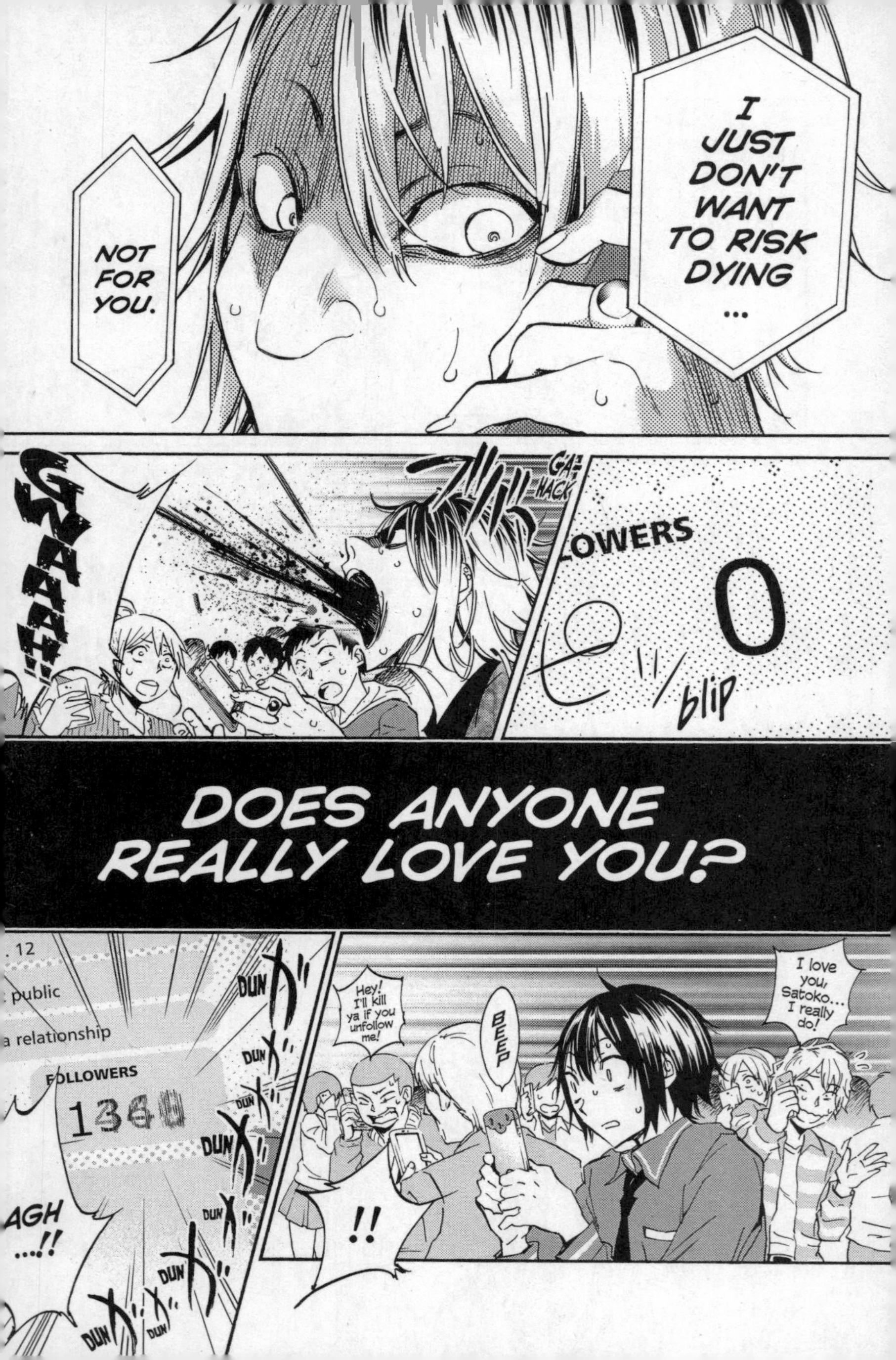
I JUST DON'T WANT TO RISK DYING ...
NOT FOR YOU.
OWERS
0
blip
GA-HACK
GWAAAH!!
DOES ANYONE REALLY LOVE YOU?
I love you, Satoko... I really do!
BEEP
Hey! I'll kill ya if you unfollow me!
!!
12
public
a relationship
FOLLOWERS
DUN
DUN
DUN
DUN
DUN
DUN
DUN
DUN
AGH ...!!

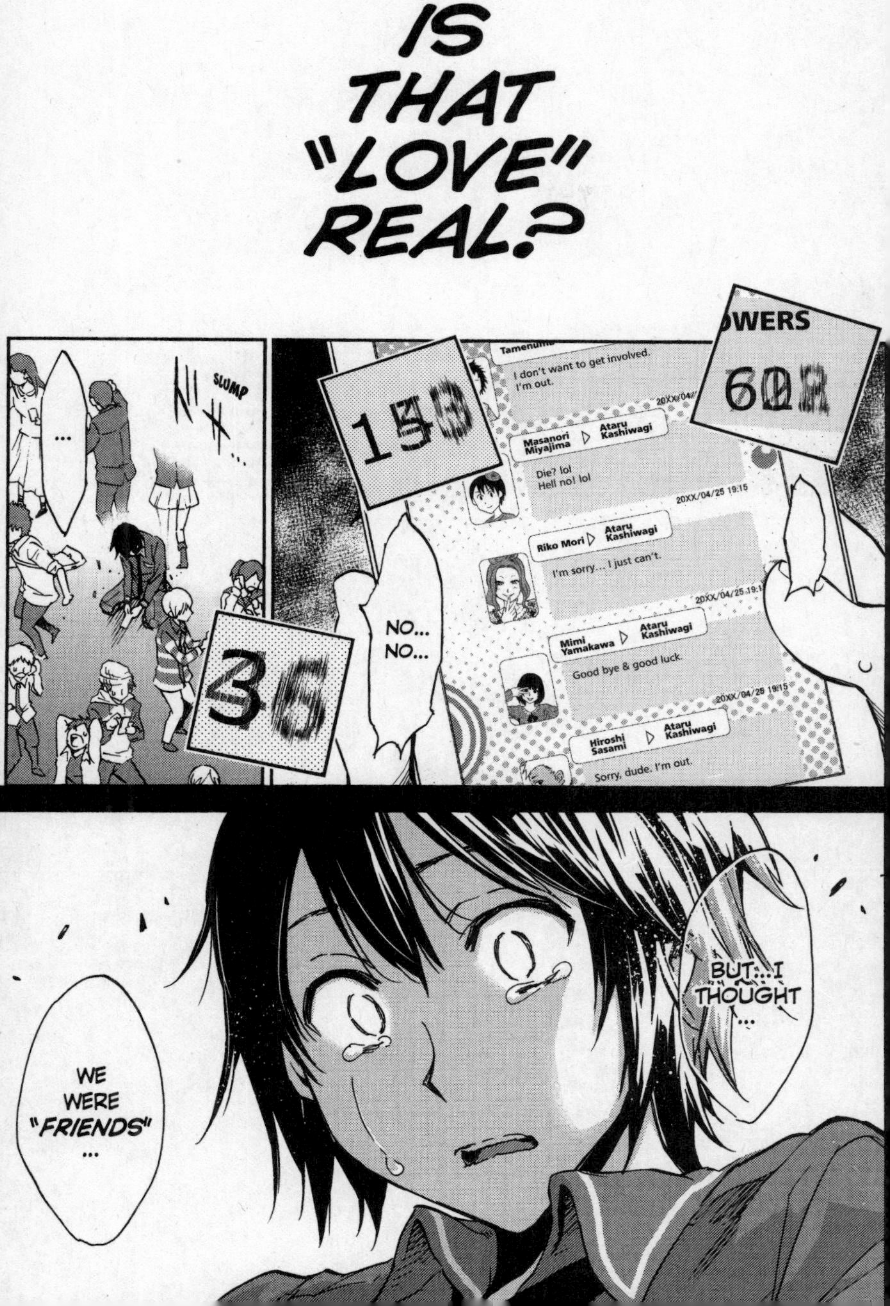
IS THAT "LOVE" REAL?
I don't want to get involved. I'm out.
Masanori Miyajima ▷ Ataru Kashiwagi
Die? lol Hell no! lol
20XX/04/25 19:15
Riko Mori ▷ Ataru Kashiwagi
I'm sorry... I just can't.
Mimi Yamakawa ▷ Ataru Kashiwagi
Good bye & good luck.
20XX/04/25 19:15
Hiroshi Sasami ▷ Ataru Kashiwagi
Sorry, dude. I'm out.
NO... NO...
SLUMP
...
BUT... I THOUGHT ...
WE WERE "FRIENDS" ...

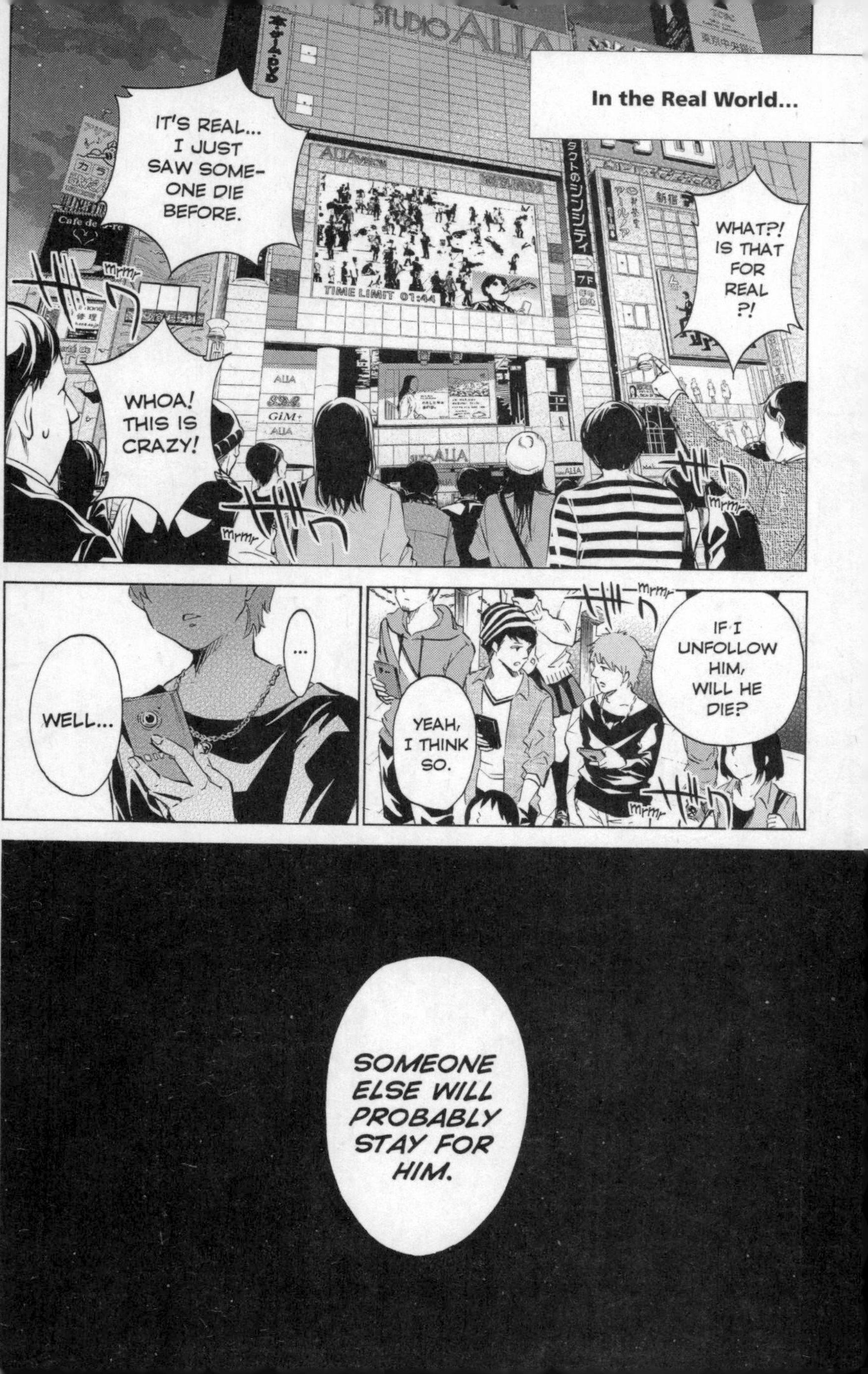
In the Real World...
WHAT?! IS THAT FOR REAL?!
IT'S REAL... I JUST SAW SOME-ONE DIE BEFORE.
mrmr
WHOA! THIS IS CRAZY!
mrmr
mrmr
TIME LIMIT 01:44
STUDIO ALTA
IF I UNFOLLOW HIM, WILL HE DIE?
mrmr
YEAH, I THINK SO.
mrmr
...
WELL...
SOMEONE ELSE WILL PROBABLY STAY FOR HIM.

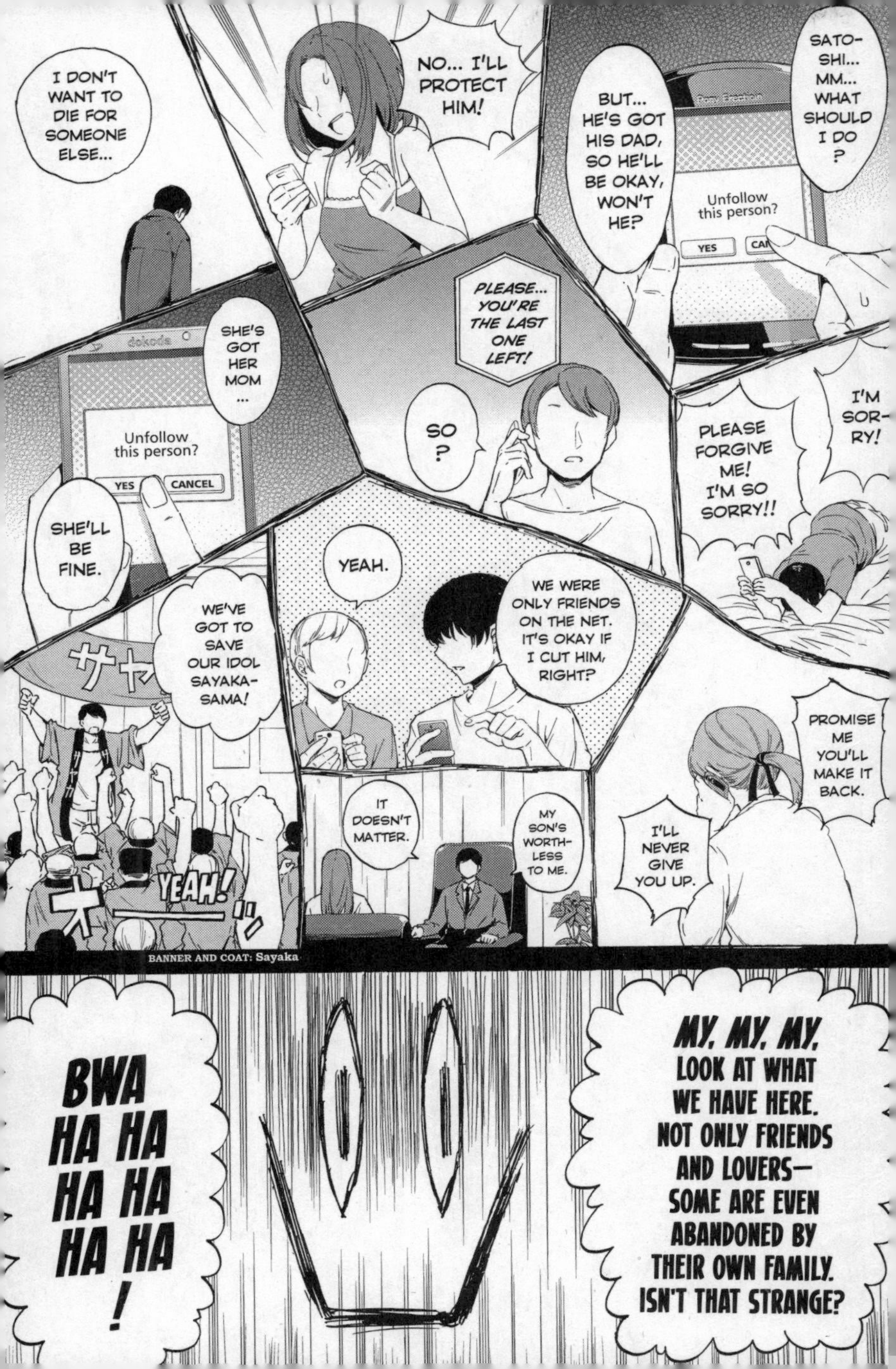
SATO-SHI... MM... WHAT SHOULD I DO?
Unfollow this person?
YES
BUT... HE'S GOT HIS DAD, SO HE'LL BE OKAY, WON'T HE?
NO... I'LL PROTECT HIM!
I DON'T WANT TO DIE FOR SOMEONE ELSE...
I'M SORRY!
PLEASE FORGIVE ME! I'M SO SORRY!!
PLEASE... YOU'RE THE LAST ONE LEFT!
SO?
SHE'S GOT HER MOM...
dokoda
Unfollow this person?
YES
CANCEL
SHE'LL BE FINE.
PROMISE ME YOU'LL MAKE IT BACK.
I'LL NEVER GIVE YOU UP.
WE WERE ONLY FRIENDS ON THE NET. IT'S OKAY IF I CUT HIM, RIGHT?
YEAH.
MY SON'S WORTHLESS TO ME.
IT DOESN'T MATTER.
WE'VE GOT TO SAVE OUR IDOL SAYAKA-SAMA!
YEAH!
BANNER AND COAT: Sayaka
MY, MY, MY, LOOK AT WHAT WE HAVE HERE. NOT ONLY FRIENDS AND LOVERS— SOME ARE EVEN ABANDONED BY THEIR OWN FAMILY. ISN'T THAT STRANGE?
BWA HA HA HA HA HA HA HA HA!

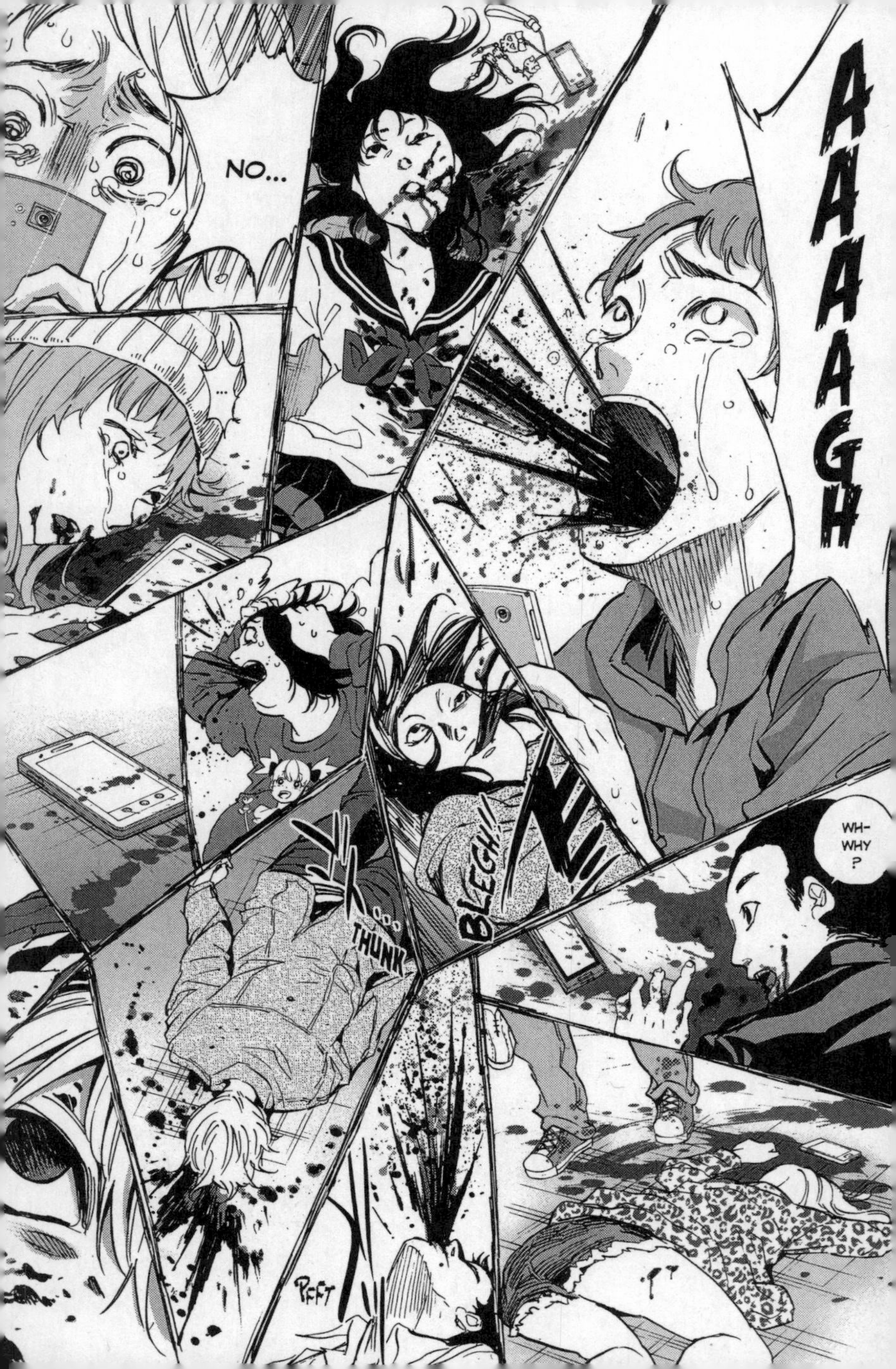
AAAAGH
NO...
...
WH-WHY?
BLECH!!
THUNK
PFFT

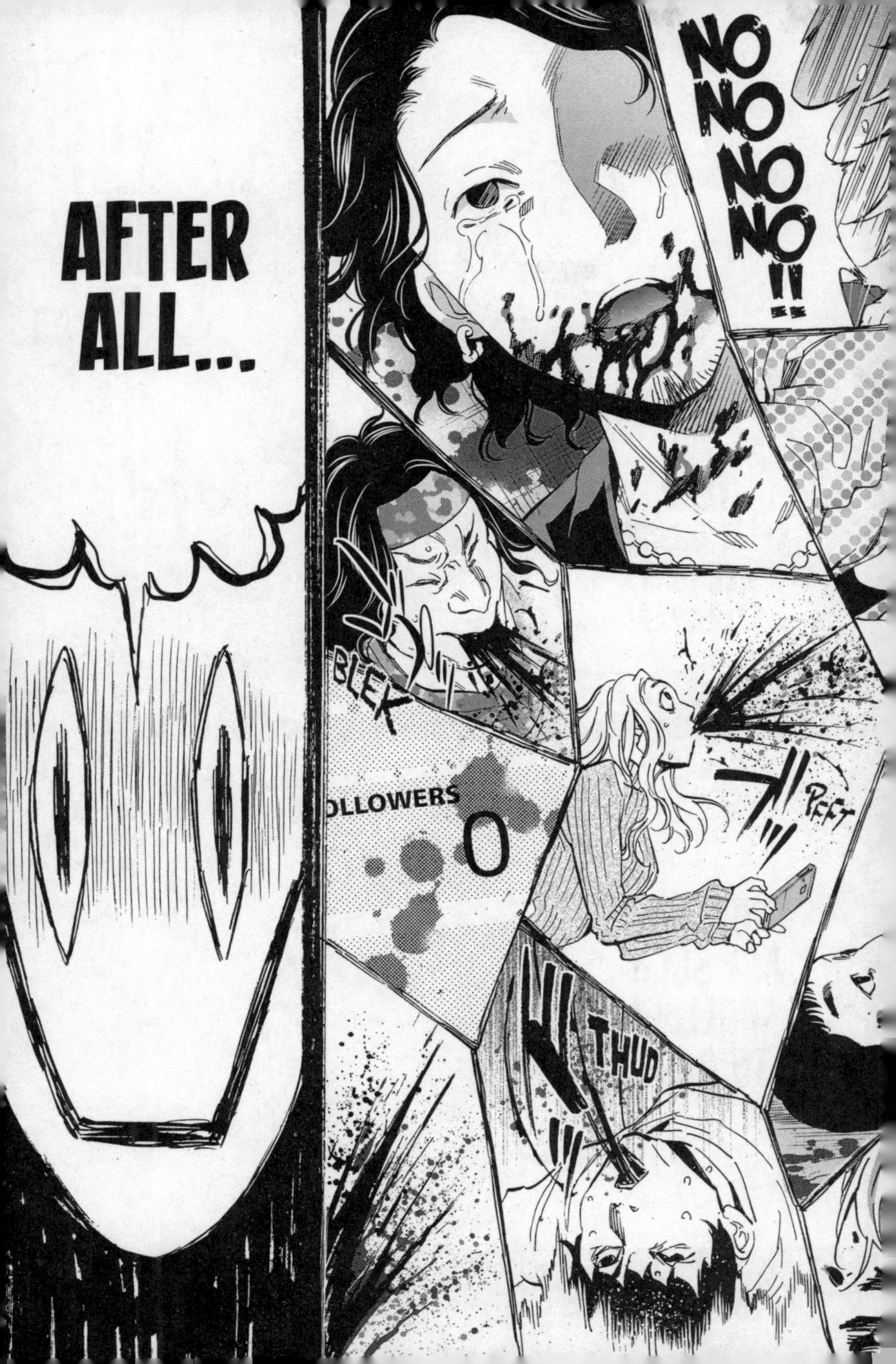
NO NO NO NO!!
BLEK
PFFT
OLLOWERS
0
THUD
AFTER ALL...

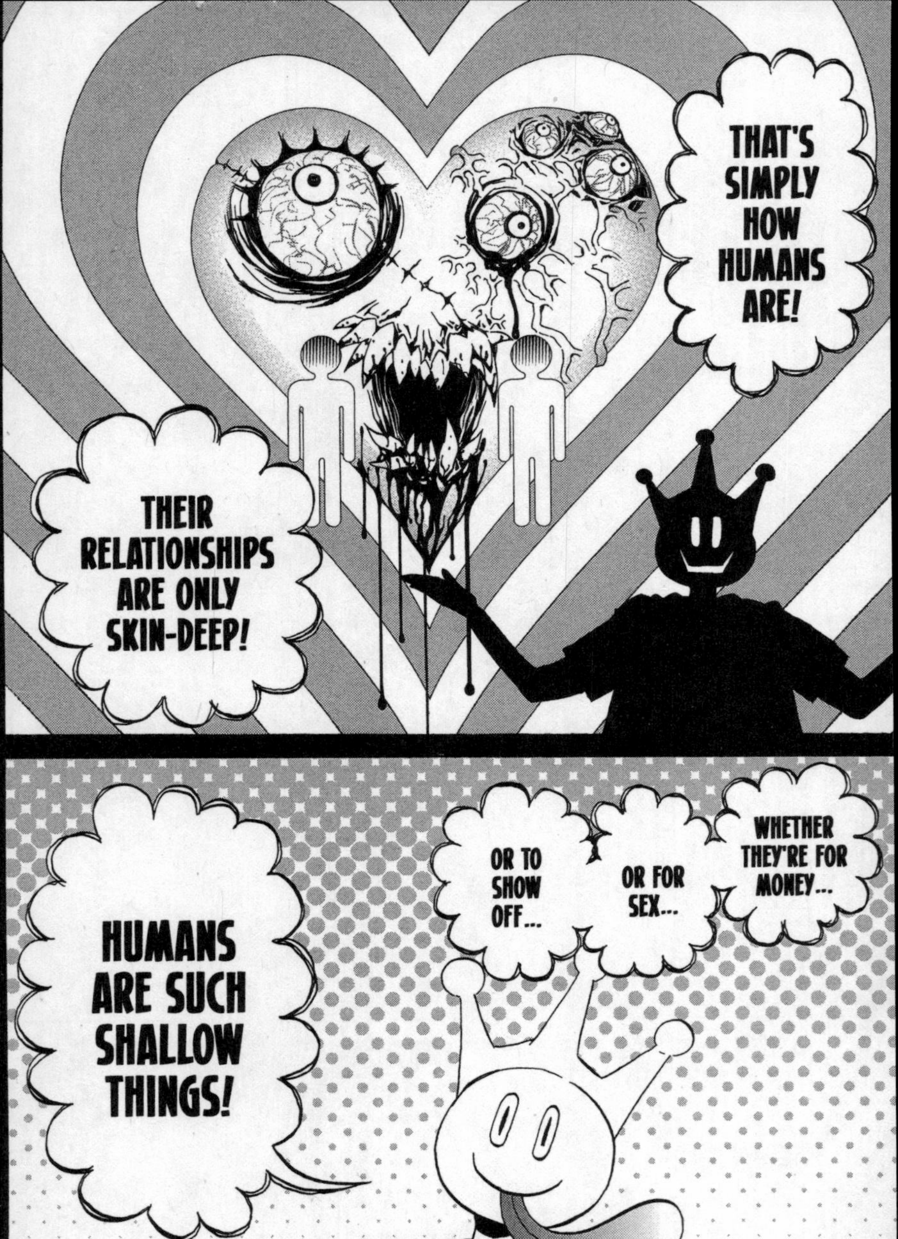
THAT'S SIMPLY HOW HUMANS ARE!
THEIR RELATIONSHIPS ARE ONLY SKIN-DEEP!
WHETHER THEY'RE FOR MONEY...
OR FOR SEX...
OR TO SHOW OFF...
HUMANS ARE SUCH SHALLOW THINGS!

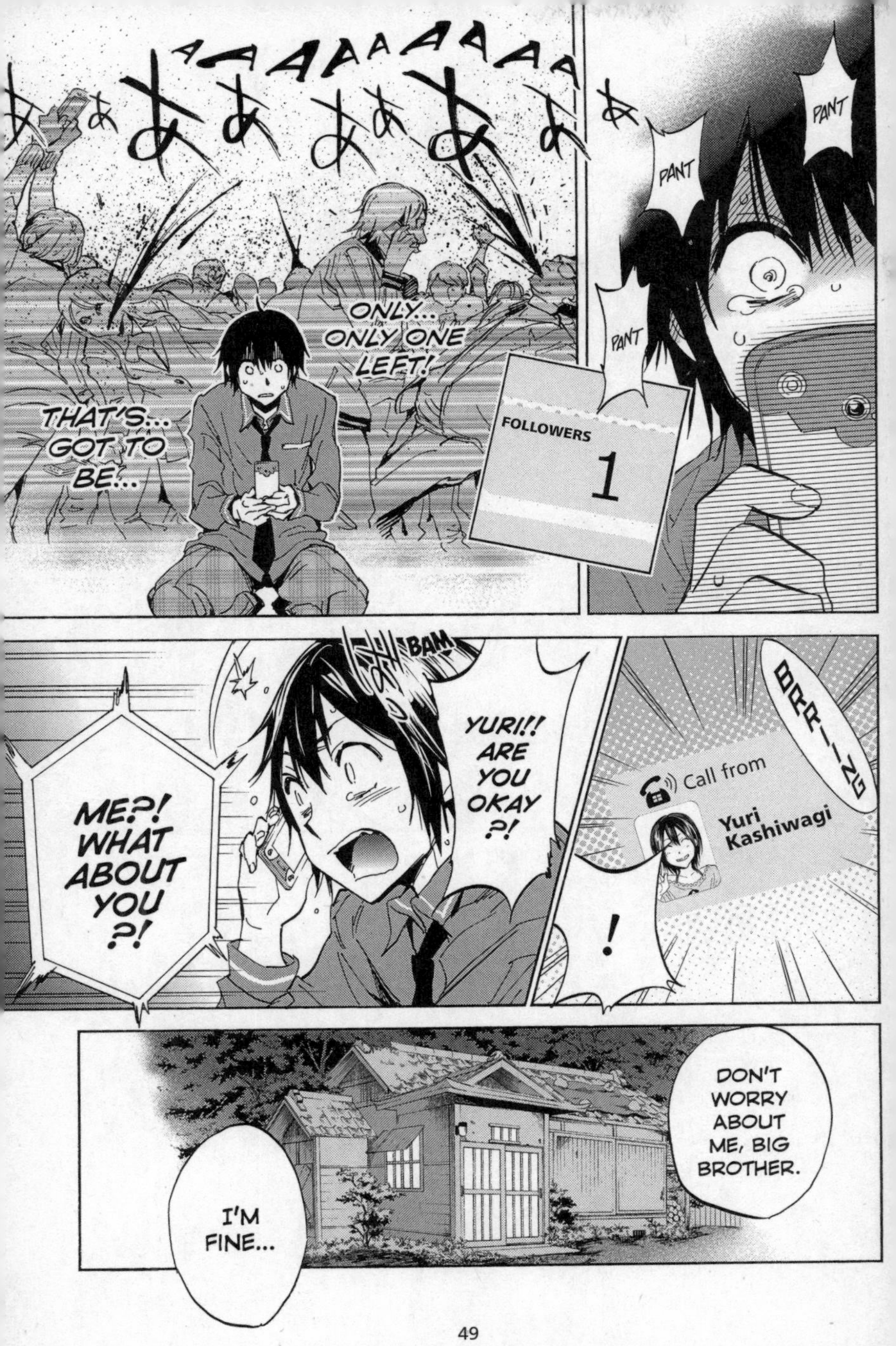
PANT
PANT
PANT
FOLLOWERS
1
AAAAAAAAAA
ONLY... ONLY ONE LEFT!
THAT'S... GOT TO BE...
BRRING
Call from
Yuri Kashiwagi
!
BAM
YURI!! ARE YOU OKAY?!
ME?! WHAT ABOUT YOU?!
DON'T WORRY ABOUT ME, BIG BROTHER.
I'M FINE...

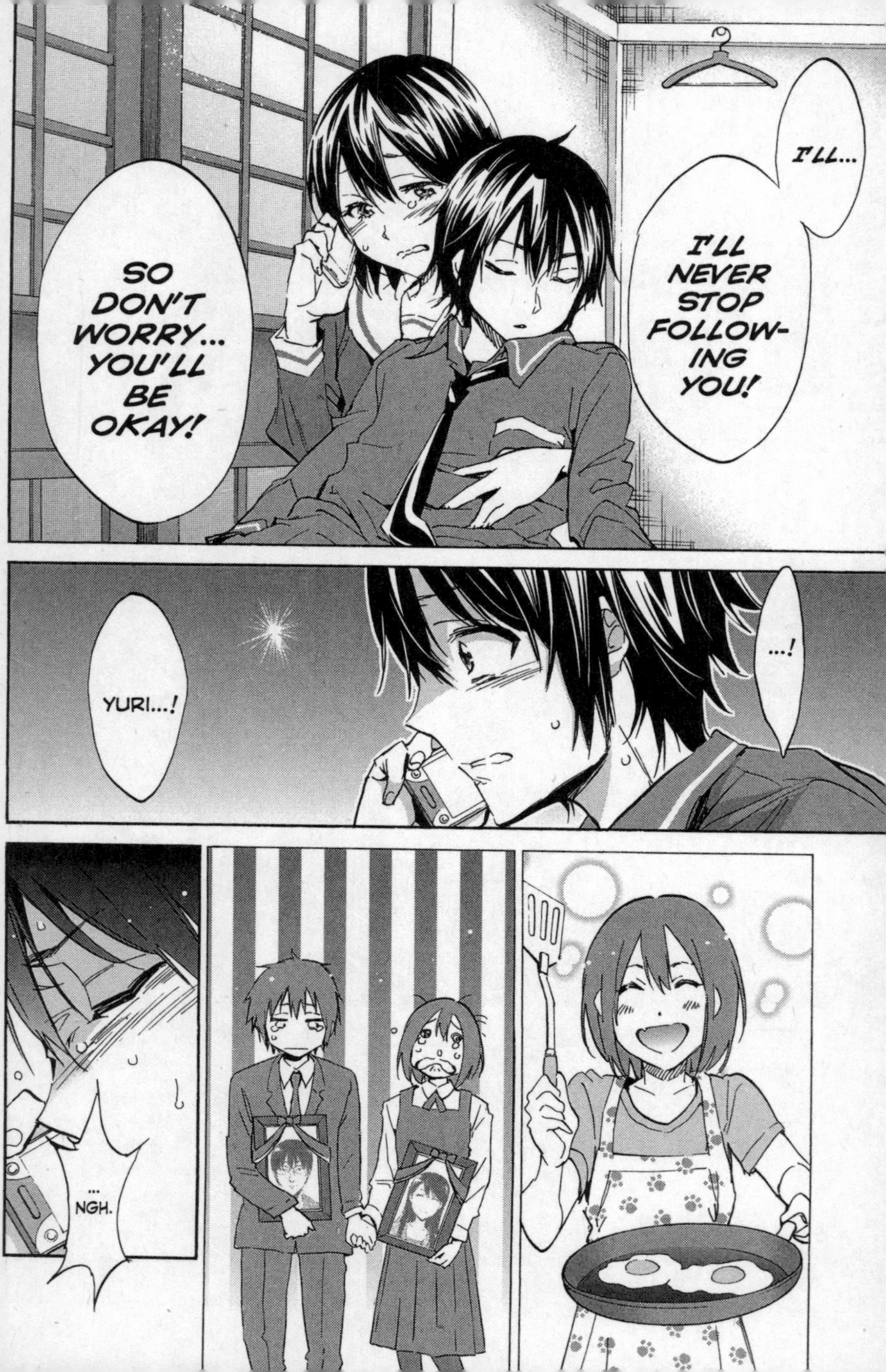
I'LL...
I'LL NEVER STOP FOLLOW-ING YOU!
SO DON'T WORRY... YOU'LL BE OKAY!
...!
YURI...!
... NGH.

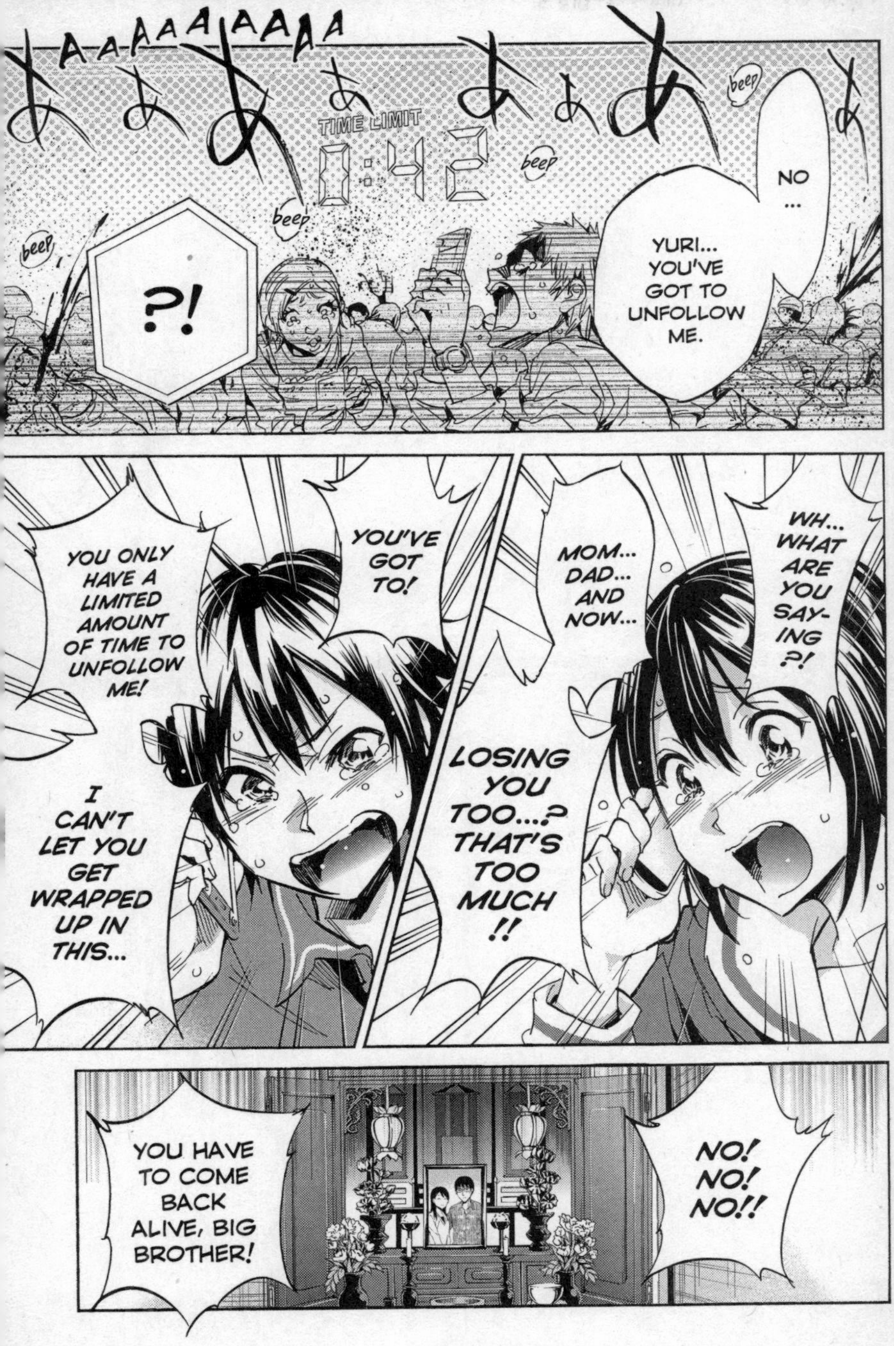
AAAAAAAAAA
TIME LIMIT
0:42
beep
beep
beep
beep
NO ...
YURI... YOU'VE GOT TO UNFOLLOW ME.
?!
WH... WHAT ARE YOU SAY-ING?!
MOM... DAD... AND NOW...
LOSING YOU TOO...? THAT'S TOO MUCH!!
YOU'VE GOT TO!
YOU ONLY HAVE A LIMITED AMOUNT OF TIME TO UNFOLLOW ME!
I CAN'T LET YOU GET WRAPPED UP IN THIS...
NO! NO! NO!!
YOU HAVE TO COME BACK ALIVE, BIG BROTHER!

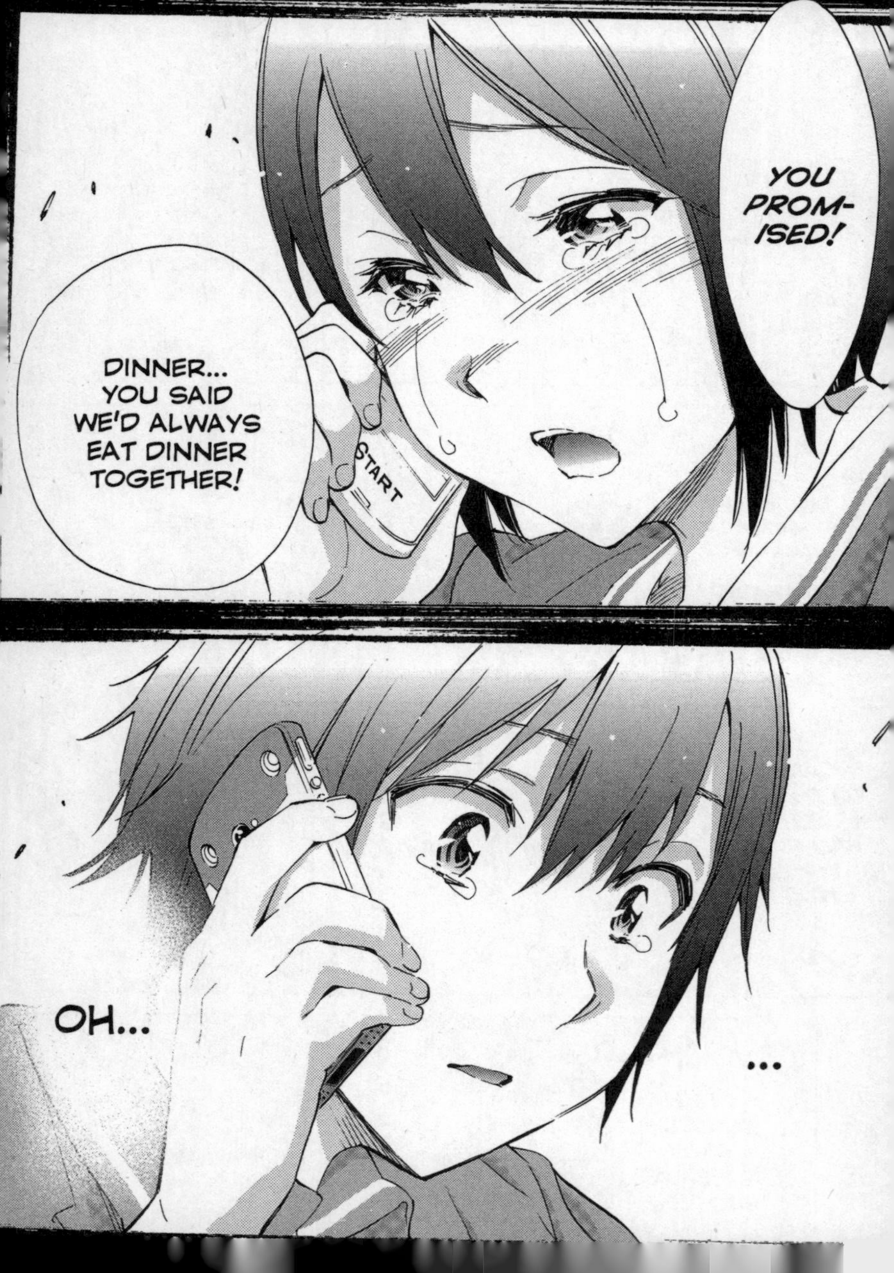
YOU PROM-ISED!
DINNER... YOU SAID WE'D ALWAYS EAT DINNER TOGETHER!
START
...
OH...

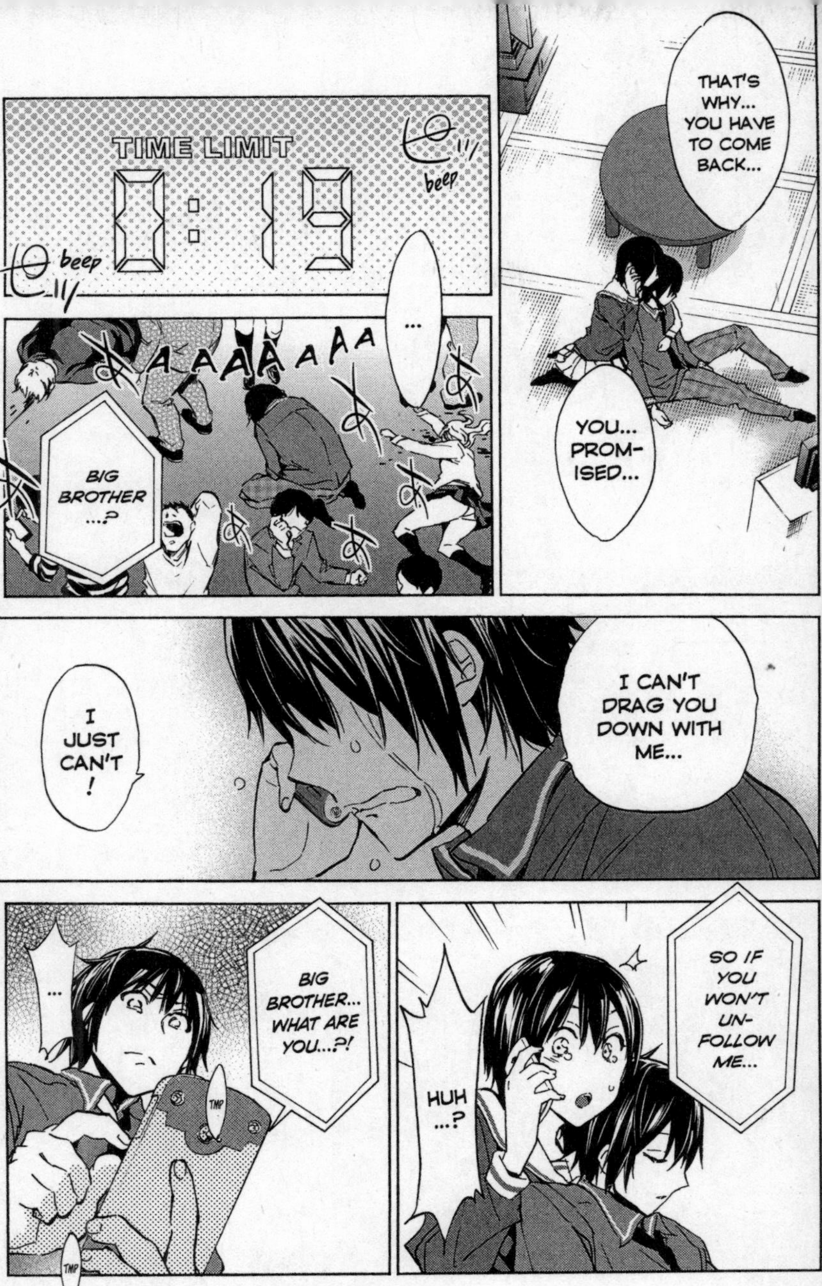
THAT'S WHY... YOU HAVE TO COME BACK...
YOU... PROMISED...
TIME LIMIT
0:19
beep
beep
...
AAAAAAAA
BIG BROTHER ...?
I CAN'T DRAG YOU DOWN WITH ME...
I JUST CAN'T!
SO IF YOU WON'T UNFOLLOW ME...
HUH ...?
BIG BROTHER... WHAT ARE YOU...?!
...
TMP
TMP

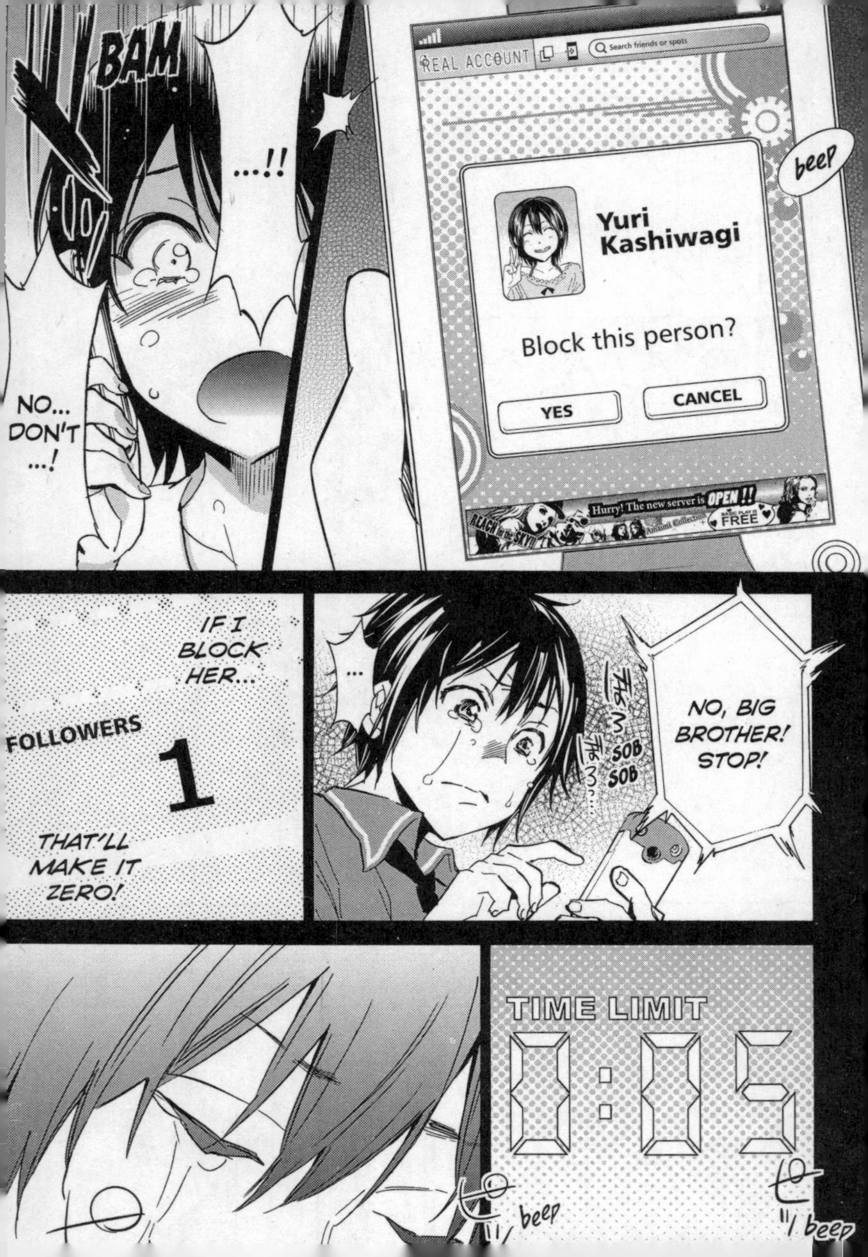
REAL ACCOUNT
Search friends or spots
beep
Yuri Kashiwagi
Block this person?
YES
CANCEL
Hurry! The new server is OPEN!!
FREE
REACH for the SKY!!
BAM
...!!
NO... DON'T ...!
NO, BIG BROTHER! STOP!
SOB SOB
...
IF I BLOCK HER...
FOLLOWERS
1
THAT'LL MAKE IT ZERO!
TIME LIMIT
0:05
beep
beep

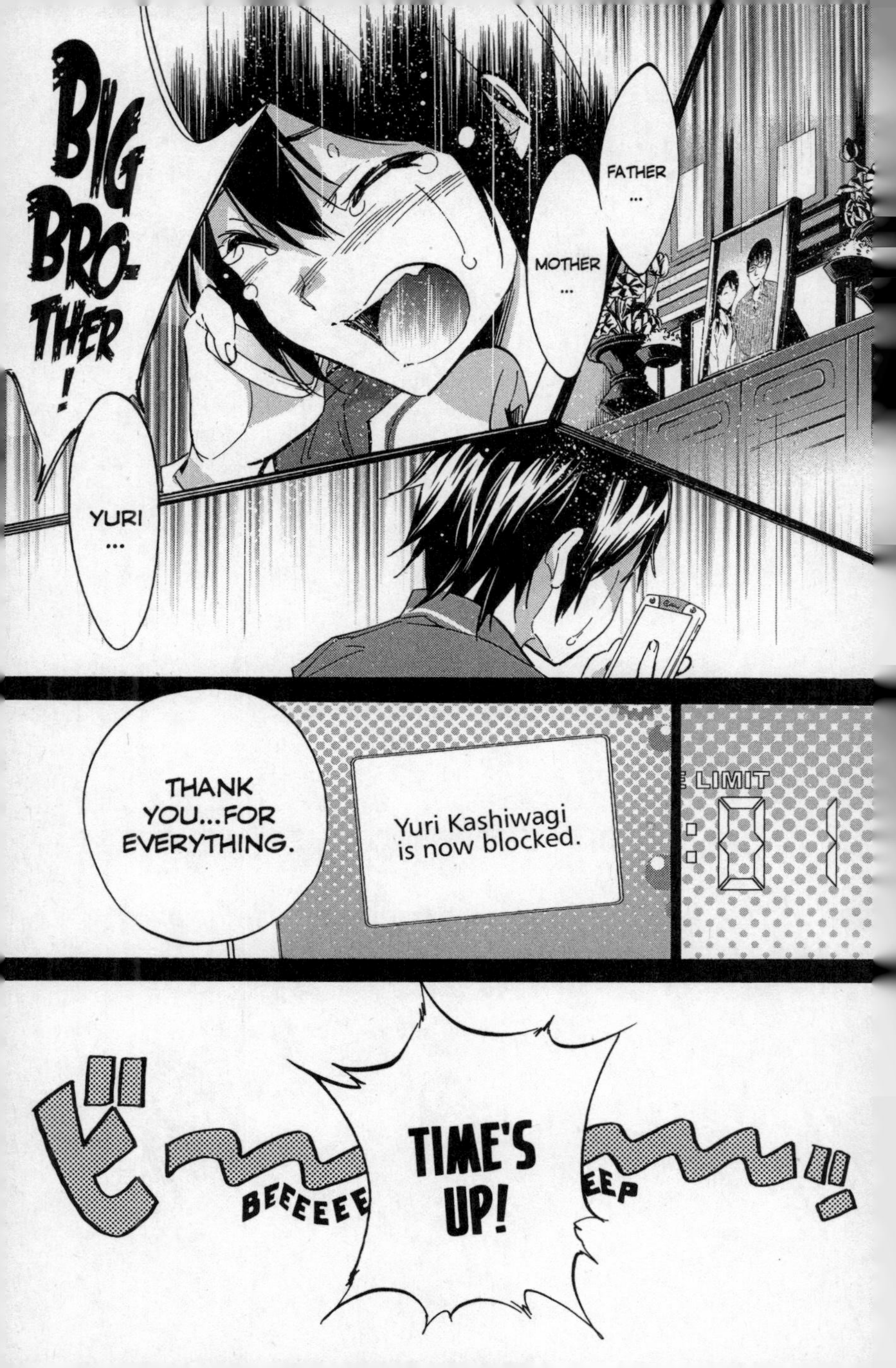
FATHER ...
MOTHER ...
BIG BRO-THER!
YURI ...
E LIMIT
:01
Yuri Kashiwagi is now blocked.
THANK YOU...FOR EVERYTHING.
ど〜〜〜〜ん!!
BEEEEEE EEP
TIME'S UP!

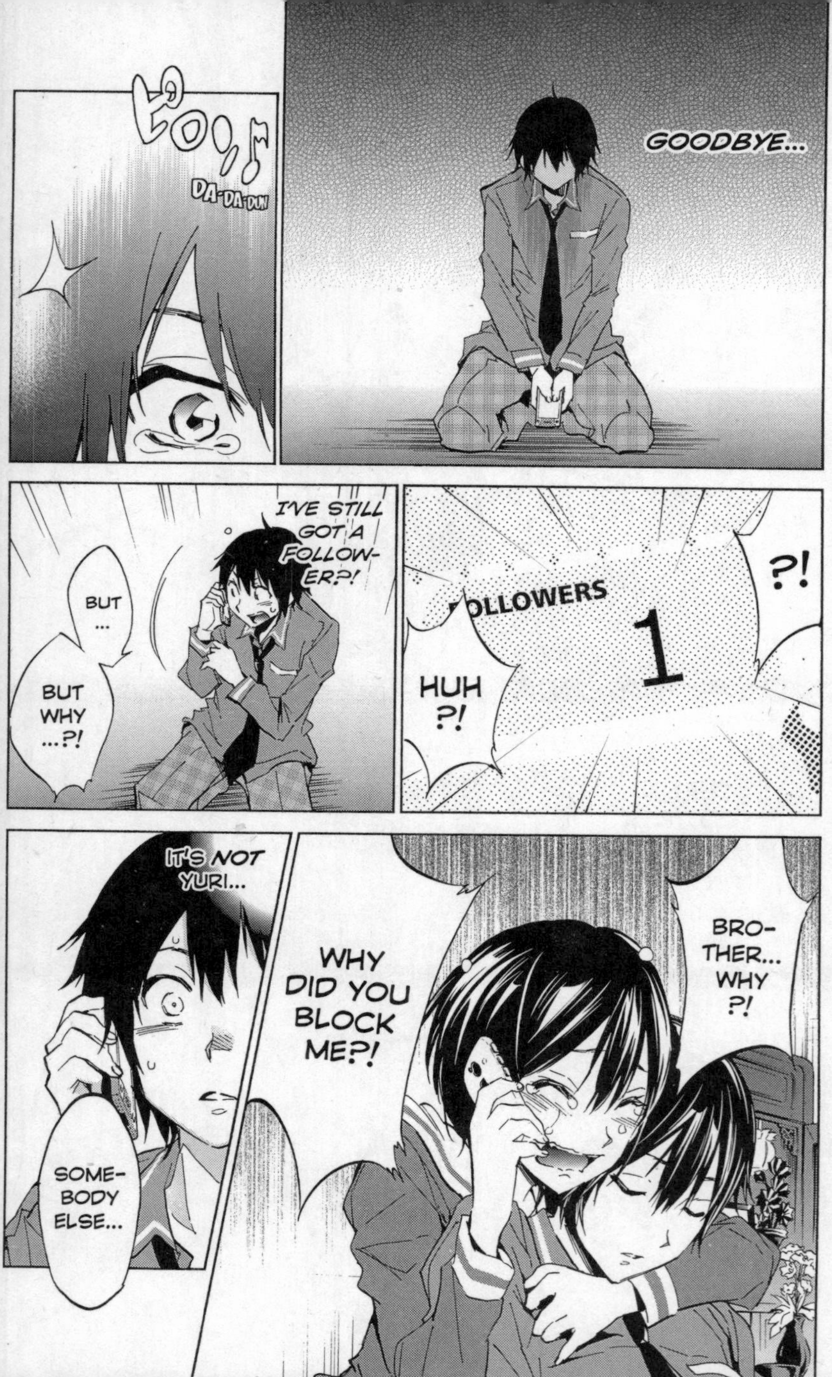
GOODBYE...
ピロッ♪
DA-DA-DUN
?!
FOLLOWERS
1
HUH ?!
I'VE STILL GOT A FOLLOWER?!
BUT ...
BUT WHY ...?!
BROTHER... WHY ?!
WHY DID YOU BLOCK ME?!
IT'S NOT YURI...
SOMEBODY ELSE...

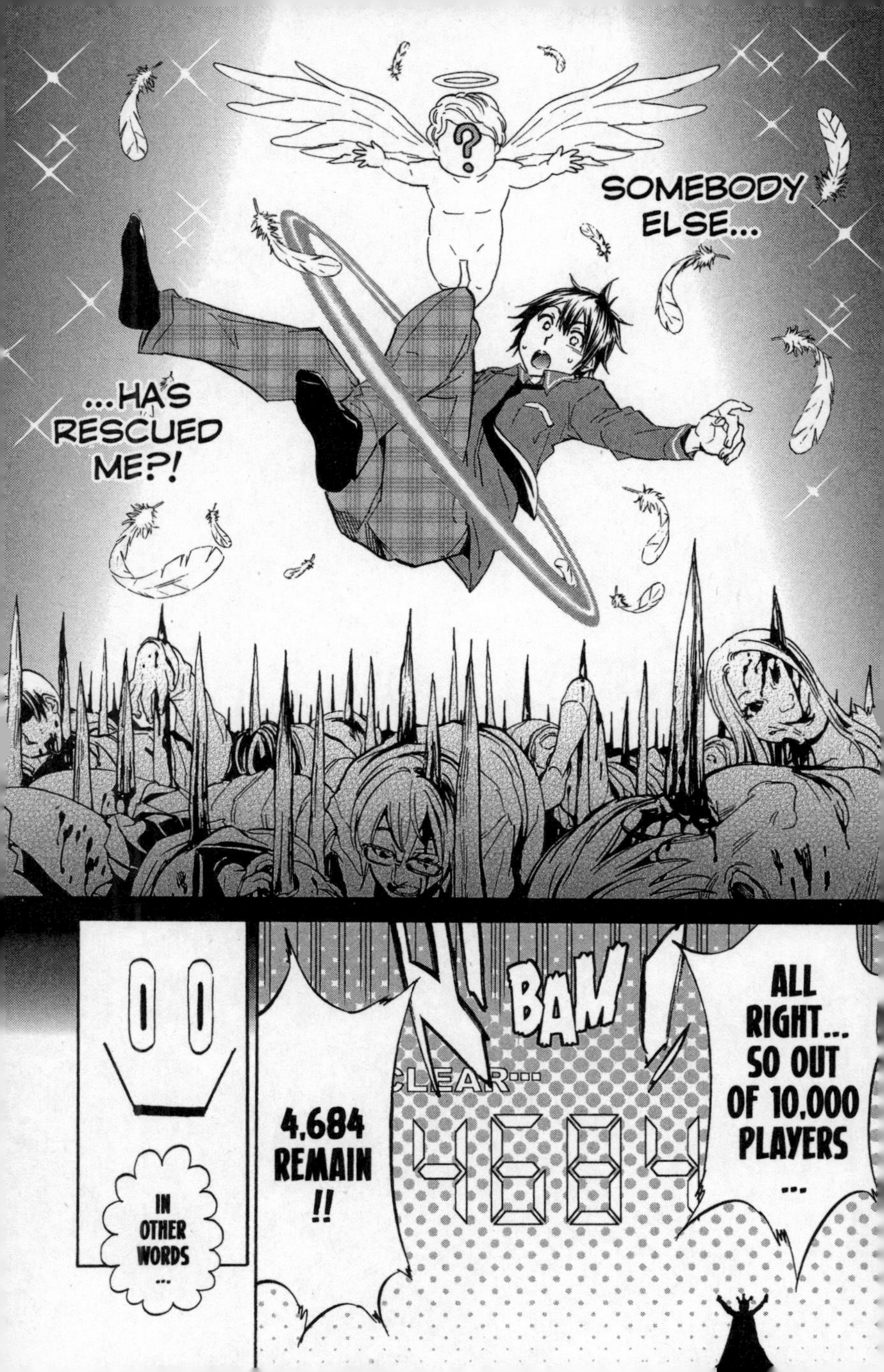
SOMEBODY ELSE...
...HAS RESCUED ME?!
ALL RIGHT... SO OUT OF 10,000 PLAYERS ...
BAM
CLEAR...
4684
4,684 REMAIN !!
IN OTHER WORDS ...

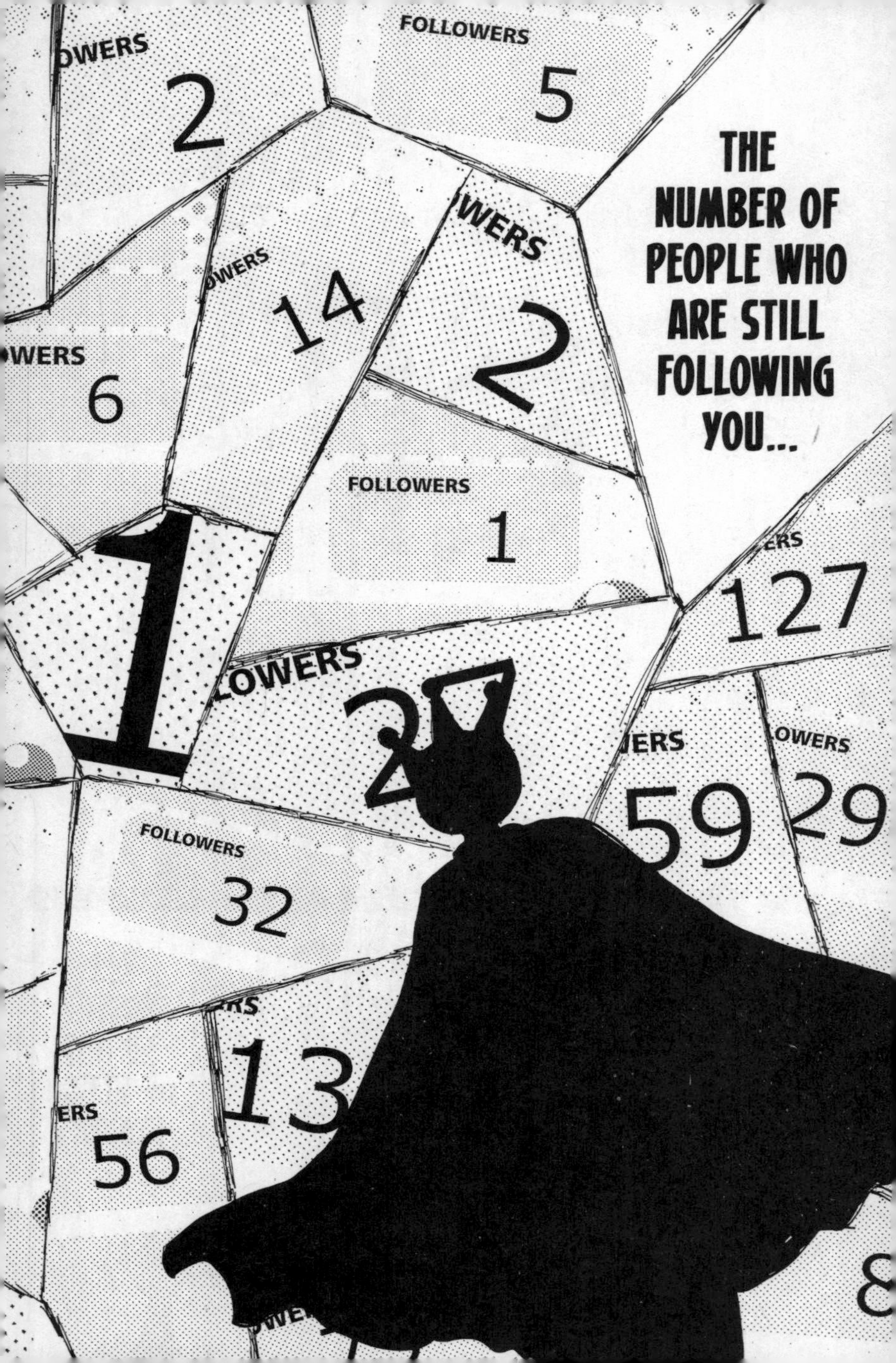
THE NUMBER OF PEOPLE WHO ARE STILL FOLLOWING YOU...
FOLLOWERS 5
FOLLOWERS 1
FOLLOWERS 32
2
14
6
2
1
127
59
29
13
56

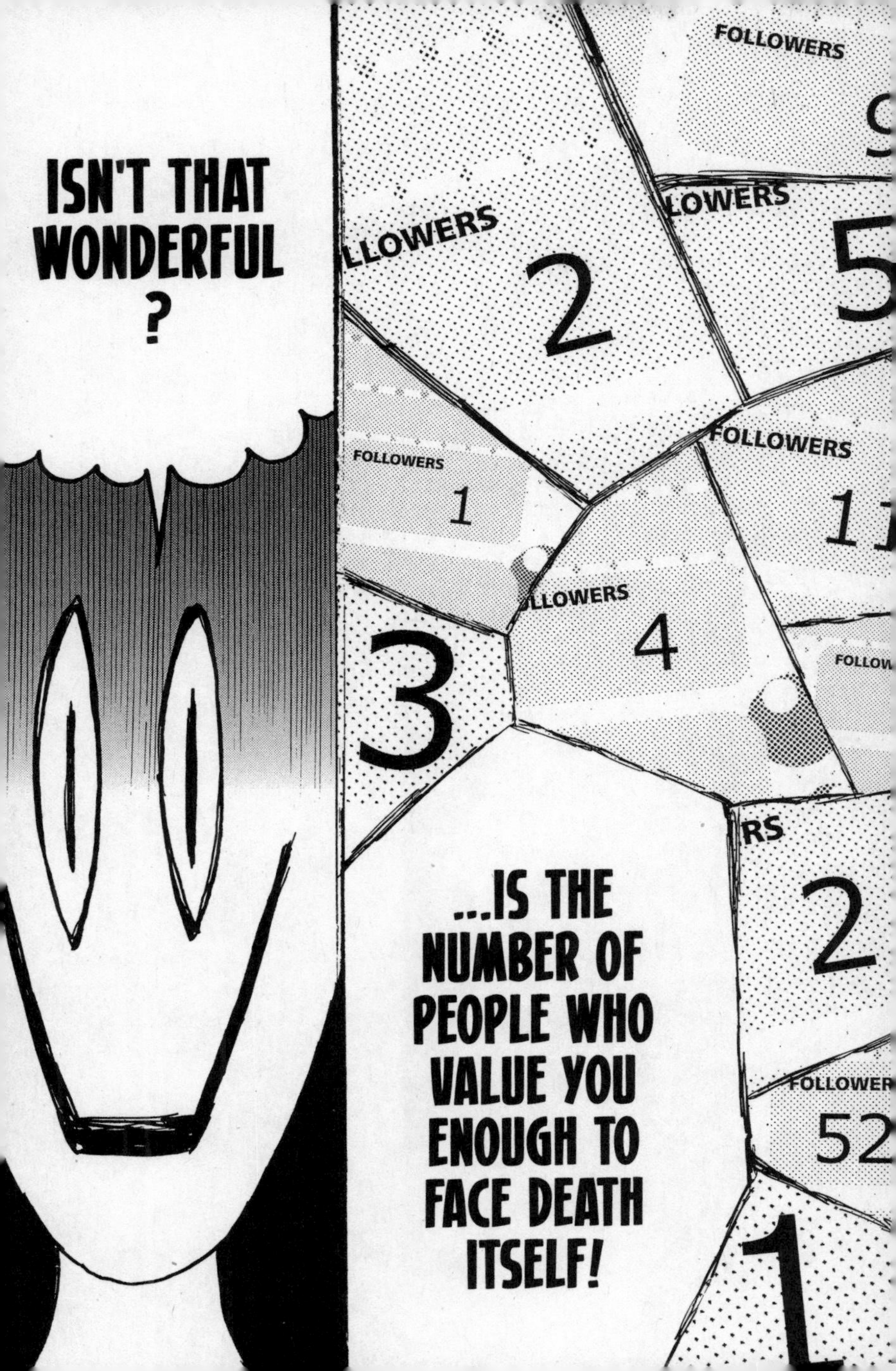
FOLLOWERS
LOWERS
5
LLOWERS
2
FOLLOWERS
1
FOLLOWERS
LLOWERS
4
3
RS
2
...IS THE NUMBER OF PEOPLE WHO VALUE YOU ENOUGH TO FACE DEATH ITSELF!
ISN'T THAT WONDERFUL?

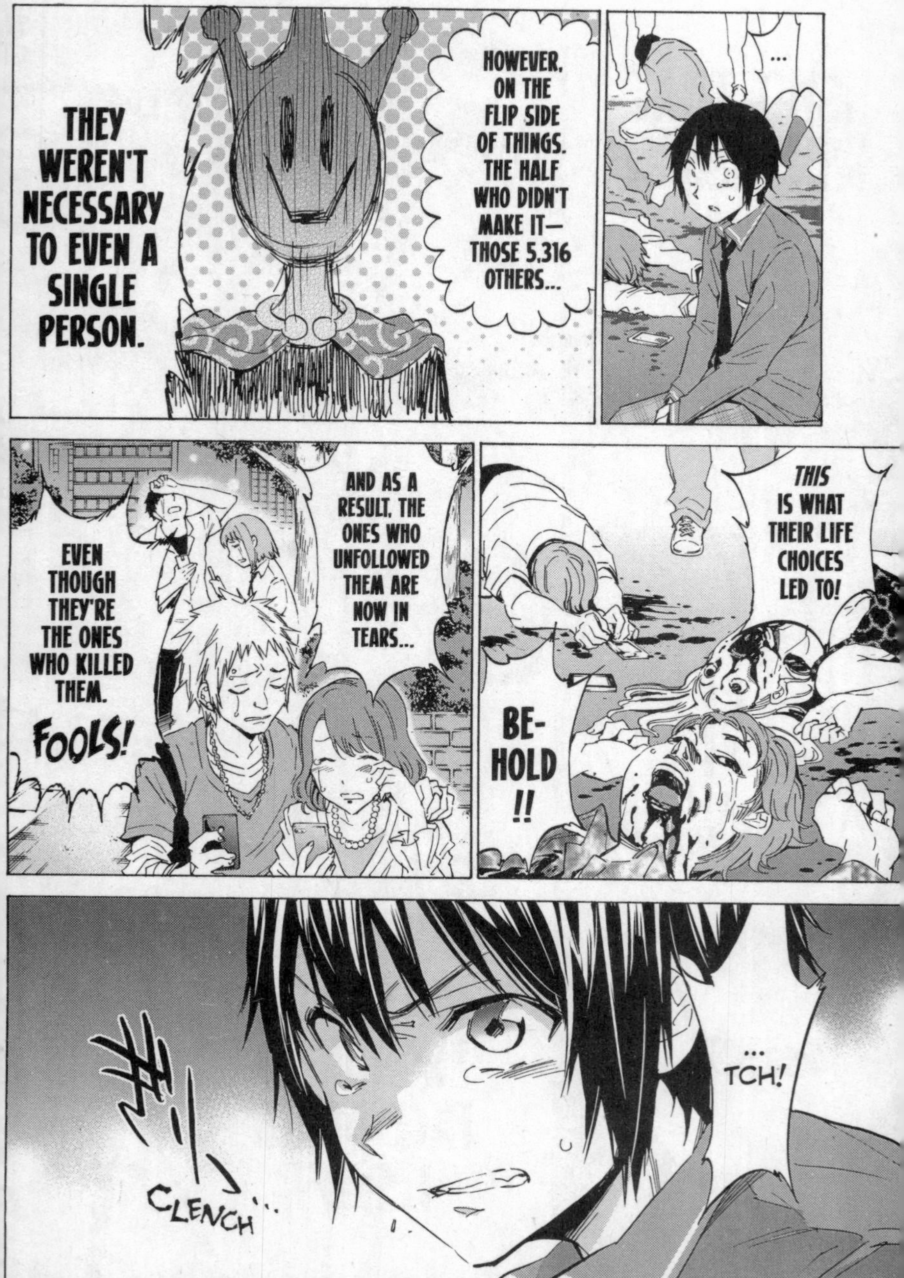
...
HOWEVER, ON THE FLIP SIDE OF THINGS. THE HALF WHO DIDN'T MAKE IT—THOSE 5,316 OTHERS...
THEY WEREN'T NECESSARY TO EVEN A SINGLE PERSON.
THIS IS WHAT THEIR LIFE CHOICES LED TO!
BE-HOLD!!
AND AS A RESULT, THE ONES WHO UNFOLLOWED THEM ARE NOW IN TEARS...
EVEN THOUGH THEY'RE THE ONES WHO KILLED THEM.
FOOLS!
...TCH!
CLENCH...

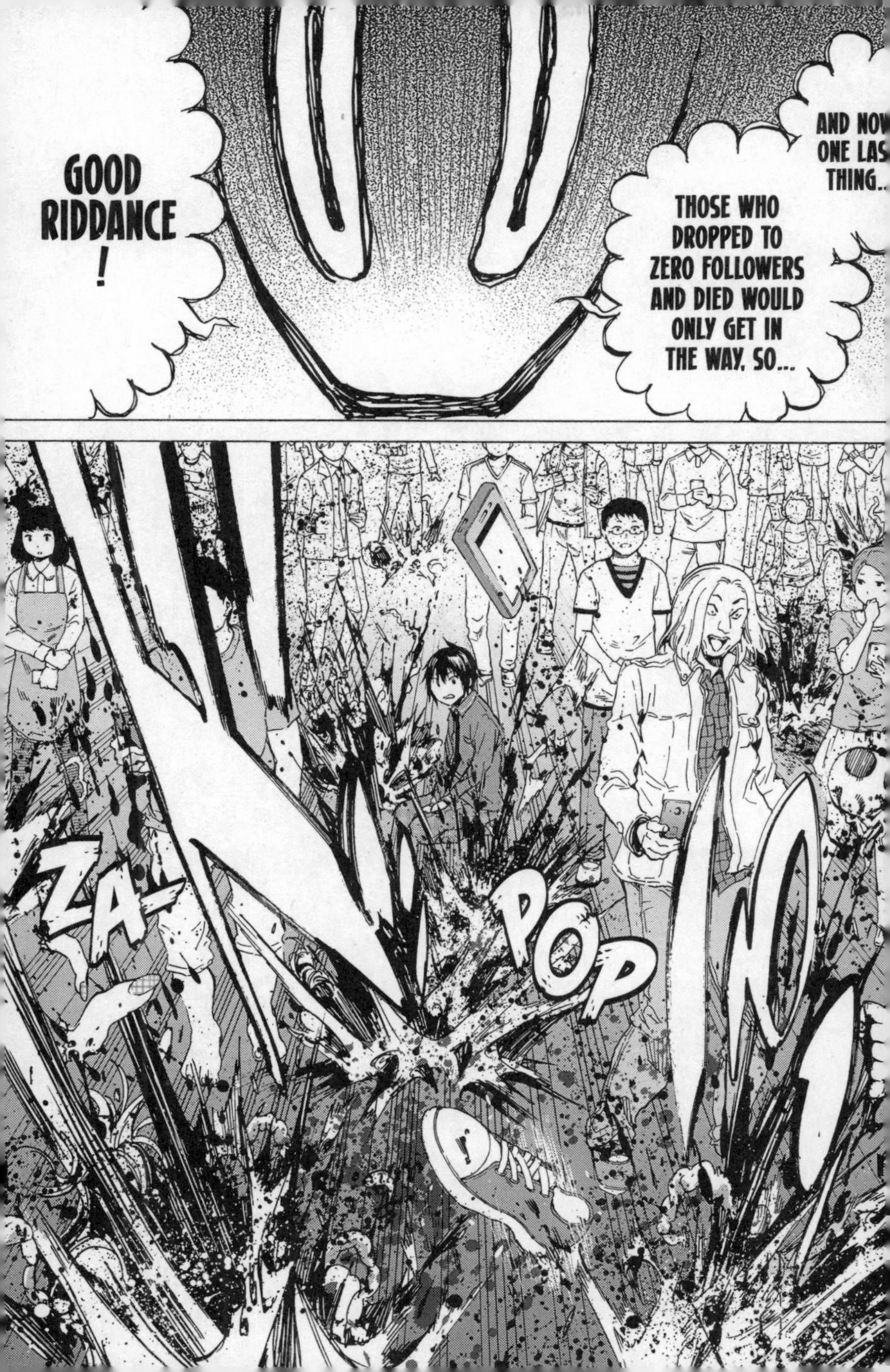
AND NOW ONE LAS THING..
THOSE WHO DROPPED TO ZERO FOLLOWERS AND DIED WOULD ONLY GET IN THE WAY, SO...
GOOD RIDDANCE!
POP
ZA-

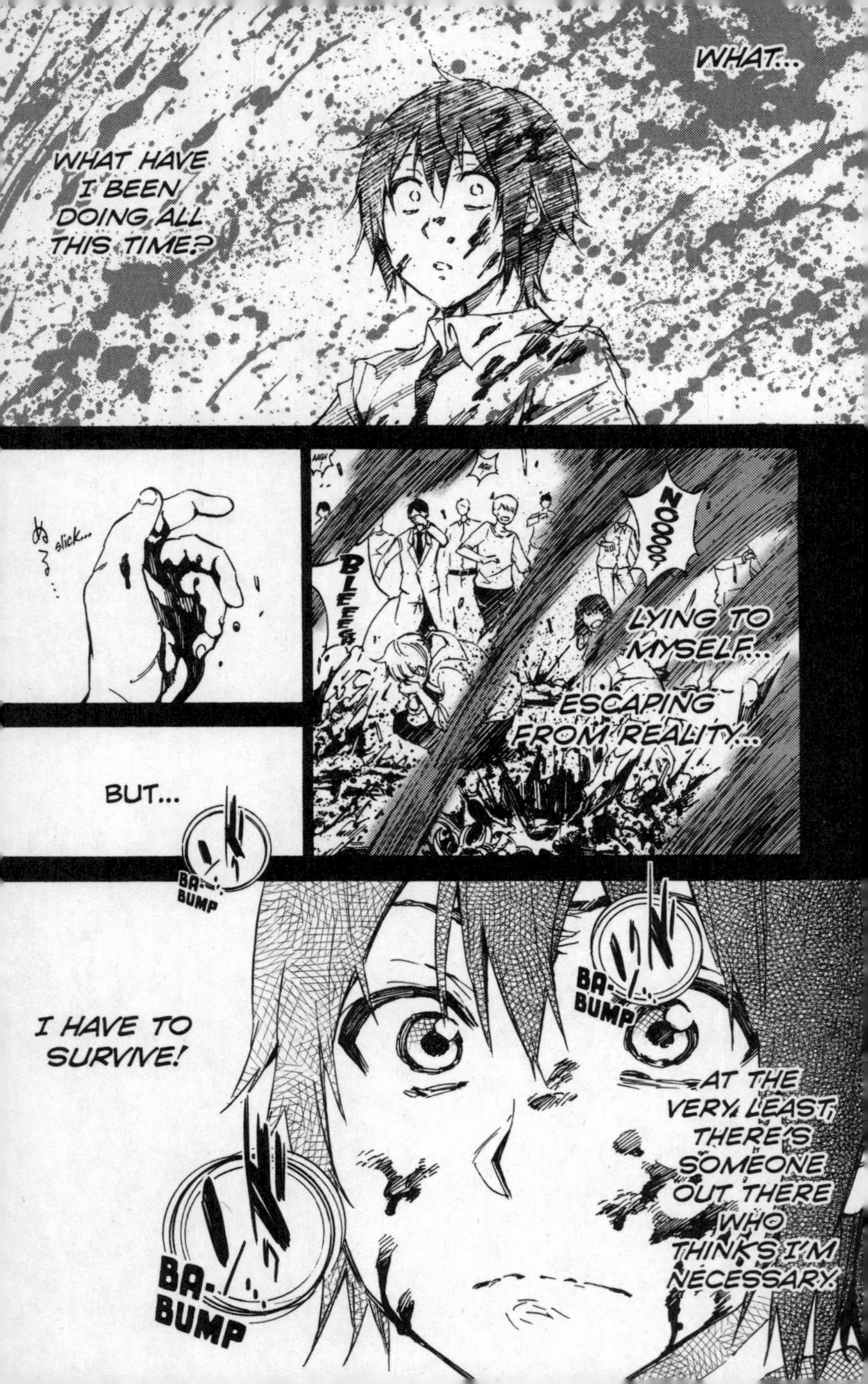
WHAT...
WHAT HAVE I BEEN DOING ALL THIS TIME?
NOOOOO
LYING TO MYSELF...
ESCAPING FROM REALITY...
ぬる... slick...
BUT...
BA-BUMP
BA-BUMP
AT THE VERY LEAST, THERE'S SOMEONE OUT THERE WHO THINKS I'M NECESSARY.
I HAVE TO SURVIVE!
BA-BUMP

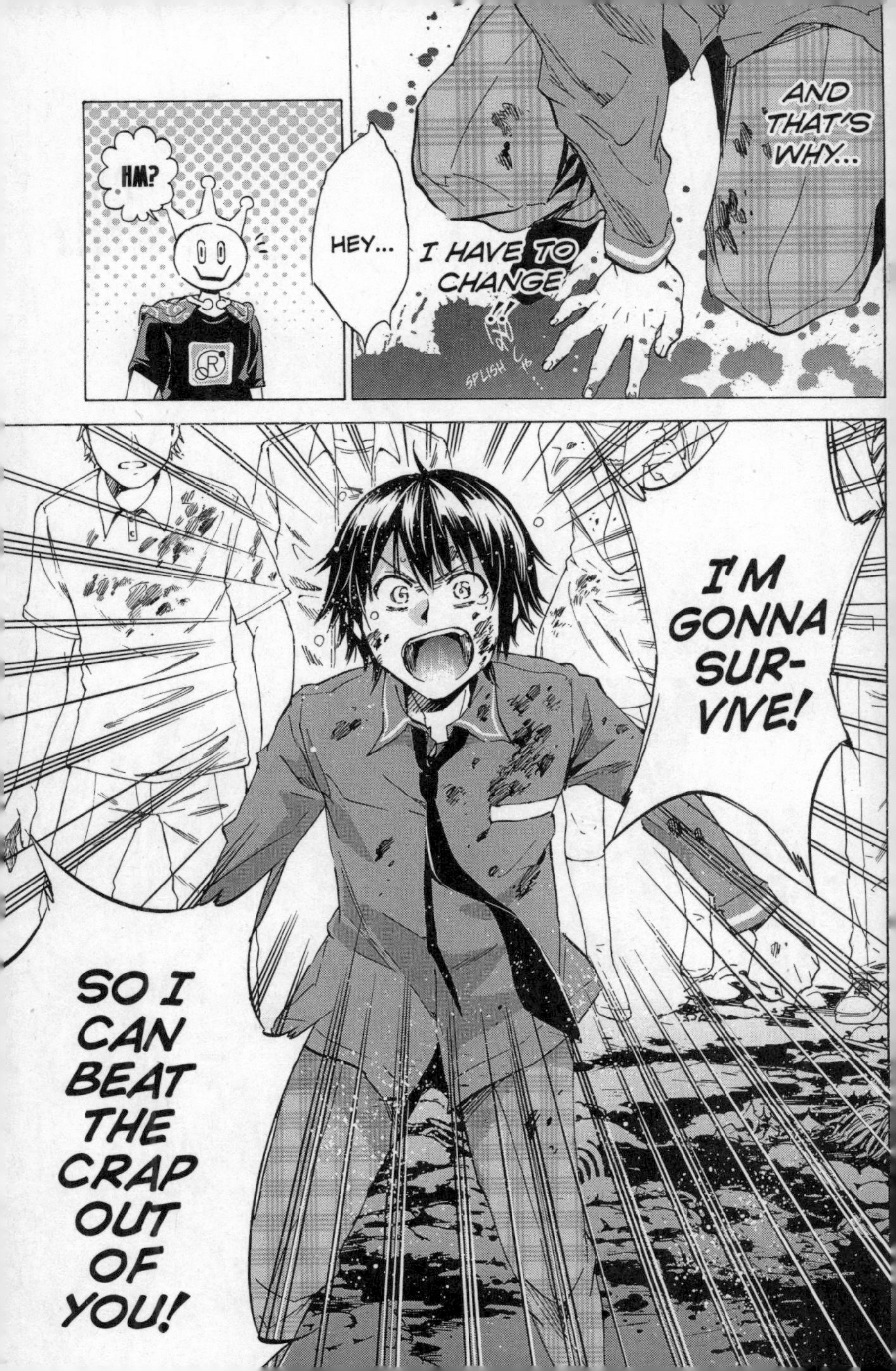
AND THAT'S WHY...
I HAVE TO CHANGE!!
HEY...
SPLISH
HM?
I'M GONNA SUR-VIVE!
SO I CAN BEAT THE CRAP OUT OF YOU!

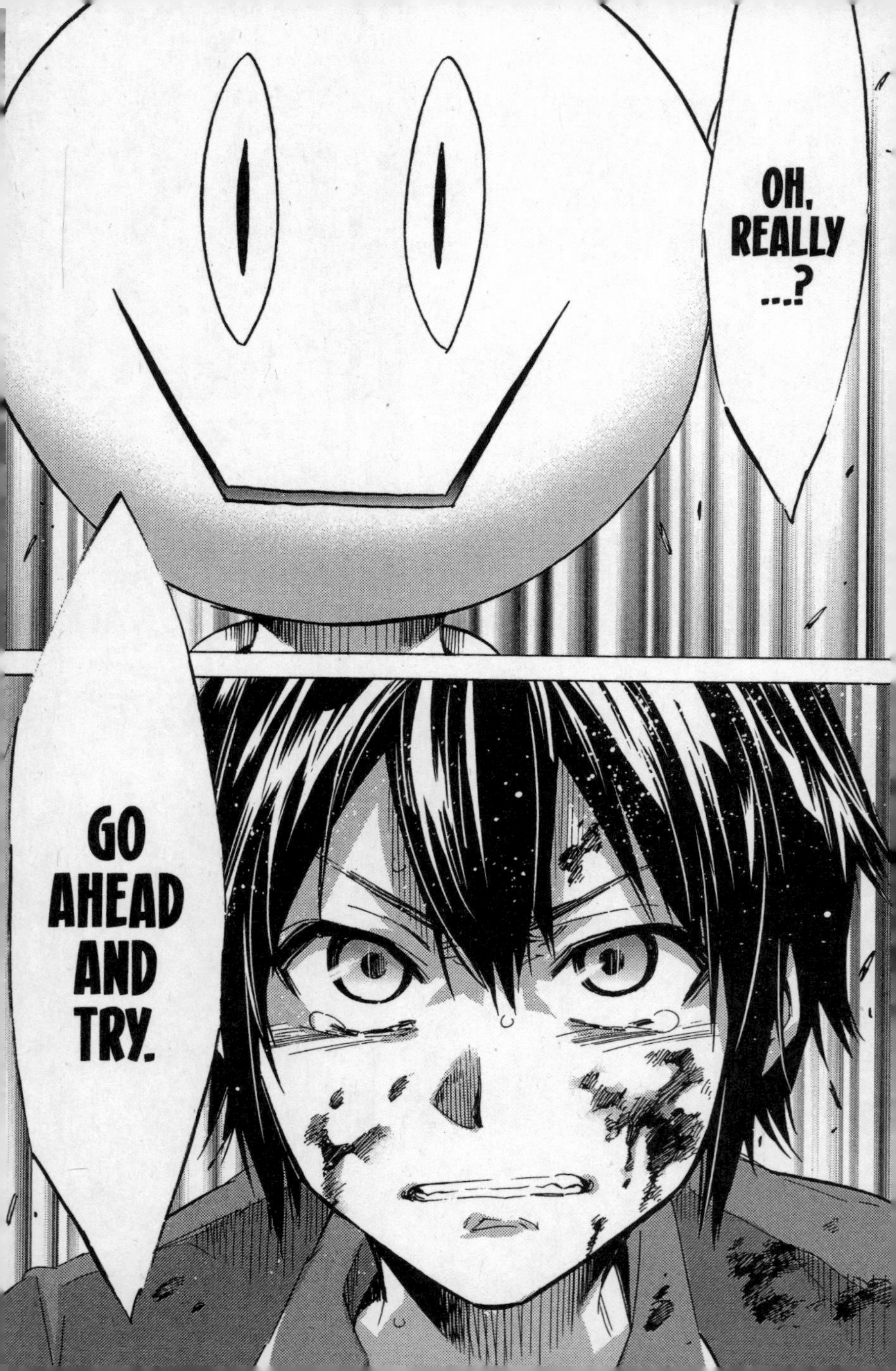
OH, REALLY ...?
GO AHEAD AND TRY.

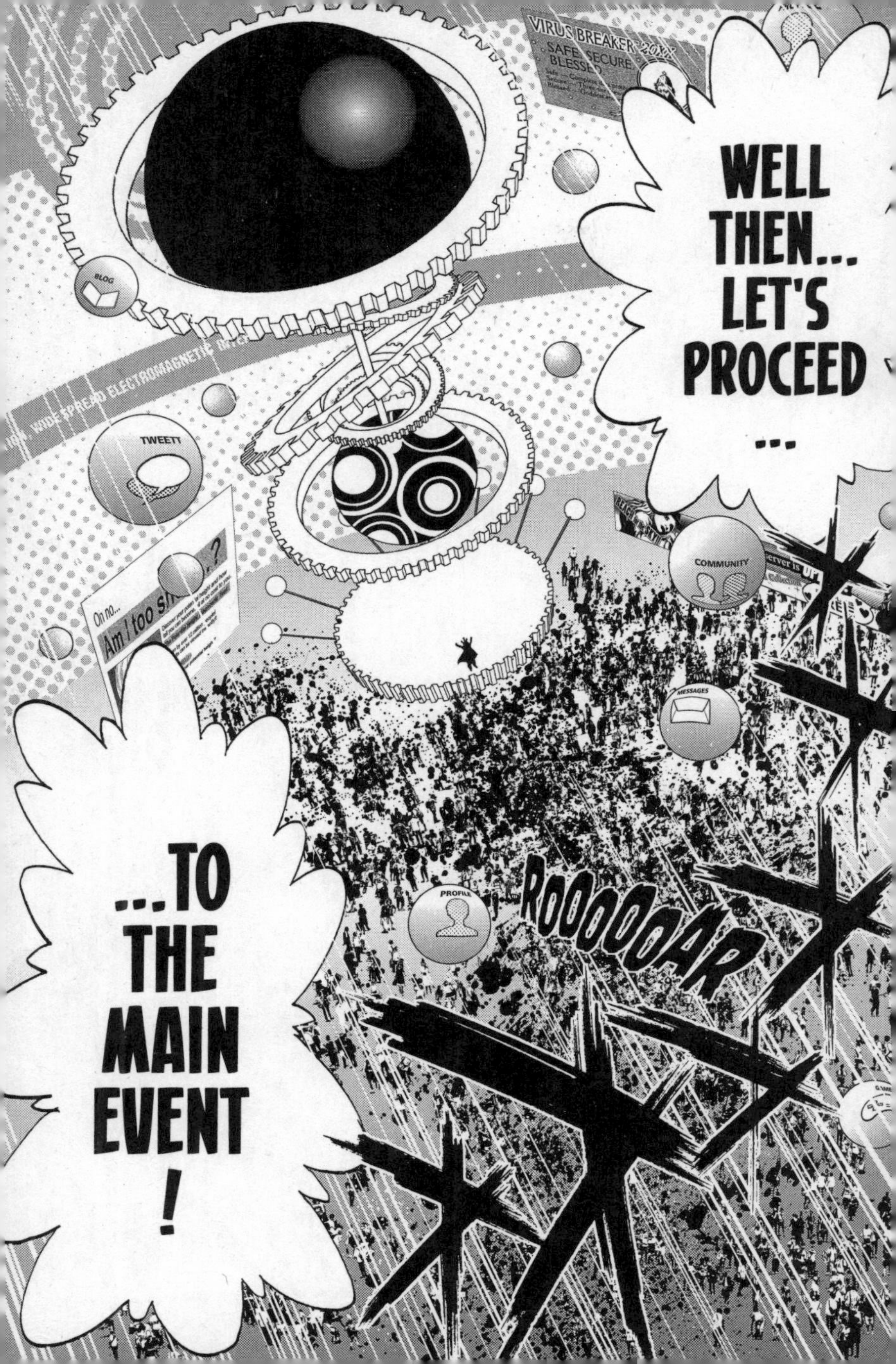
VIRUS BREAKER 20XX
SAFE SECURE BLESSED
WELL THEN... LET'S PROCEED ...
BLOG
TWEETT
COMMUNITY
MESSAGES
...TO THE MAIN EVENT !
ROOOOOAR
PROFILE

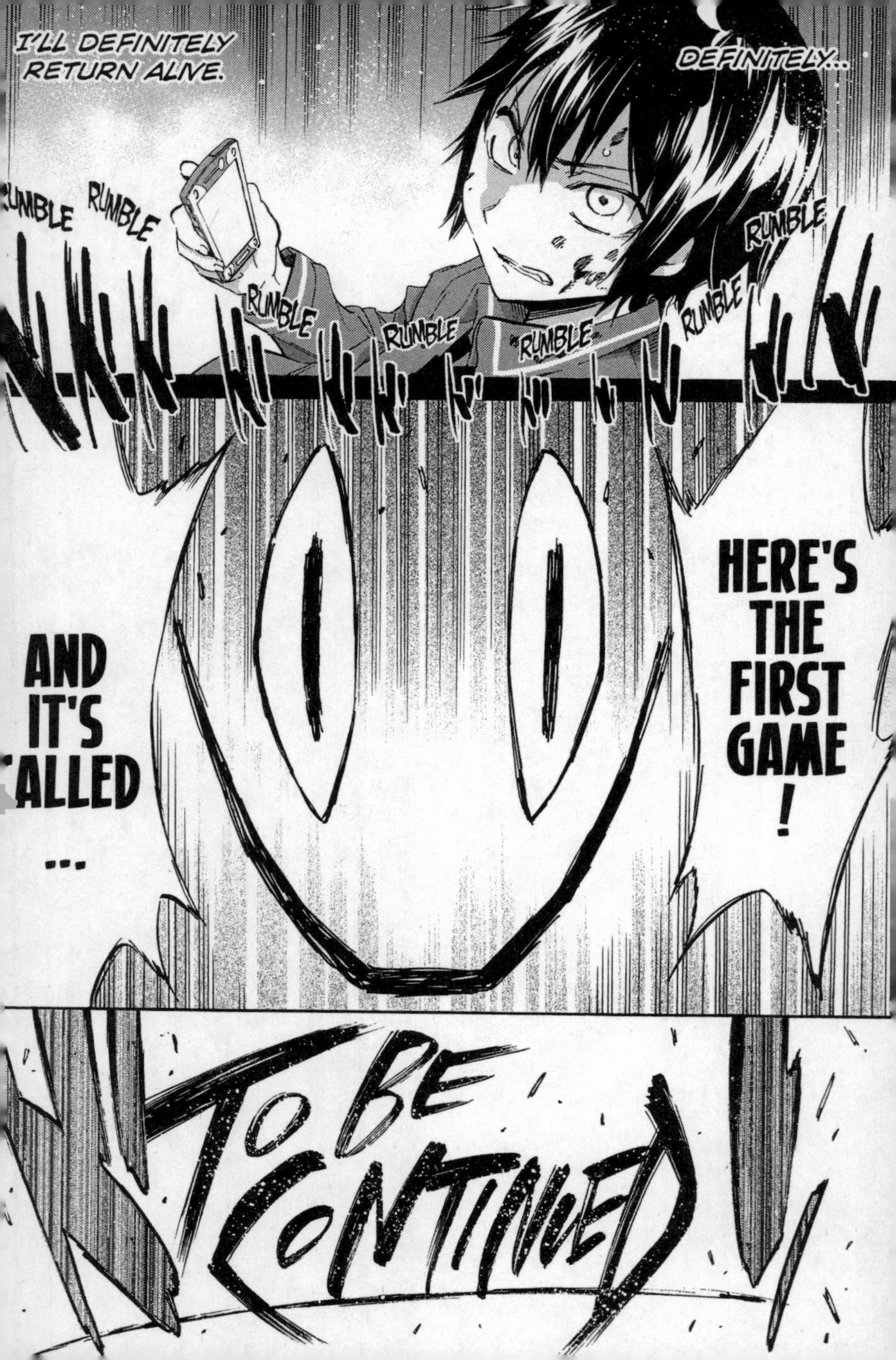
DEFINITELY...
I'LL DEFINITELY RETURN ALIVE.
RUMBLE RUMBLE RUMBLE RUMBLE RUMBLE RUMBLE RUMBLE RUMBLE
HERE'S THE FIRST GAME!
AND IT'S CALLED...
TO BE CONTINUED

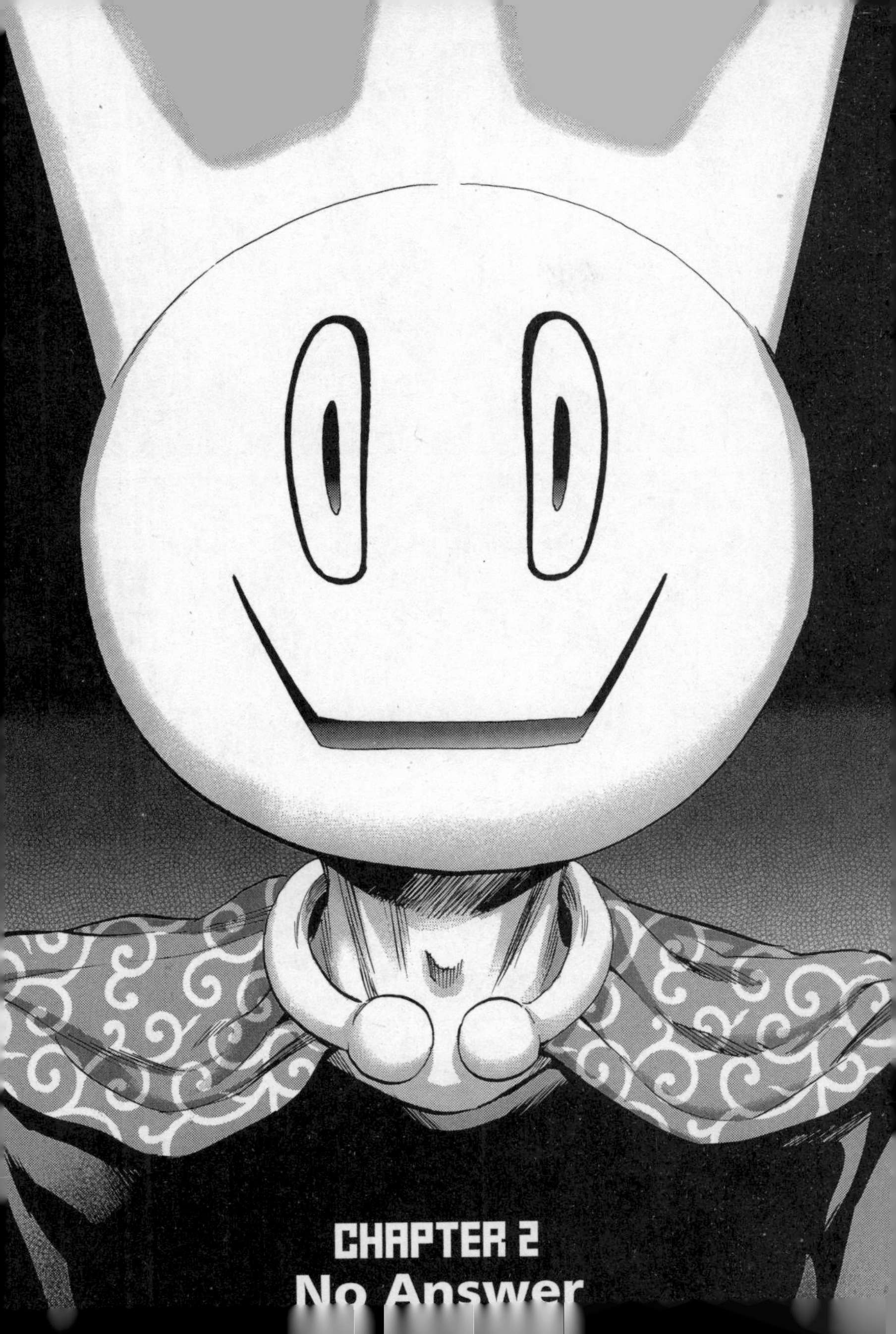

CHAPTER 2
No Answer

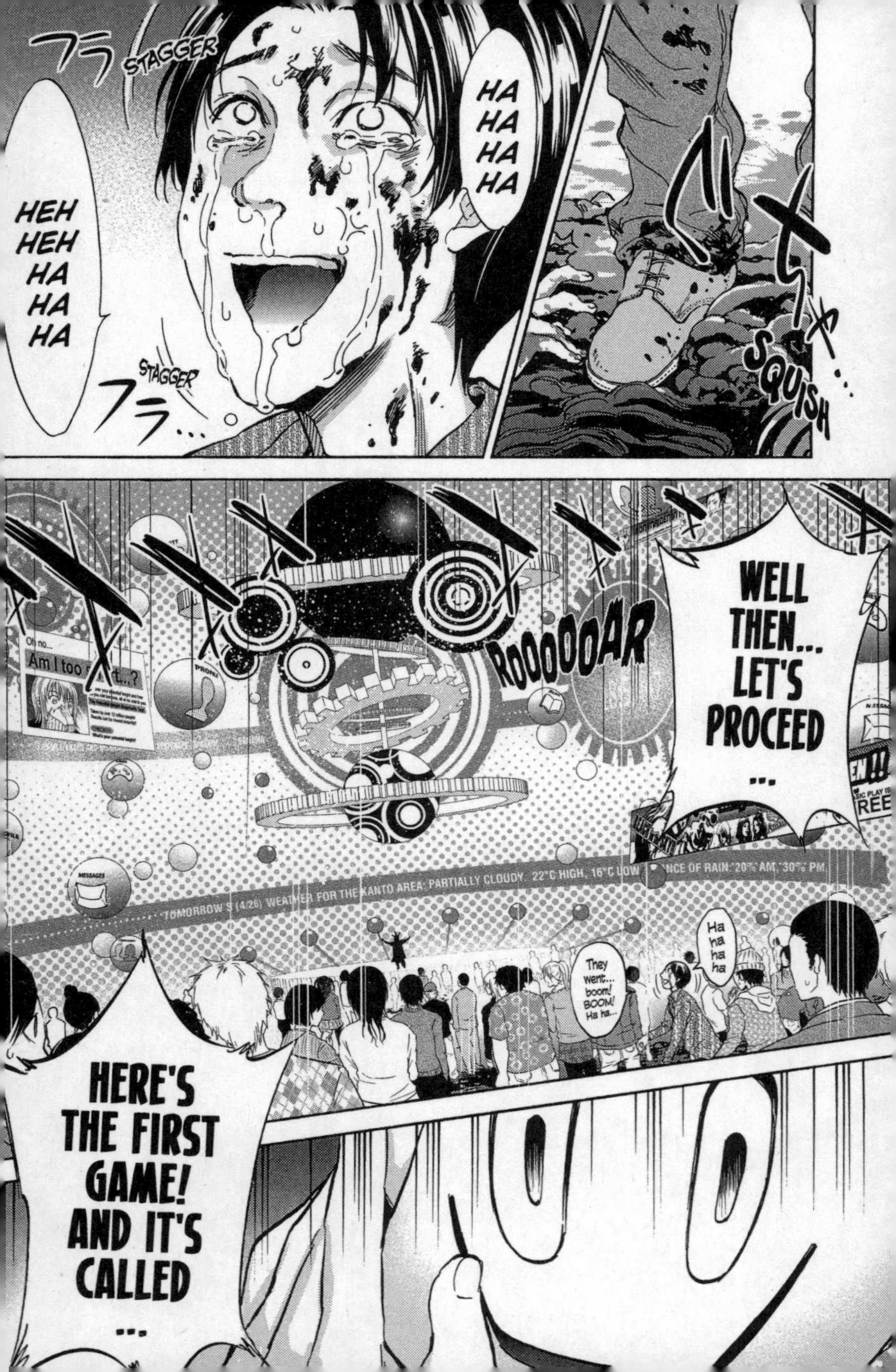
SQUISH
HA HA HA HA
フラ STAGGER
HEH HEH HA HA HA
STAGGER フラ...
WELL THEN... LET'S PROCEED...
ROOOOOAR
Oh no...
TOMORROW'S (4/26) WEATHER FOR THE KANTO AREA: PARTIALLY CLOUDY. 22°C HIGH, 16°C LOW
NCE OF RAIN: 20% AM, 30% PM
MESSAGES
Ha ha ha ha
They went... boom! BOOM! Ha ha...
HERE'S THE FIRST GAME! AND IT'S CALLED ...

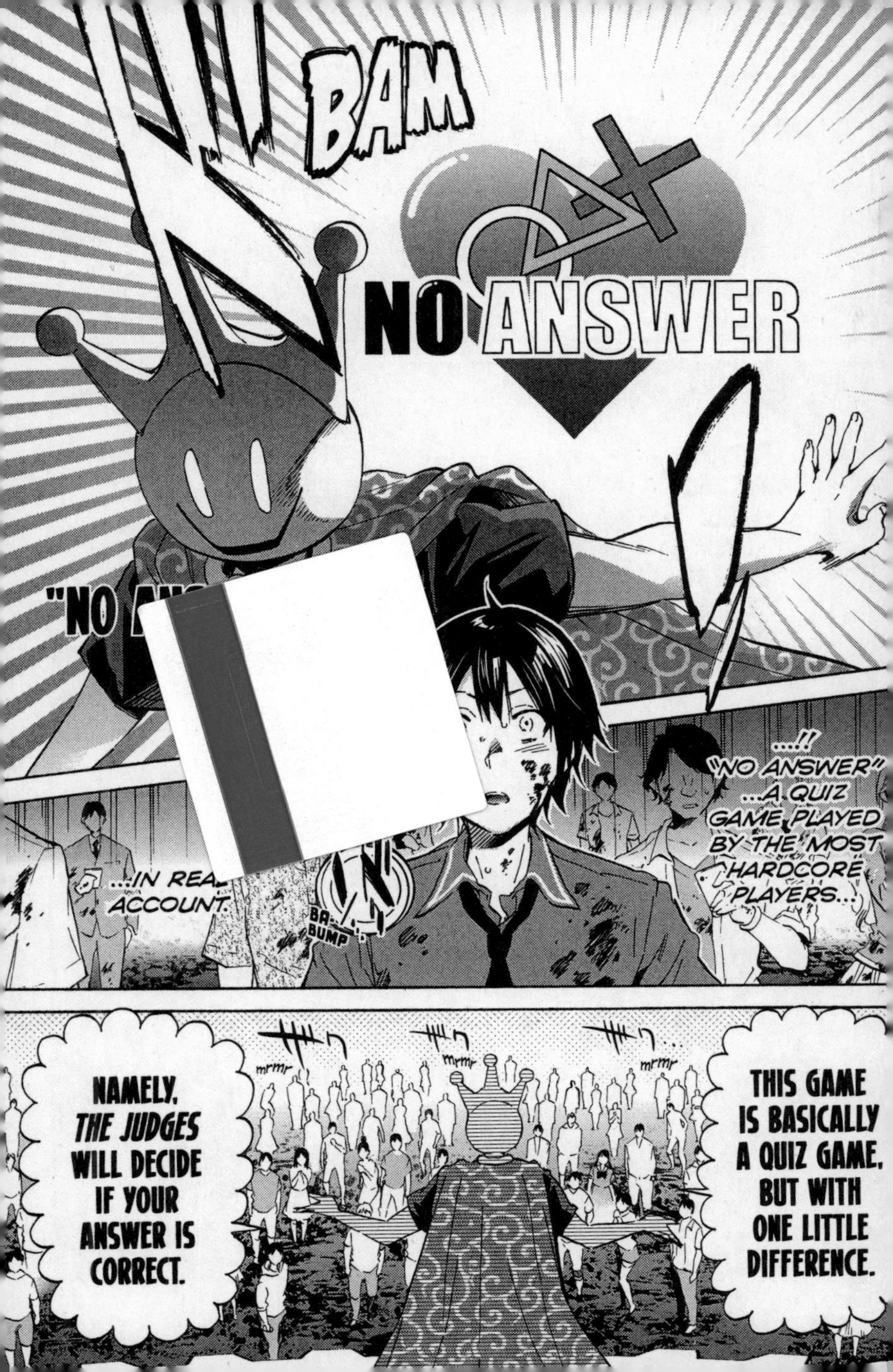
BAM
NO ANSWER
...!!
"NO ANSWER" ...A QUIZ GAME PLAYED BY THE MOST HARDCORE PLAYERS...
...IN REA
ACCOUNT.
BA-BUMP
THIS GAME IS BASICALLY A QUIZ GAME. BUT WITH ONE LITTLE DIFFERENCE.
mrmr
mrmr
mrmr
NAMELY, THE JUDGES WILL DECIDE IF YOUR ANSWER IS CORRECT.

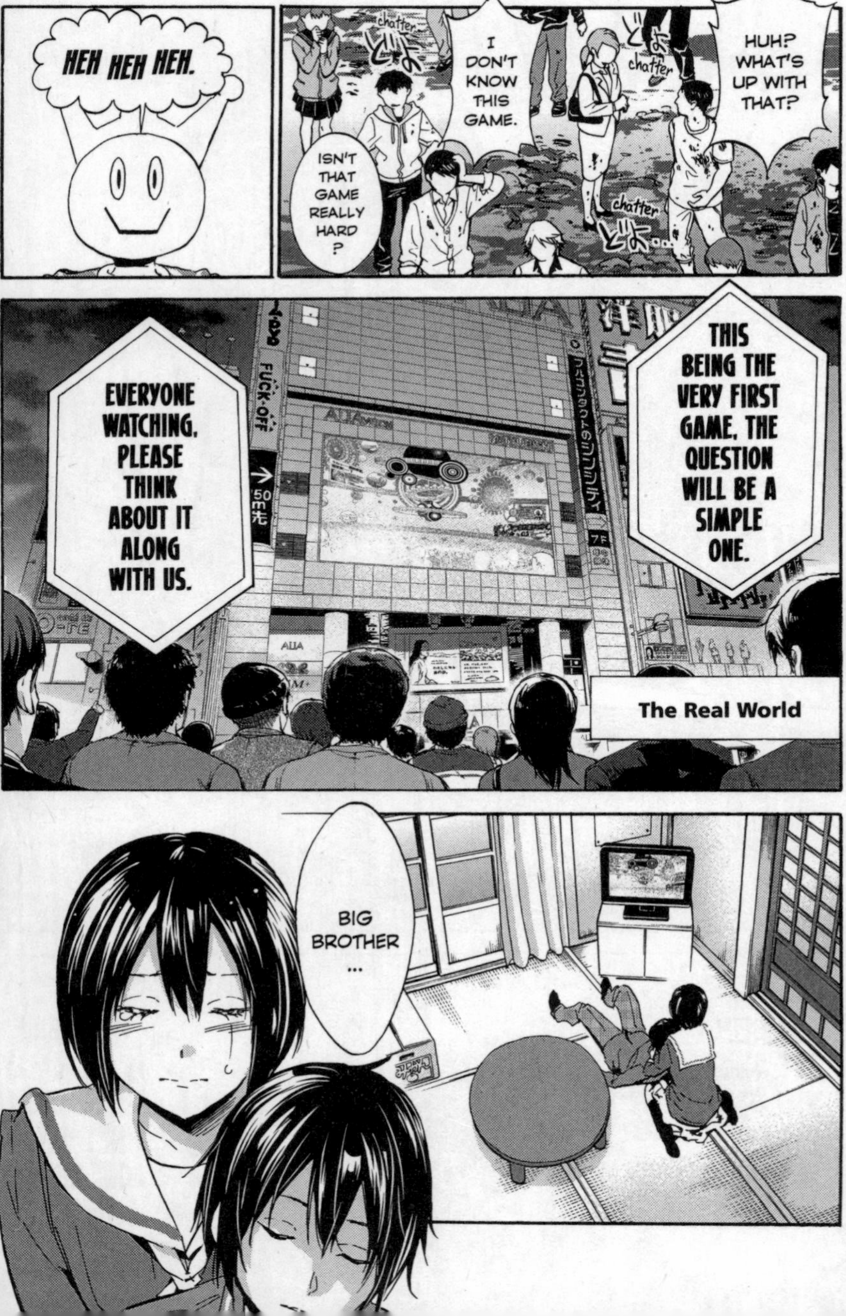
HUH? WHAT'S UP WITH THAT?
chatter どよ
I DON'T KNOW THIS GAME.
chatter どよ
ISN'T THAT GAME REALLY HARD?
chatter どよ...
HEH HEH HEH.
THIS BEING THE VERY FIRST GAME, THE QUESTION WILL BE A SIMPLE ONE.
FUCK-OFF
EVERYONE WATCHING, PLEASE THINK ABOUT IT ALONG WITH US.
The Real World
BIG BROTHER ...

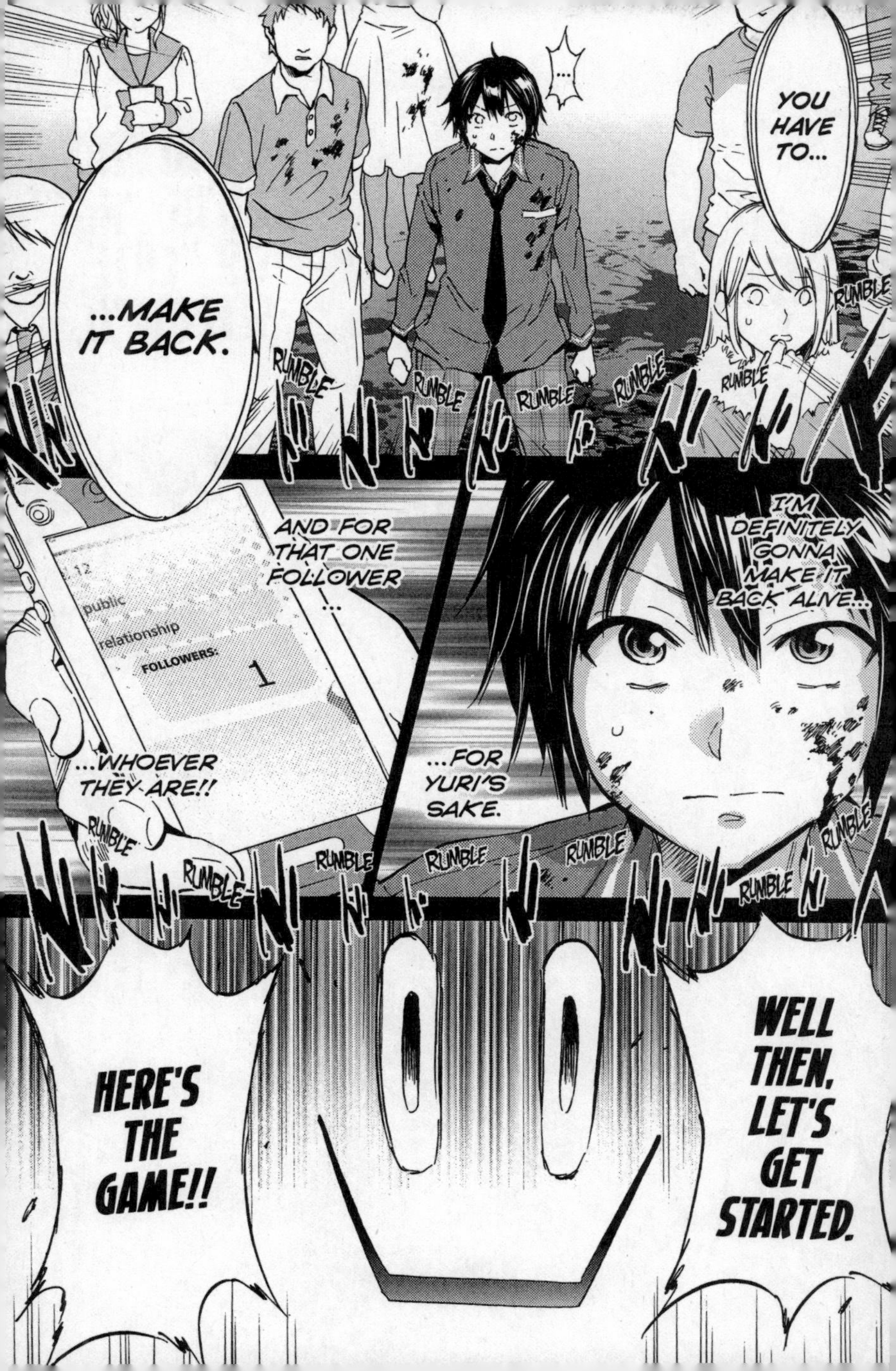

YOU HAVE TO...
...
...MAKE IT BACK.
RUMBLE RUMBLE RUMBLE RUMBLE RUMBLE RUMBLE
I'M DEFINITELY GONNA MAKE IT BACK ALIVE...
...FOR YURI'S SAKE.
AND FOR THAT ONE FOLLOWER...
12
public
relationship
FOLLOWERS:
1
...WHOEVER THEY ARE!!
RUMBLE RUMBLE RUMBLE RUMBLE RUMBLE RUMBLE RUMBLE
WELL THEN, LET'S GET STARTED.
HERE'S THE GAME!!

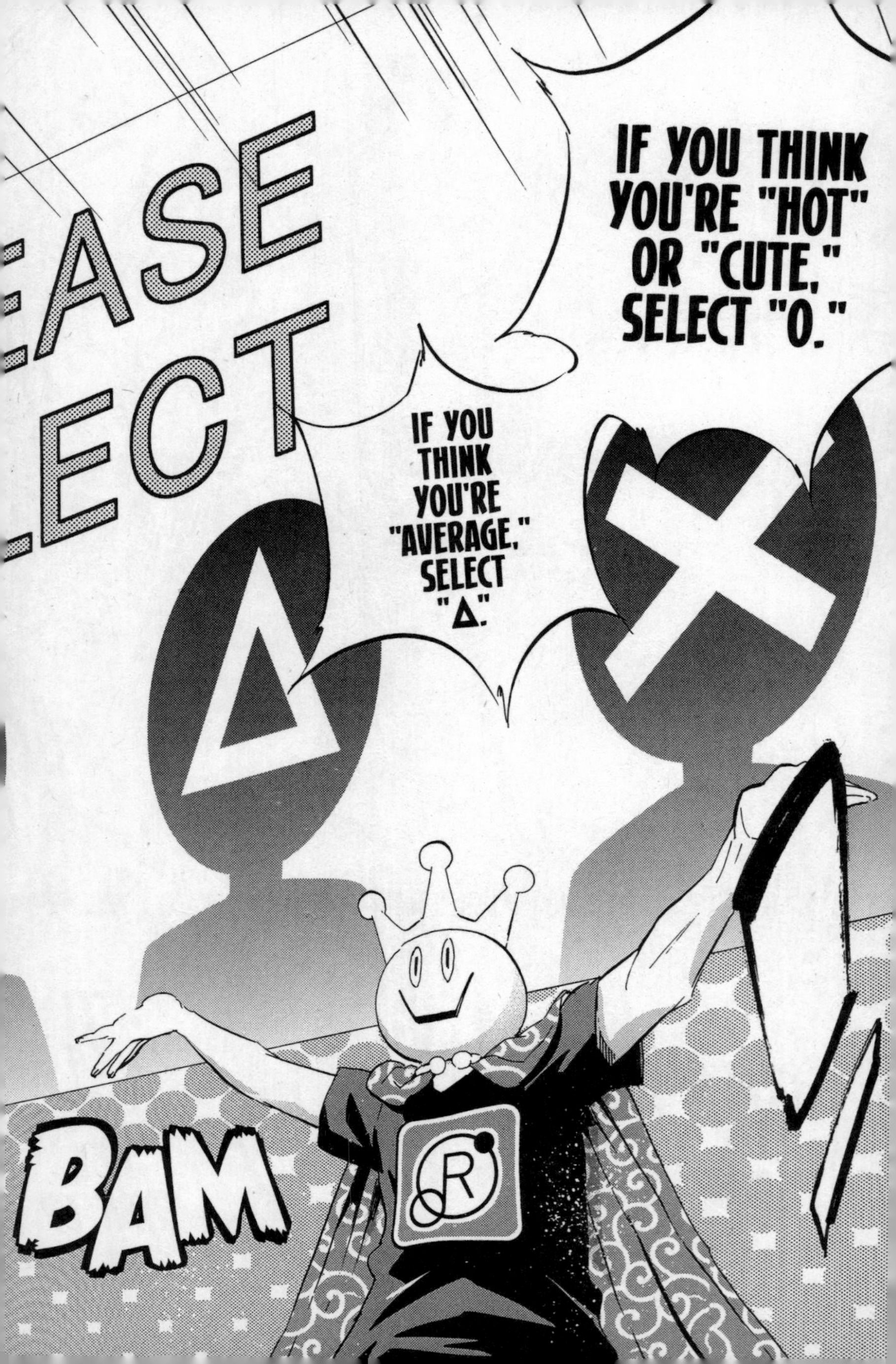
IF YOU THINK YOU'RE "HOT" OR "CUTE," SELECT "O."
EASE
ECT
IF YOU THINK YOU'RE "AVERAGE," SELECT "Δ."
BAM

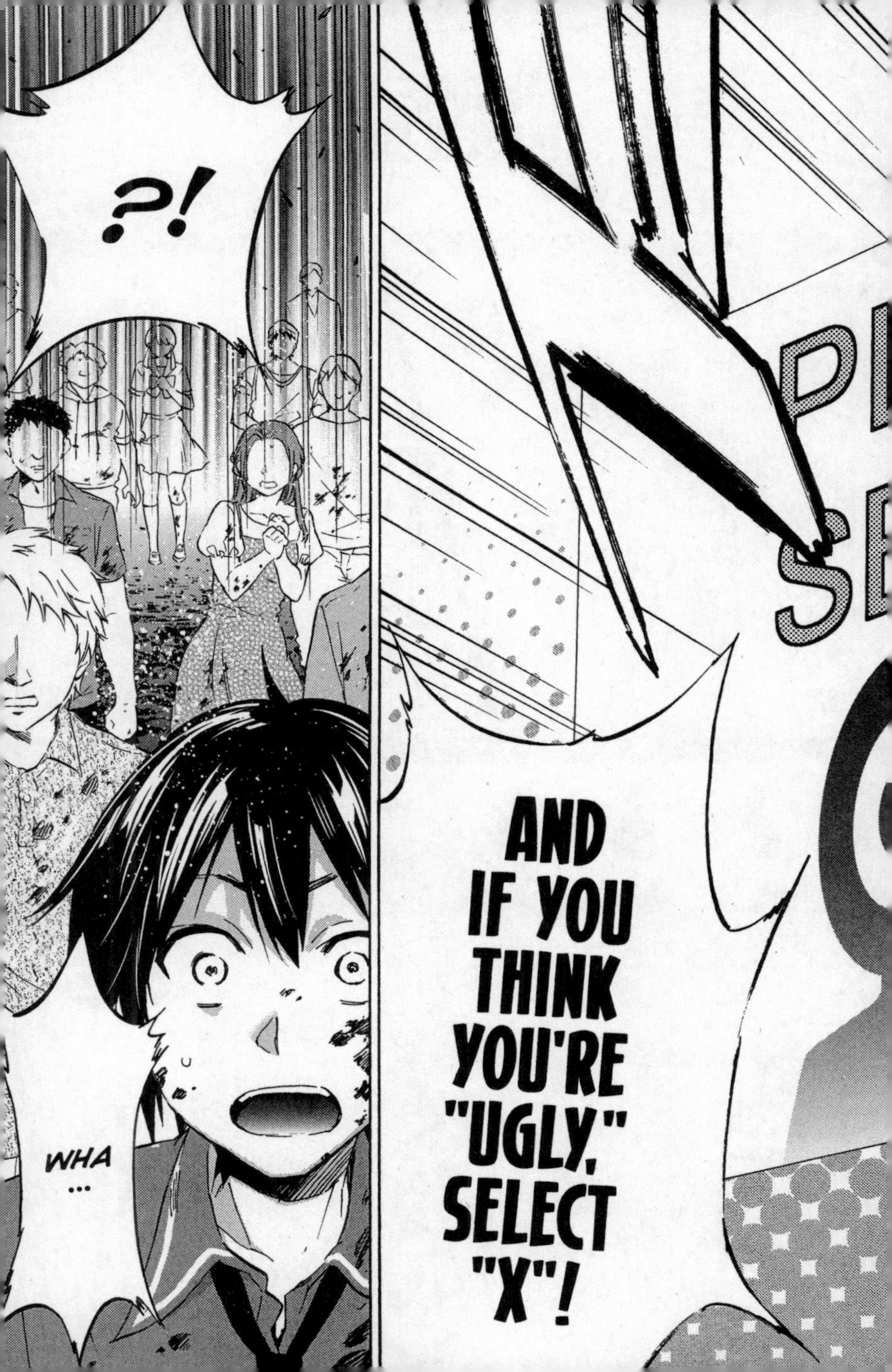
AND IF YOU THINK YOU'RE "UGLY," SELECT "X"!
?!
WHA ...

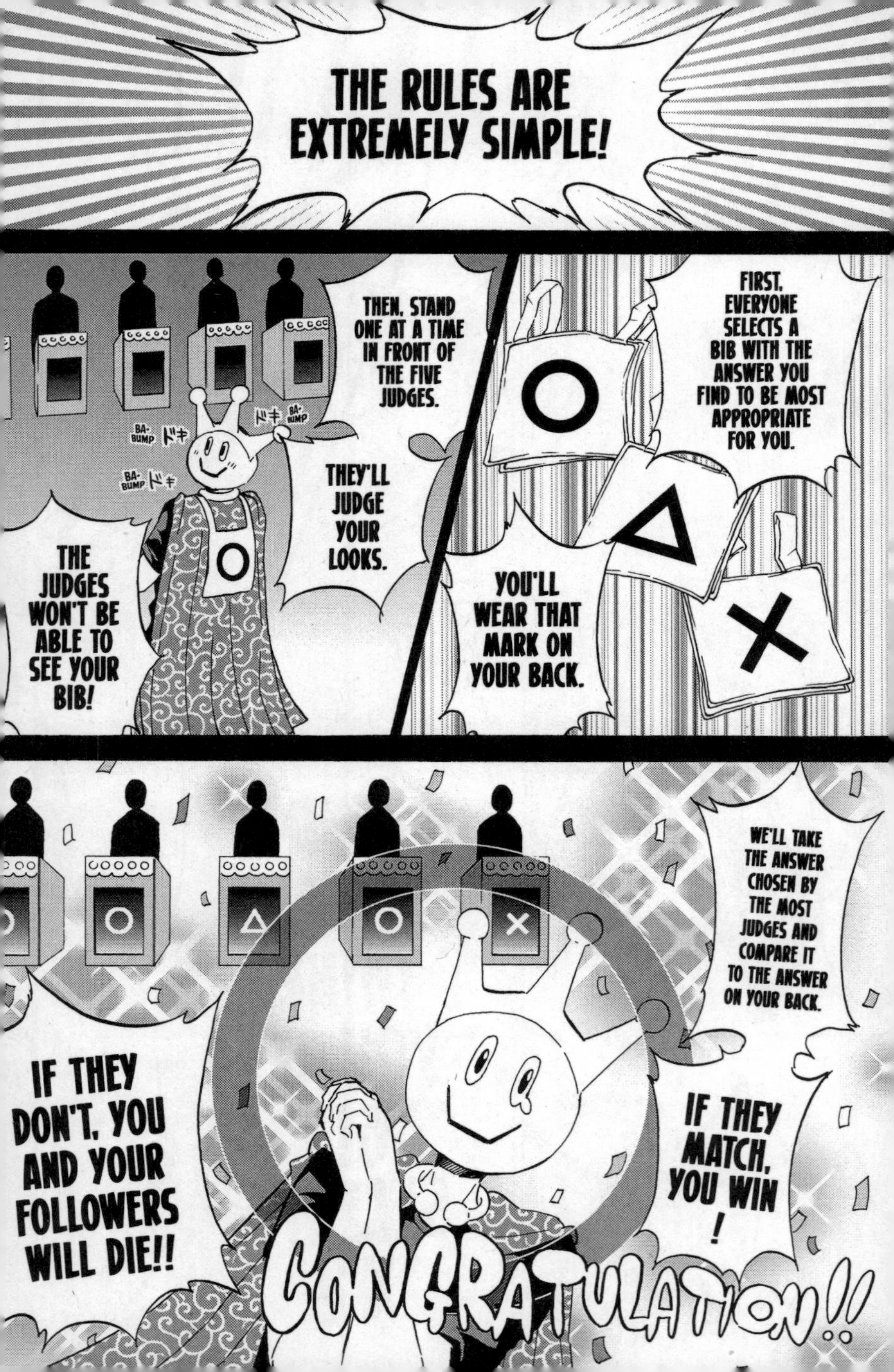

THE RULES ARE EXTREMELY SIMPLE!
FIRST, EVERYONE SELECTS A BIB WITH THE ANSWER YOU FIND TO BE MOST APPROPRIATE FOR YOU.
YOU'LL WEAR THAT MARK ON YOUR BACK.
THEN, STAND ONE AT A TIME IN FRONT OF THE FIVE JUDGES.
THEY'LL JUDGE YOUR LOOKS.
BA-BUMP ドキ
BA-BUMP ドキ
BA-BUMP ドキ
THE JUDGES WON'T BE ABLE TO SEE YOUR BIB!
WE'LL TAKE THE ANSWER CHOSEN BY THE MOST JUDGES AND COMPARE IT TO THE ANSWER ON YOUR BACK.
IF THEY MATCH, YOU WIN!
CONGRATULATION!!
IF THEY DON'T, YOU AND YOUR FOLLOWERS WILL DIE!!

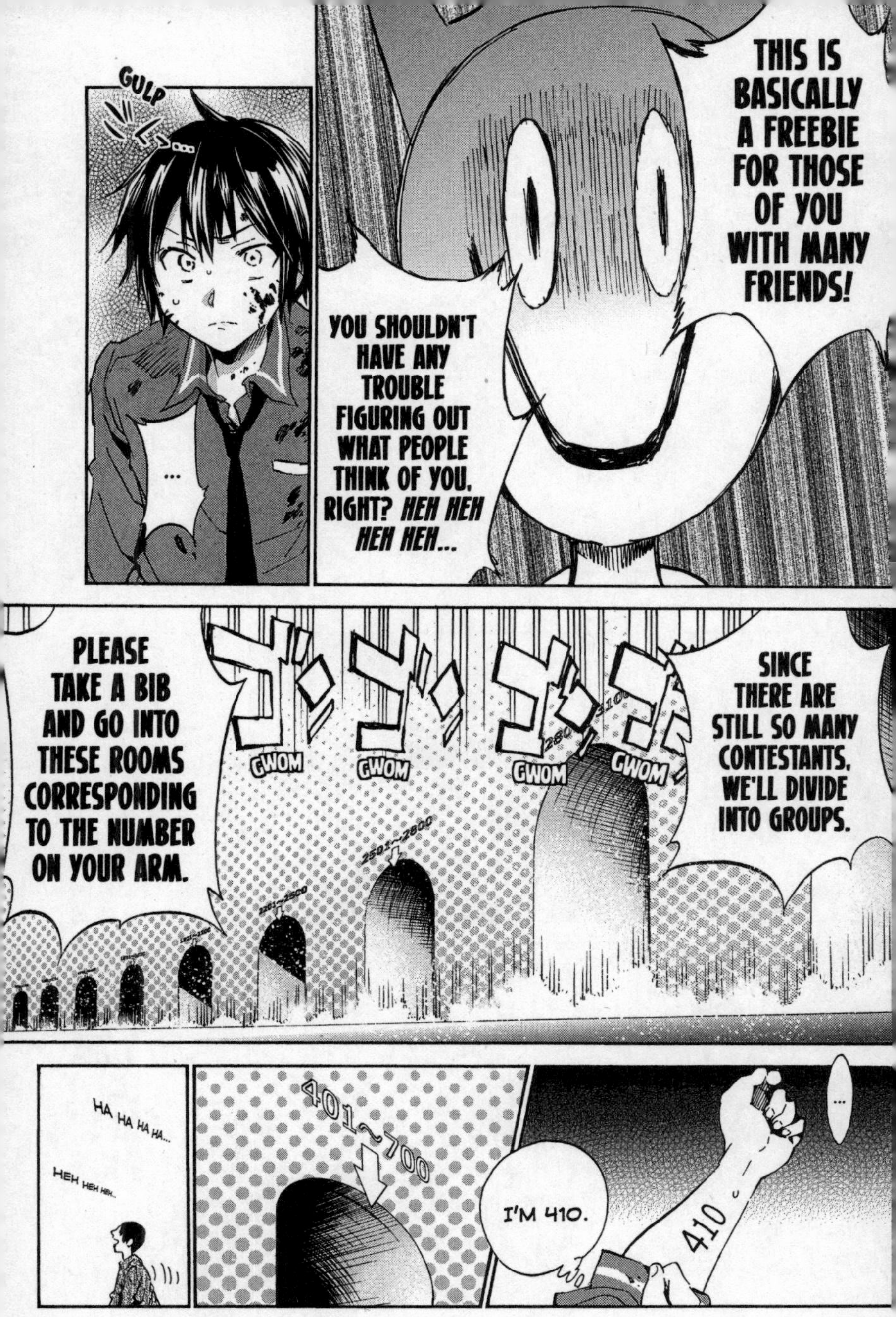
THIS IS BASICALLY A FREEBIE FOR THOSE OF YOU WITH MANY FRIENDS!
YOU SHOULDN'T HAVE ANY TROUBLE FIGURING OUT WHAT PEOPLE THINK OF YOU, RIGHT? *HEH HEH HEH HEH...*
GULP
...
SINCE THERE ARE STILL SO MANY CONTESTANTS, WE'LL DIVIDE INTO GROUPS.
GWOM
GWOM
GWOM
GWOM
2501~2800
PLEASE TAKE A BIB AND GO INTO THESE ROOMS CORRESPONDING TO THE NUMBER ON YOUR ARM.
...
I'M 410.
410
401~700
HA HA HA HA...
HEH HEH HEH..

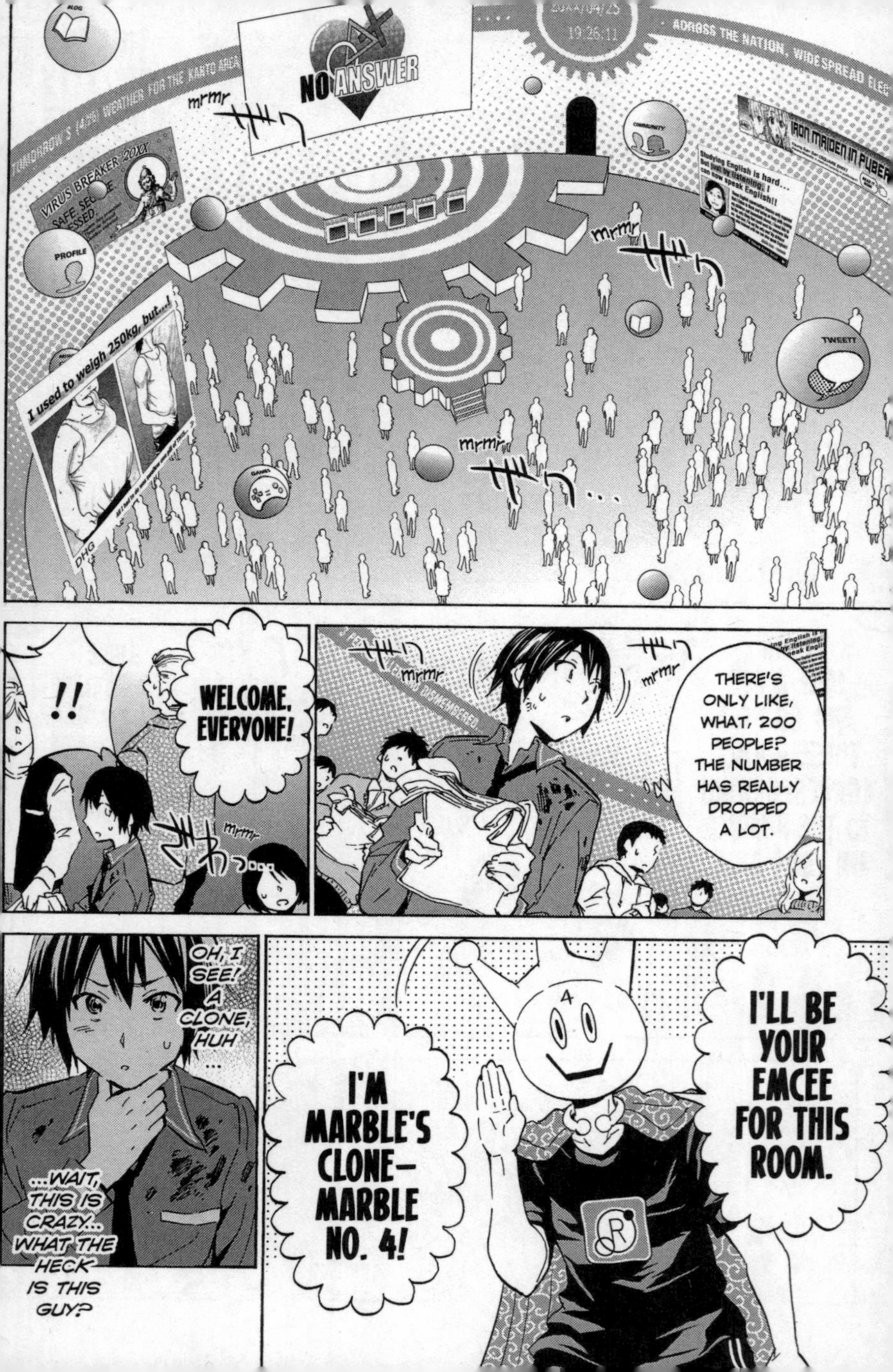
19:26:11
ACROSS THE NATION, WIDESPREAD ELEC
NO ANSWER
BLOG
mrmr
IRON MAIDEN IN PUBER
COMMUNITY
Studying English is hard... But just by listening, I can now speak English!!
VIRUS BREAKER 20XX
PROFILE
mrmr
TWEET!
I used to weigh 250kg, but...!
DHG
GAMES
mrmr
...
THERE'S ONLY LIKE, WHAT, 200 PEOPLE? THE NUMBER HAS REALLY DROPPED A LOT.
mrmr
mrmr
WELCOME, EVERYONE!
!!
mrmr
I'LL BE YOUR EMCEE FOR THIS ROOM.
I'M MARBLE'S CLONE— MARBLE NO. 4!
OH, I SEE! A CLONE, HUH...
...WAIT, THIS IS CRAZY... WHAT THE HECK IS THIS GUY?

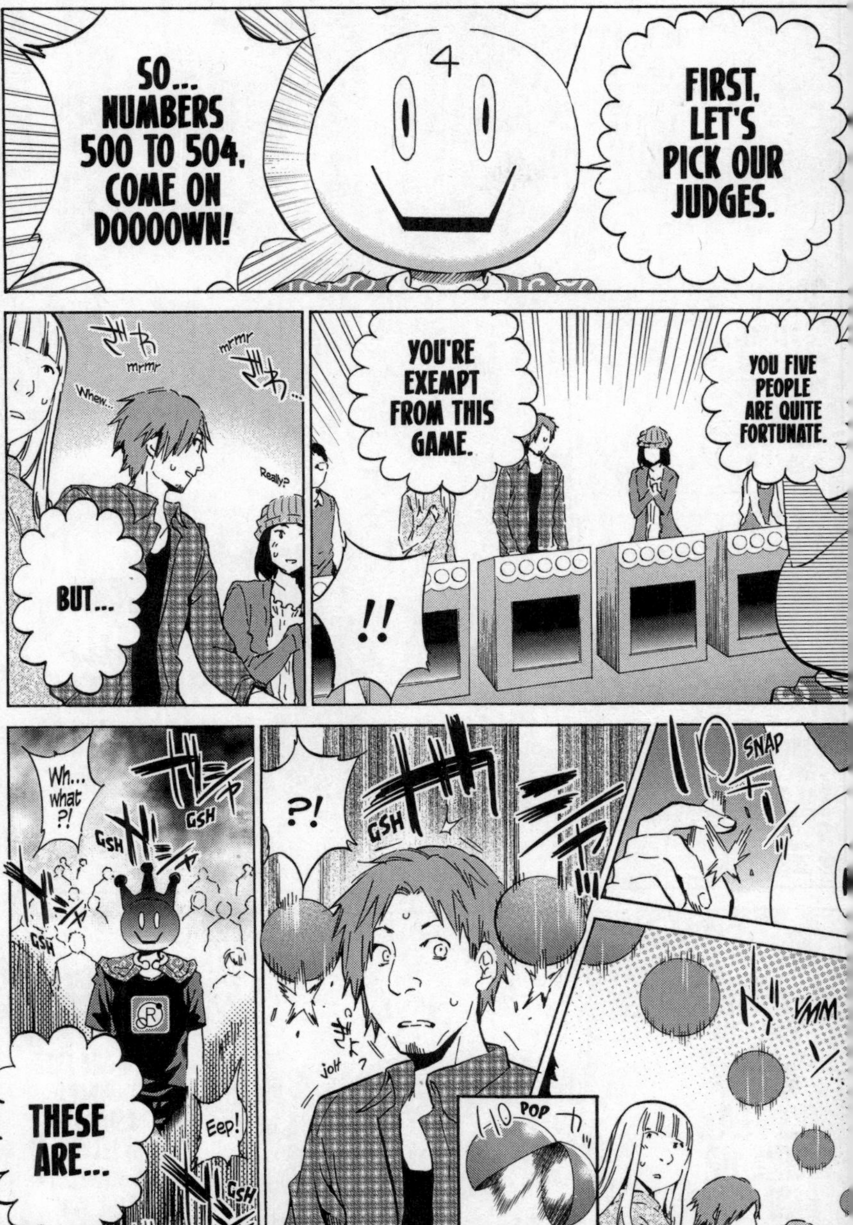
FIRST. LET'S PICK OUR JUDGES.
SO... NUMBERS 500 TO 504. COME ON DOOOOWN!
YOU FIVE PEOPLE ARE QUITE FORTUNATE.
YOU'RE EXEMPT FROM THIS GAME.
!!
mrmr
mrmr
Whew...
Really?
BUT...
SNAP
VMM
POP
?!
GSH
jolt
Wh... what ?!
GSH
GSH
GSH
THESE ARE...
Eep!
GSH
GSH

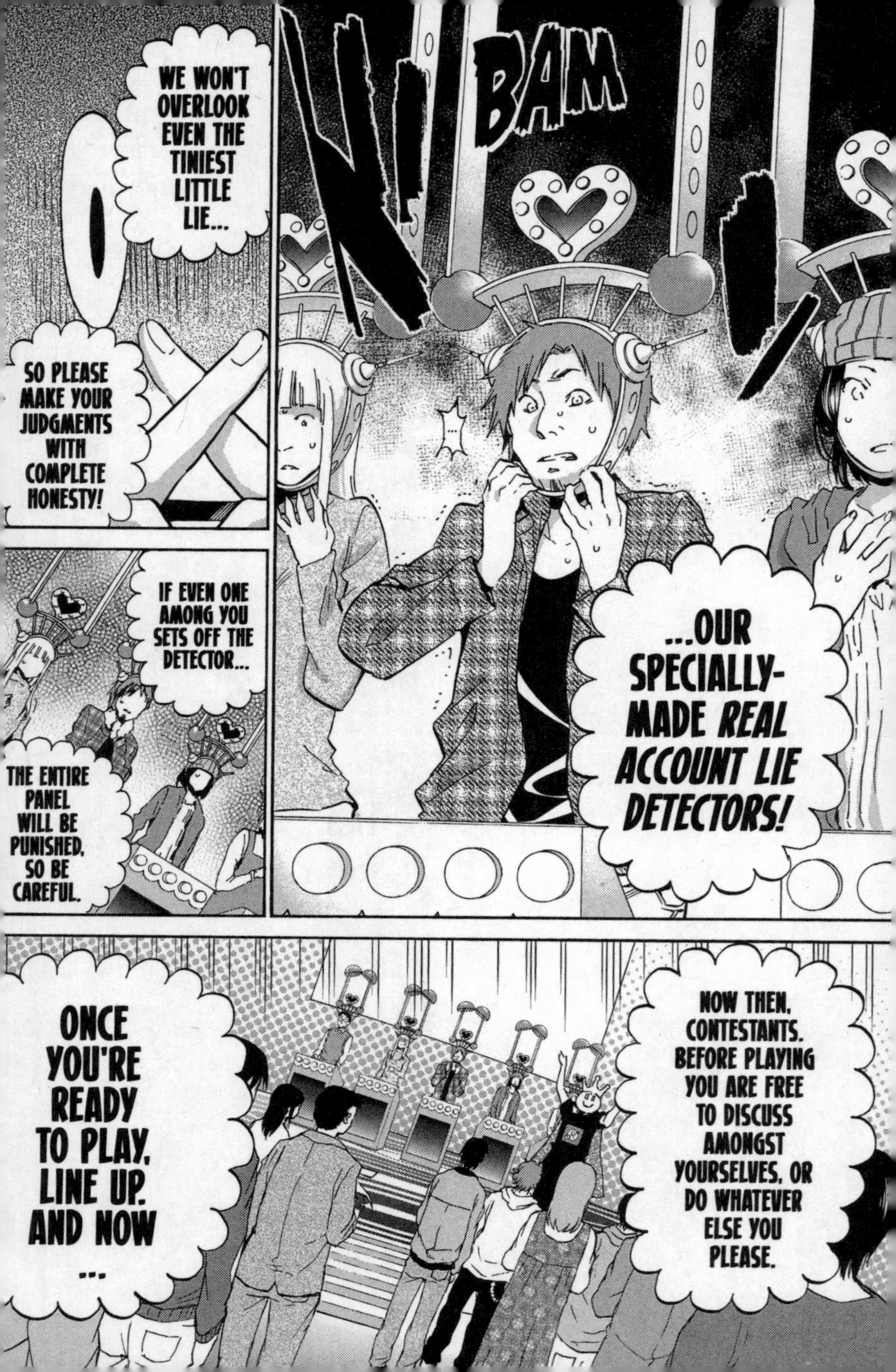
BAM
...
...OUR SPECIALLY-MADE *REAL ACCOUNT LIE DETECTORS!*
WE WON'T OVERLOOK EVEN THE TINIEST LITTLE LIE...
SO PLEASE MAKE YOUR JUDGMENTS WITH COMPLETE HONESTY!
IF EVEN ONE AMONG YOU SETS OFF THE DETECTOR...
THE ENTIRE PANEL WILL BE PUNISHED, SO BE CAREFUL.
NOW THEN, CONTESTANTS. BEFORE PLAYING YOU ARE FREE TO DISCUSS AMONGST YOURSELVES, OR DO WHATEVER ELSE YOU PLEASE.
ONCE YOU'RE READY TO PLAY, LINE UP. AND NOW ...

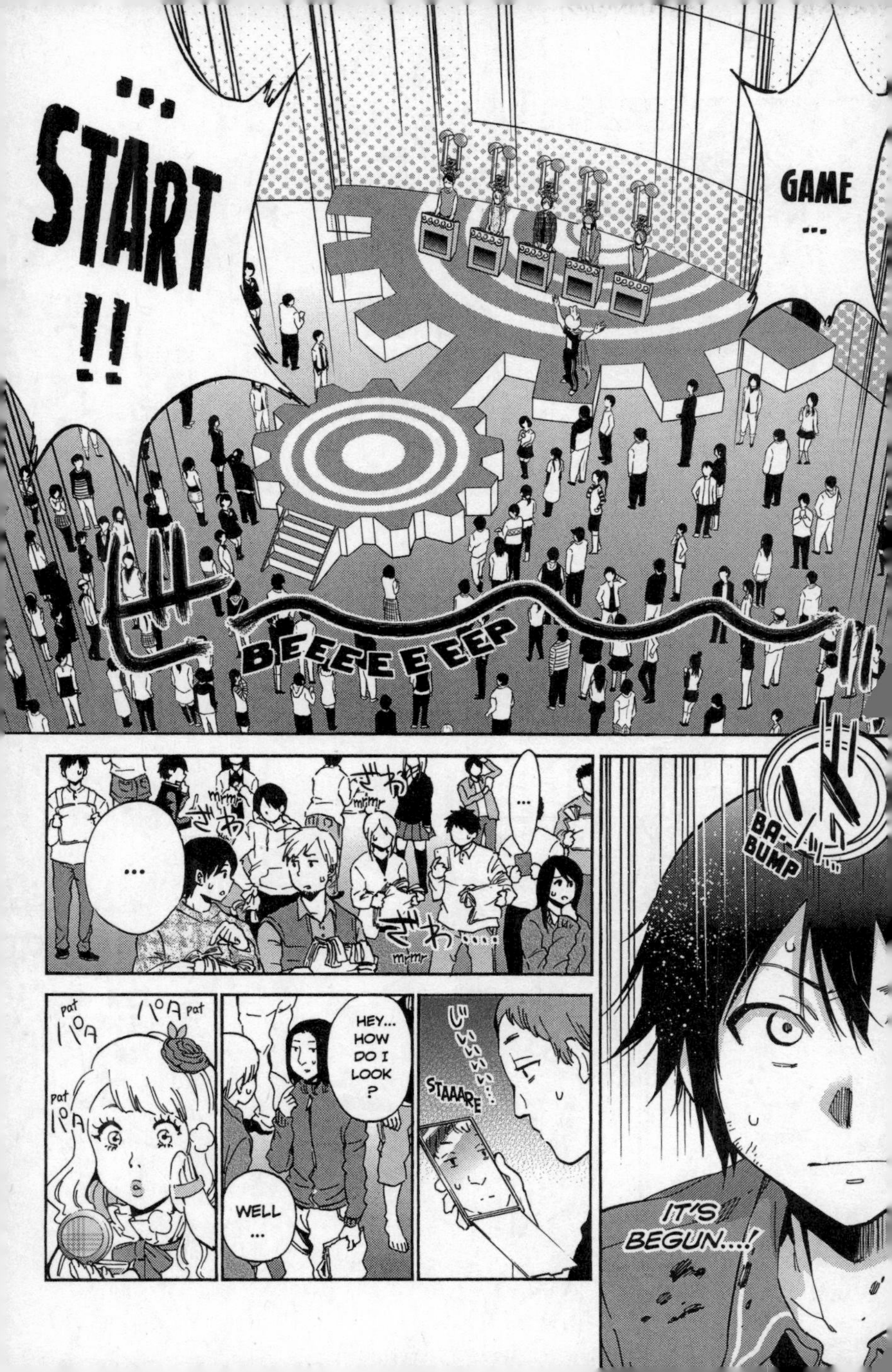

GAME ...
...START!!
BEEEEEEEP
BA-BUMP
IT'S BEGUN...!
...
...
mrmr
mrmr
mrmr
STAAARE...
HEY... HOW DO I LOOK?
WELL ...
pat
pat
pat

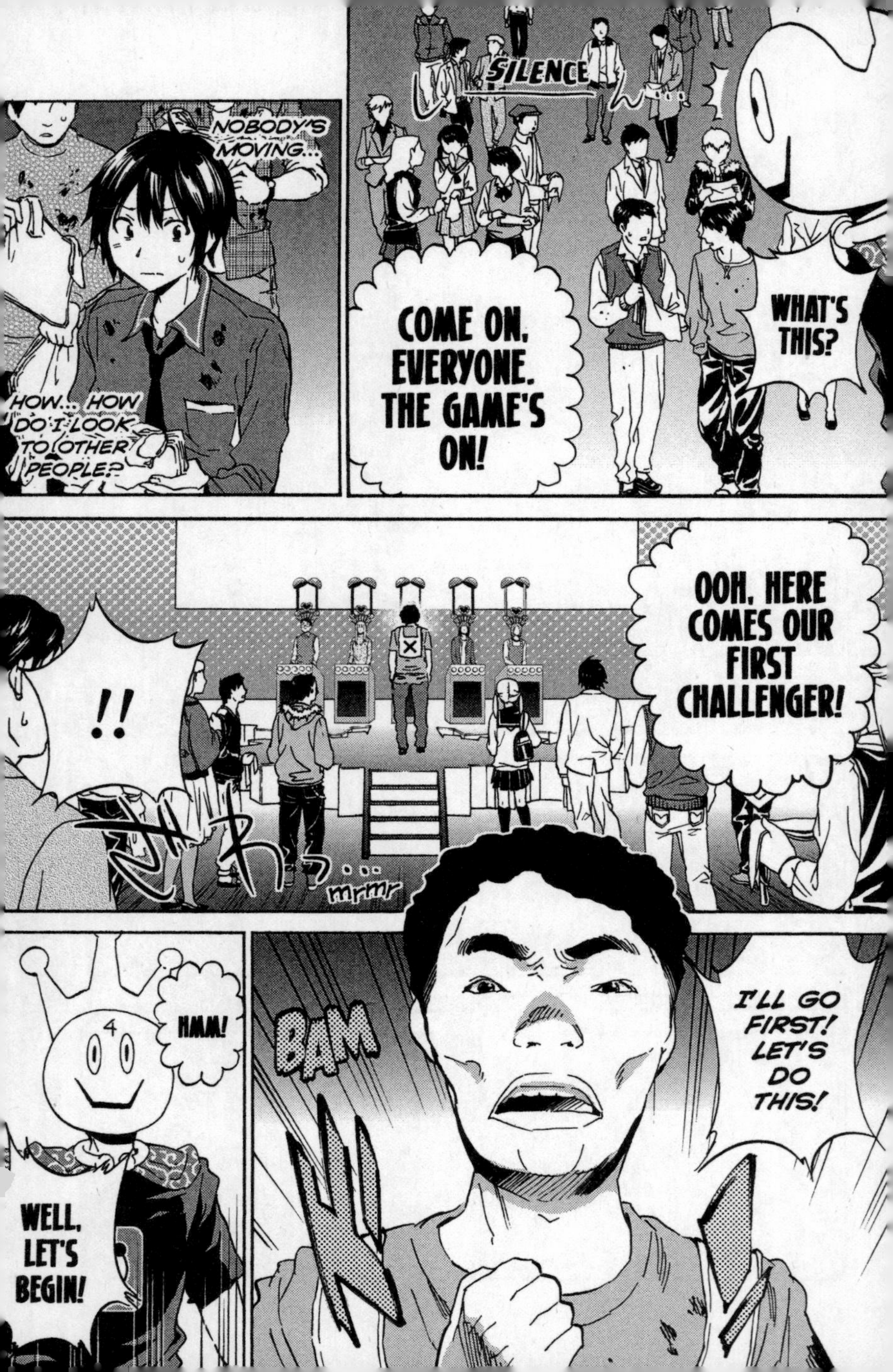
SILENCE
WHAT'S THIS?
COME ON, EVERYONE. THE GAME'S ON!
NOBODY'S MOVING...
HOW... HOW DO I LOOK TO OTHER PEOPLE?
OOH, HERE COMES OUR FIRST CHALLENGER!
!!
mrmr
I'LL GO FIRST! LET'S DO THIS!
BAM
HMM!
WELL, LET'S BEGIN!

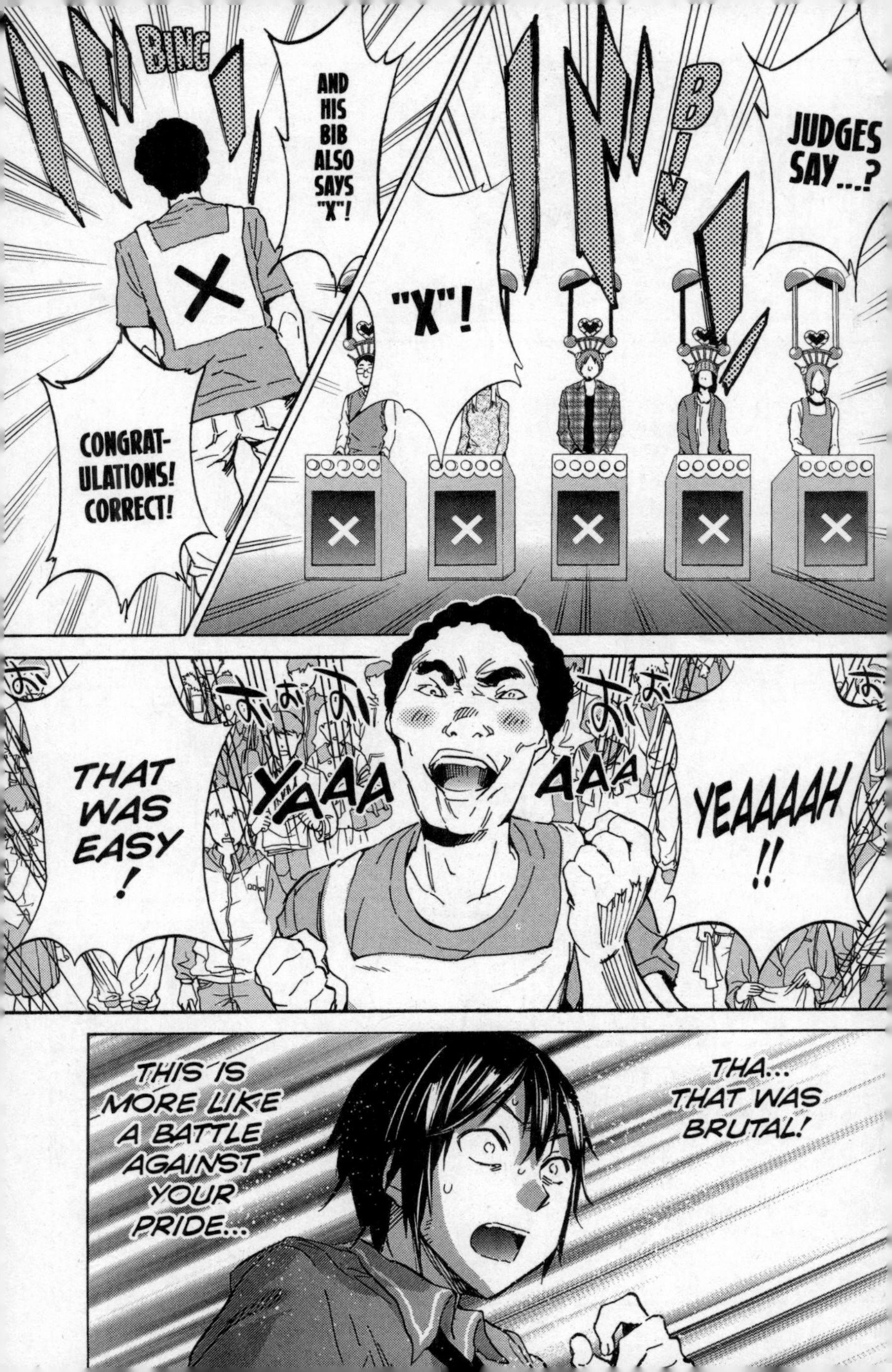
JUDGES SAY...?
BIB
"X"!
BING
AND HIS BIB ALSO SAYS "X"!
CONGRAT-ULATIONS! CORRECT!
YEAAAAH!!
YAAAAAA
THAT WAS EASY!
THA... THAT WAS BRUTAL!
THIS IS MORE LIKE A BATTLE AGAINST YOUR PRIDE...

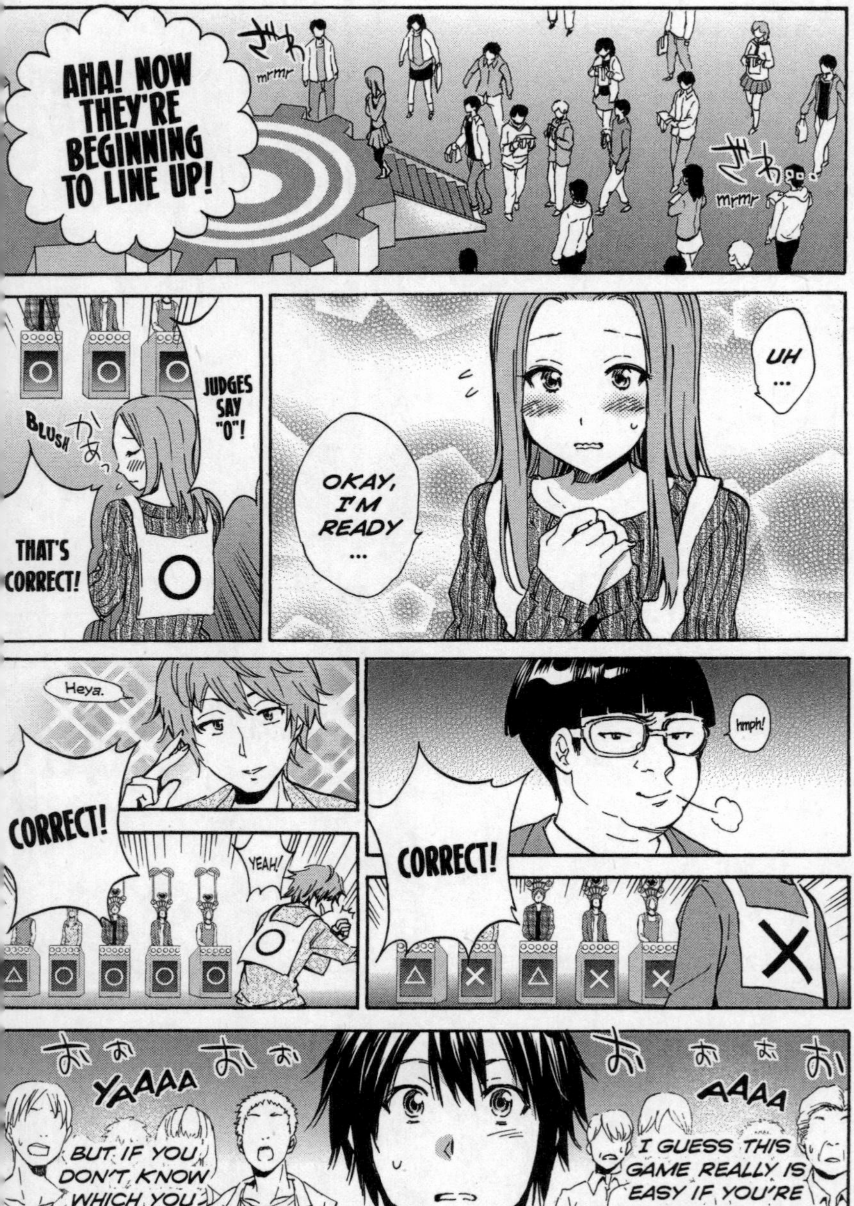
ざわ
mrmr
AHA! NOW THEY'RE BEGINNING TO LINE UP!
ざわ
mrmr
UH ...
OKAY, I'M READY ...
JUDGES SAY "O"!
BLUSH
THAT'S CORRECT!
hmph!
CORRECT!
Heya.
CORRECT!
YEAH!
AAAA
I GUESS THIS GAME REALLY IS EASY IF YOU'RE CLEARLY BEAUTIFUL OR UGLY.
YAAAA
BUT IF YOU DON'T KNOW WHICH YOU ARE...!!

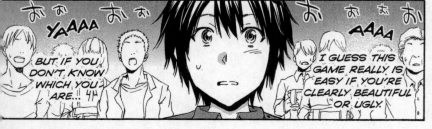

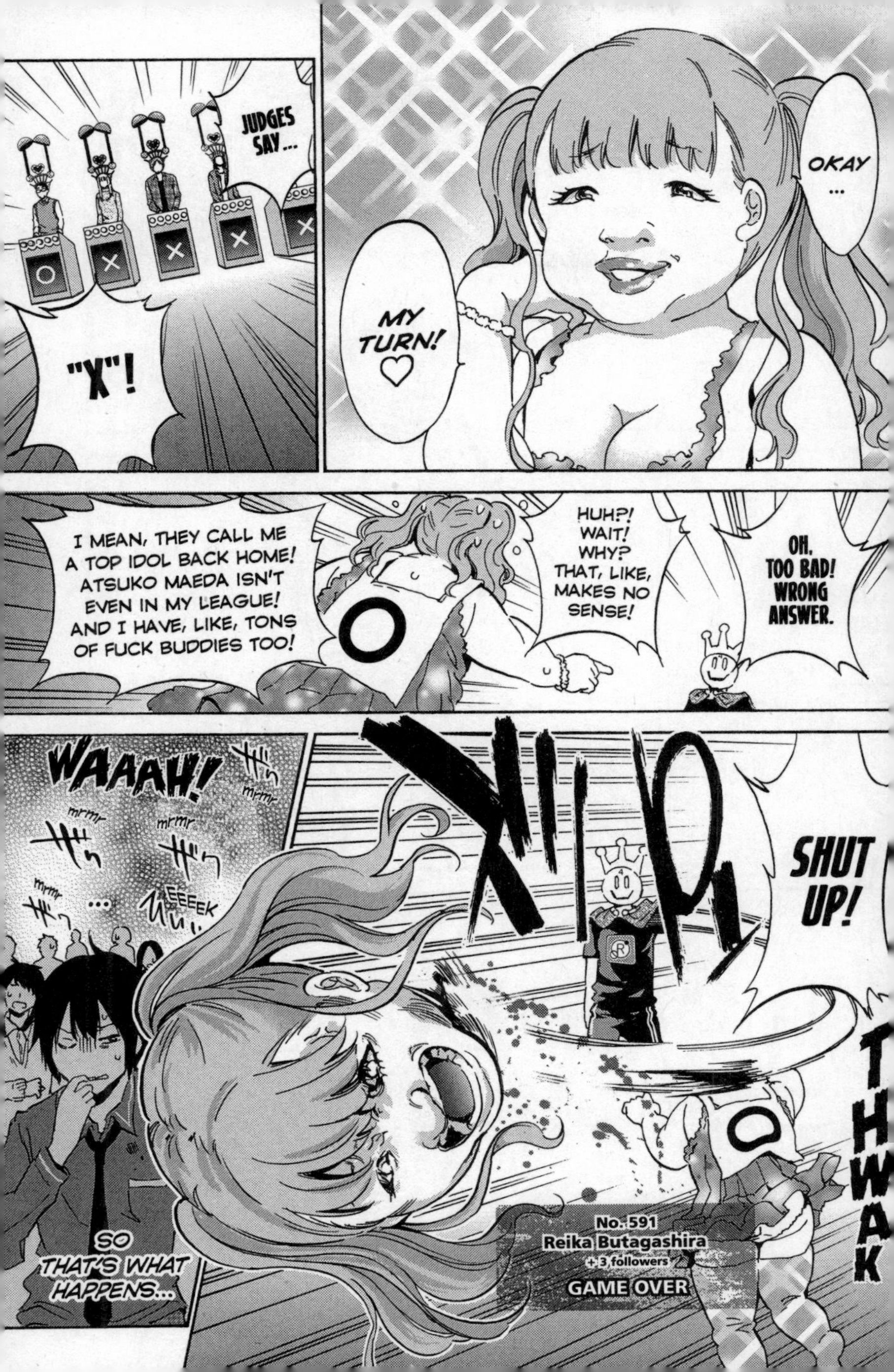
OKAY ...
MY TURN! ♡
JUDGES SAY...
"X"!
OH, TOO BAD! WRONG ANSWER.
HUH?! WAIT! WHY? THAT, LIKE, MAKES NO SENSE!
I MEAN, THEY CALL ME A TOP IDOL BACK HOME! ATSUKO MAEDA ISN'T EVEN IN MY LEAGUE! AND I HAVE, LIKE, TONS OF FUCK BUDDIES TOO!
SHUT UP!
THWAK
No. 591
Reika Butagashira
+ 3 followers
GAME OVER
WAAAH!
mrmr
mrmr
mrmr
mrmr
...
EEEEK
SO THAT'S WHAT HAPPENS...

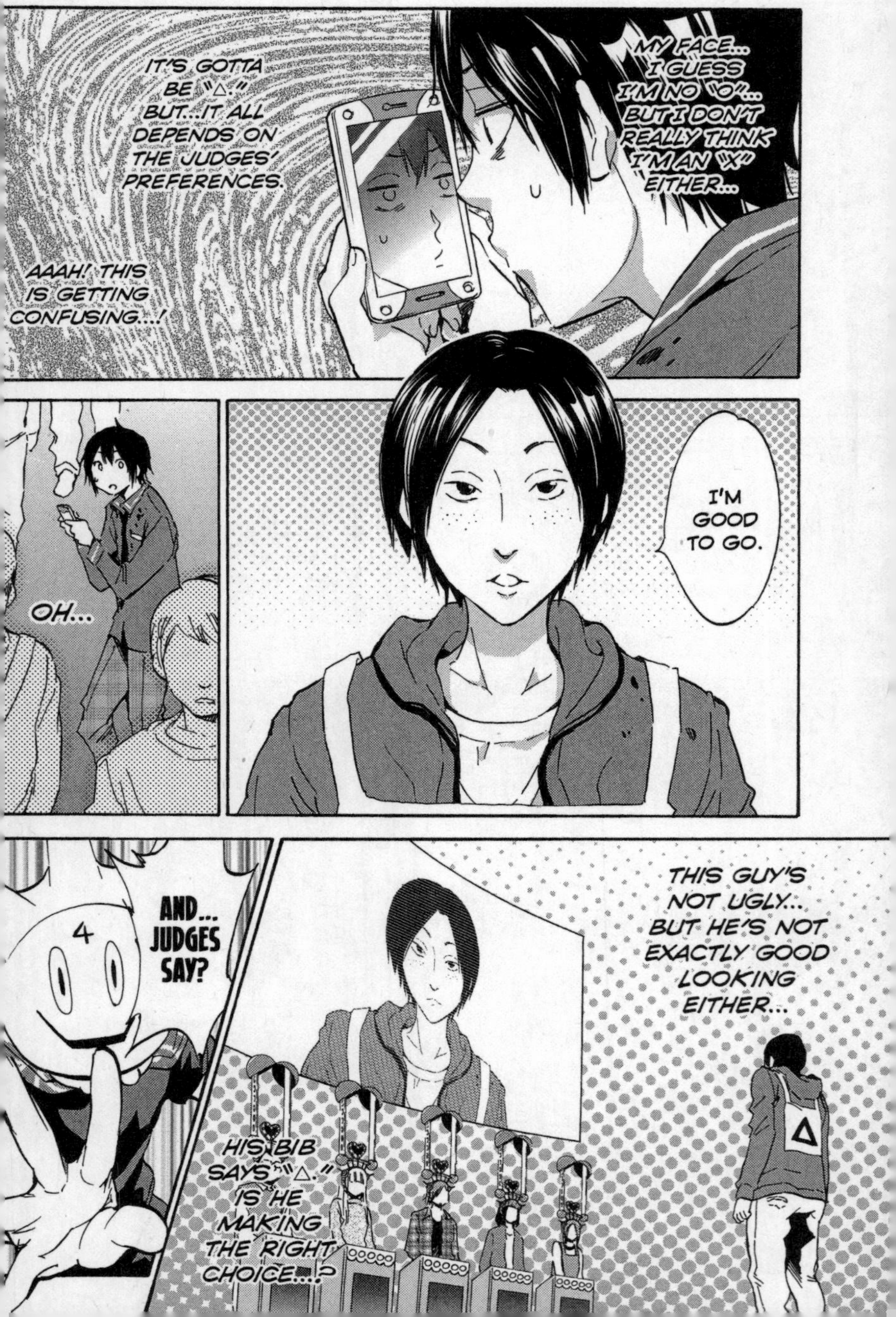
MY FACE... I GUESS I'M NO "O"... BUT I DON'T REALLY THINK I'M AN "X" EITHER...
IT'S GOTTA BE "△." BUT...IT ALL DEPENDS ON THE JUDGES' PREFERENCES.
AAAH! THIS IS GETTING CONFUSING...!
I'M GOOD TO GO.
OH...
THIS GUY'S NOT UGLY... BUT HE'S NOT EXACTLY GOOD LOOKING EITHER...
HIS BIB SAYS "△." IS HE MAKING THE RIGHT CHOICE...!?
△
4
AND... JUDGES SAY?

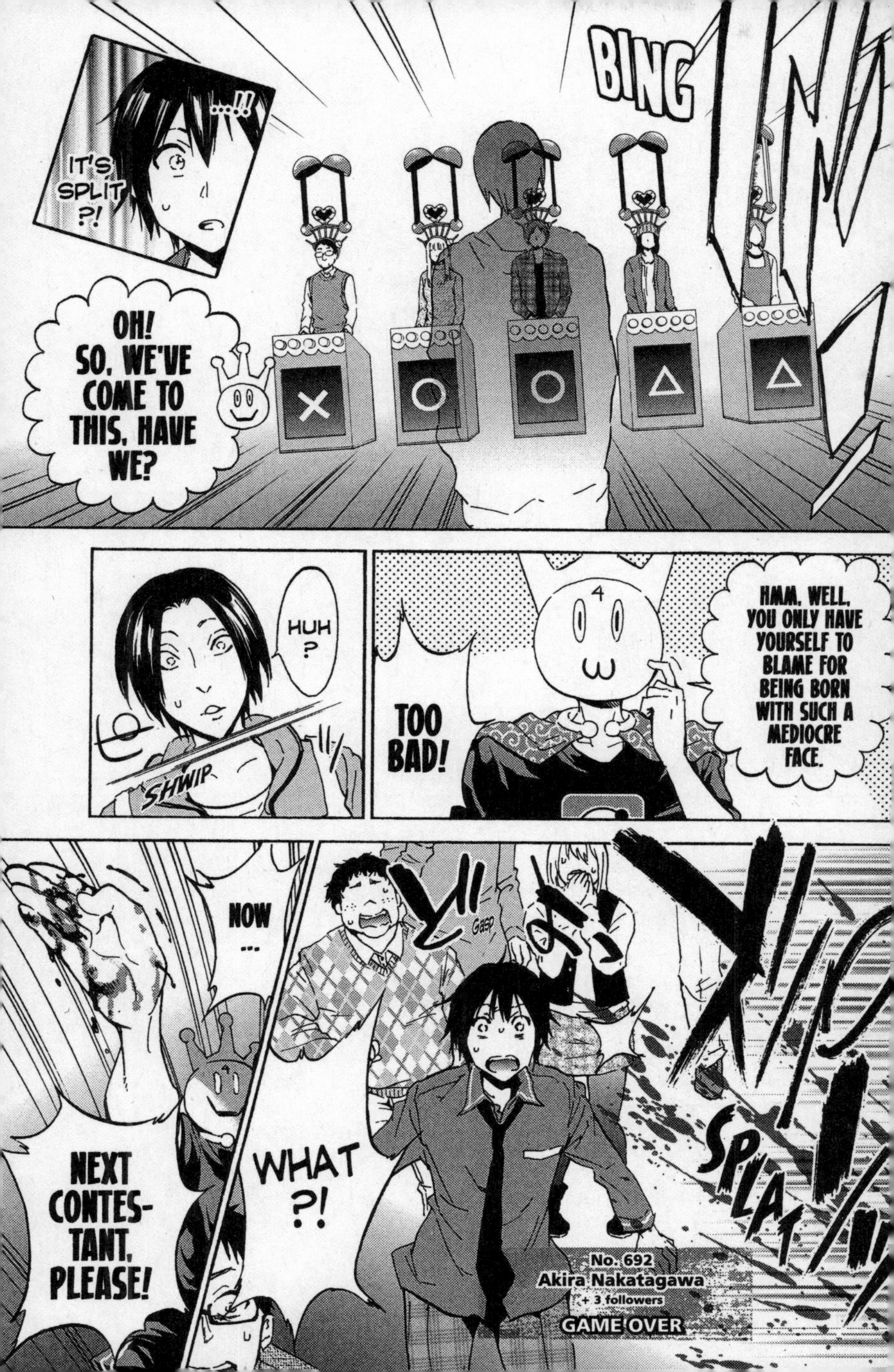
BING
...!!
IT'S SPLIT?!
OH! SO, WE'VE COME TO THIS, HAVE WE?
HMM. WELL, YOU ONLY HAVE YOURSELF TO BLAME FOR BEING BORN WITH SUCH A MEDIOCRE FACE.
TOO BAD!
HUH?
SHWIP
SPLAT
Gasp
WHAT?!
No. 692
Akira Nakatagawa
+ 3 followers
GAME OVER
NOW...
NEXT CONTESTANT, PLEASE!

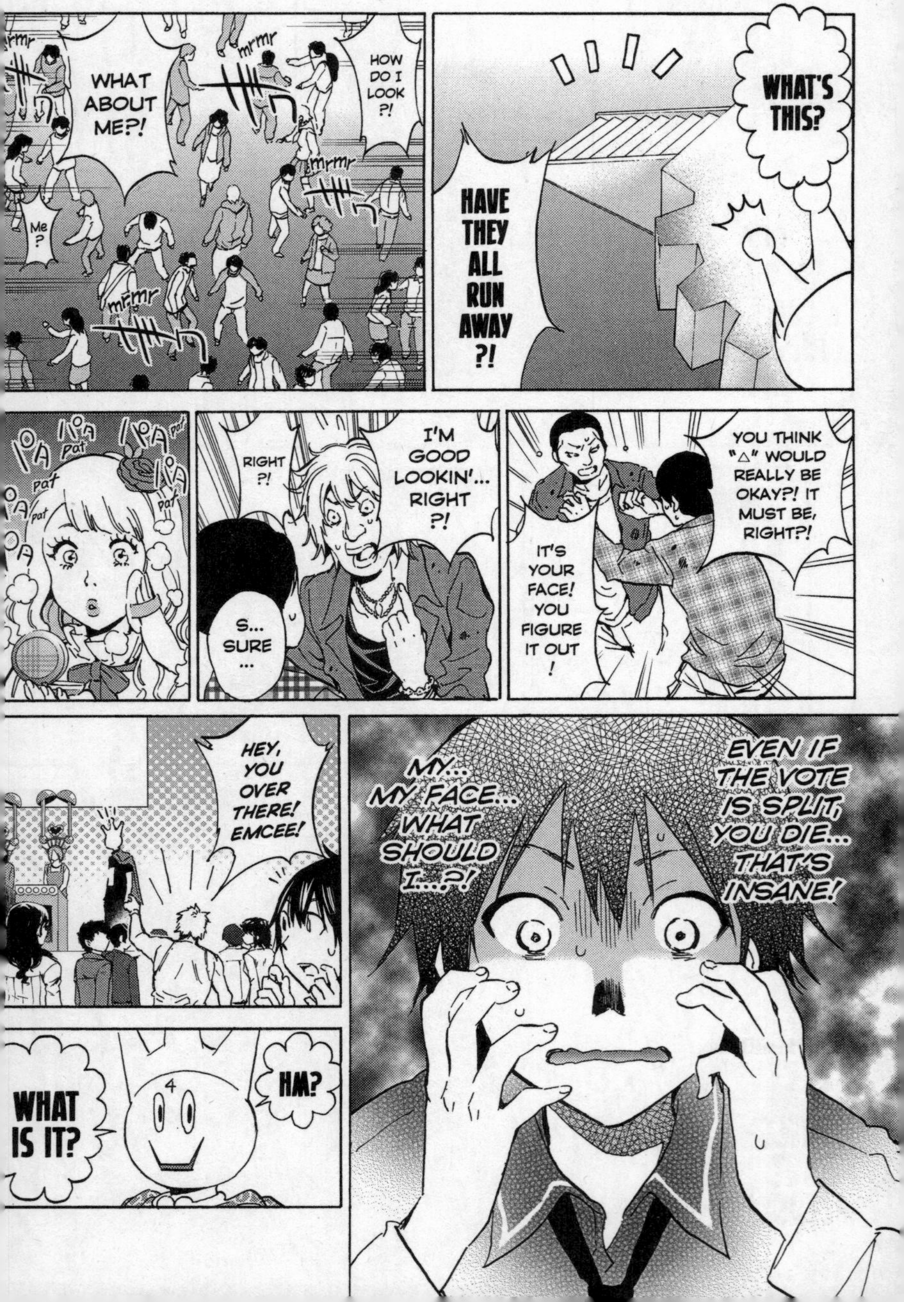
WHAT'S THIS?
HAVE THEY ALL RUN AWAY?!
HOW DO I LOOK?!
mrmr
WHAT ABOUT ME?!
Me?
YOU THINK "△" WOULD REALLY BE OKAY?! IT MUST BE, RIGHT?!
IT'S YOUR FACE! YOU FIGURE IT OUT!
I'M GOOD LOOKIN'... RIGHT?!
RIGHT?!
S... SURE...
pat
EVEN IF THE VOTE IS SPLIT, YOU DIE... THAT'S INSANE!
MY... MY FACE... WHAT SHOULD I...?!
HEY, YOU OVER THERE! EMCEE!
HM?
WHAT IS IT?

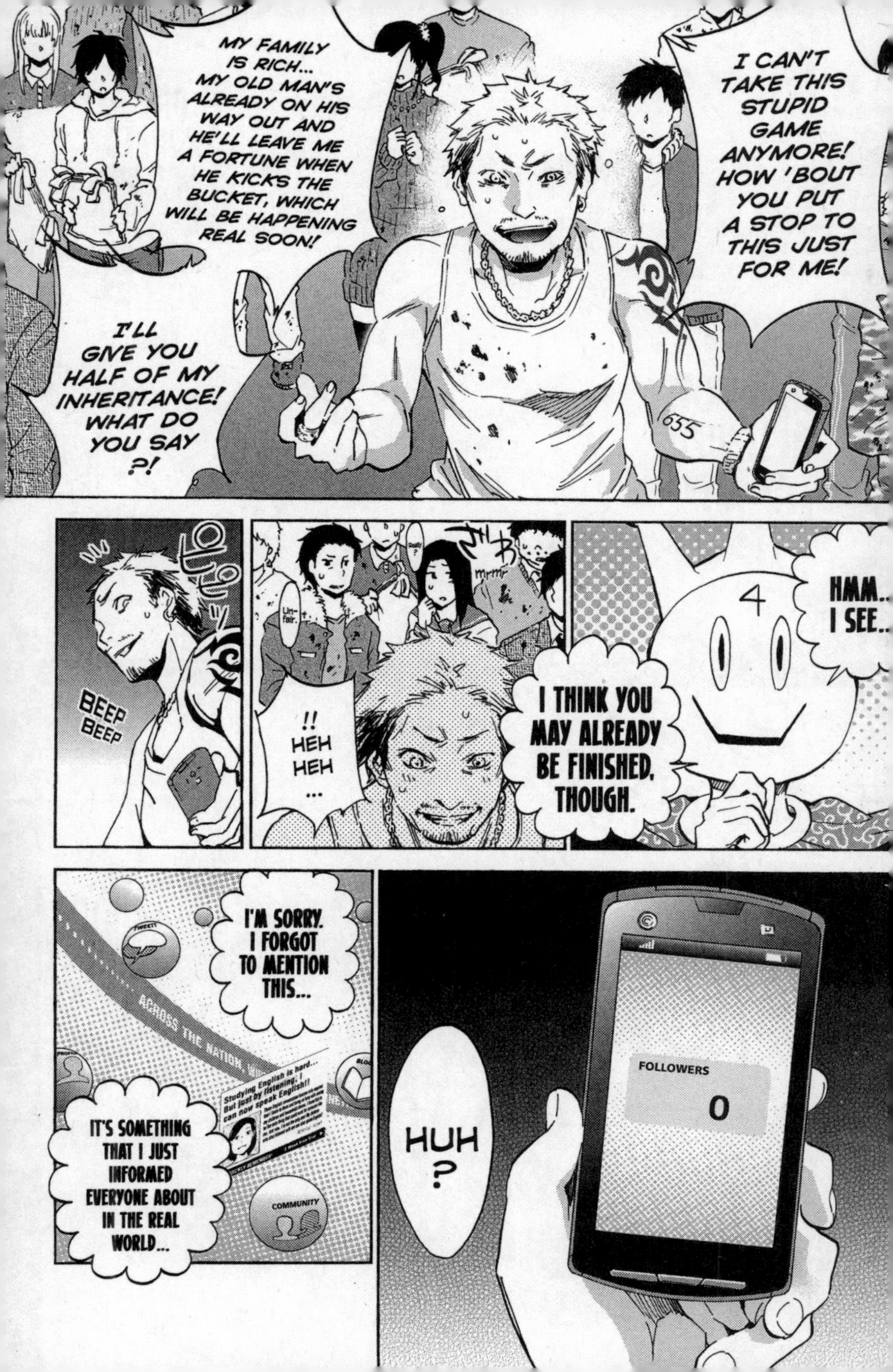
I CAN'T TAKE THIS STUPID GAME ANYMORE! HOW 'BOUT YOU PUT A STOP TO THIS JUST FOR ME!
MY FAMILY IS RICH... MY OLD MAN'S ALREADY ON HIS WAY OUT AND HE'LL LEAVE ME A FORTUNE WHEN HE KICKS THE BUCKET, WHICH WILL BE HAPPENING REAL SOON!
I'LL GIVE YOU HALF OF MY INHERITANCE! WHAT DO YOU SAY ?!
655
HMM.. I SEE..
4
I THINK YOU MAY ALREADY BE FINISHED, THOUGH.
!! HEH HEH ...
Really?
mrmr
Un-fair.
BEEP BEEP
FOLLOWERS
0
HUH ?
I'M SORRY. I FORGOT TO MENTION THIS...
TWEET
ACROSS THE NATION
Studying English is hard... But just by listening, I can now speak English!!
COMMUNITY
IT'S SOMETHING THAT I JUST INFORMED EVERYONE ABOUT IN THE REAL WORLD...

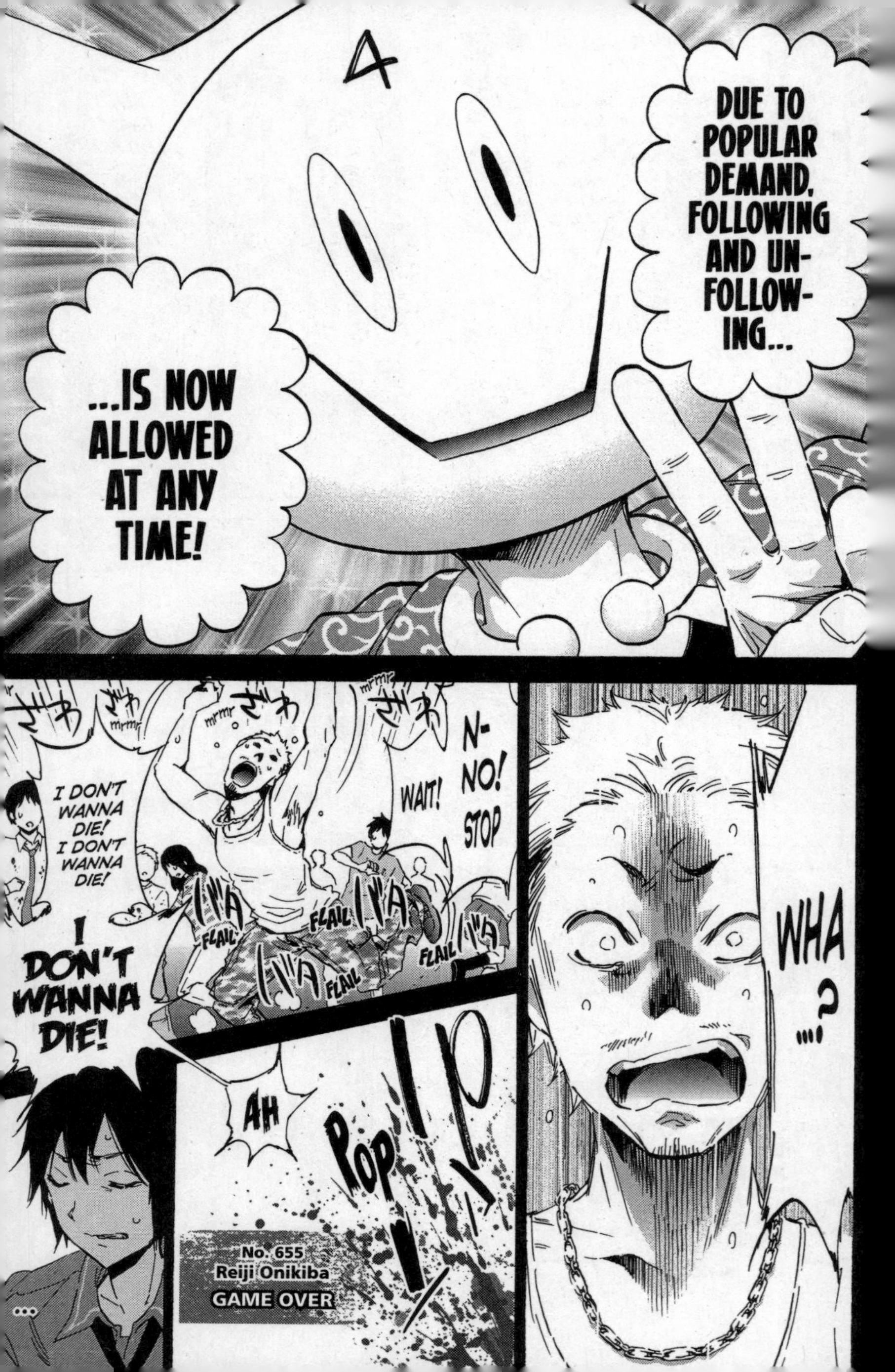
DUE TO POPULAR DEMAND, FOLLOWING AND UN-FOLLOWING...
...IS NOW ALLOWED AT ANY TIME!
WHA ...?
ざわ ざわ mrmr
N-NO! STOP
WAIT!
I DON'T WANNA DIE! I DON'T WANNA DIE!
I DON'T WANNA DIE!
FLAIL FLAIL FLAIL FLAIL
POP
AH
No. 655
Reiji Onikiba
GAME OVER
...

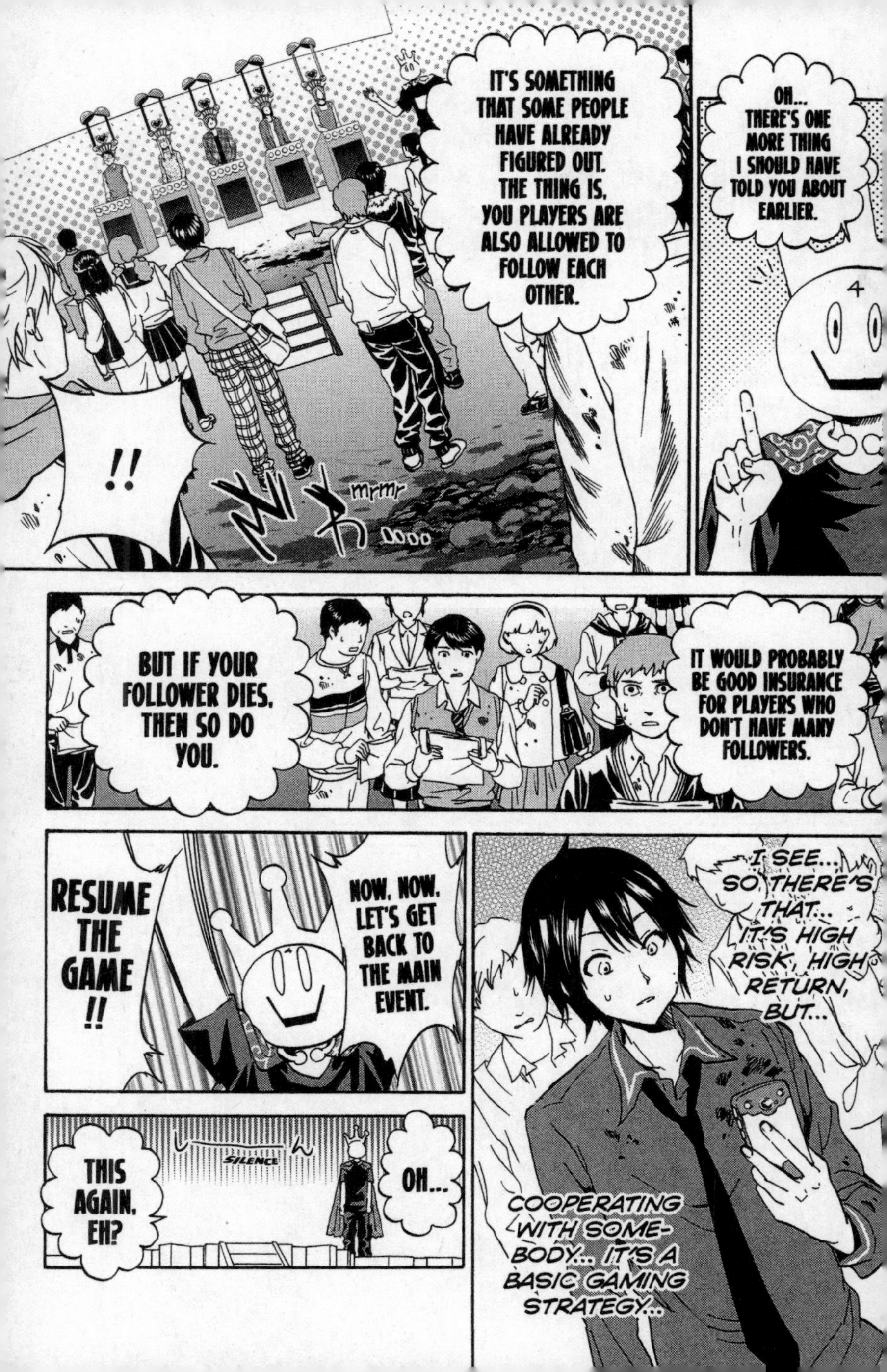
OH... THERE'S ONE MORE THING I SHOULD HAVE TOLD YOU ABOUT EARLIER.
IT'S SOMETHING THAT SOME PEOPLE HAVE ALREADY FIGURED OUT. THE THING IS, YOU PLAYERS ARE ALSO ALLOWED TO FOLLOW EACH OTHER.
!!
mrmr
IT WOULD PROBABLY BE GOOD INSURANCE FOR PLAYERS WHO DON'T HAVE MANY FOLLOWERS.
BUT IF YOUR FOLLOWER DIES, THEN SO DO YOU.
I SEE... SO THERE'S THAT... IT'S HIGH RISK, HIGH RETURN, BUT...
COOPERATING WITH SOME-BODY... IT'S A BASIC GAMING STRATEGY...
NOW, NOW. LET'S GET BACK TO THE MAIN EVENT.
RESUME THE GAME !!
OH...
SILENCE
THIS AGAIN, EH?

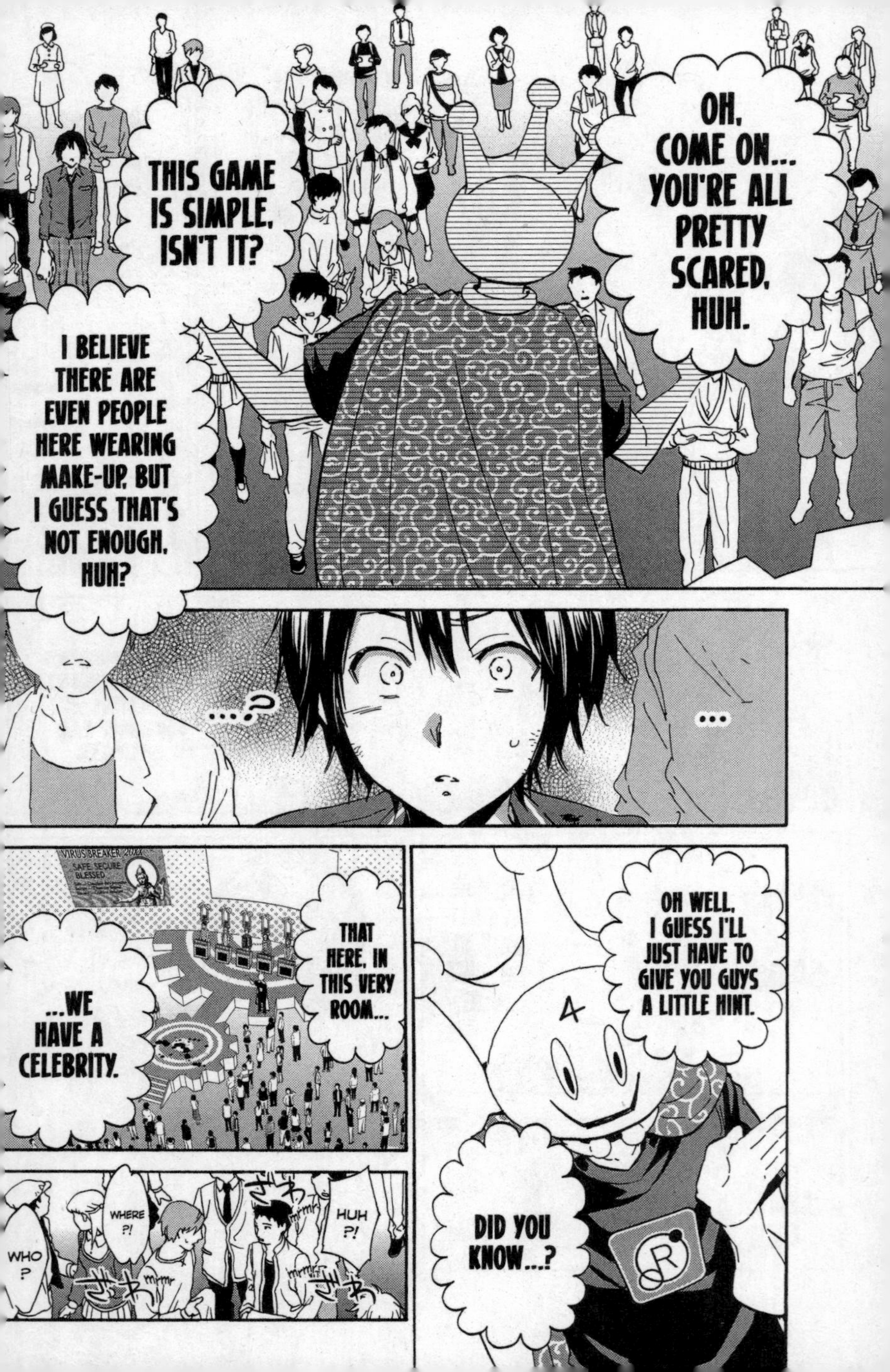
OH, COME ON... YOU'RE ALL PRETTY SCARED, HUH.
THIS GAME IS SIMPLE, ISN'T IT?
I BELIEVE THERE ARE EVEN PEOPLE HERE WEARING MAKE-UP, BUT I GUESS THAT'S NOT ENOUGH, HUH?
...
...?
OH WELL, I GUESS I'LL JUST HAVE TO GIVE YOU GUYS A LITTLE HINT.
DID YOU KNOW...?
VIRUS BREAKER 20XX
SAFE. SECURE. BLESSED.
THAT HERE, IN THIS VERY ROOM...
...WE HAVE A CELEBRITY.
HUH ?!
mrmr
WHERE ?!
WHO ?
mrmr
mrmr

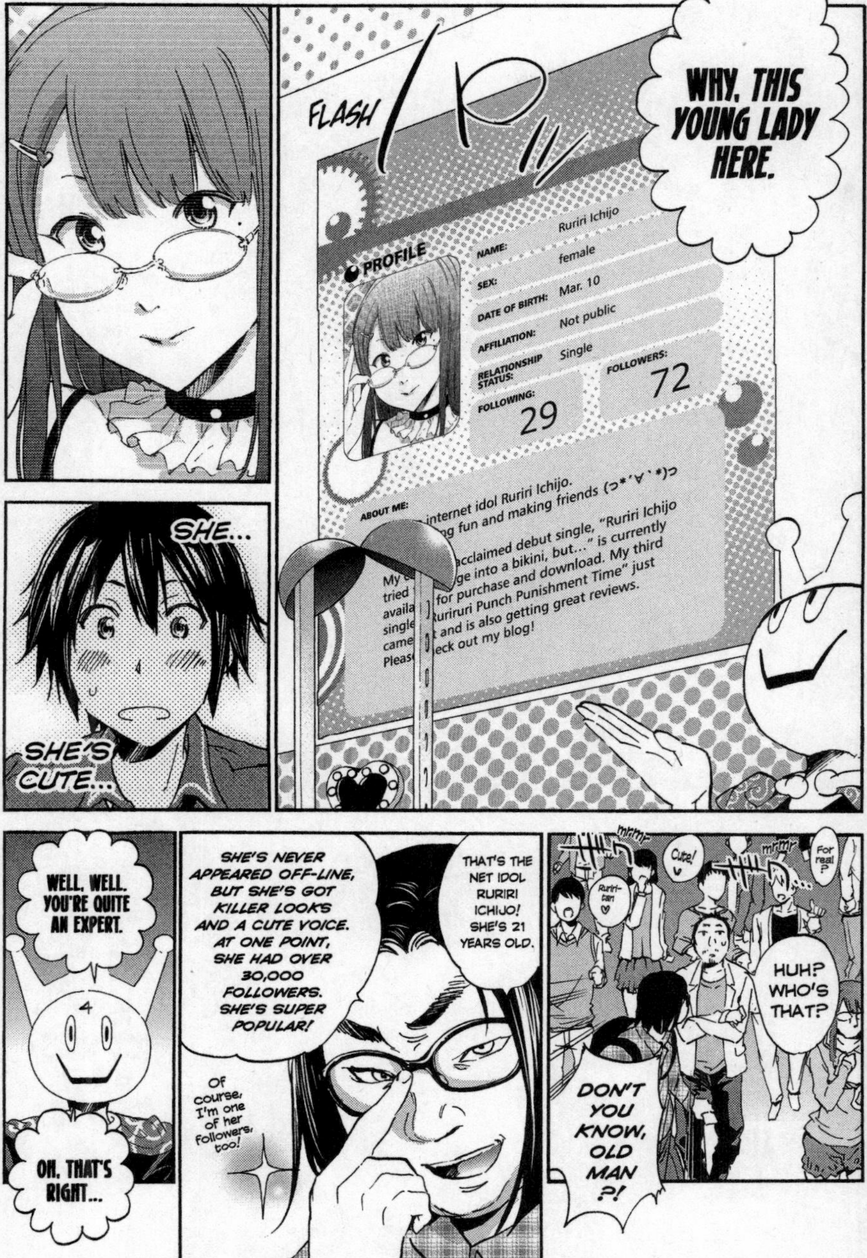
WHY, THIS YOUNG LADY HERE.
FLASH
PROFILE
NAME: Ruriri Ichijo
SEX: female
DATE OF BIRTH: Mar. 10
AFFILIATION: Not public
RELATIONSHIP STATUS: Single
FOLLOWERS: 72
FOLLOWING: 29
ABOUT ME:
internet idol Ruriri Ichijo.
ng fun and making friends (っ*´∀`*)っ
My acclaimed debut single, "Ruriri Ichijo
tried ge into a bikini, but..." is currently
availa for purchase and download. My third
single Ruriruri Punch Punishment Time" just
came t and is also getting great reviews.
Pleas eck out my blog!
SHE...
SHE'S CUTE...
mrmr
Cute! ♥
Ruriri-tan ♥
mrmr
For real?
HUH? WHO'S THAT?
DON'T YOU KNOW, OLD MAN ?!
THAT'S THE NET IDOL RURIRI ICHIJO! SHE'S 21 YEARS OLD.
SHE'S NEVER APPEARED OFF-LINE, BUT SHE'S GOT KILLER LOOKS AND A CUTE VOICE. AT ONE POINT, SHE HAD OVER 30,000 FOLLOWERS. SHE'S SUPER POPULAR!
Of course, I'm one of her followers, too!
WELL, WELL. YOU'RE QUITE AN EXPERT.
OH, THAT'S RIGHT...

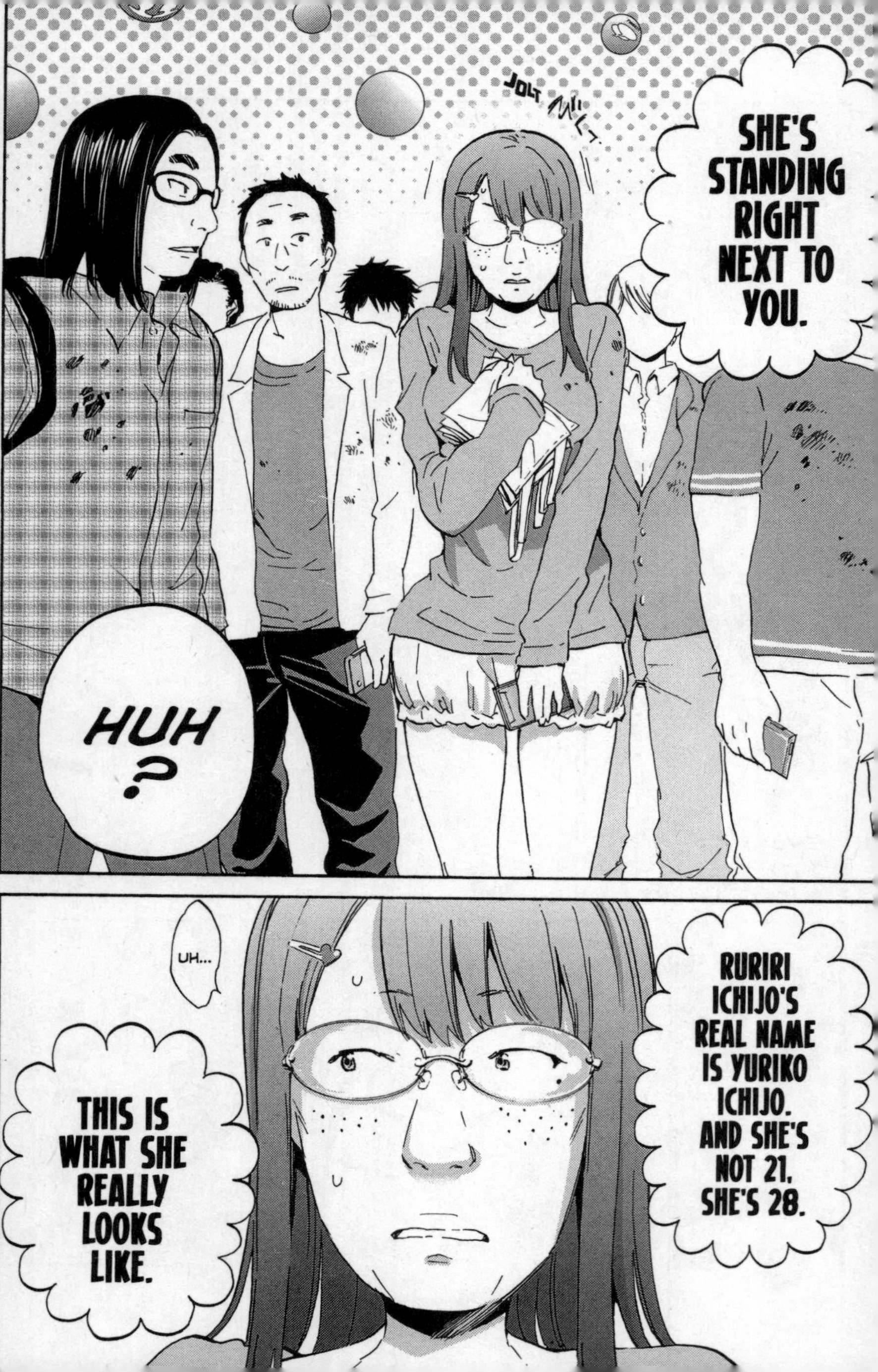
SHE'S STANDING RIGHT NEXT TO YOU.
JOLT
HUH?
RURIRI ICHIJO'S REAL NAME IS YURIKO ICHIJO. AND SHE'S NOT 21, SHE'S 28.
UH...
THIS IS WHAT SHE REALLY LOOKS LIKE.

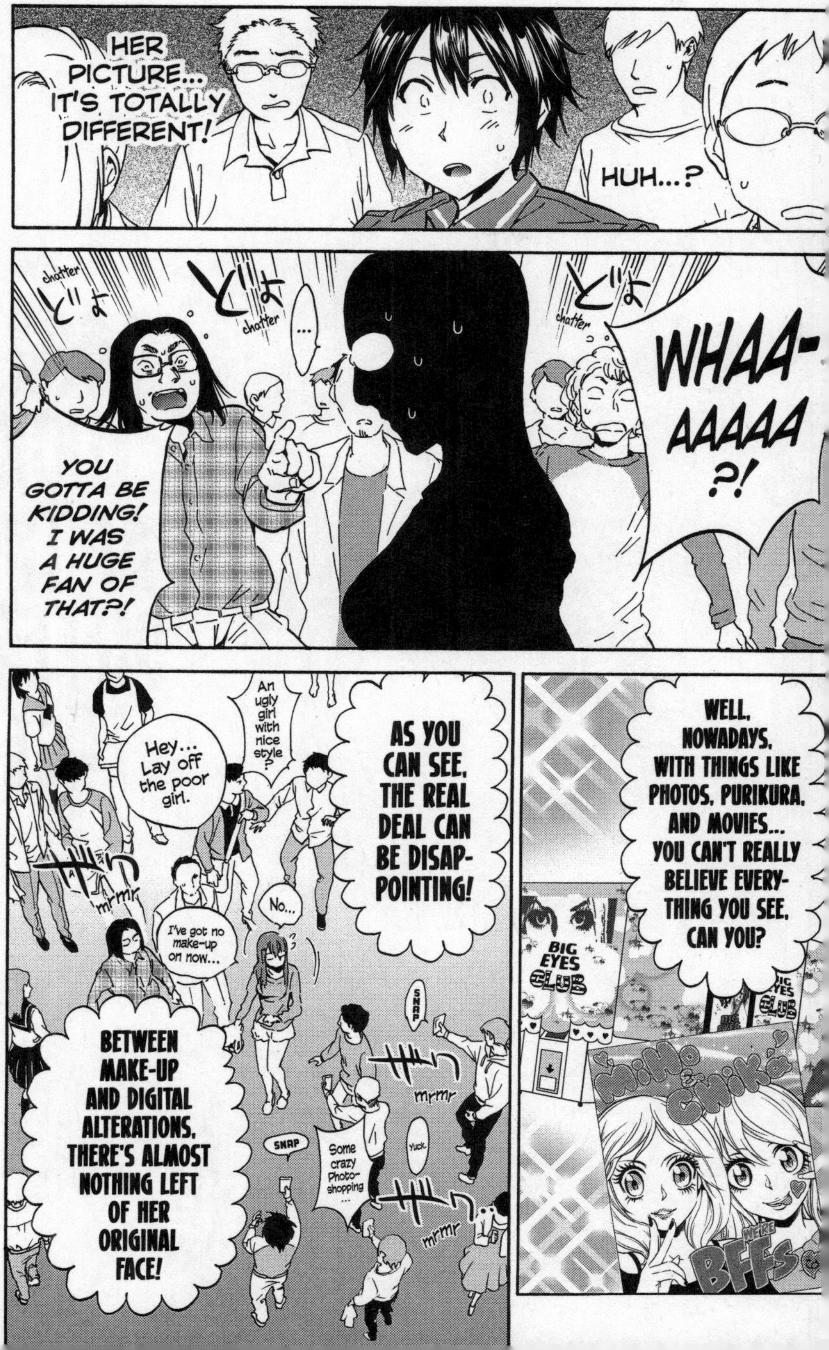
HER PICTURE... IT'S TOTALLY DIFFERENT!
HUH...?
WHAA-AAAAA?!
どよ chatter
...
どよ chatter
どよ chatter
YOU GOTTA BE KIDDING! I WAS A HUGE FAN OF THAT?!
WELL, NOWADAYS, WITH THINGS LIKE PHOTOS, PURIKURA, AND MOVIES... YOU CAN'T REALLY BELIEVE EVERY-THING YOU SEE, CAN YOU?
BIG EYES CLUB
BIG EYES CLUB
WE'RE BFFS
AS YOU CAN SEE, THE REAL DEAL CAN BE DISAP-POINTING!
An ugly girl with nice style?
Hey... Lay off the poor girl.
mrmr
No...
I've got no make-up on now...
BETWEEN MAKE-UP AND DIGITAL ALTERATIONS, THERE'S ALMOST NOTHING LEFT OF HER ORIGINAL FACE!
SNAP
mrmr
SNAP
Yuck.
Some crazy Photo-shopping...
mrmr

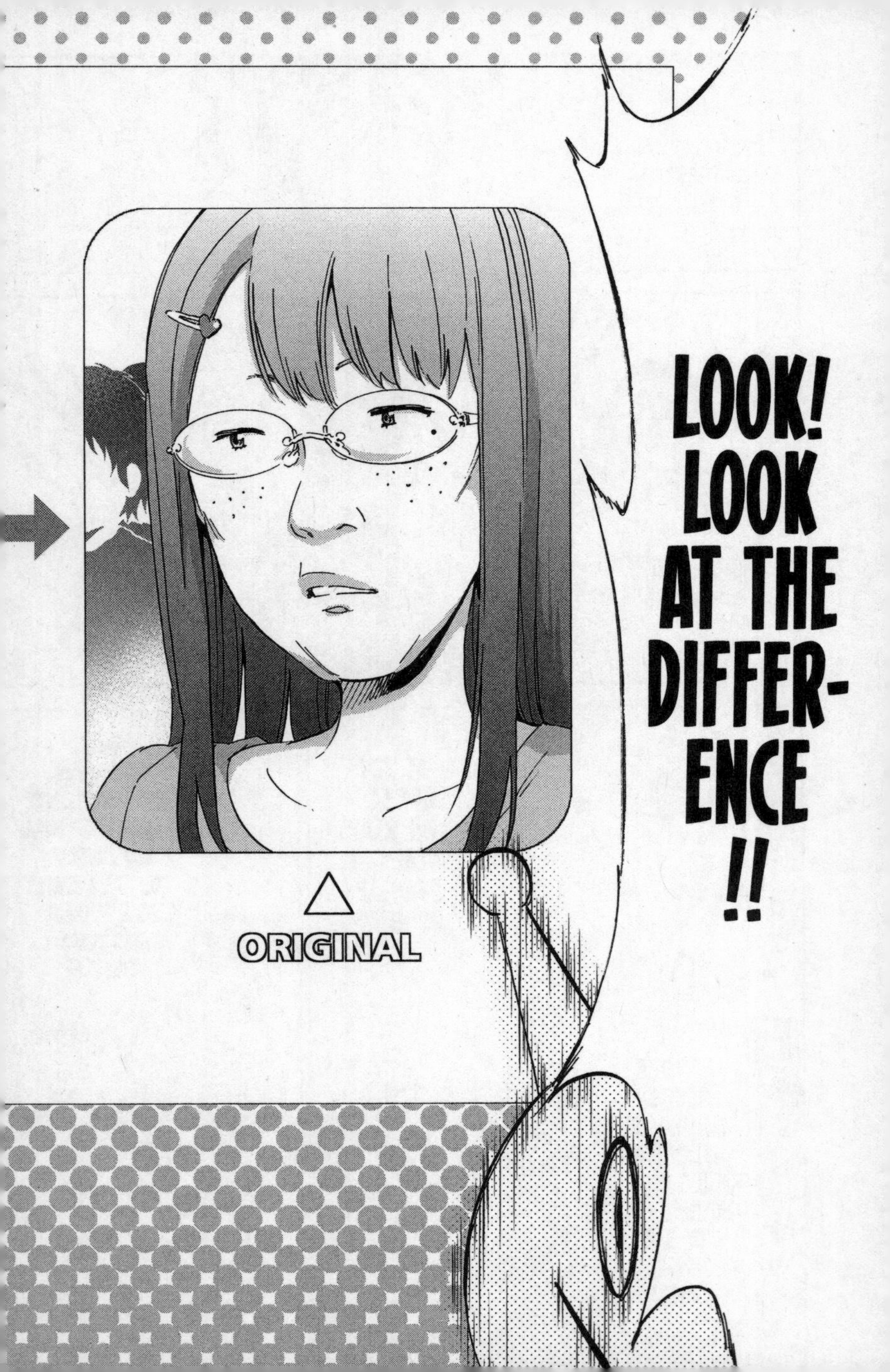
LOOK! LOOK AT THE DIFFER-ENCE!!
ORIGINAL

FWAAAAAH!!

△
ICON

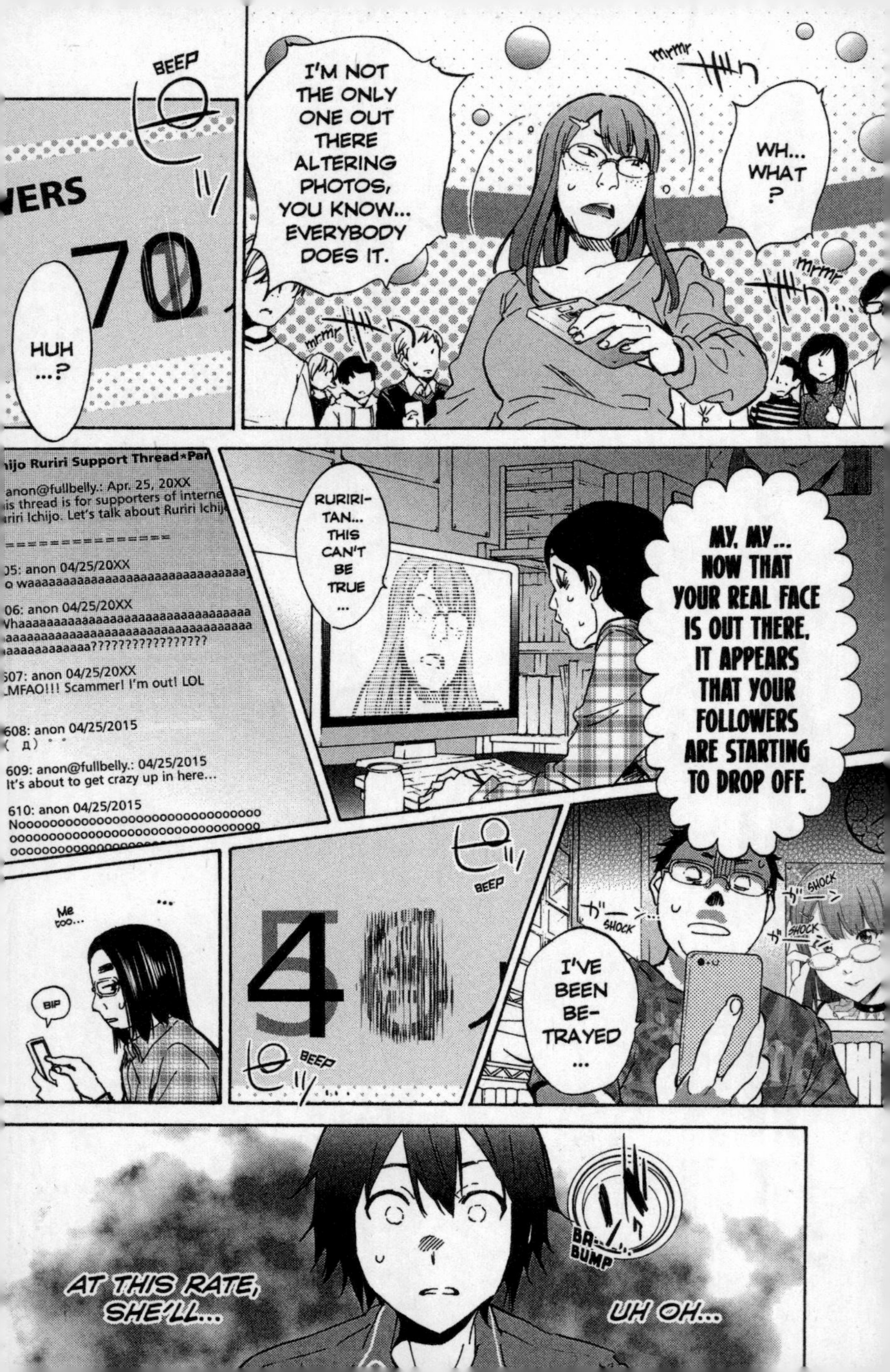

mrmr
I'M NOT THE ONLY ONE OUT THERE ALTERING PHOTOS, YOU KNOW... EVERYBODY DOES IT.
WH... WHAT?
mrmr
mrmr
BEEP
WERS
70
HUH...?
MY, MY... NOW THAT YOUR REAL FACE IS OUT THERE, IT APPEARS THAT YOUR FOLLOWERS ARE STARTING TO DROP OFF.
RURIRI-TAN... THIS CAN'T BE TRUE...
hijo Ruriri Support Thread*Par
anon@fullbelly.: Apr. 25, 20XX
is thread is for supporters of interne
riri Ichijo. Let's talk about Ruriri Ichij
===============
05: anon 04/25/20XX
o waaaaaaaaaaaaaaaaaaaaaaaaaaaaaaaay
06: anon 04/25/20XX
Vhaaaaaaaaaaaaaaaaaaaaaaaaaaaaaaaaa
aaaaaaaaaaaaaaaaaaaaaaaaaaaaaaaaaaaa
aaaaaaaaaaaaa????????????????
607: anon 04/25/20XX
LMFAO!!! Scammer! I'm out! LOL
608: anon 04/25/2015
(д) ° °
609: anon@fullbelly.: 04/25/2015
It's about to get crazy up in here...
610: anon 04/25/2015
Noooooooooooooooooooooooooooooooooo
ooooooooooooooooooooooooooooooooooo
ooooooooooooooooooooooooooooooooooo
SHOCK
SHOCK
SHOCK
I'VE BEEN BE-TRAYED...
BEEP
4
BEEP
...
Me too...
BIP
BA-BUMP
UH OH...
AT THIS RATE, SHE'LL...

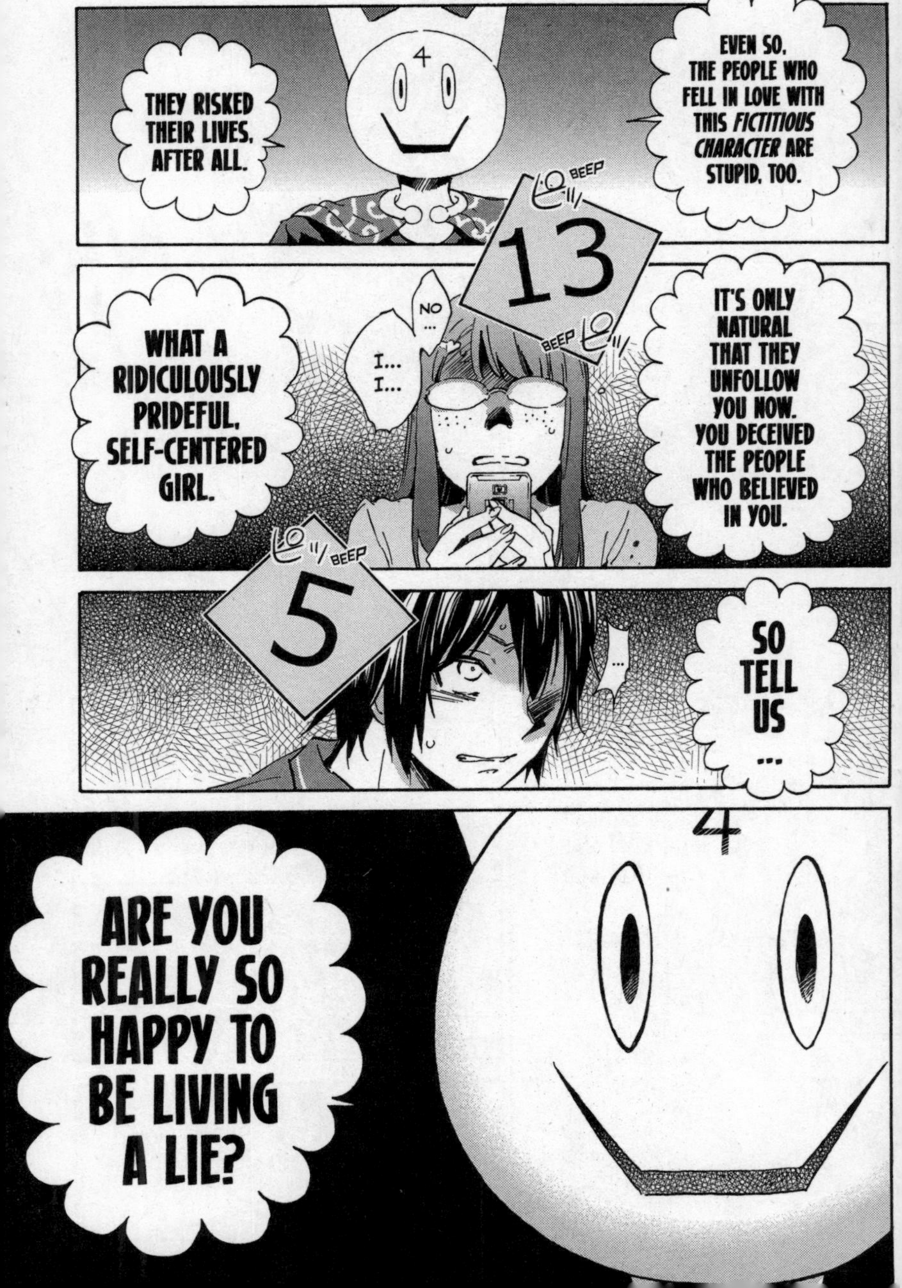
EVEN SO, THE PEOPLE WHO FELL IN LOVE WITH THIS *FICTITIOUS CHARACTER* ARE STUPID, TOO.
THEY RISKED THEIR LIVES, AFTER ALL.
BEEP
13
BEEP
IT'S ONLY NATURAL THAT THEY UNFOLLOW YOU NOW. YOU DECEIVED THE PEOPLE WHO BELIEVED IN YOU.
NO ...
I... I...
WHAT A RIDICULOUSLY PRIDEFUL, SELF-CENTERED GIRL.
BEEP
5
SO TELL US ...
...
ARE YOU REALLY SO HAPPY TO BE LIVING A LIE?

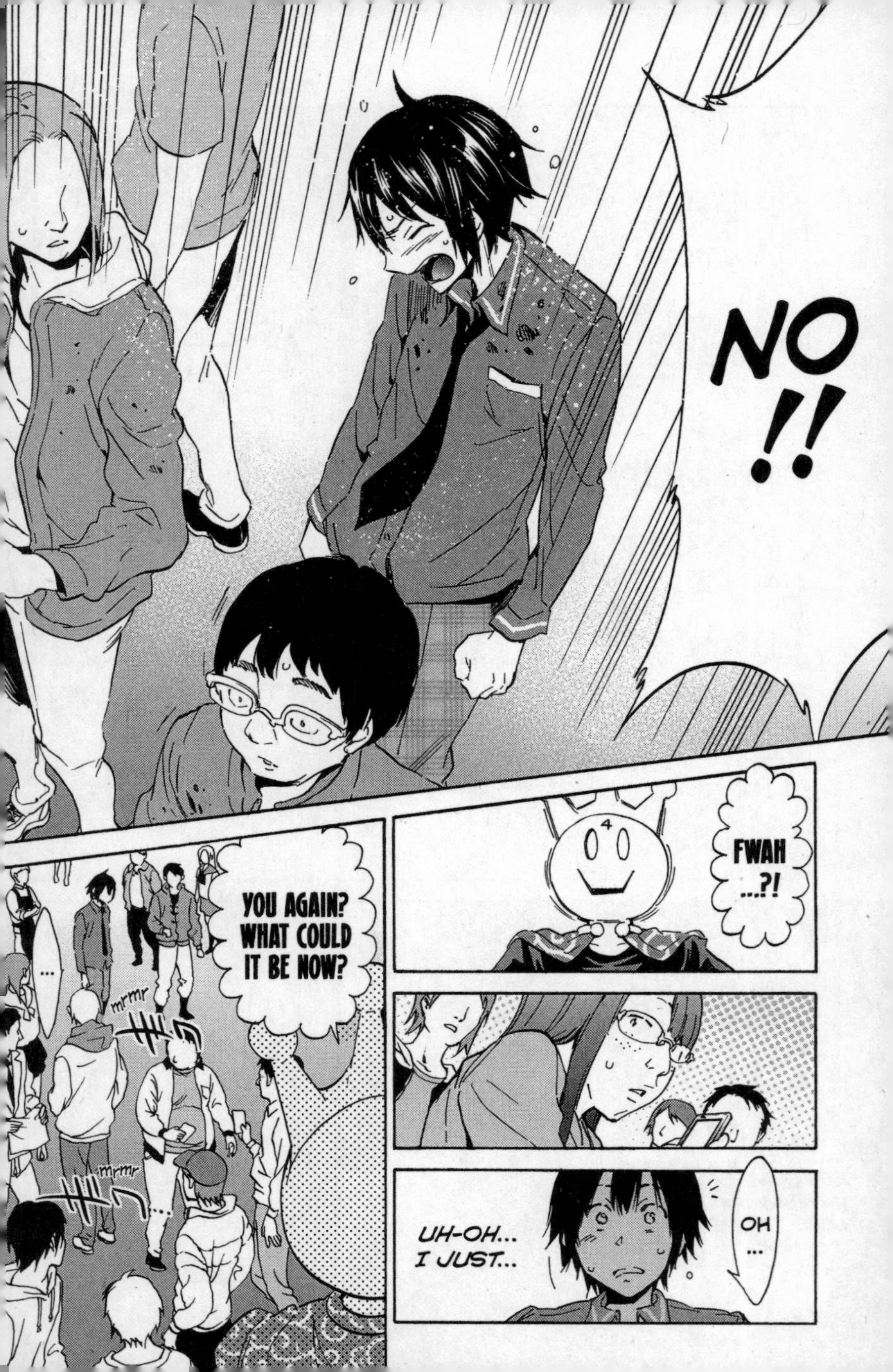
NO!!
FWAH ...?!
OH ...
UH-OH... I JUST...
YOU AGAIN? WHAT COULD IT BE NOW?
...
mrmr
mrmr

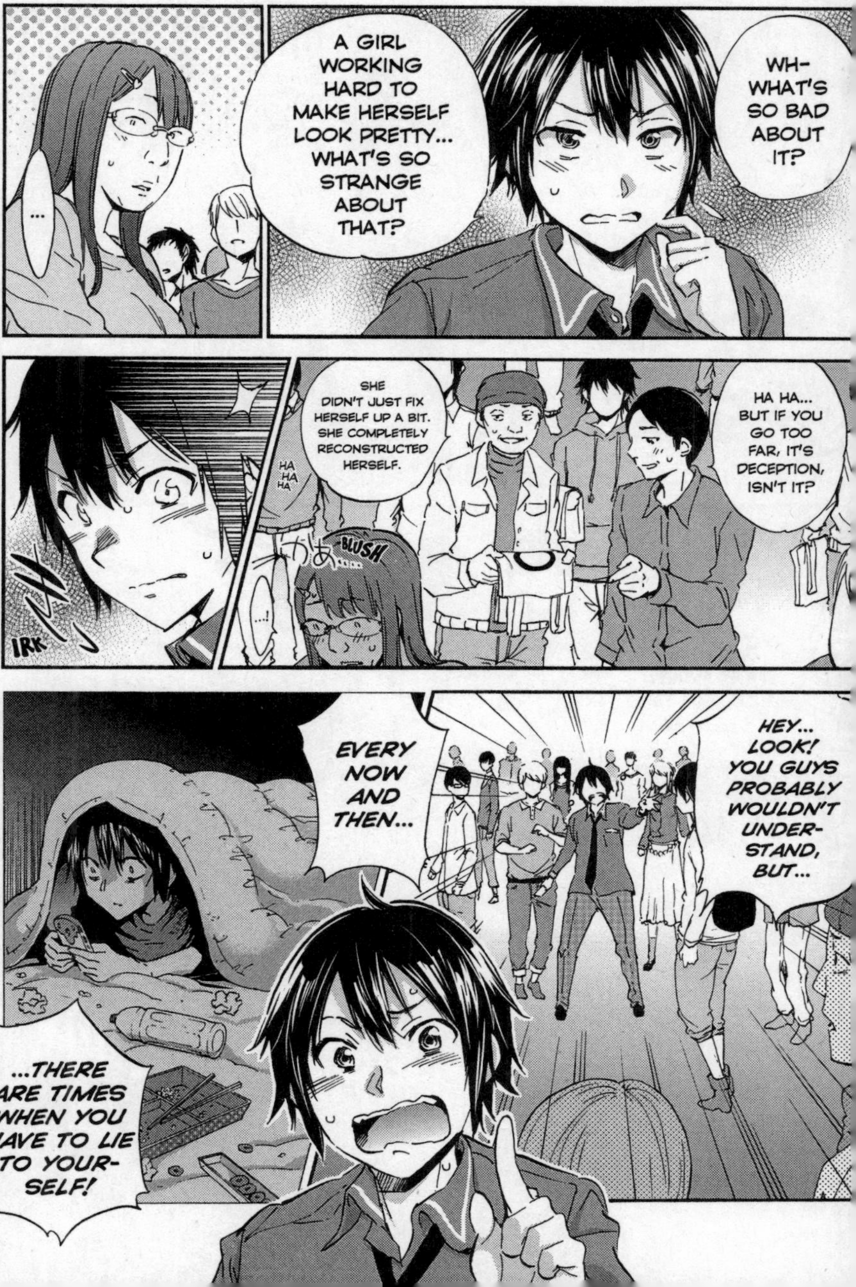
WH- WHAT'S SO BAD ABOUT IT?
A GIRL WORKING HARD TO MAKE HERSELF LOOK PRETTY... WHAT'S SO STRANGE ABOUT THAT?
...
HA HA... BUT IF YOU GO TOO FAR, IT'S DECEPTION, ISN'T IT?
SHE DIDN'T JUST FIX HERSELF UP A BIT. SHE COMPLETELY RECONSTRUCTED HERSELF.
HA HA HA
BLUSH
...!
IRK
HEY... LOOK! YOU GUYS PROBABLY WOULDN'T UNDER-STAND, BUT...
EVERY NOW AND THEN...
...THERE ARE TIMES WHEN YOU HAVE TO LIE TO YOUR-SELF!

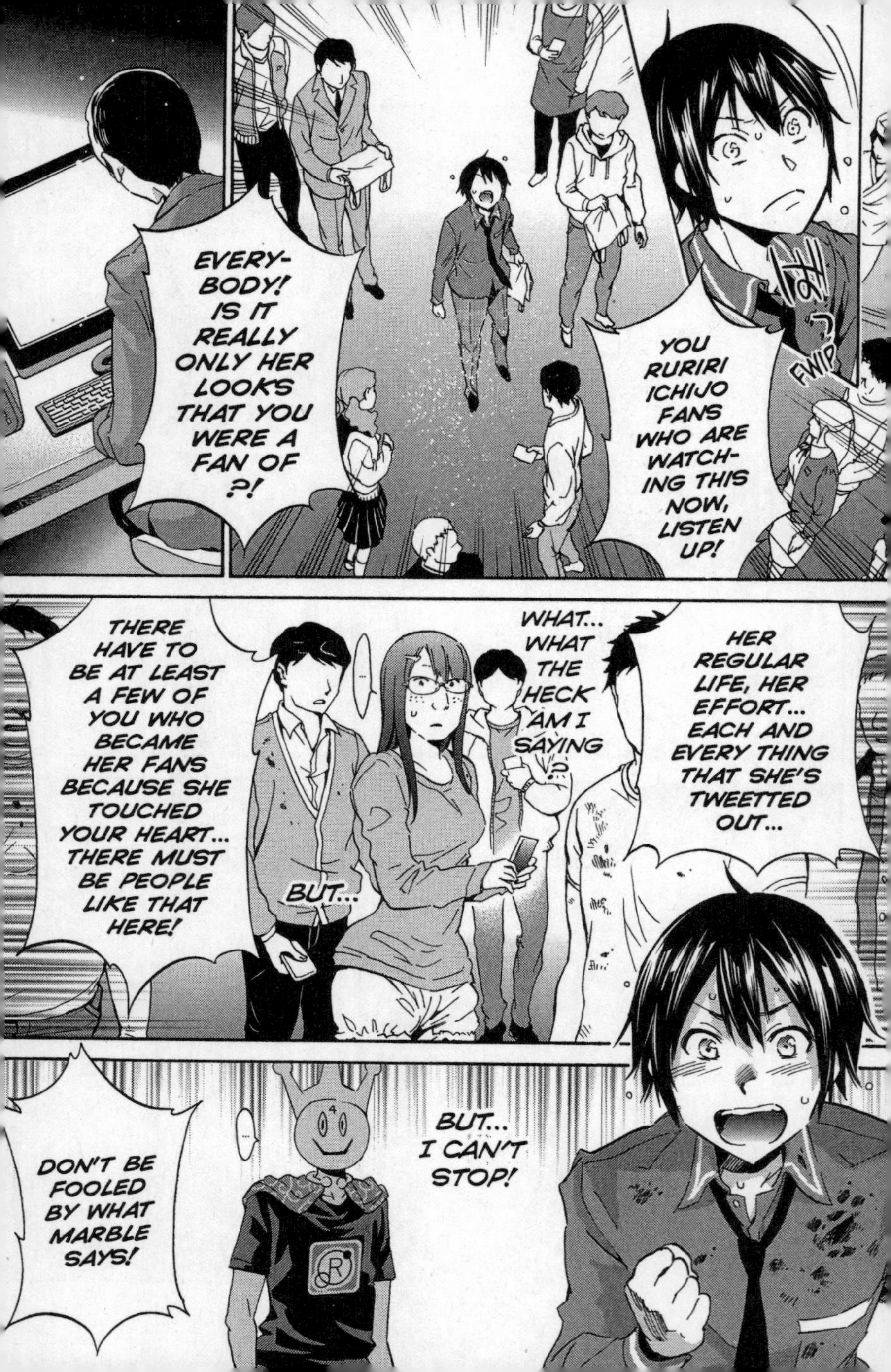
FWIP
YOU RURIRI ICHIJO FANS WHO ARE WATCHING THIS NOW, LISTEN UP!
EVERYBODY! IS IT REALLY ONLY HER LOOKS THAT YOU WERE A FAN OF ?!
HER REGULAR LIFE, HER EFFORT... EACH AND EVERY THING THAT SHE'S TWEETTED OUT...
WHAT... WHAT THE HECK AM I SAYING ?
...
THERE HAVE TO BE AT LEAST A FEW OF YOU WHO BECAME HER FANS BECAUSE SHE TOUCHED YOUR HEART... THERE MUST BE PEOPLE LIKE THAT HERE!
BUT...
BUT... I CAN'T STOP!
...
DON'T BE FOOLED BY WHAT MARBLE SAYS!

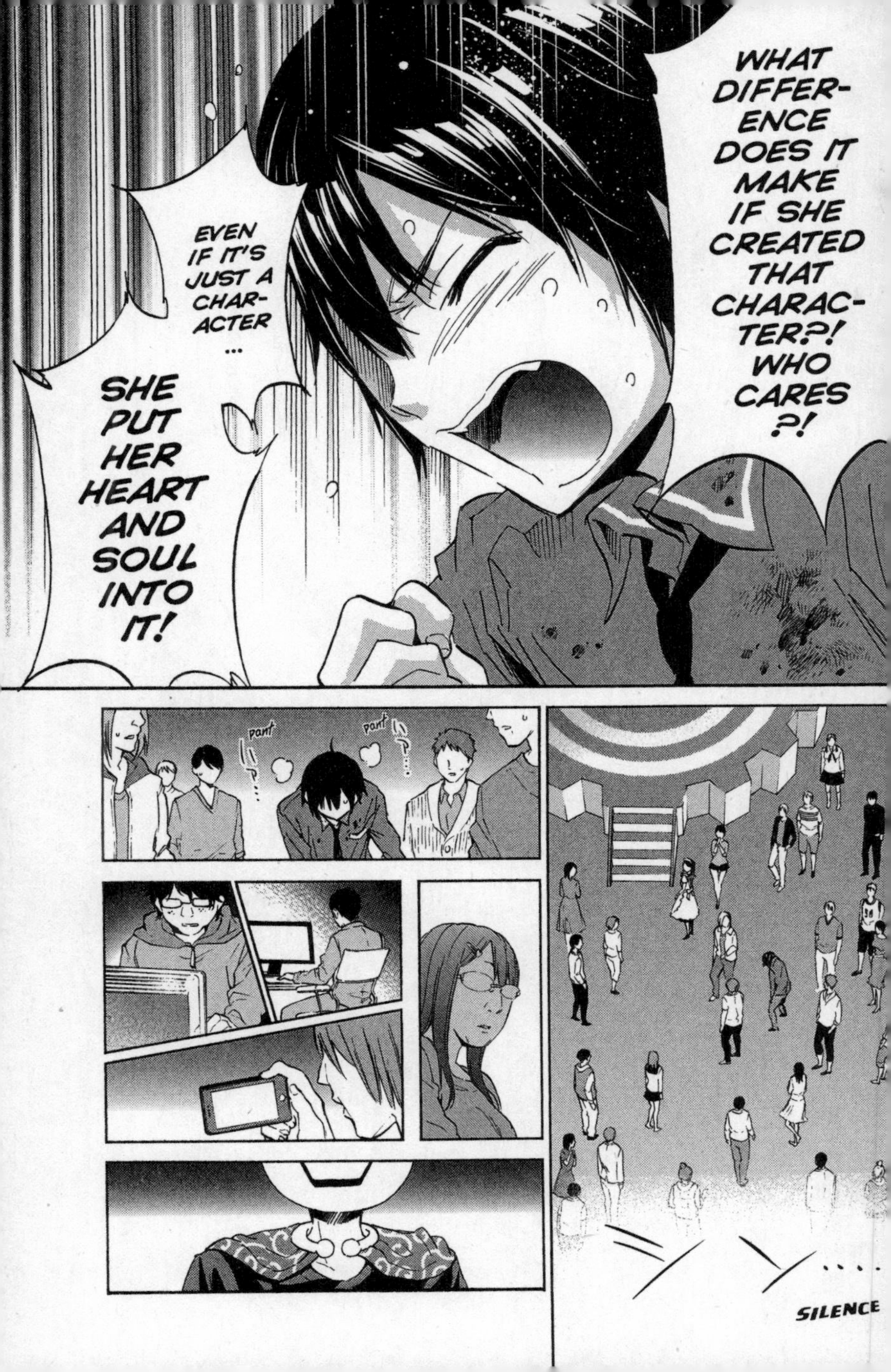
WHAT DIFFERENCE DOES IT MAKE IF SHE CREATED THAT CHARACTER?! WHO CARES?!
EVEN IF IT'S JUST A CHARACTER...
SHE PUT HER HEART AND SOUL INTO IT!
SILENCE
pant
pant

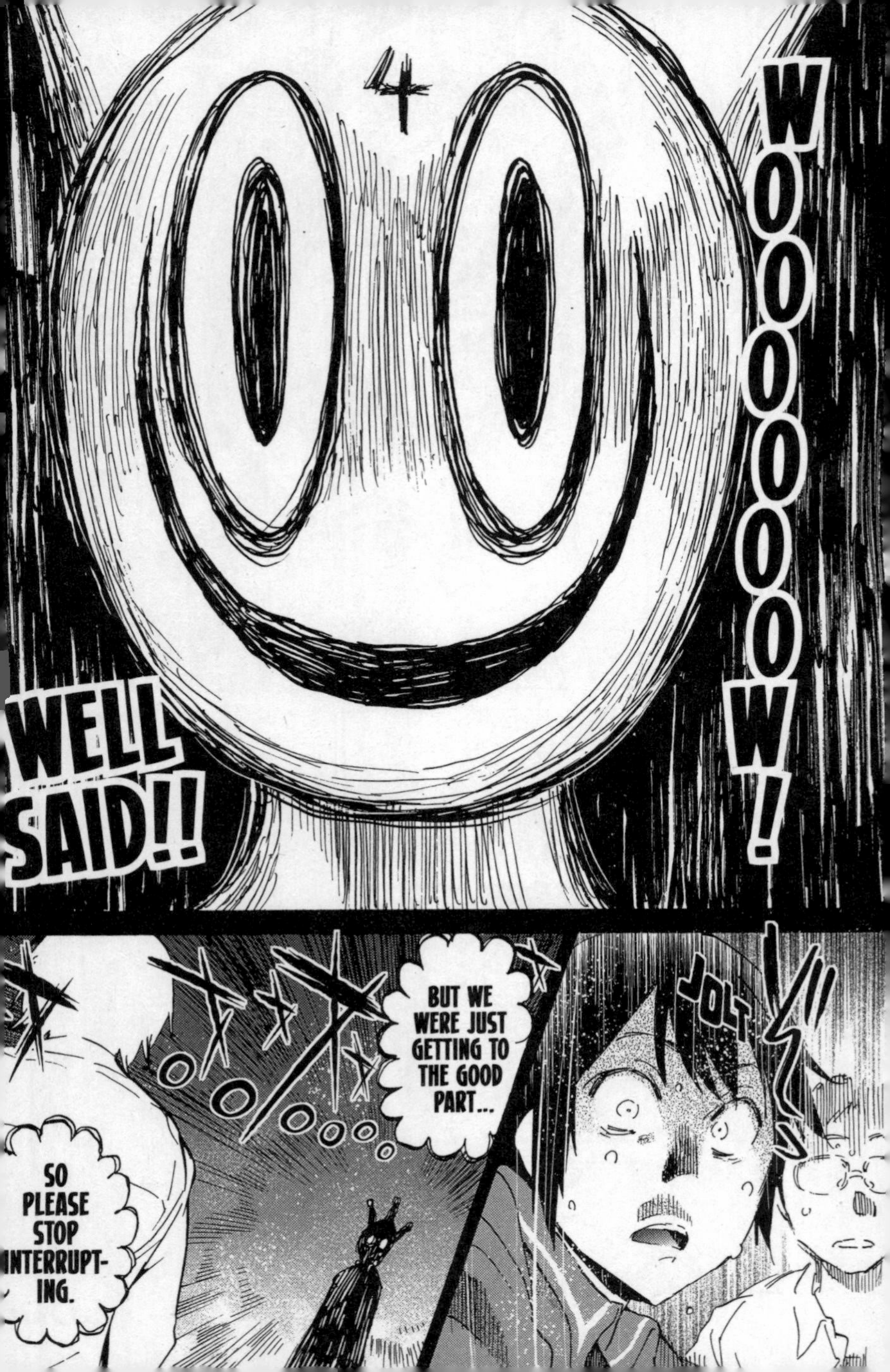
WOOOOOOW!
WELL SAID!!
JOLT
BUT WE WERE JUST GETTING TO THE GOOD PART...
SO PLEASE STOP INTERRUPTING.

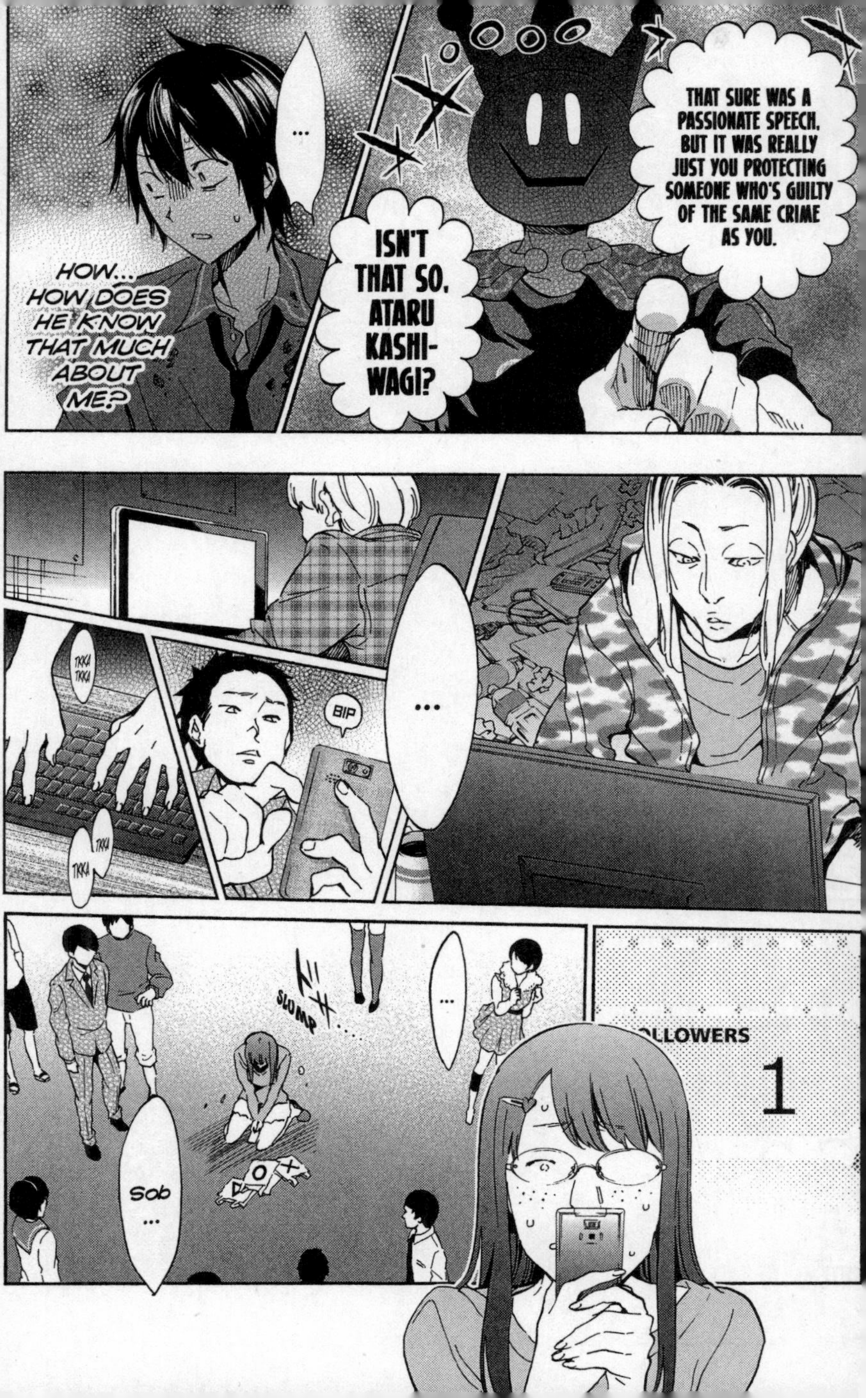

THAT SURE WAS A PASSIONATE SPEECH, BUT IT WAS REALLY JUST YOU PROTECTING SOMEONE WHO'S GUILTY OF THE SAME CRIME AS YOU.
ISN'T THAT SO, ATARU KASHI-WAGI?
...
HOW... HOW DOES HE KNOW THAT MUCH ABOUT ME?
...
TKKA TKKA
BIP
TKKA TKKA
OLLOWERS
1
...
SLUMP
Sob ...

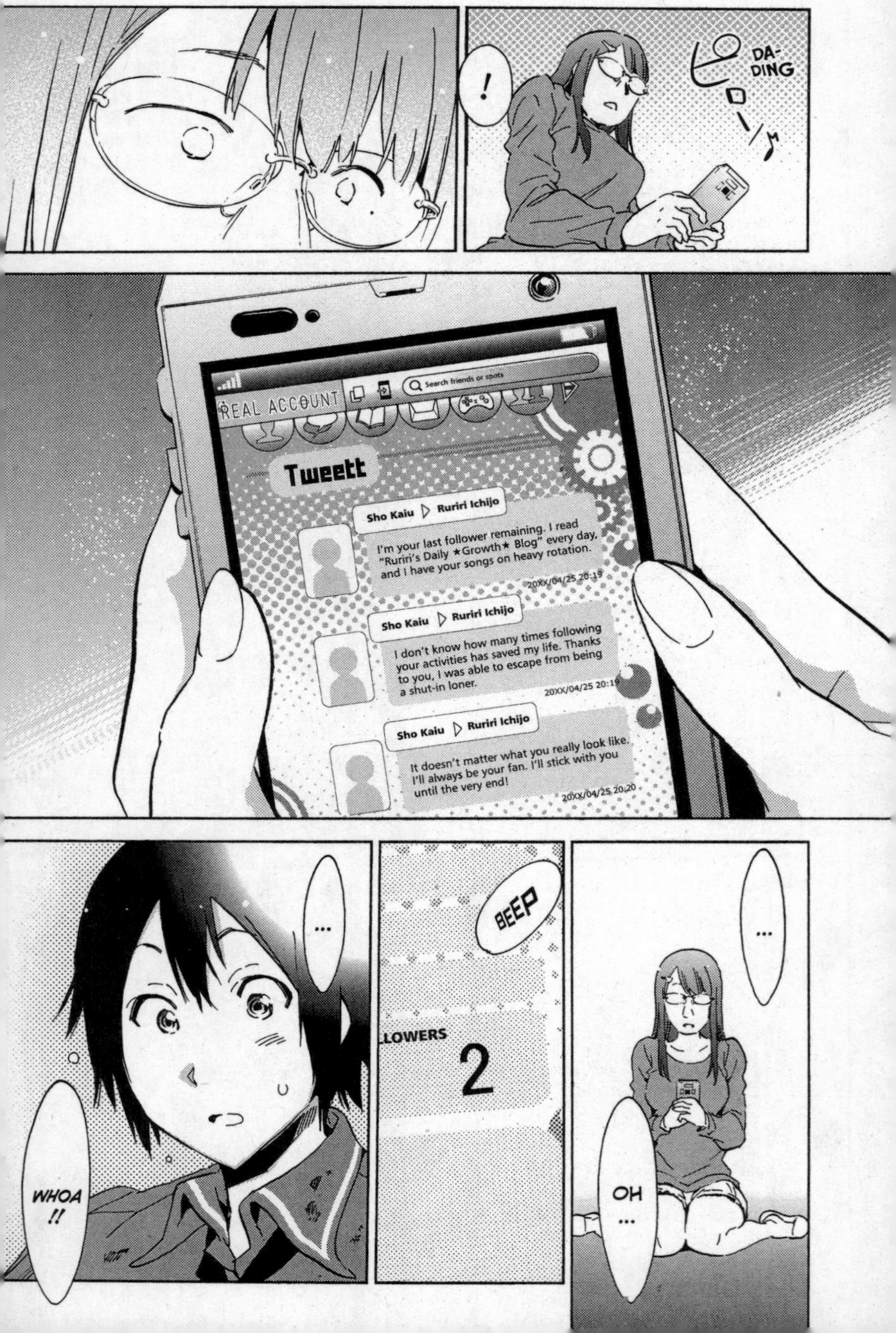
DA-DING
!
REAL ACCOUNT
Search friends or spots
Tweett
Sho Kaiu ▷ Ruriri Ichijo
I'm your last follower remaining. I read "Ruriri's Daily ★Growth★ Blog" every day, and I have your songs on heavy rotation.
20XX/04/25 20:19
Sho Kaiu ▷ Ruriri Ichijo
I don't know how many times following your activities has saved my life. Thanks to you, I was able to escape from being a shut-in loner.
20XX/04/25 20:19
Sho Kaiu ▷ Ruriri Ichijo
It doesn't matter what you really look like. I'll always be your fan. I'll stick with you until the very end!
20XX/04/25 20:20
...
OH ...
BEEP
LLOWERS
2
...
WHOA !!

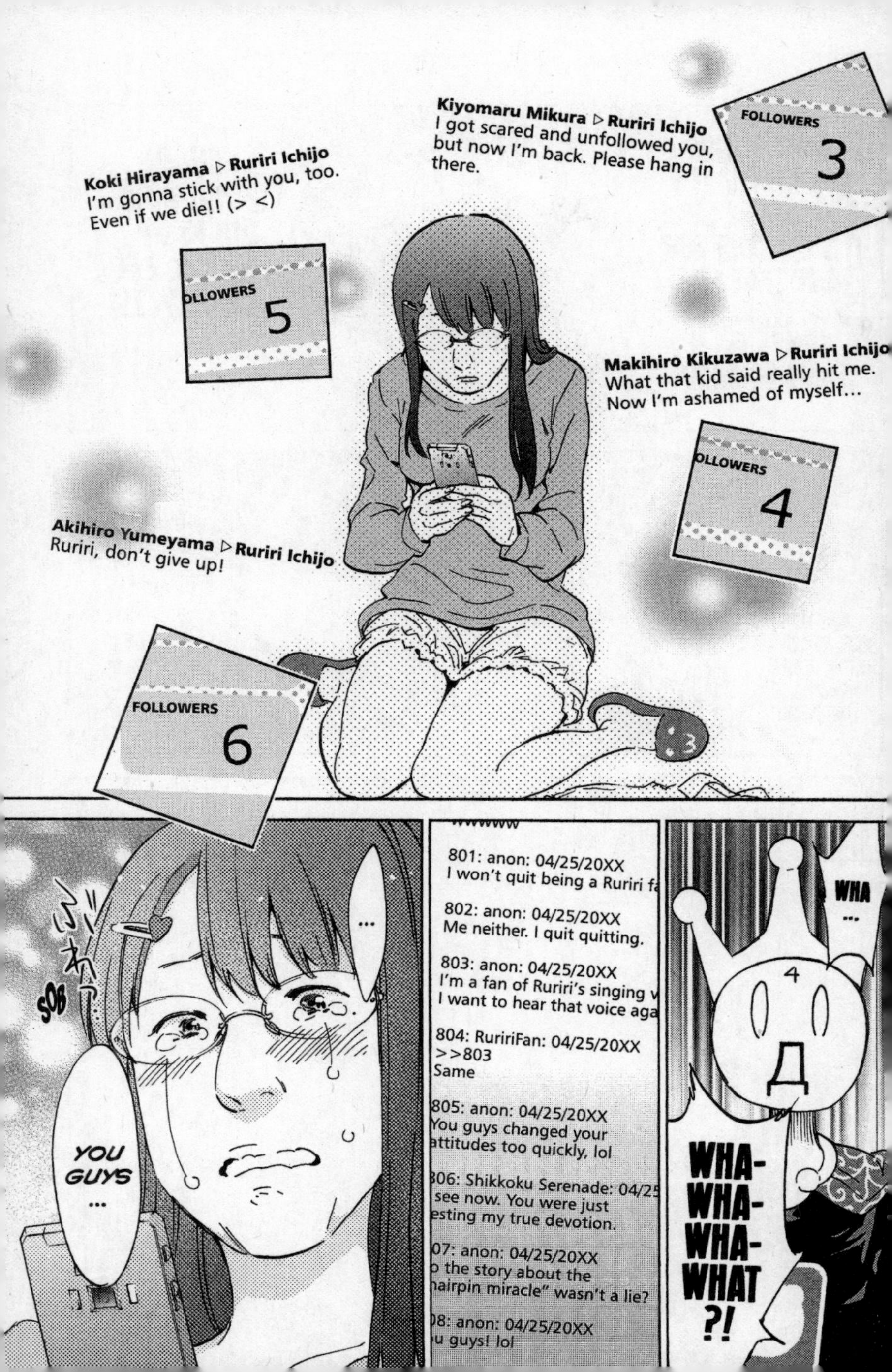
FOLLOWERS
3
Kiyomaru Mikura ▷ Ruriri Ichijo
I got scared and unfollowed you, but now I'm back. Please hang in there.
Makihiro Kikuzawa ▷ Ruriri Ichijo
What that kid said really hit me. Now I'm ashamed of myself…
Koki Hirayama ▷ Ruriri Ichijo
I'm gonna stick with you, too. Even if we die!! (> <)
OLLOWERS
5
OLLOWERS
4
Akihiro Yumeyama ▷ Ruriri Ichijo
Ruriri, don't give up!
FOLLOWERS
6
WHA …
WHA-WHA-WHA-WHAT?!
801: anon: 04/25/20XX
I won't quit being a Ruriri fa
802: anon: 04/25/20XX
Me neither. I quit quitting.
803: anon: 04/25/20XX
I'm a fan of Ruriri's singing v
I want to hear that voice aga
804: RuririFan: 04/25/20XX
>>803
Same
805: anon: 04/25/20XX
You guys changed your attitudes too quickly, lol
306: Shikkoku Serenade: 04/25
see now. You were just esting my true devotion.
07: anon: 04/25/20XX
o the story about the hairpin miracle" wasn't a lie?
08: anon: 04/25/20XX
u guys! lol
…
SOB
YOU GUYS …

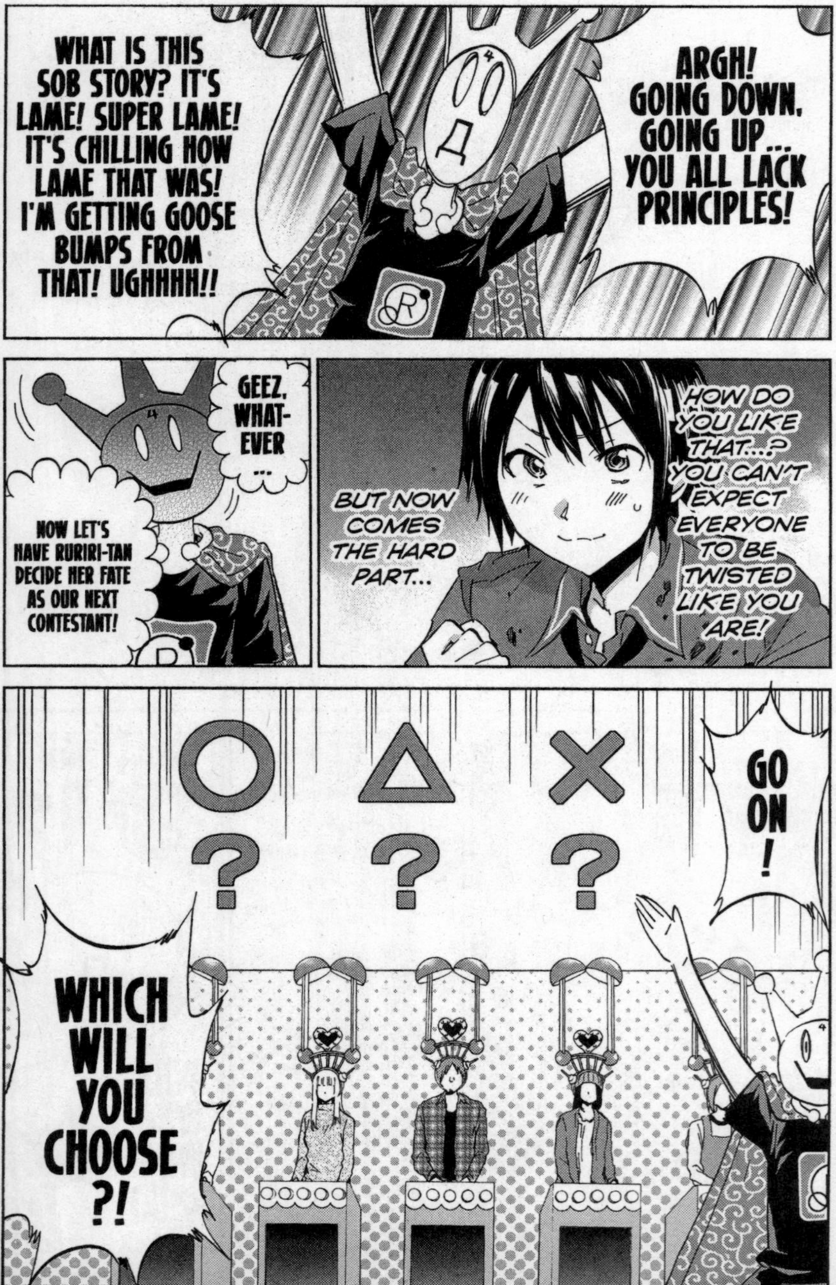
ARGH! GOING DOWN, GOING UP... YOU ALL LACK PRINCIPLES!
WHAT IS THIS SOB STORY? IT'S LAME! SUPER LAME! IT'S CHILLING HOW LAME THAT WAS! I'M GETTING GOOSE BUMPS FROM THAT! UGHHHH!!
HOW DO YOU LIKE THAT...? YOU CAN'T EXPECT EVERYONE TO BE TWISTED LIKE YOU ARE!
BUT NOW COMES THE HARD PART...
GEEZ, WHAT-EVER...
NOW LET'S HAVE RURIRI-TAN DECIDE HER FATE AS OUR NEXT CONTESTANT!
GO ON!
WHICH WILL YOU CHOOSE?!

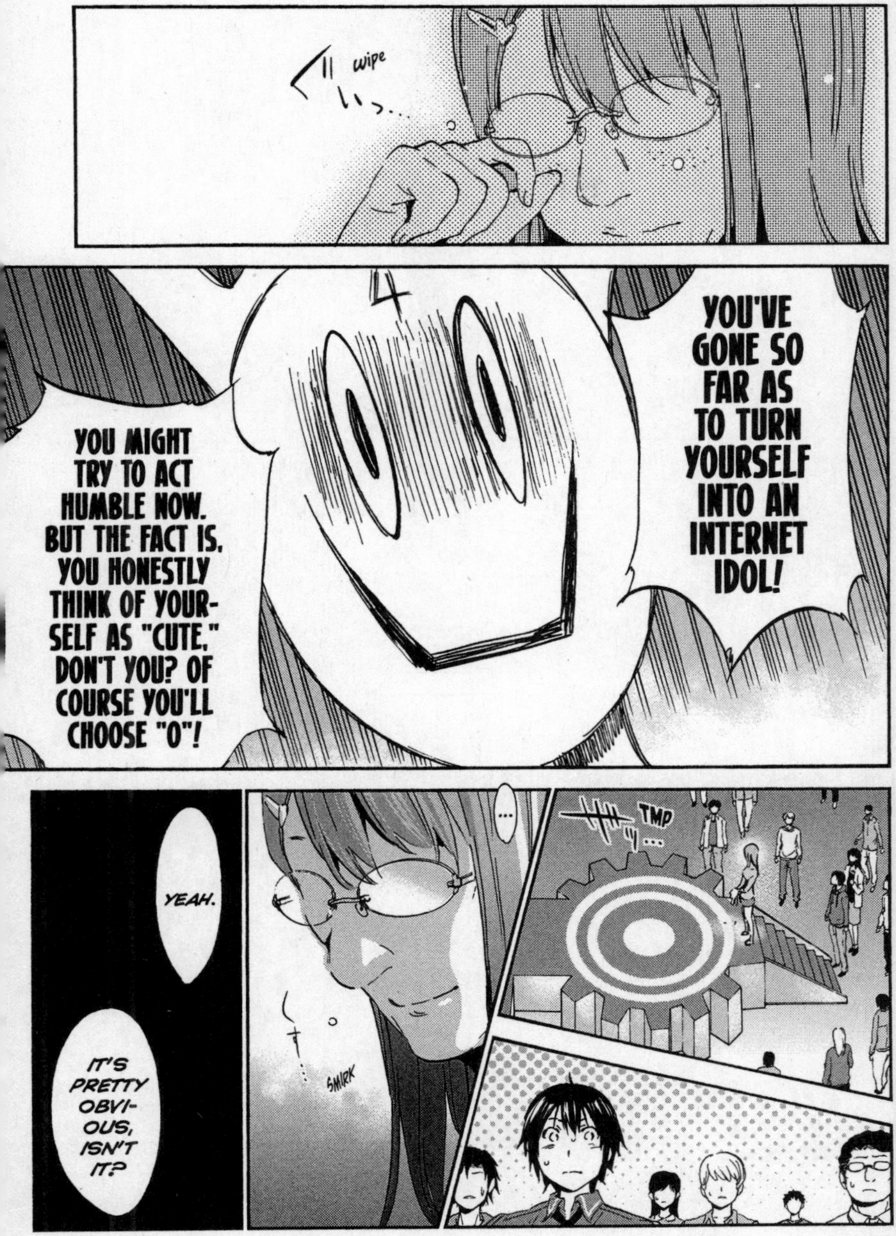

wipe
YOU'VE GONE SO FAR AS TO TURN YOURSELF INTO AN INTERNET IDOL!
YOU MIGHT TRY TO ACT HUMBLE NOW. BUT THE FACT IS, YOU HONESTLY THINK OF YOUR-SELF AS "CUTE," DON'T YOU? OF COURSE YOU'LL CHOOSE "O"!
TMP
...
SMIRK
YEAH.
IT'S PRETTY OBVI-OUS, ISN'T IT?

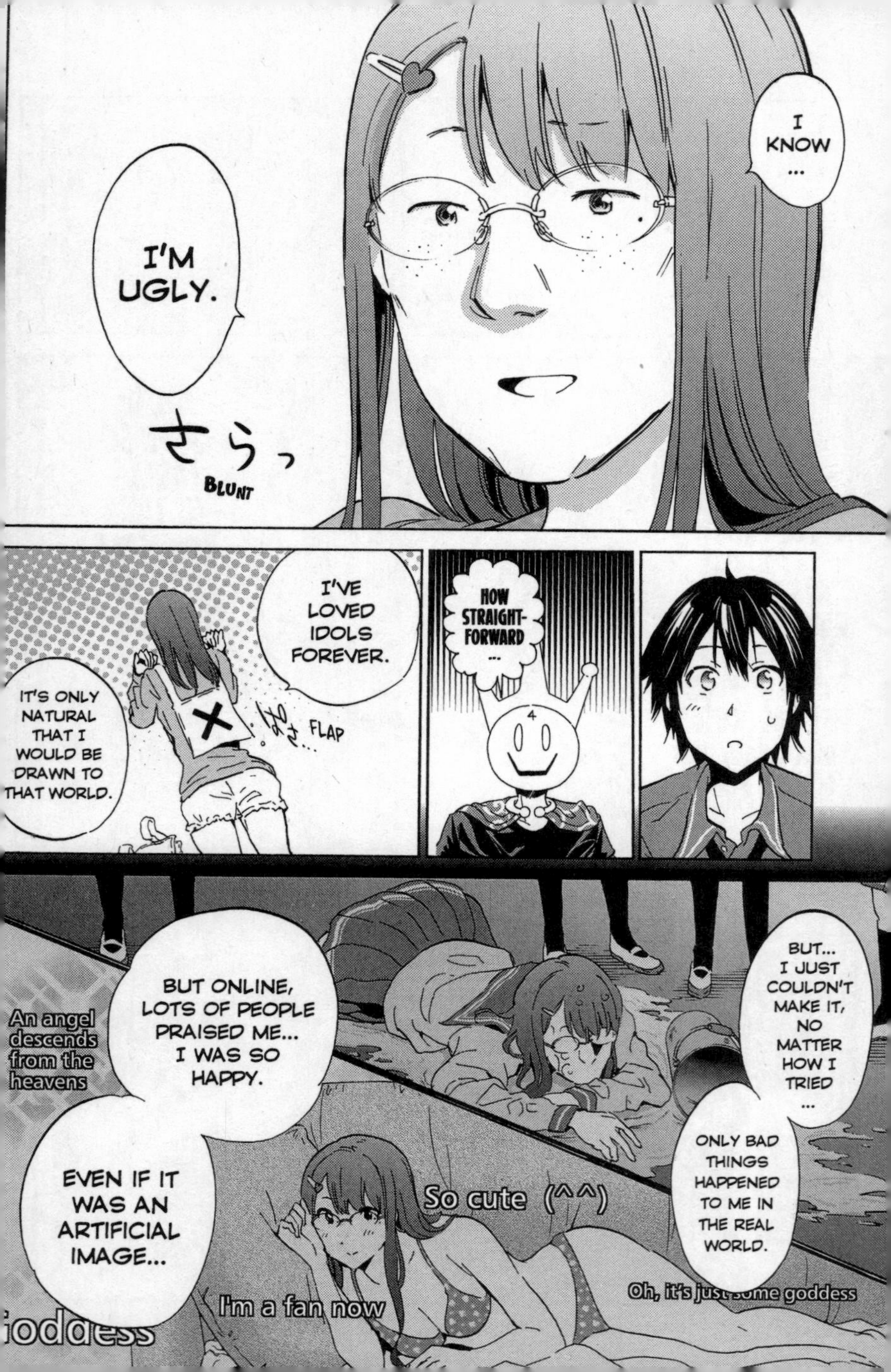
I KNOW...
I'M UGLY.
さらっ
BLUNT
HOW STRAIGHTFORWARD...
I'VE LOVED IDOLS FOREVER.
ぱさ...
FLAP
IT'S ONLY NATURAL THAT I WOULD BE DRAWN TO THAT WORLD.
BUT... I JUST COULDN'T MAKE IT, NO MATTER HOW I TRIED...
ONLY BAD THINGS HAPPENED TO ME IN THE REAL WORLD.
Oh, it's just some goddess
BUT ONLINE, LOTS OF PEOPLE PRAISED ME... I WAS SO HAPPY.
So cute (^^)
EVEN IF IT WAS AN ARTIFICIAL IMAGE...
An angel descends from the heavens
I'm a fan now

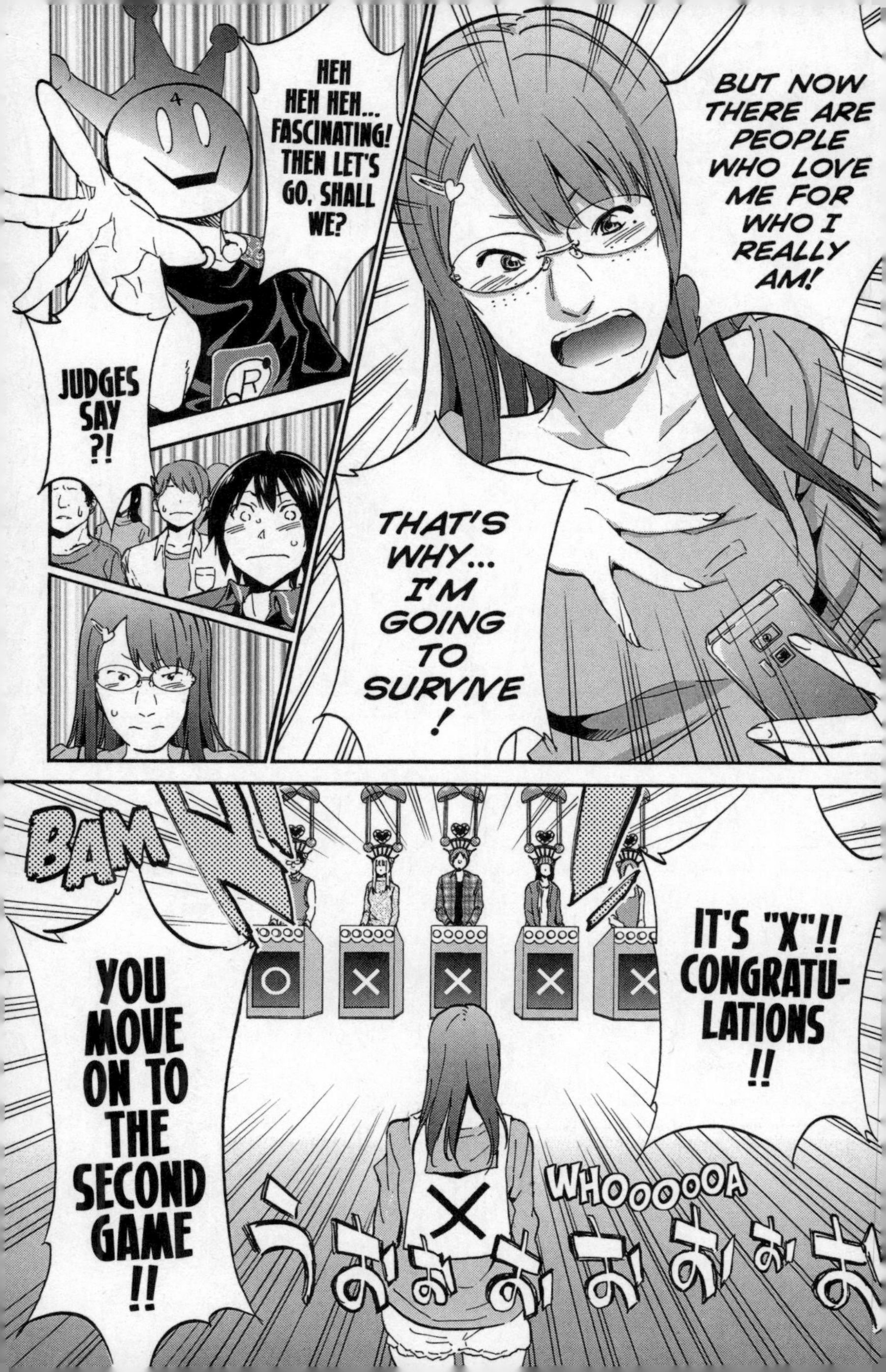
BUT NOW THERE ARE PEOPLE WHO LOVE ME FOR WHO I REALLY AM!
THAT'S WHY... I'M GOING TO SURVIVE!
HEH HEH HEH... FASCINATING! THEN LET'S GO, SHALL WE?
JUDGES SAY ?!
IT'S "X"!! CONGRATU-LATIONS!!
BAM
YOU MOVE ON TO THE SECOND GAME!!
WHOOOOOA

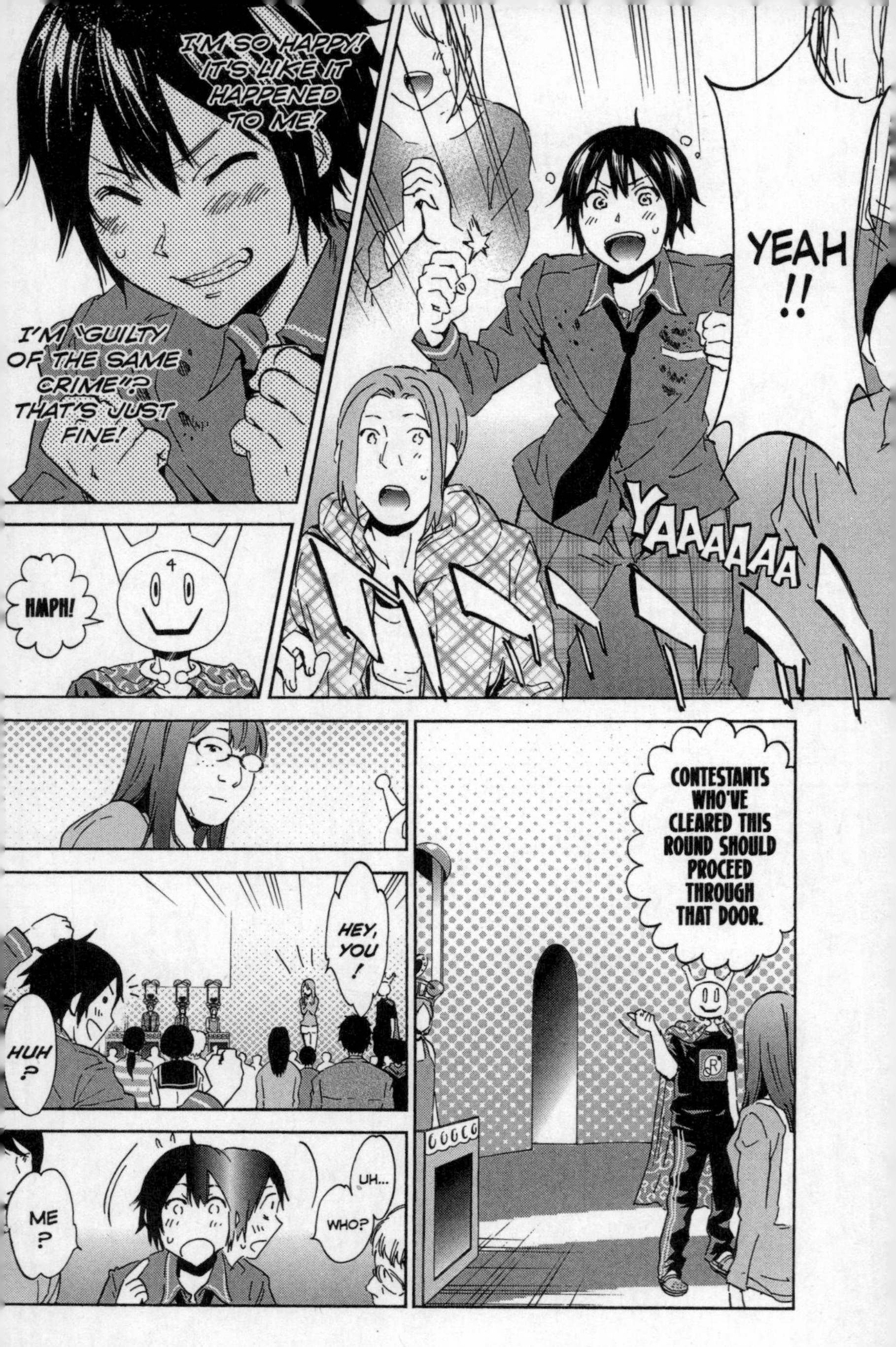
YEAH !!
YAAAAAA
I'M SO HAPPY! IT'S LIKE IT HAPPENED TO ME!
I'M "GUILTY OF THE SAME CRIME"? THAT'S JUST FINE!
HMPH!
CONTESTANTS WHO'VE CLEARED THIS ROUND SHOULD PROCEED THROUGH THAT DOOR.
HEY, YOU!
HUH?
UH... WHO?
ME?

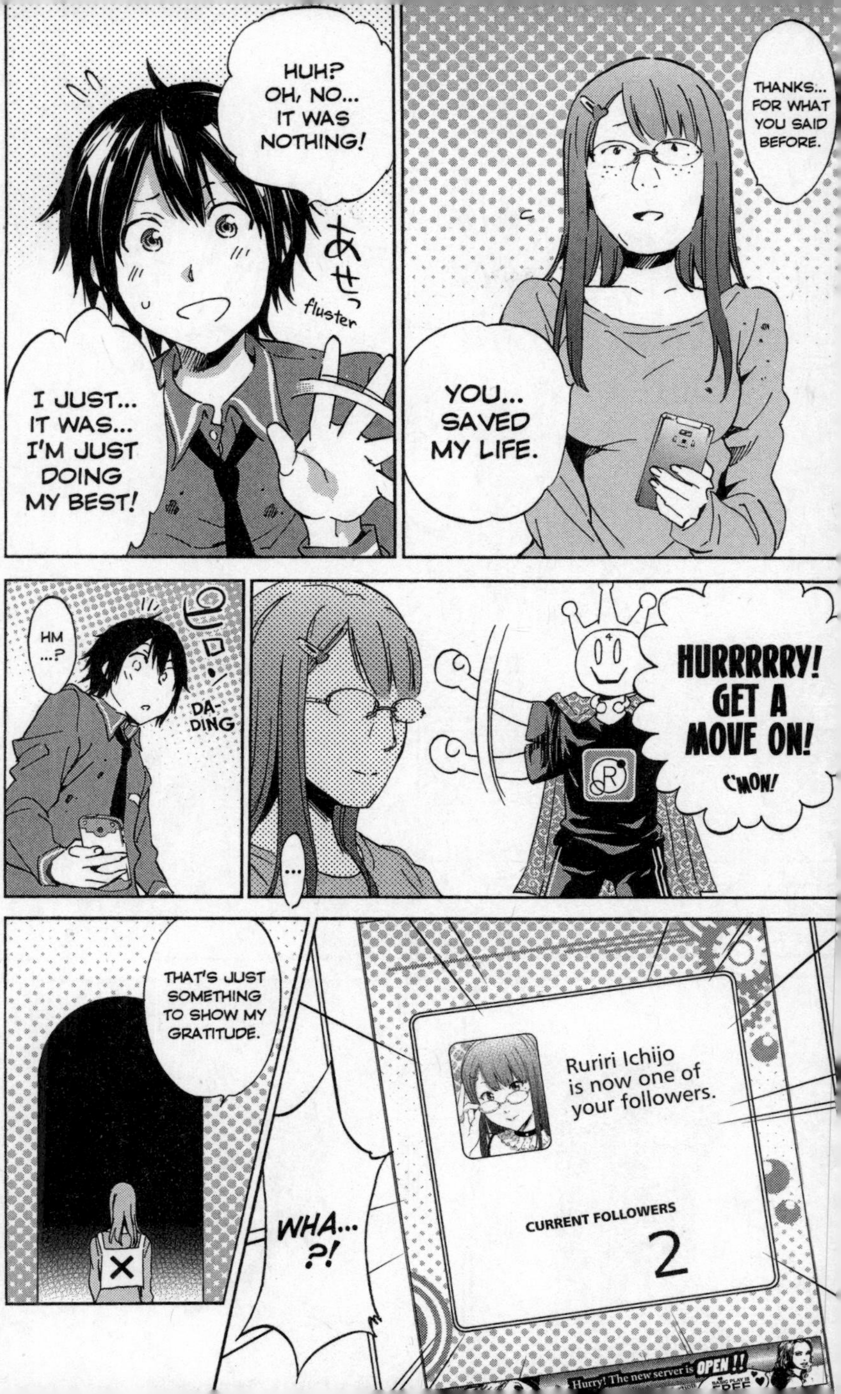
THANKS... FOR WHAT YOU SAID BEFORE.
YOU... SAVED MY LIFE.
HUH? OH, NO... IT WAS NOTHING!
あせっ
fluster
I JUST... IT WAS... I'M JUST DOING MY BEST!
HURRRRRY! GET A MOVE ON!
C'MON!
...
DA-DING
HM ...?
Ruriri Ichijo is now one of your followers.
CURRENT FOLLOWERS
2
WHA... ?!
Hurry! The new server is OPEN!!
THAT'S JUST SOMETHING TO SHOW MY GRATITUDE.

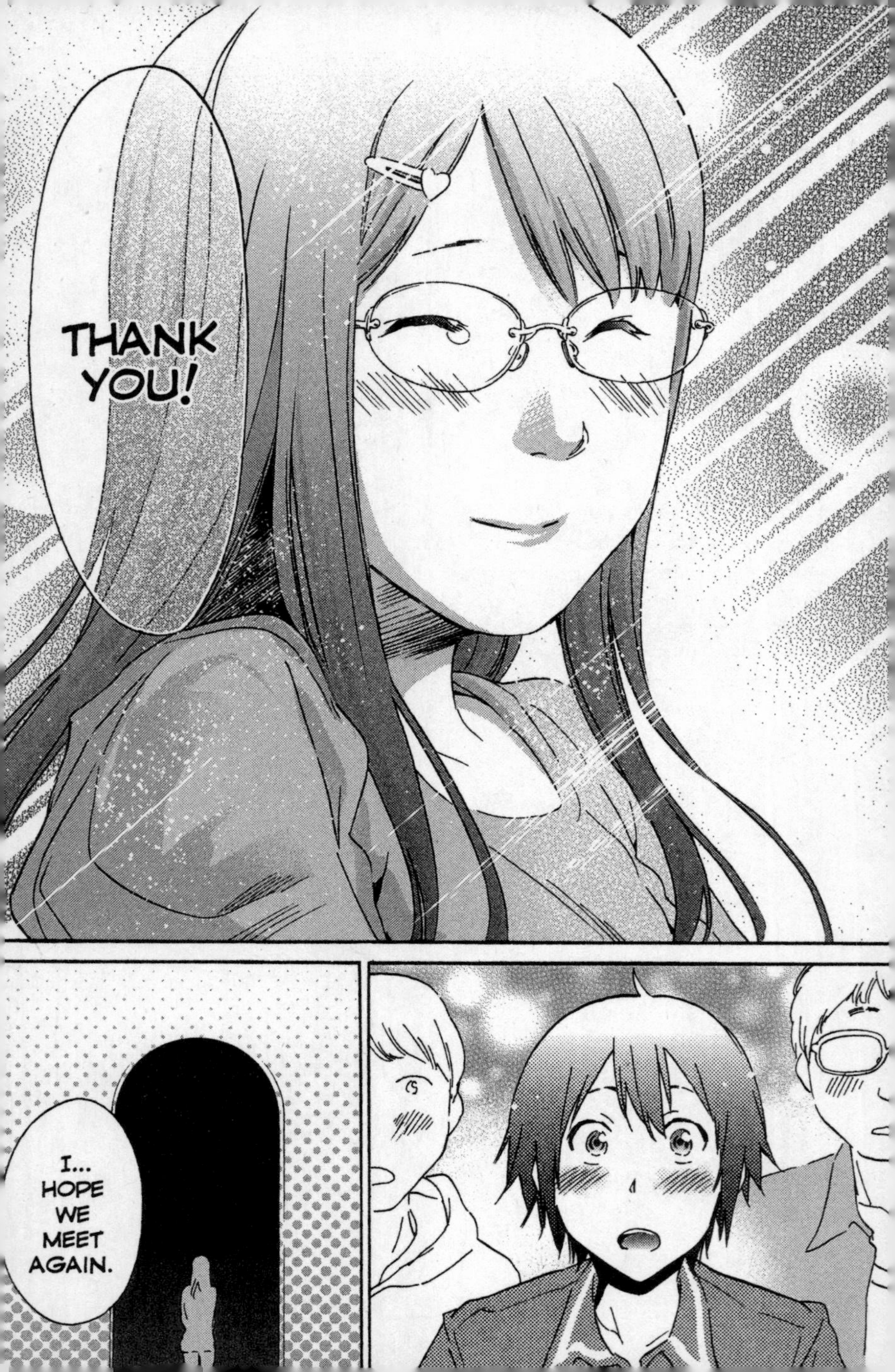
THANK YOU!
I... HOPE WE MEET AGAIN.

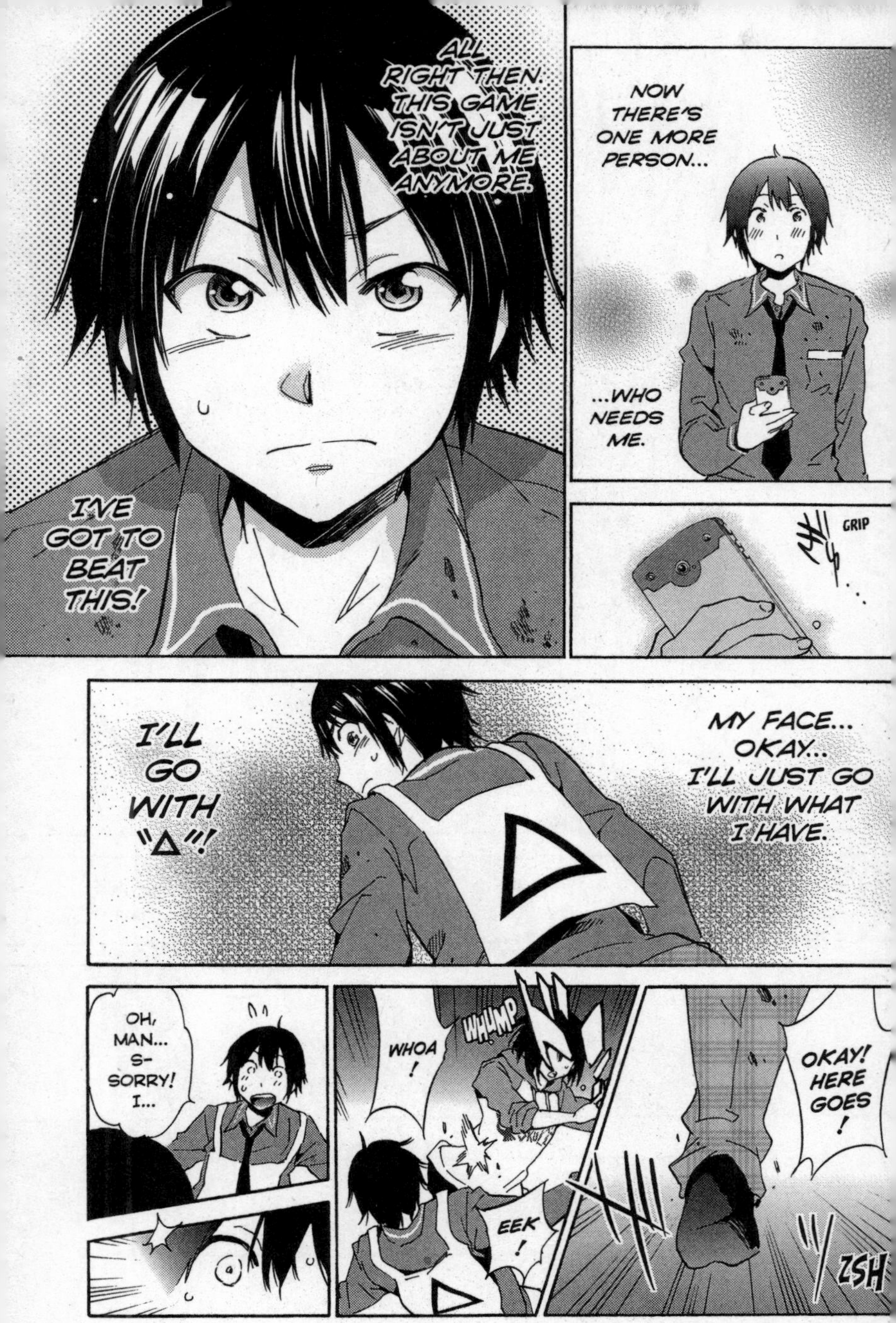
NOW THERE'S ONE MORE PERSON...
...WHO NEEDS ME.
GRIP
ALL RIGHT THEN. THIS GAME ISN'T JUST ABOUT ME ANYMORE.
I'VE GOT TO BEAT THIS!
MY FACE... OKAY... I'LL JUST GO WITH WHAT I HAVE.
I'LL GO WITH "△"!
OKAY! HERE GOES!
ZSH
WHUMP
WHOA!
EEK!
OH, MAN... S-SORRY! I...

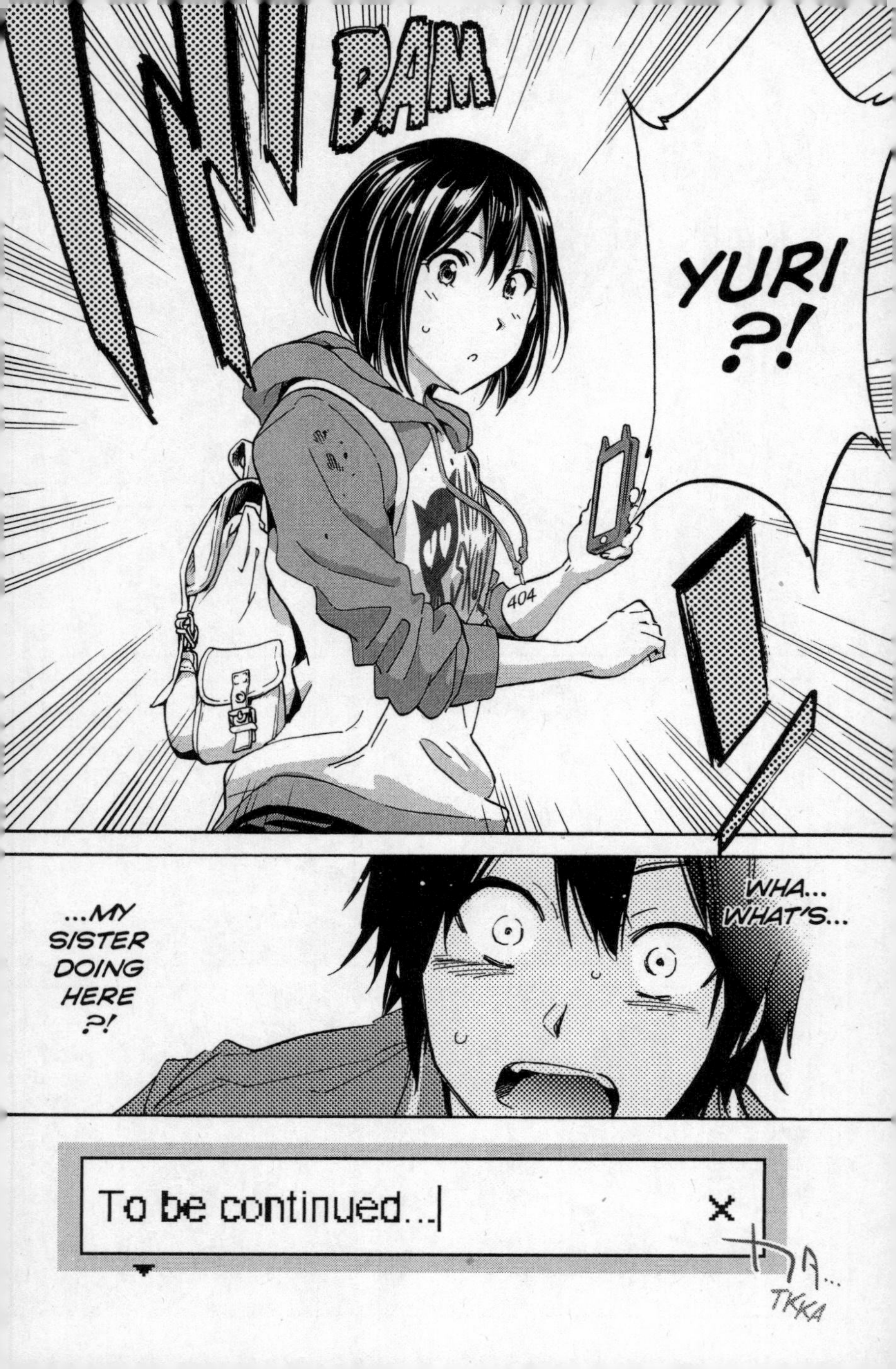
YURI ?!
BAM
WHA... WHAT'S...
...MY SISTER DOING HERE ?!
To be continued...
TKKA

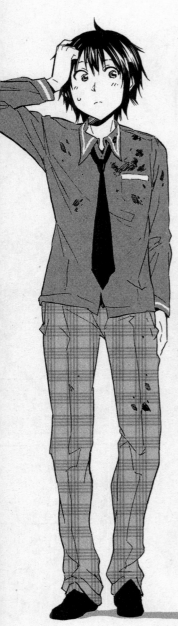

CHAPTER 3
No Answer, Part 2

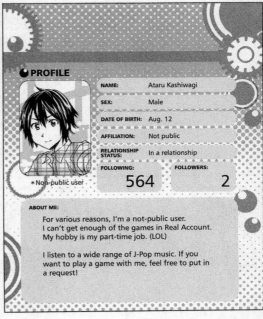

PROFILE

*Non-public user

NAME:	Ataru Kashiwagi
SEX:	Male
DATE OF BIRTH:	Aug. 12
AFFILIATION:	Not public
RELATIONSHIP STATUS:	In a relationship
FOLLOWING: 564	FOLLOWERS: 2

ABOUT ME:

For various reasons, I'm a not-public user.
I can't get enough of the games in Real Account.
My hobby is my part-time job. (LOL)

I listen to a wide range of J-Pop music. If you want to play a game with me, feel free to put in a request!

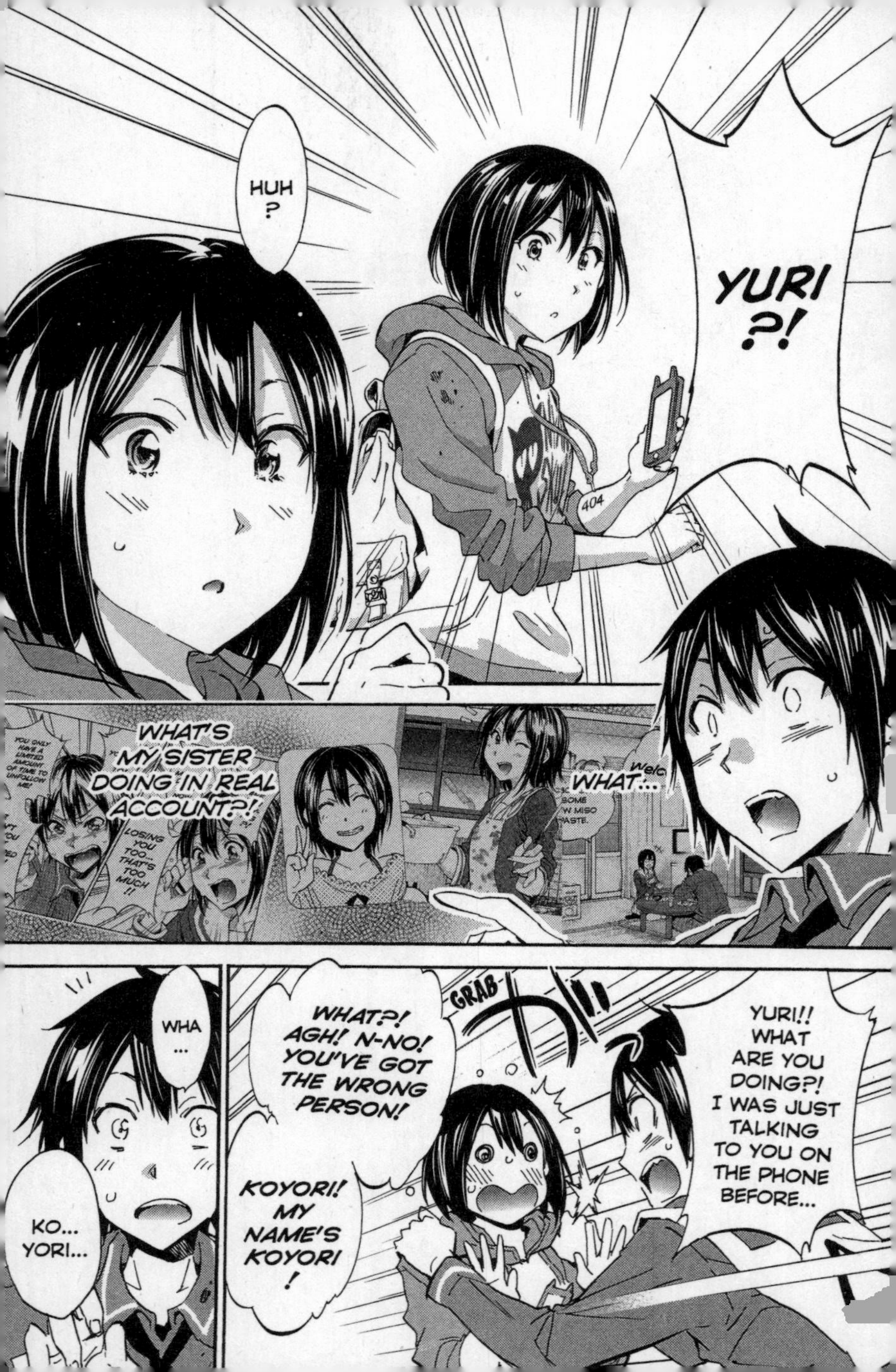

YURI ?!
HUH ?
WHAT...
WHAT'S MY SISTER DOING IN REAL ACCOUNT?!
LOSING YOU TOO... THAT'S TOO MUCH !!
YOU ONLY HAVE A LIMITED AMOUNT OF TIME TO UNFOLLOW ME!
YURI!! WHAT ARE YOU DOING?! I WAS JUST TALKING TO YOU ON THE PHONE BEFORE...
GRAB
WHAT?! AGH! N-NO! YOU'VE GOT THE WRONG PERSON!
KOYORI! MY NAME'S KOYORI !
WHA ...
KO... YORI...

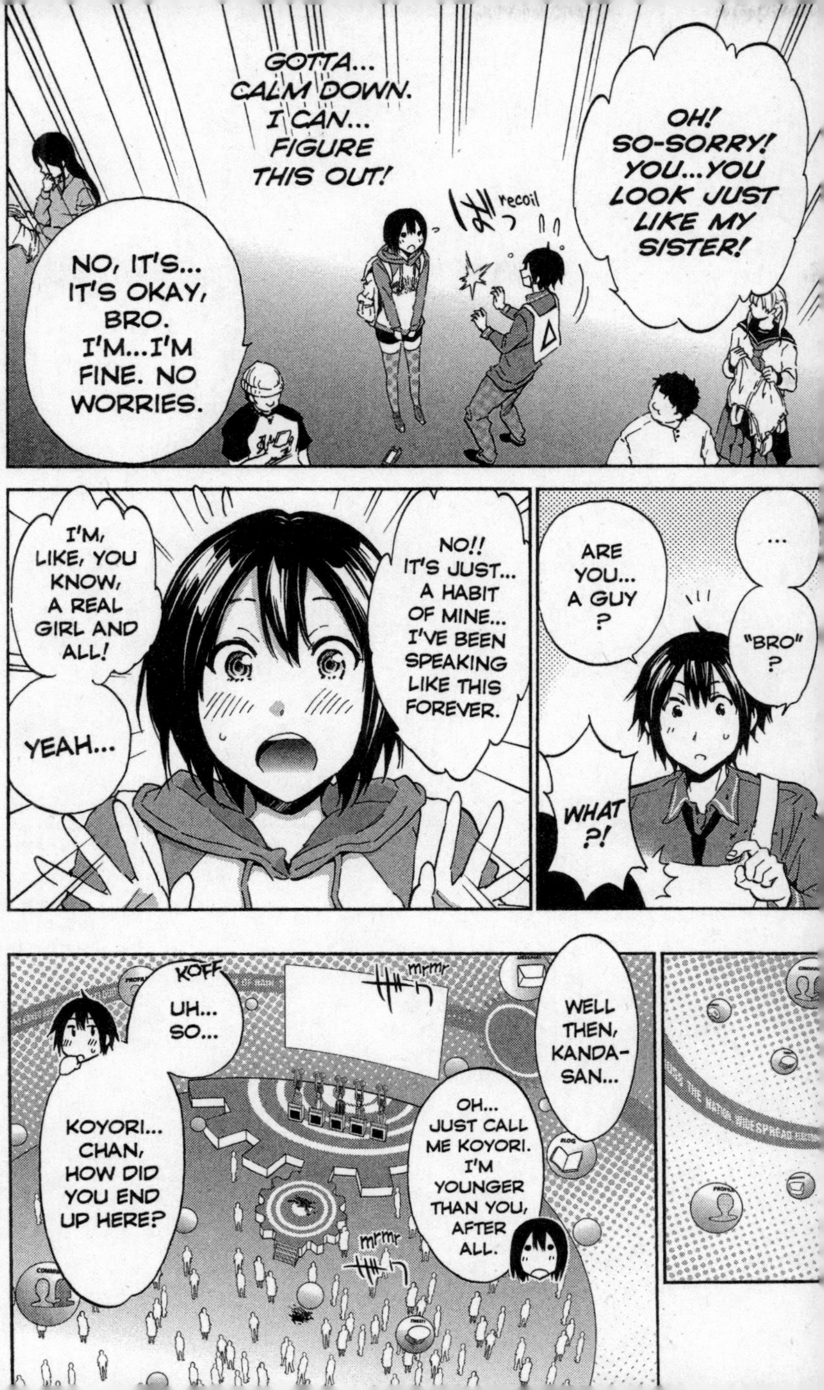
OH! SO-SORRY! YOU...YOU LOOK JUST LIKE MY SISTER!
recoil
GOTTA... CALM DOWN. I CAN... FIGURE THIS OUT!
NO, IT'S... IT'S OKAY, BRO. I'M...I'M FINE. NO WORRIES.
...
"BRO" ?
ARE YOU... A GUY ?
WHAT ?!
NO!! IT'S JUST... A HABIT OF MINE... I'VE BEEN SPEAKING LIKE THIS FOREVER.
I'M, LIKE, YOU KNOW, A REAL GIRL AND ALL!
YEAH...
WELL THEN, KANDA-SAN...
OH... JUST CALL ME KOYORI. I'M YOUNGER THAN YOU, AFTER ALL.
mrmr
mrmr
KOFF
UH... SO...
KOYORI... CHAN, HOW DID YOU END UP HERE?

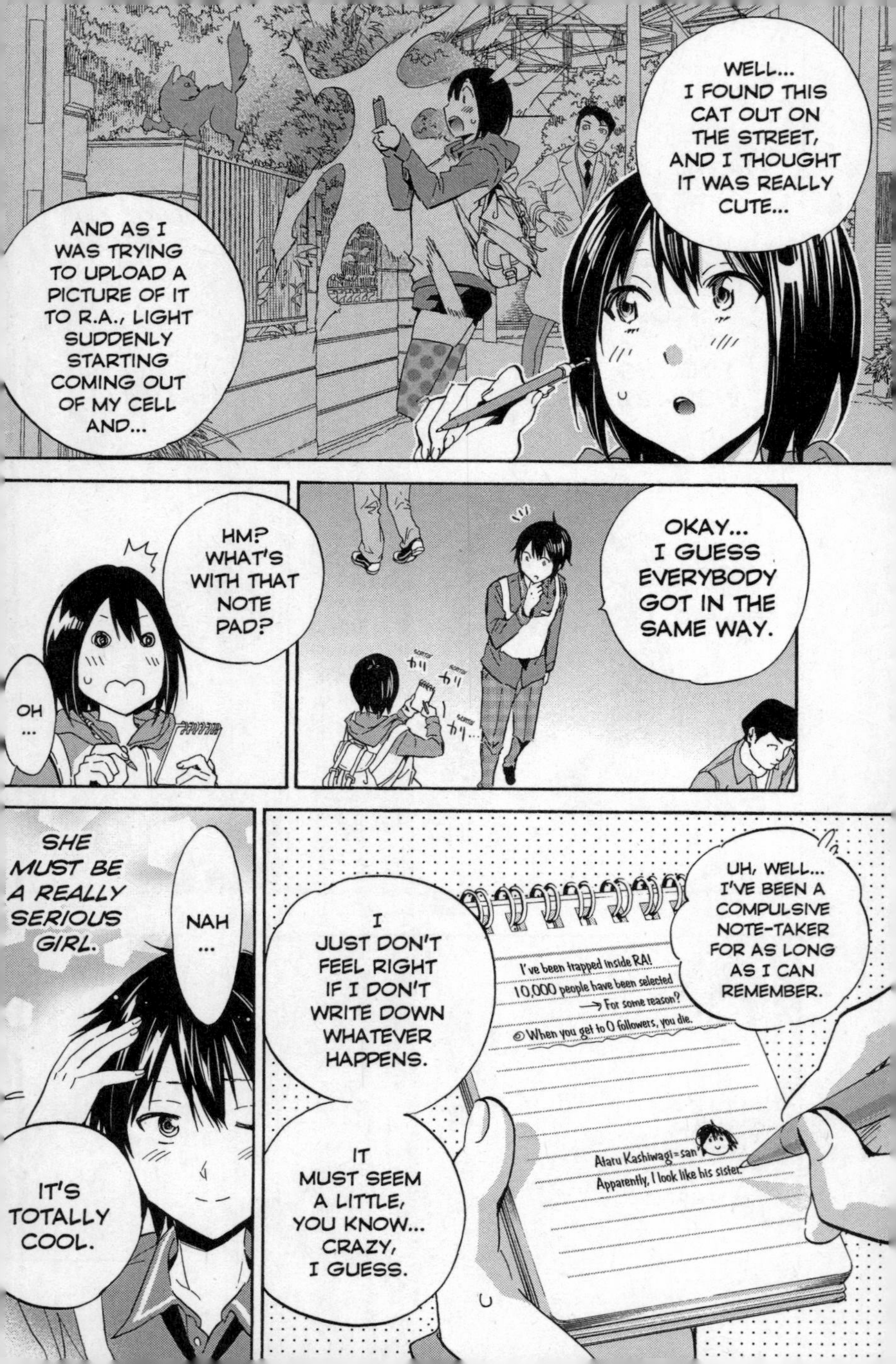
WELL... I FOUND THIS CAT OUT ON THE STREET, AND I THOUGHT IT WAS REALLY CUTE...
AND AS I WAS TRYING TO UPLOAD A PICTURE OF IT TO R.A., LIGHT SUDDENLY STARTING COMING OUT OF MY CELL AND...
OKAY... I GUESS EVERYBODY GOT IN THE SAME WAY.
HM? WHAT'S WITH THAT NOTE PAD?
OH ...
UH, WELL... I'VE BEEN A COMPULSIVE NOTE-TAKER FOR AS LONG AS I CAN REMEMBER.
I JUST DON'T FEEL RIGHT IF I DON'T WRITE DOWN WHATEVER HAPPENS.
I've been trapped inside RA!
10,000 people have been selected
→ For some reason?
◎ When you get to 0 followers, you die.
Ataru Kashiwagi=san
Apparently, I look like his sister.
IT MUST SEEM A LITTLE, YOU KNOW... CRAZY, I GUESS.
SHE MUST BE A REALLY SERIOUS GIRL.
NAH ...
IT'S TOTALLY COOL.

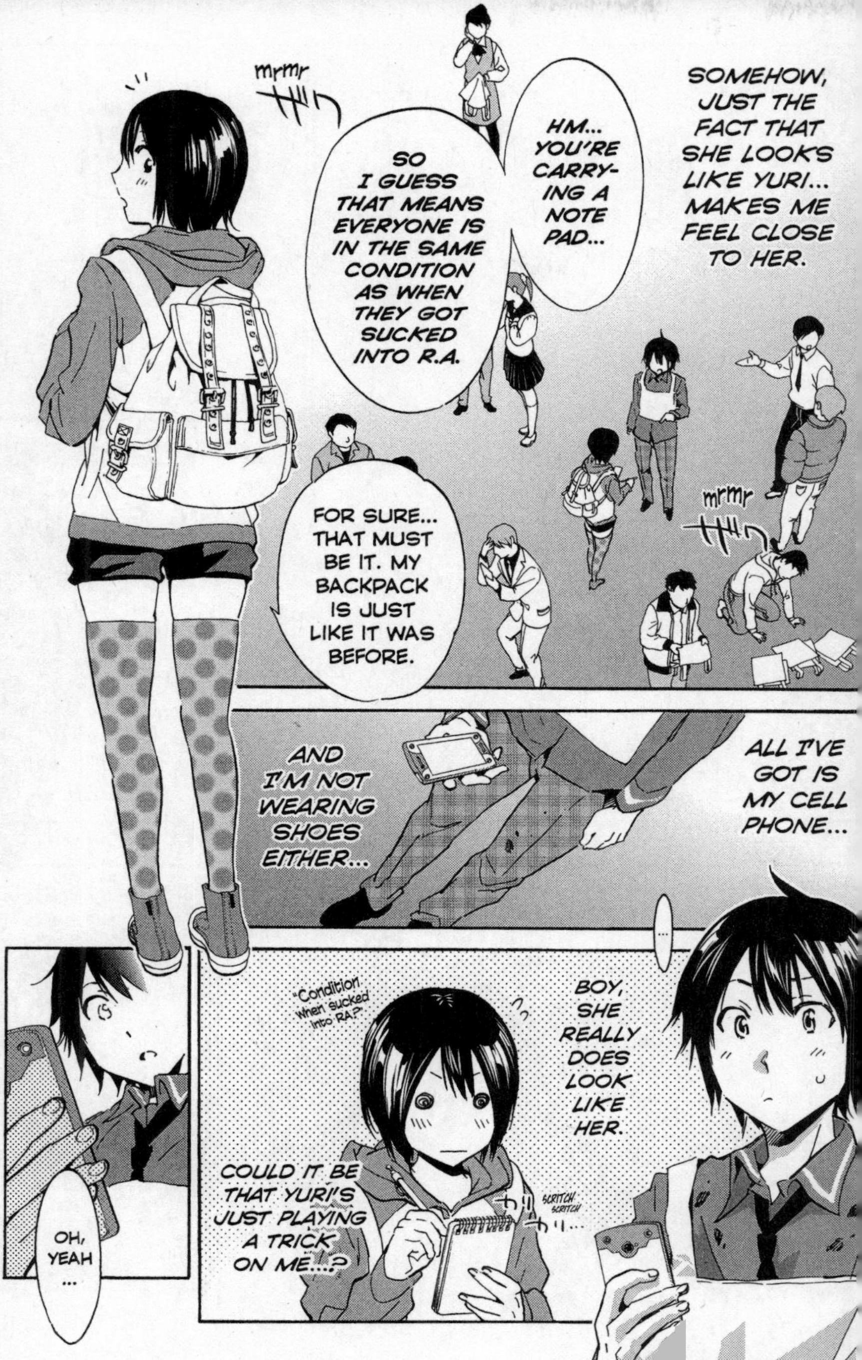

SOMEHOW, JUST THE FACT THAT SHE LOOKS LIKE YURI... MAKES ME FEEL CLOSE TO HER.
HM... YOU'RE CARRYING A NOTE PAD...
mrmr
SO I GUESS THAT MEANS EVERYONE IS IN THE SAME CONDITION AS WHEN THEY GOT SUCKED INTO R.A.
mrmr
FOR SURE... THAT MUST BE IT. MY BACKPACK IS JUST LIKE IT WAS BEFORE.
ALL I'VE GOT IS MY CELL PHONE...
AND I'M NOT WEARING SHOES EITHER...
...
BOY, SHE REALLY DOES LOOK LIKE HER.
"Condition when sucked into RA?"
SCRITCH SCRITCH
COULD IT BE THAT YURI'S JUST PLAYING A TRICK ON ME...?
OH, YEAH ...

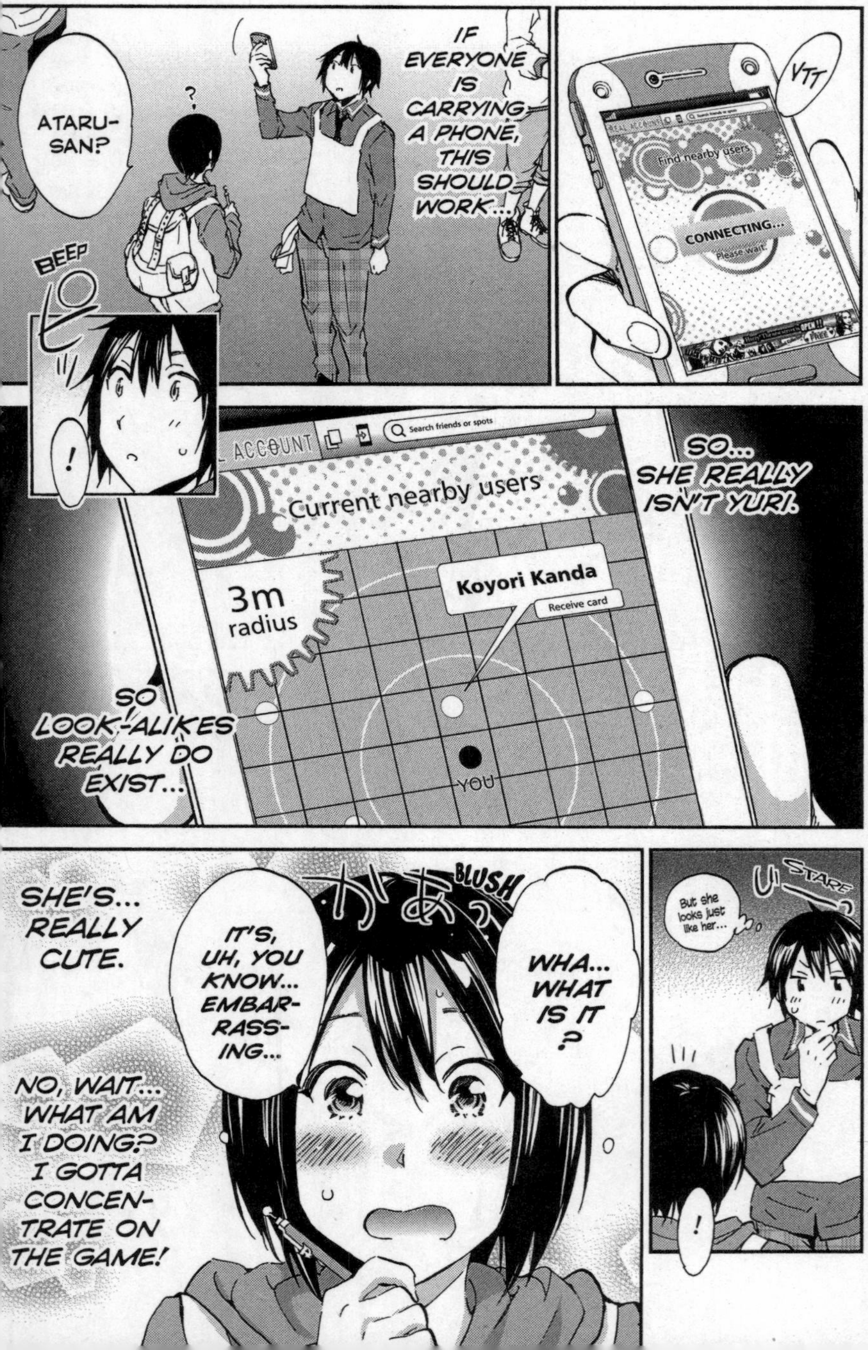
VTT
REAL ACCOUNT
Find nearby users
CONNECTING...
Please wait.
IF EVERYONE IS CARRYING A PHONE, THIS SHOULD WORK...
?
ATARU-SAN?
BEEP
!
SO... SHE REALLY ISN'T YURI.
ACCOUNT
Search friends or spots
Current nearby users
Koyori Kanda
Receive card
3m radius
YOU
SO LOOK-ALIKES REALLY DO EXIST...
STARE
But she looks just like her...
!
BLUSH
WHA... WHAT IS IT?
IT'S, UH, YOU KNOW... EMBARRASSING...
SHE'S... REALLY CUTE.
NO, WAIT... WHAT AM I DOING? I GOTTA CONCENTRATE ON THE GAME!

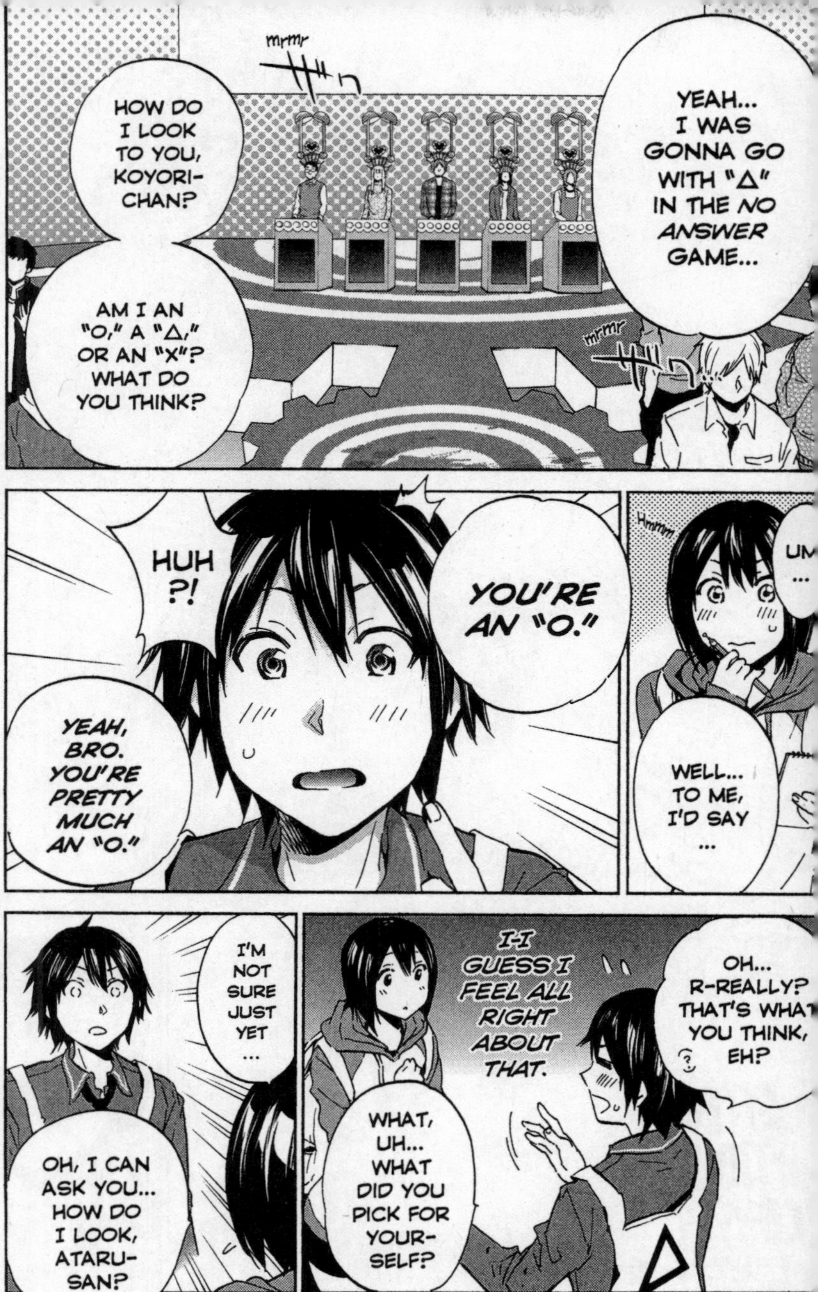
YEAH... I WAS GONNA GO WITH "Δ" IN THE NO ANSWER GAME...
mrmr
mrmr
HOW DO I LOOK TO YOU, KOYORI-CHAN?
AM I AN "O," A "Δ," OR AN "X"? WHAT DO YOU THINK?
Hmmm
UM...
WELL... TO ME, I'D SAY ...
YOU'RE AN "O."
HUH ?!
YEAH, BRO. YOU'RE PRETTY MUCH AN "O."
OH... R-REALLY? THAT'S WHAT YOU THINK, EH?
I-I GUESS I FEEL ALL RIGHT ABOUT THAT.
WHAT, UH... WHAT DID YOU PICK FOR YOURSELF?
I'M NOT SURE JUST YET ...
OH, I CAN ASK YOU... HOW DO I LOOK, ATARU-SAN?

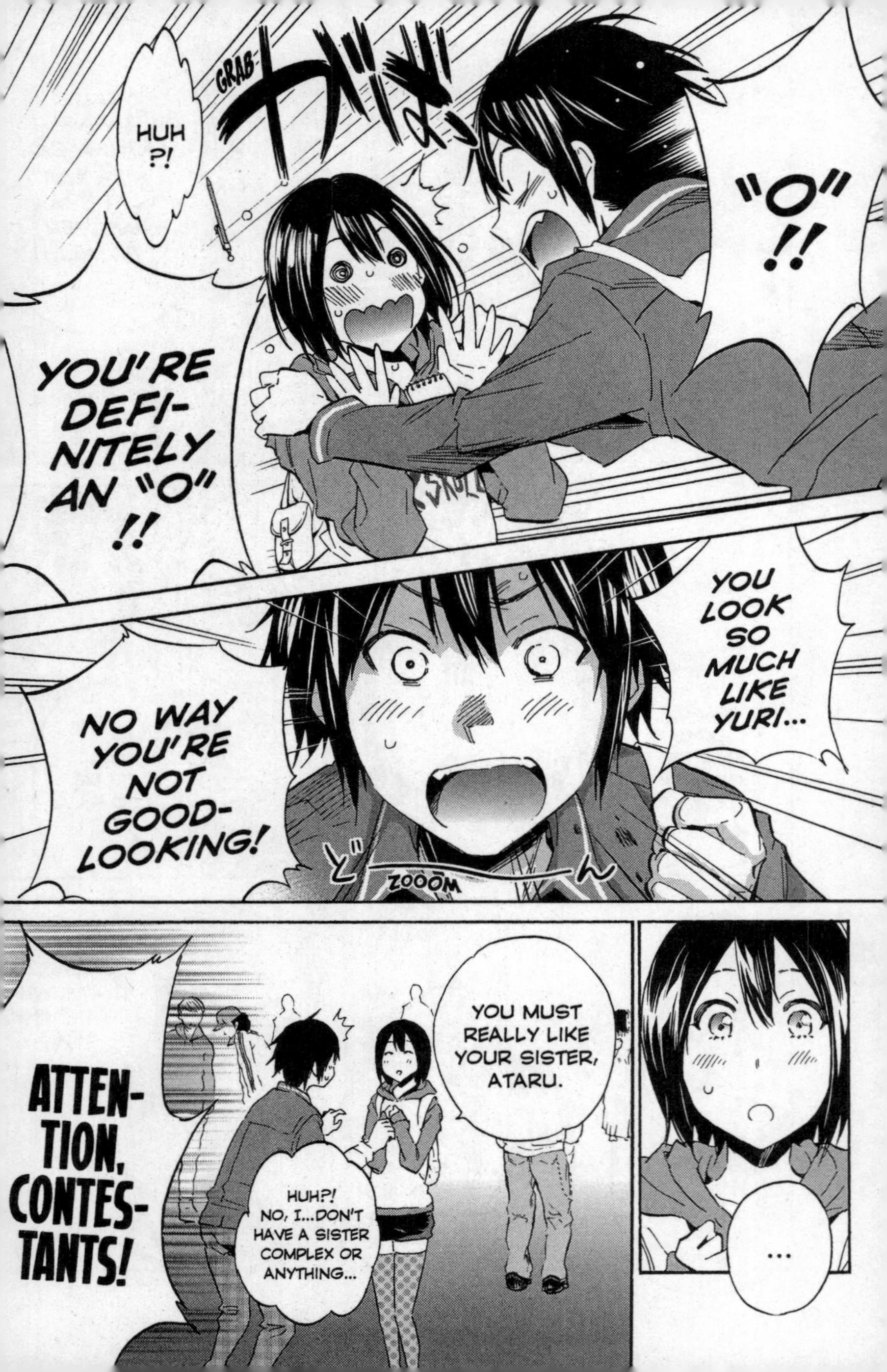
"O" !!
GRAB
HUH ?!
YOU'RE DEFI- NITELY AN "O" !!
YOU LOOK SO MUCH LIKE YURI...
NO WAY YOU'RE NOT GOOD- LOOKING!
ZOOOM
...
YOU MUST REALLY LIKE YOUR SISTER, ATARU.
HUH?! NO, I...DON'T HAVE A SISTER COMPLEX OR ANYTHING...
ATTEN- TION, CONTES- TANTS!

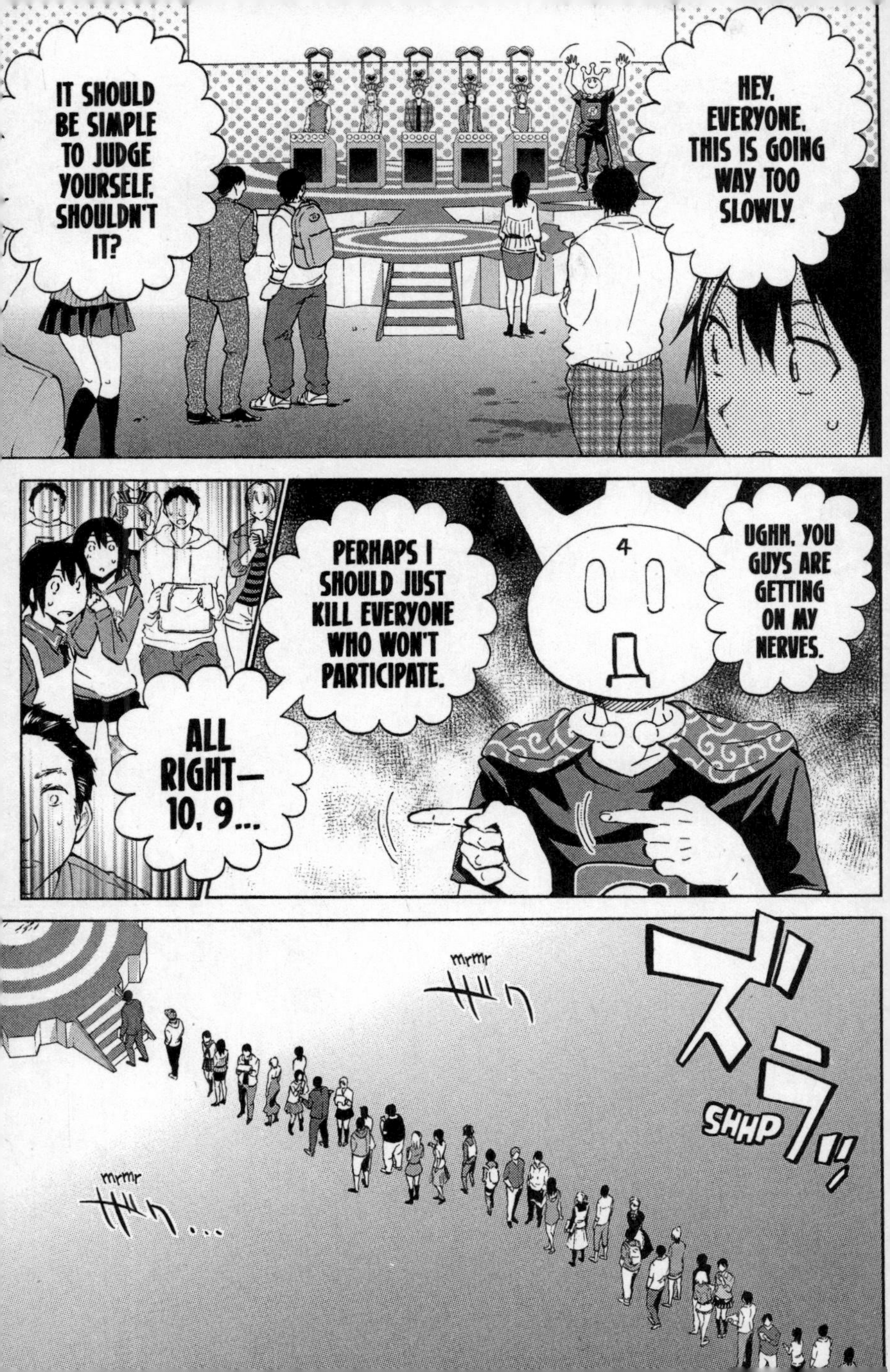
HEY, EVERYONE, THIS IS GOING WAY TOO SLOWLY.
IT SHOULD BE SIMPLE TO JUDGE YOURSELF, SHOULDN'T IT?
UGHH, YOU GUYS ARE GETTING ON MY NERVES.
PERHAPS I SHOULD JUST KILL EVERYONE WHO WON'T PARTICIPATE.
ALL RIGHT— 10, 9...
SHHP
mrmr
mrmr...

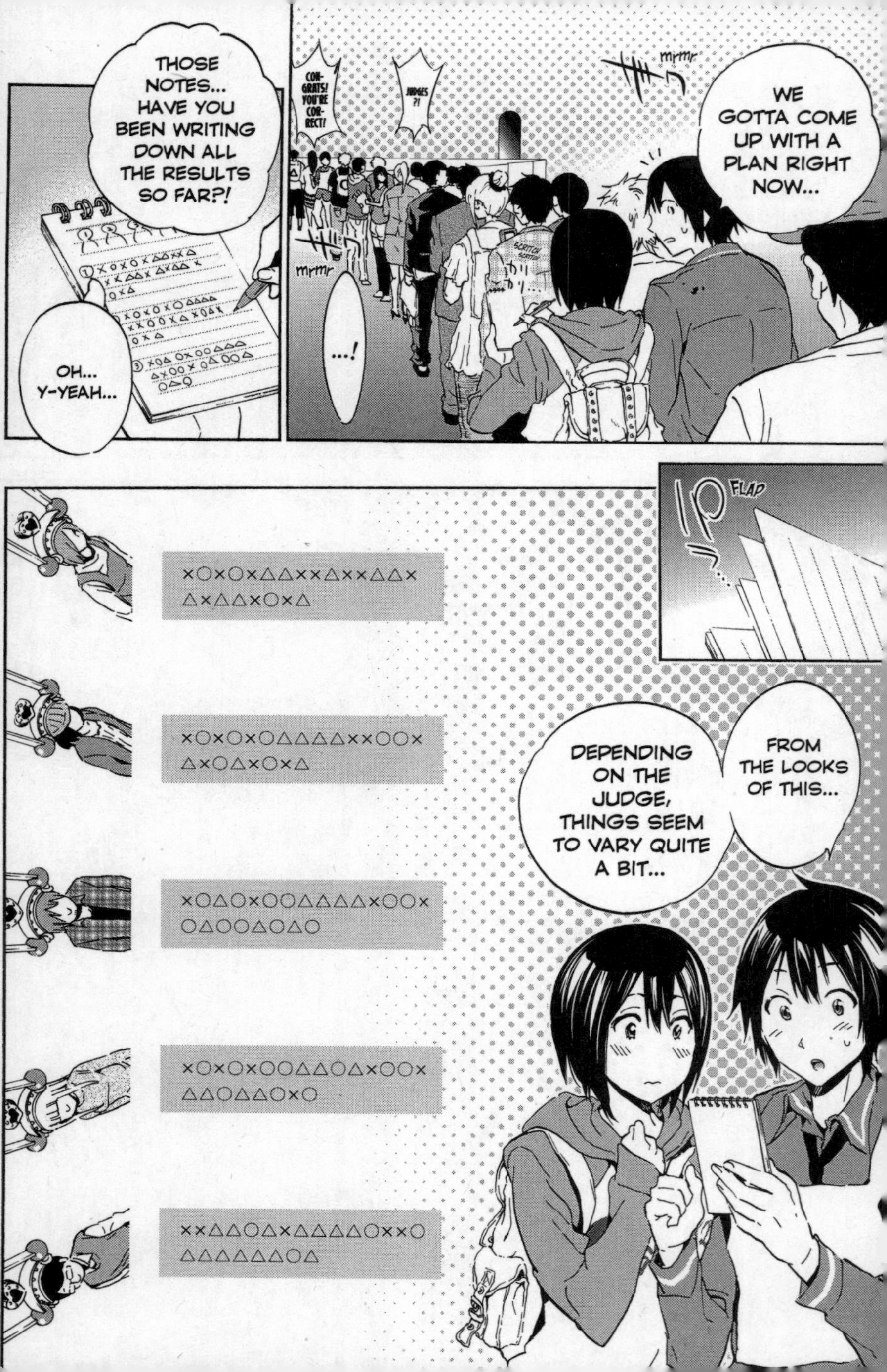
mrmr
WE GOTTA COME UP WITH A PLAN RIGHT NOW...
JUDGES?!
CON-GRATS! YOU'RE COR-RECT!
SCRITCH SCRITCH
mrmr
...!
THOSE NOTES... HAVE YOU BEEN WRITING DOWN ALL THE RESULTS SO FAR?!
OH... Y-YEAH...
FLAP
FROM THE LOOKS OF THIS...
DEPENDING ON THE JUDGE, THINGS SEEM TO VARY QUITE A BIT...
×○×○×△△××△××△△× △×△△×○×△
×○×○×○△△△△××○○× △×○△×○×△
×○△○×○○△△△△×○○× ○△○○△○△○
×○×○×○○△△○△×○○× △△○△△○×○
××△△○△×△△△△○××○ △△△△△△○△

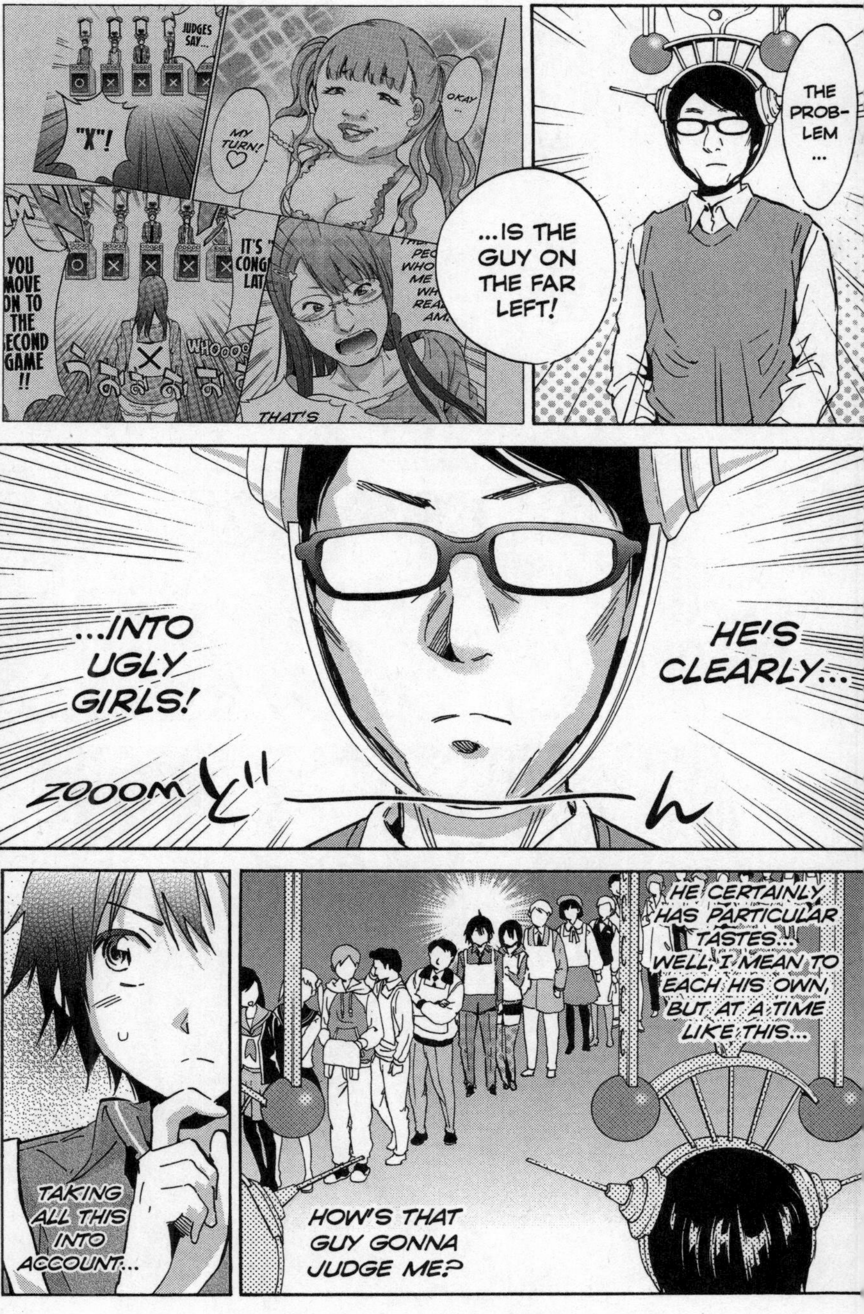
THE PROB-LEM ...
...IS THE GUY ON THE FAR LEFT!
OKAY ...
MY TURN! ♡
JUDGES SAY...
"X"!
THAT'S
YOU MOVE ON TO THE SECOND GAME !!
HE'S CLEARLY...
...INTO UGLY GIRLS!
ZOOOM
HE CERTAINLY HAS PARTICULAR TASTES... WELL, I MEAN TO EACH HIS OWN, BUT AT A TIME LIKE THIS...
HOW'S THAT GUY GONNA JUDGE ME?
TAKING ALL THIS INTO ACCOUNT...

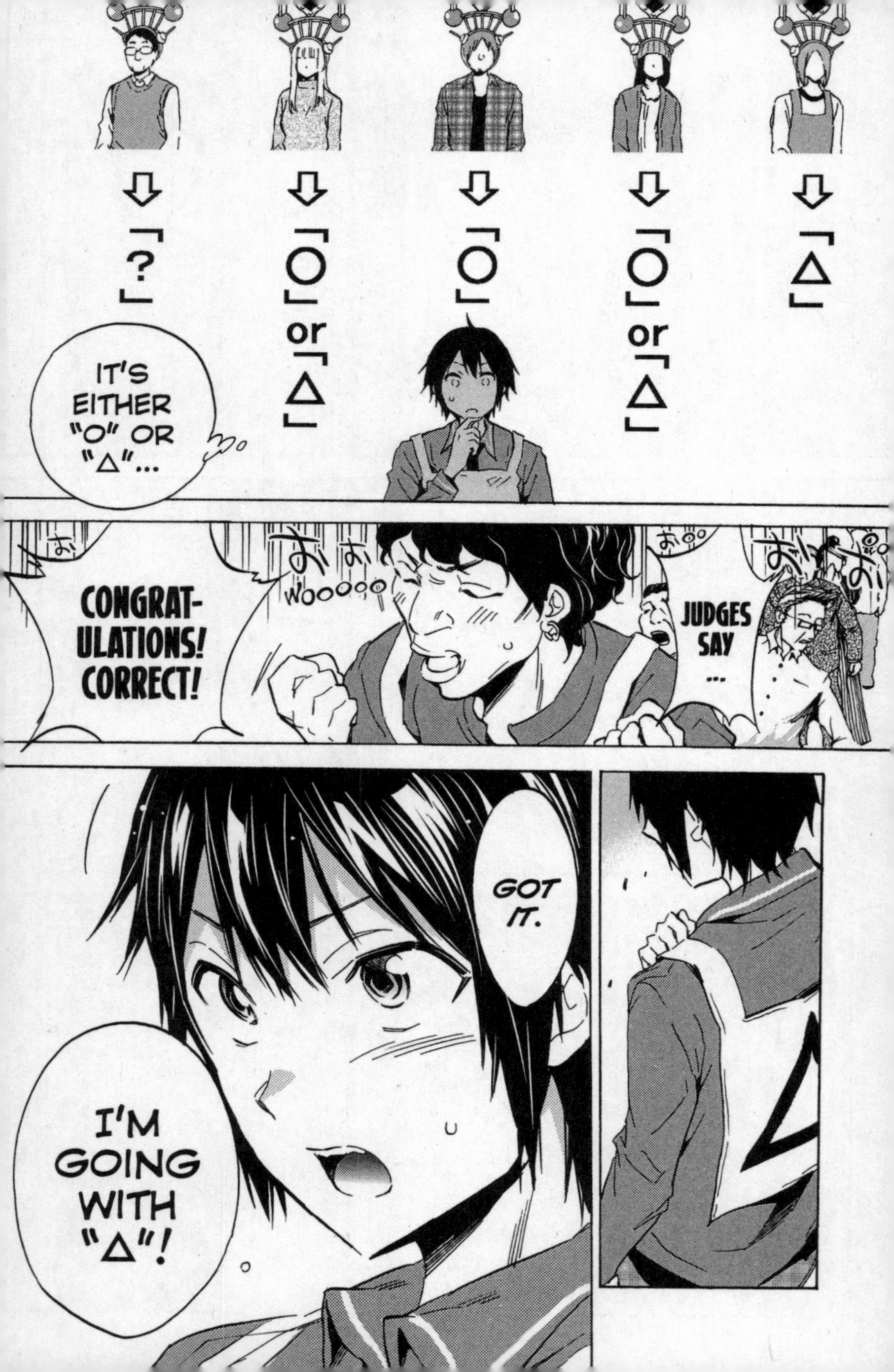
「△」
「○」or「△」
「○」
「○」or「△」
「?」
IT'S EITHER "O" OR "△"...
JUDGES SAY ...
WOOOO
CONGRAT-ULATIONS! CORRECT!
GOT IT.
I'M GOING WITH "△"!

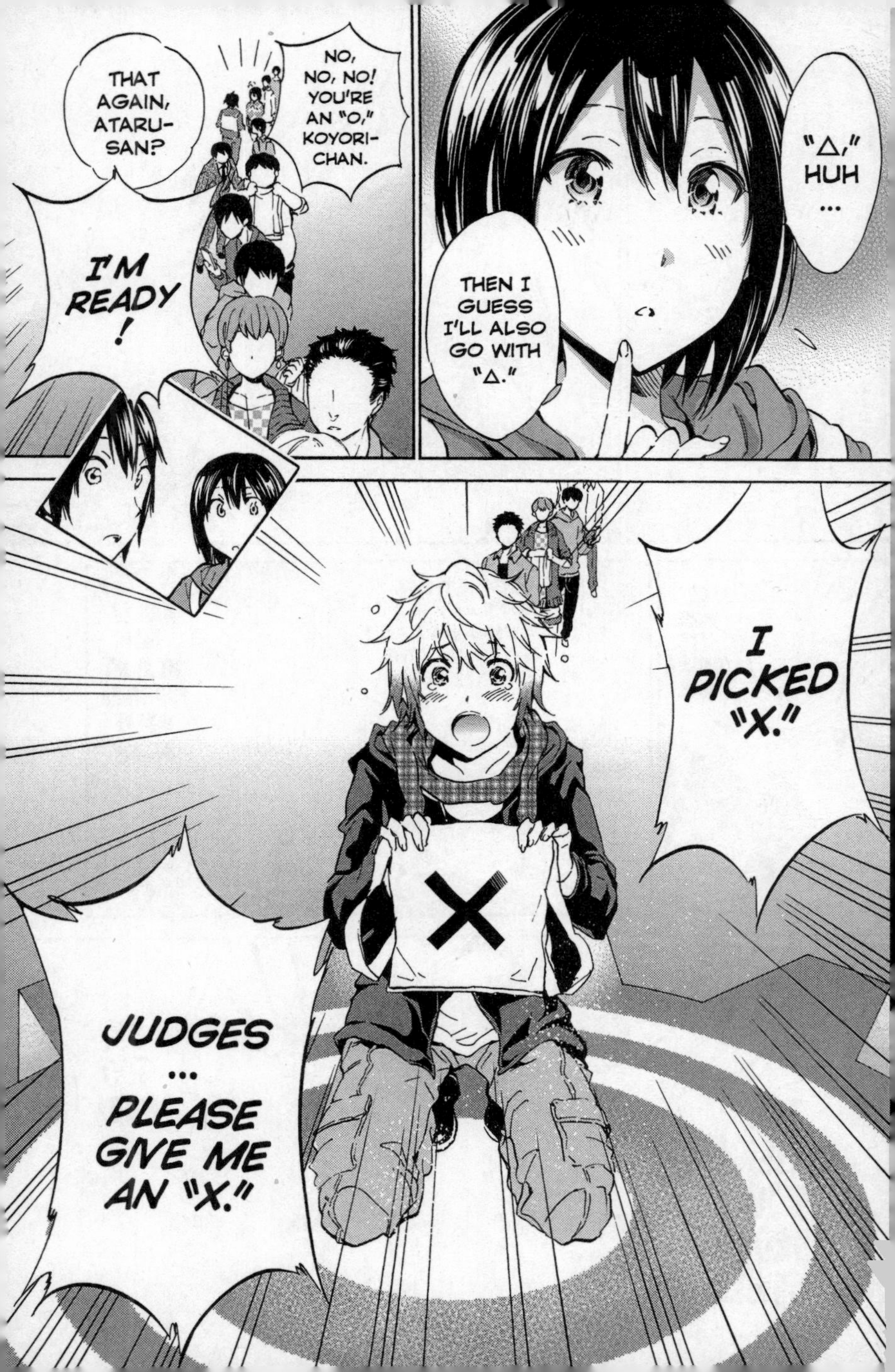
"△," HUH ...
THEN I GUESS I'LL ALSO GO WITH "△."
NO, NO, NO! YOU'RE AN "O," KOYORI-CHAN.
THAT AGAIN, ATARU-SAN?
I'M READY!
I PICKED "X."
JUDGES ... PLEASE GIVE ME AN "X."

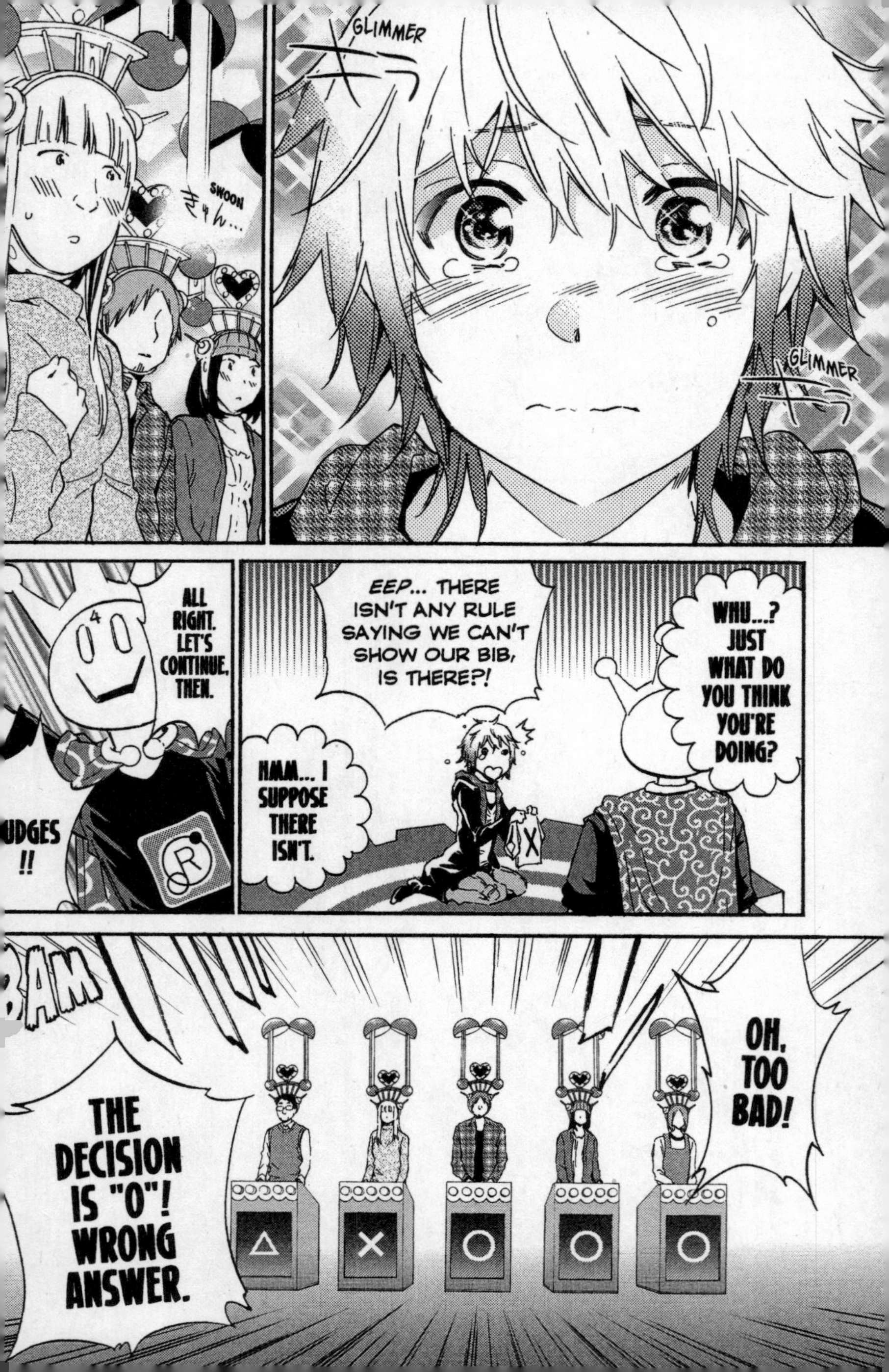
GLIMMER
GLIMMER
SWOON
きゅん…
WHU...? JUST WHAT DO YOU THINK YOU'RE DOING?
EEP... THERE ISN'T ANY RULE SAYING WE CAN'T SHOW OUR BIB, IS THERE?!
HMM... I SUPPOSE THERE ISN'T.
ALL RIGHT. LET'S CONTINUE, THEN.
UDGES !!
OH, TOO BAD!
BAM
THE DECISION IS "O"! WRONG ANSWER.

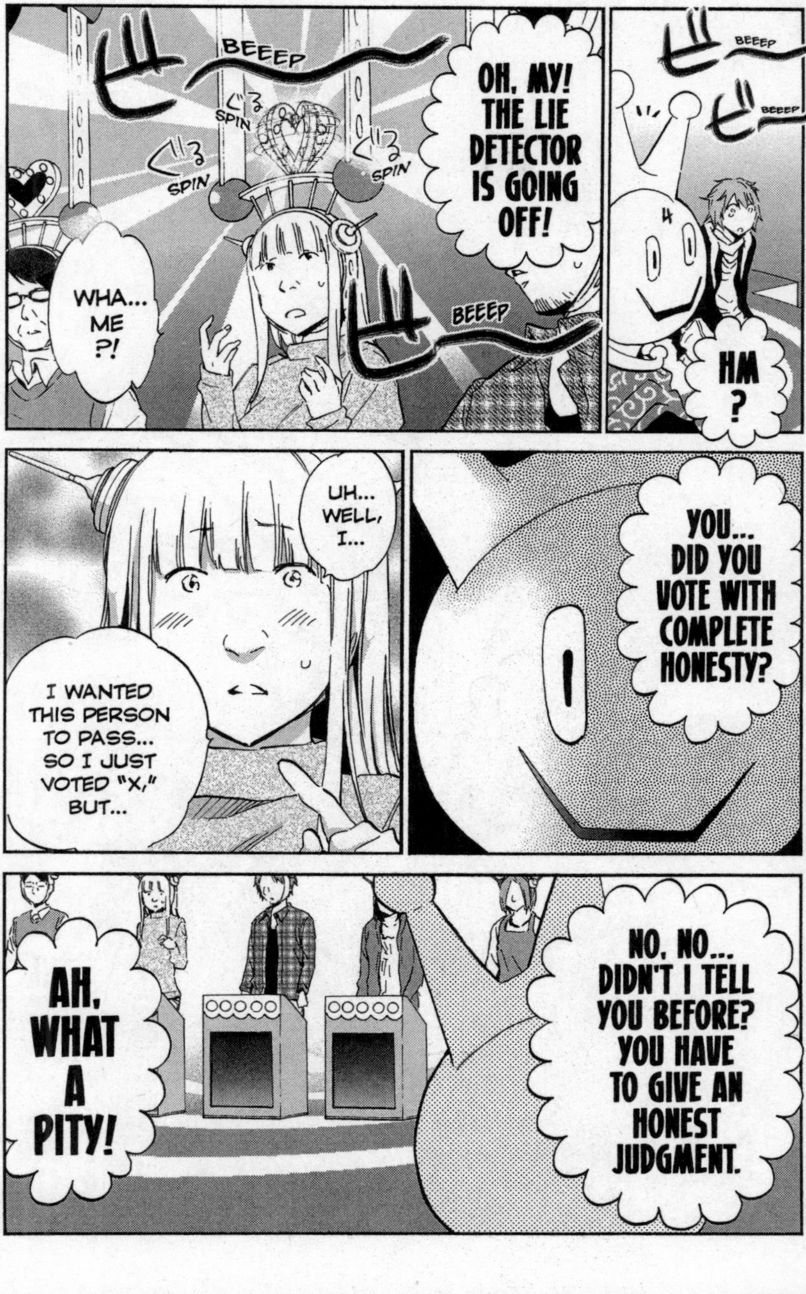

BEEEP
BEEEP
HM ?
OH, MY! THE LIE DETECTOR IS GOING OFF!
BEEEP
SPIN
SPIN
SPIN
BEEEP
WHA... ME ?!
YOU... DID YOU VOTE WITH COMPLETE HONESTY?
UH... WELL, I...
I WANTED THIS PERSON TO PASS... SO I JUST VOTED "X," BUT...
NO, NO... DIDN'T I TELL YOU BEFORE? YOU HAVE TO GIVE AN HONEST JUDGMENT.
AH, WHAT A PITY!

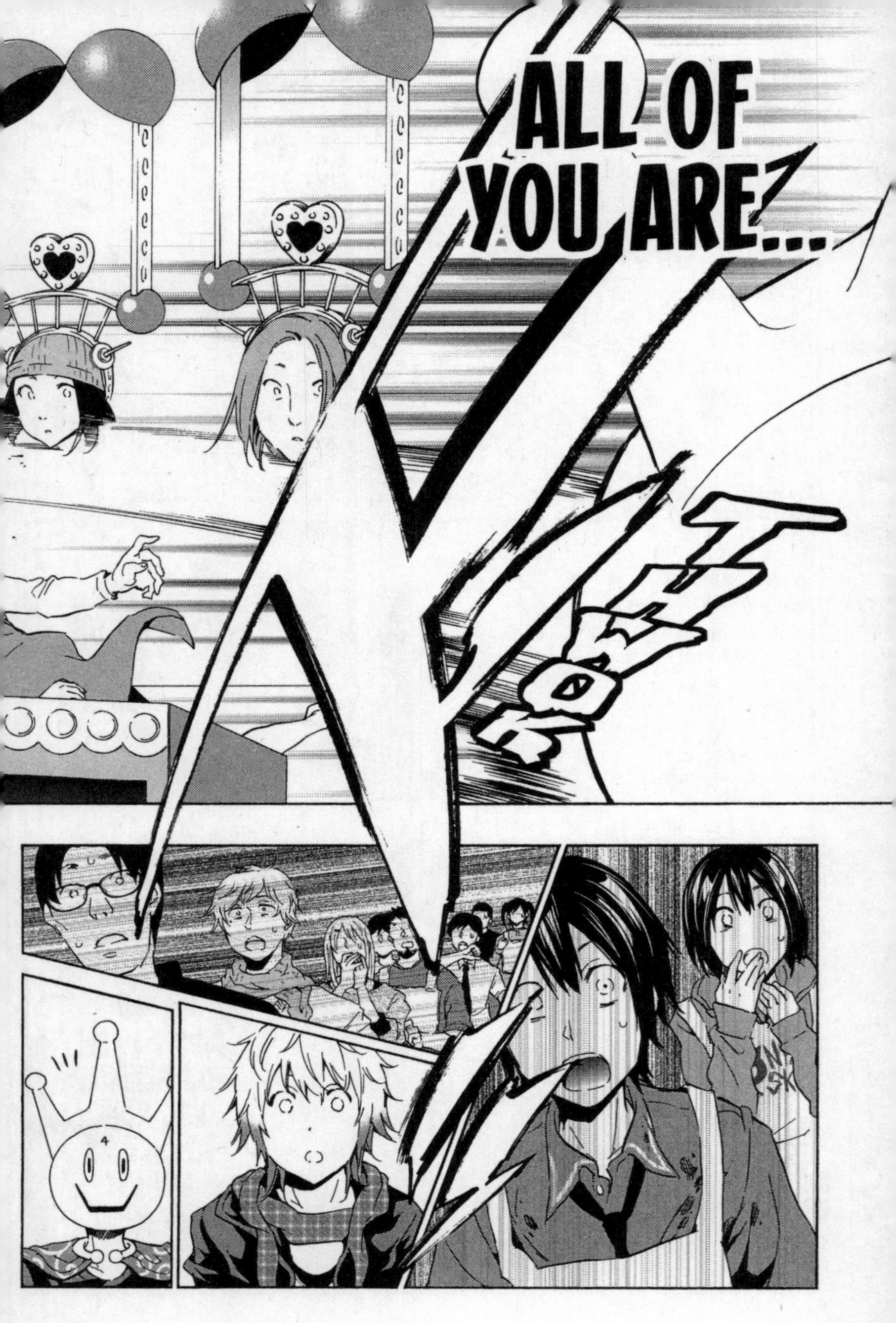
ALL OF YOU ARE...
THOK

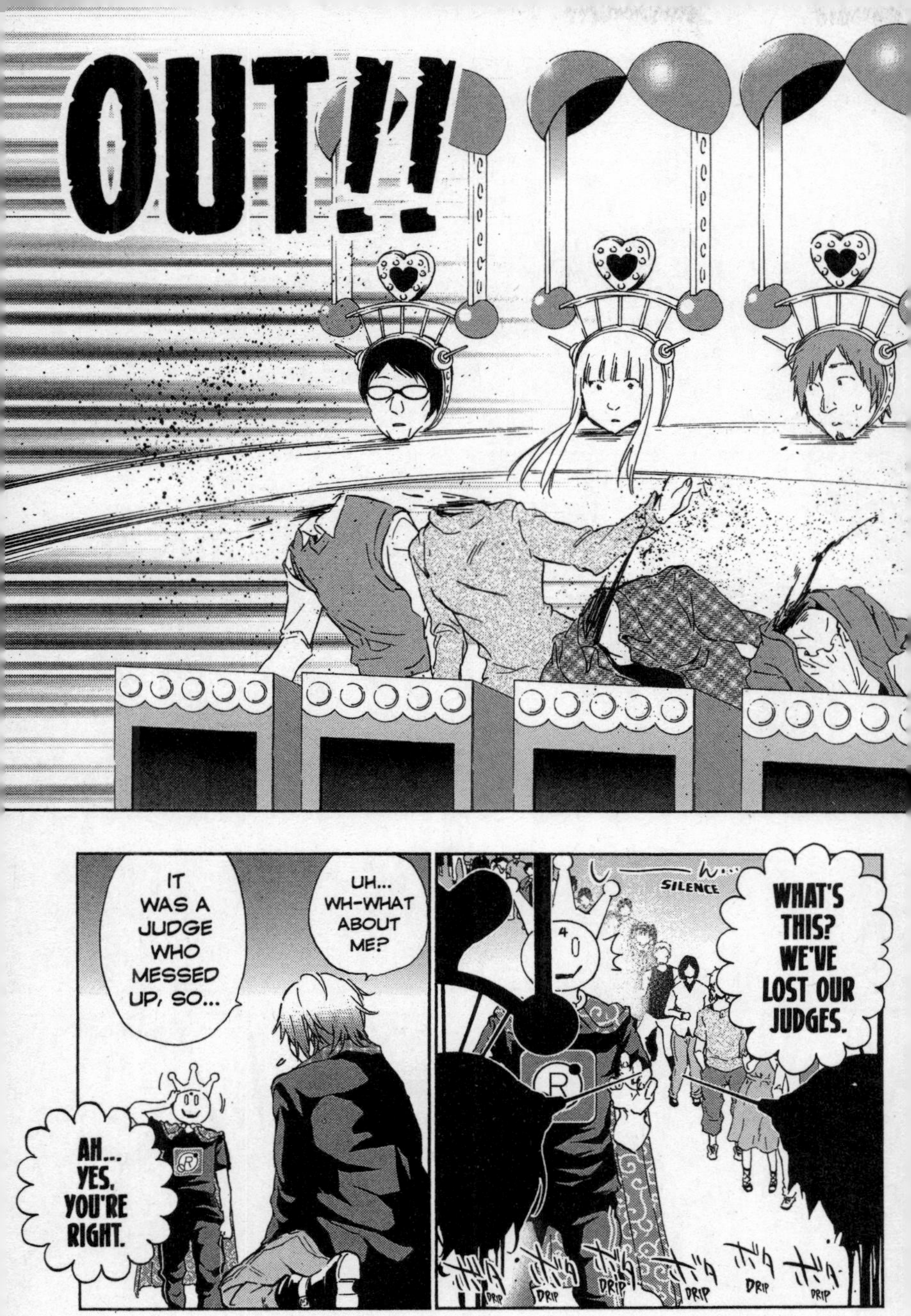
OUT!!
SILENCE
WHAT'S THIS? WE'VE LOST OUR JUDGES.
DRIP
DRIP
DRIP
DRIP
DRIP
DRIP
UH... WH-WHAT ABOUT ME?
IT WAS A JUDGE WHO MESSED UP, SO...
AH... YES. YOU'RE RIGHT.

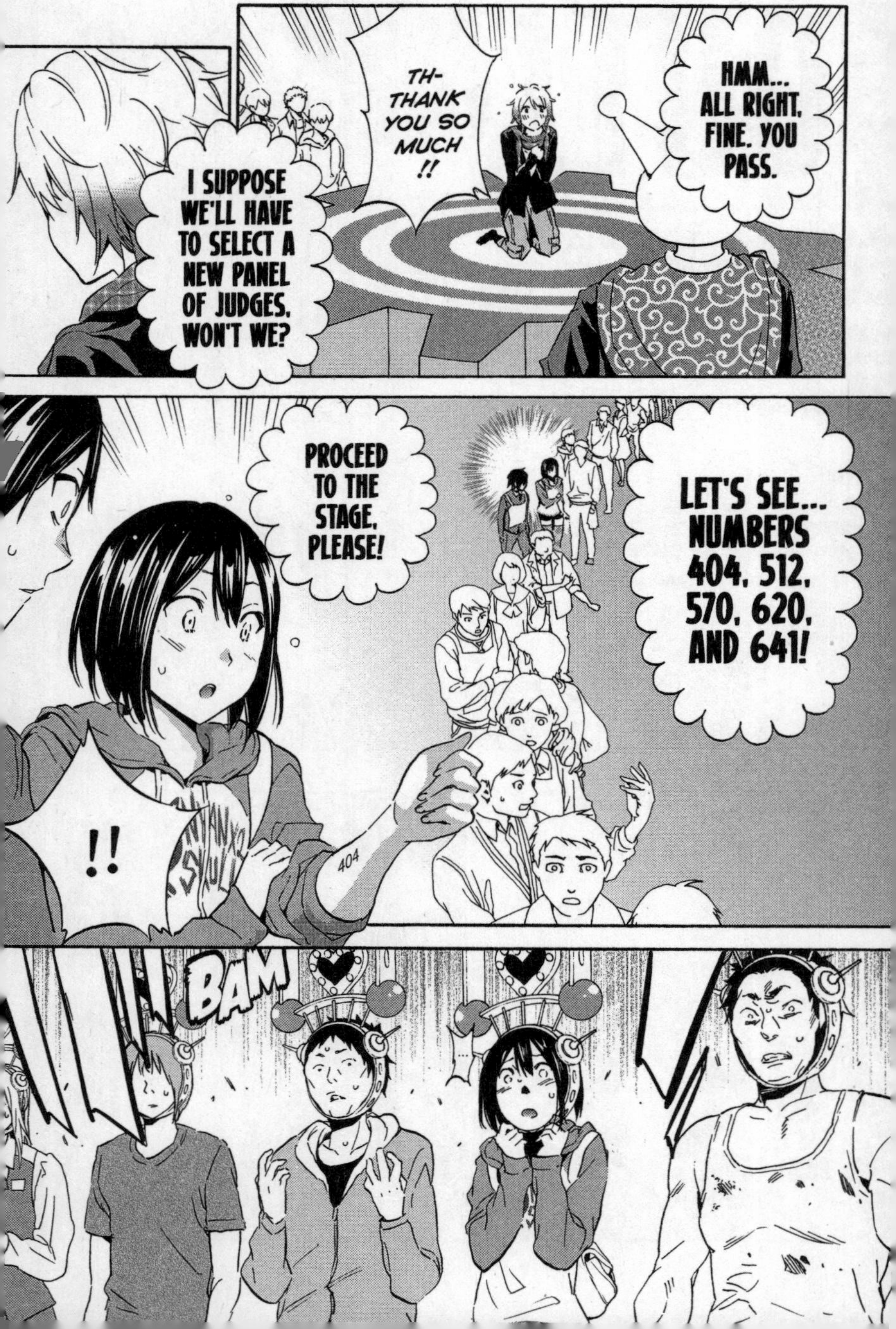
HMM... ALL RIGHT, FINE. YOU PASS.
TH-THANK YOU SO MUCH!!
I SUPPOSE WE'LL HAVE TO SELECT A NEW PANEL OF JUDGES, WON'T WE?
LET'S SEE... NUMBERS 404, 512, 570, 620, AND 641!
PROCEED TO THE STAGE, PLEASE!
!!
404
BAM

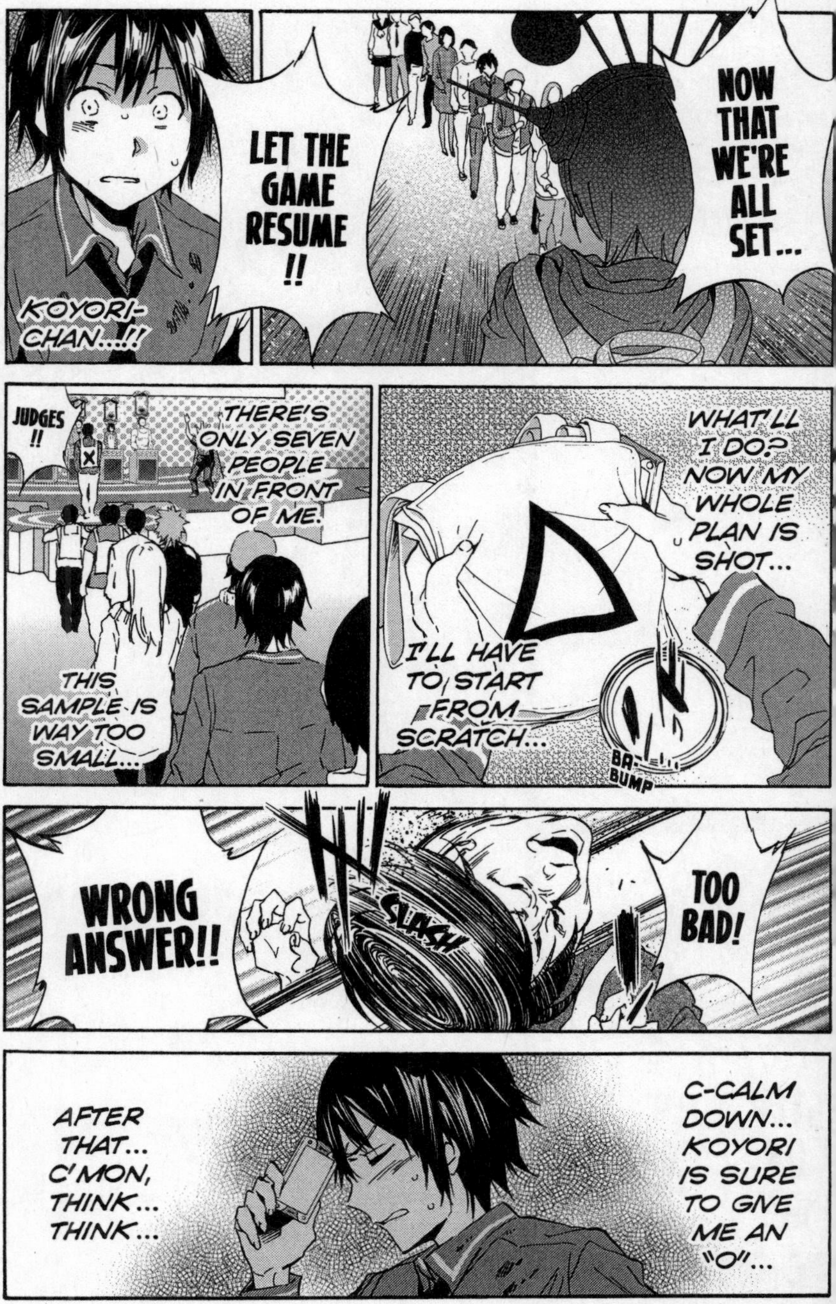
NOW THAT WE'RE ALL SET...
LET THE GAME RESUME!!
KOYORI-CHAN...!!
WHAT'LL I DO? NOW MY WHOLE PLAN IS SHOT...
I'LL HAVE TO START FROM SCRATCH...
BA-BUMP
THERE'S ONLY SEVEN PEOPLE IN FRONT OF ME.
JUDGES!!
THIS SAMPLE IS WAY TOO SMALL...
TOO BAD!
SLASH
WRONG ANSWER!!
C-CALM DOWN... KOYORI IS SURE TO GIVE ME AN "O"...
AFTER THAT... C'MON, THINK... THINK...

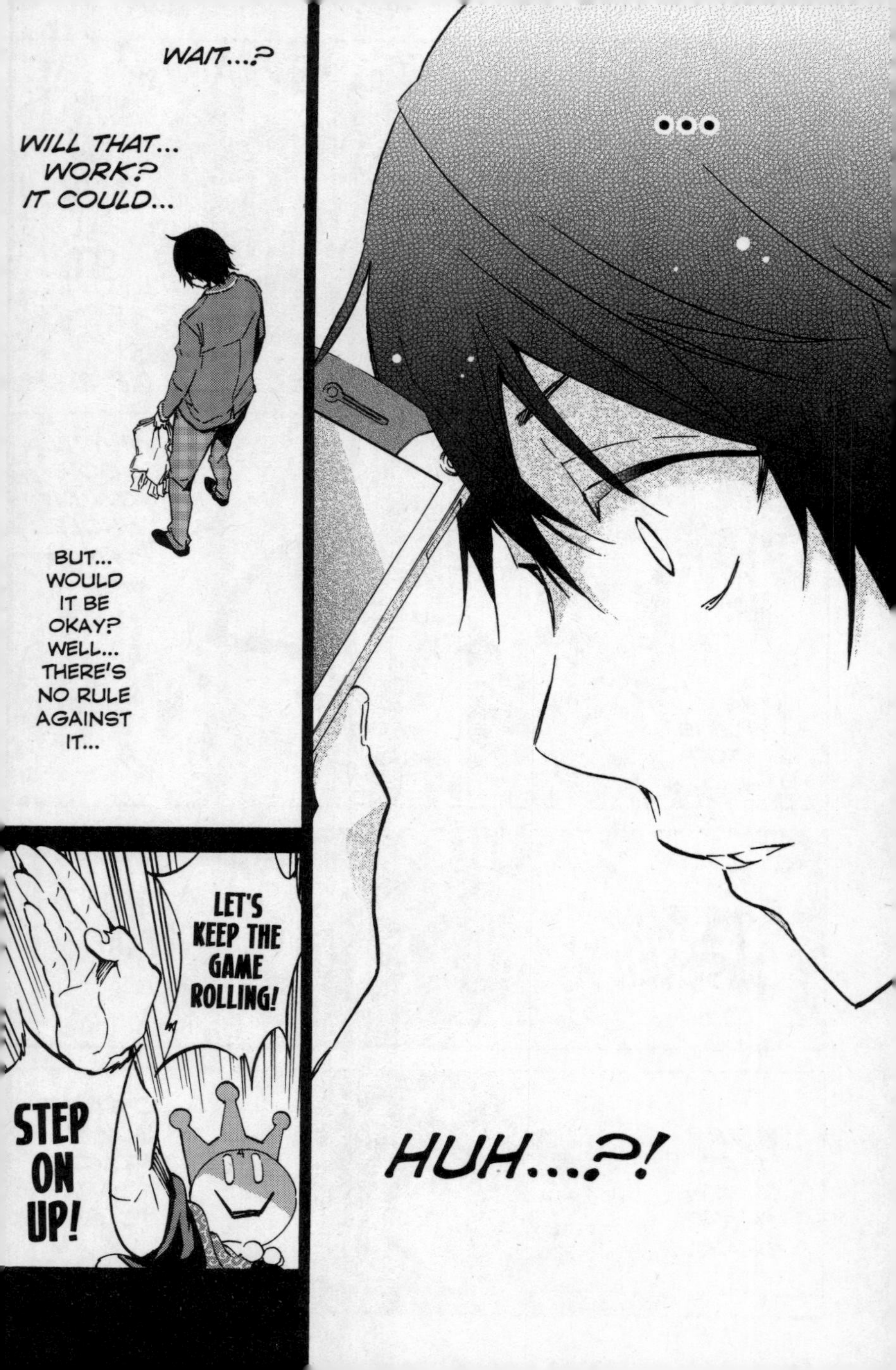
...
HUH...?!
WAIT...?
WILL THAT... WORK? IT COULD...
BUT... WOULD IT BE OKAY? WELL... THERE'S NO RULE AGAINST IT...
LET'S KEEP THE GAME ROLLING!
STEP ON UP!

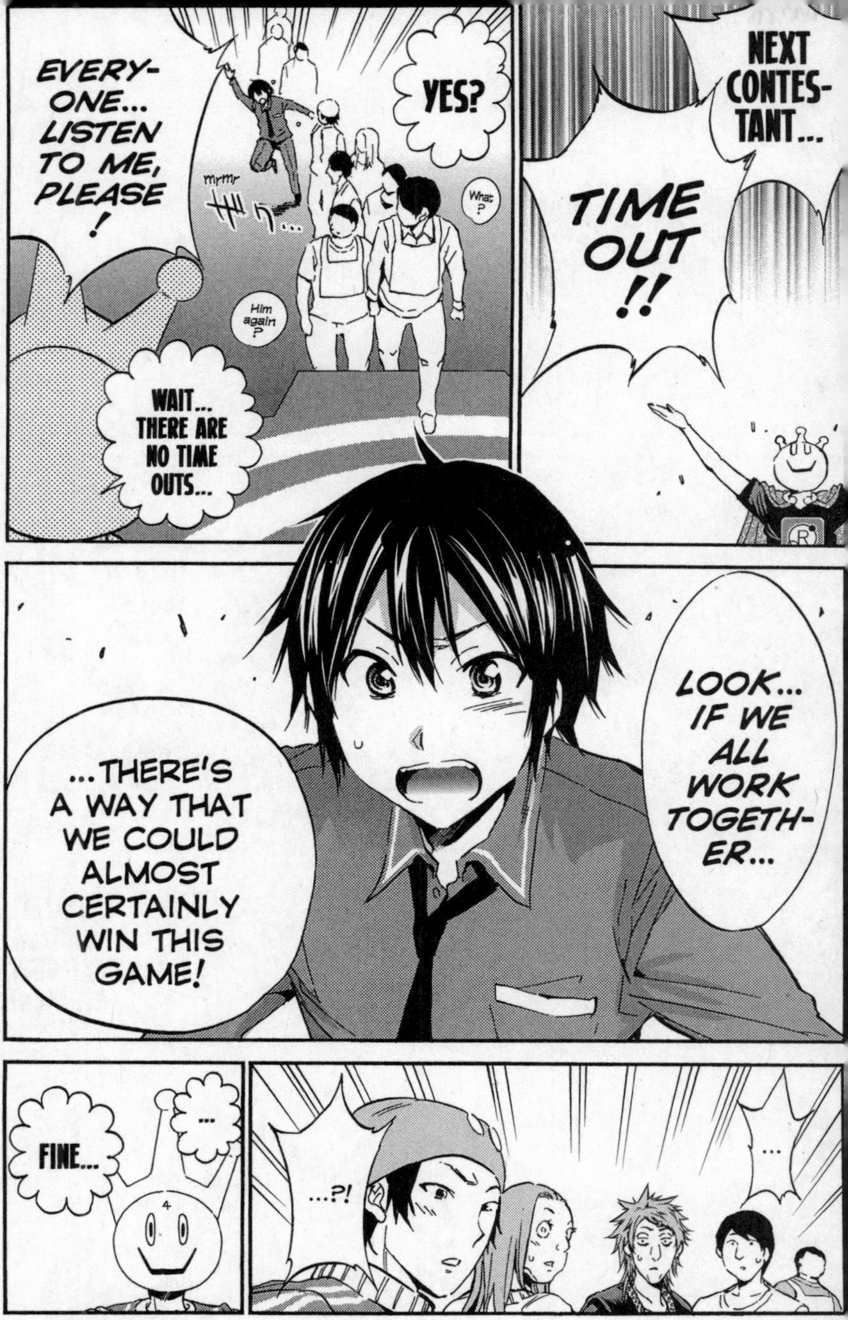

NEXT CONTESTANT...
TIME OUT!!
EVERYONE... LISTEN TO ME, PLEASE!
YES?
mrmr
What?
Him again?
WAIT... THERE ARE NO TIME OUTS...
LOOK... IF WE ALL WORK TOGETHER...
...THERE'S A WAY THAT WE COULD ALMOST CERTAINLY WIN THIS GAME!
...
...?!
...
FINE...

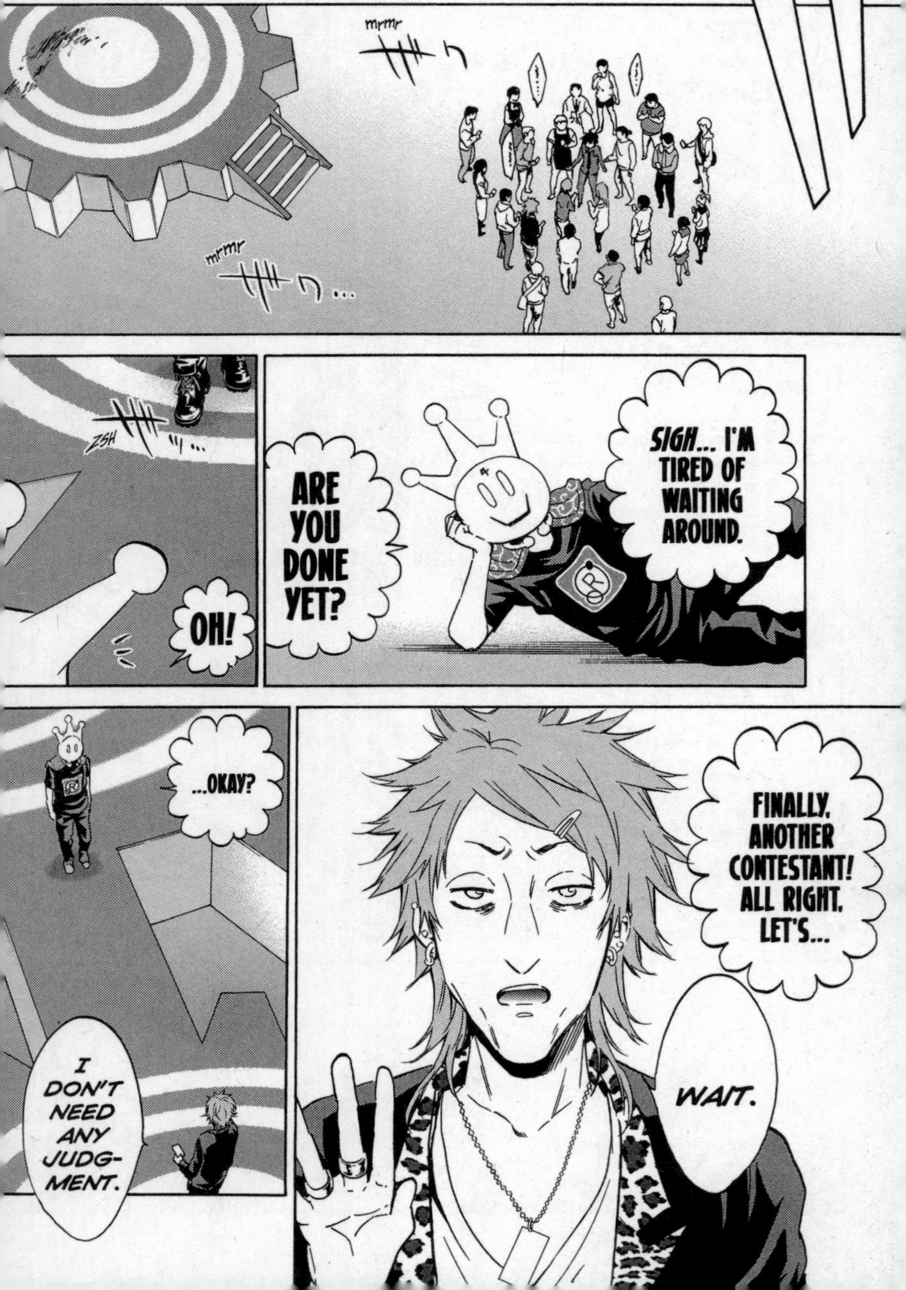
mrmr
mrmr ...
SIGH... I'M TIRED OF WAITING AROUND.
ARE YOU DONE YET?
ZSH
OH!
FINALLY, ANOTHER CONTESTANT! ALL RIGHT, LET'S...
WAIT.
...OKAY?
I DON'T NEED ANY JUDGMENT.

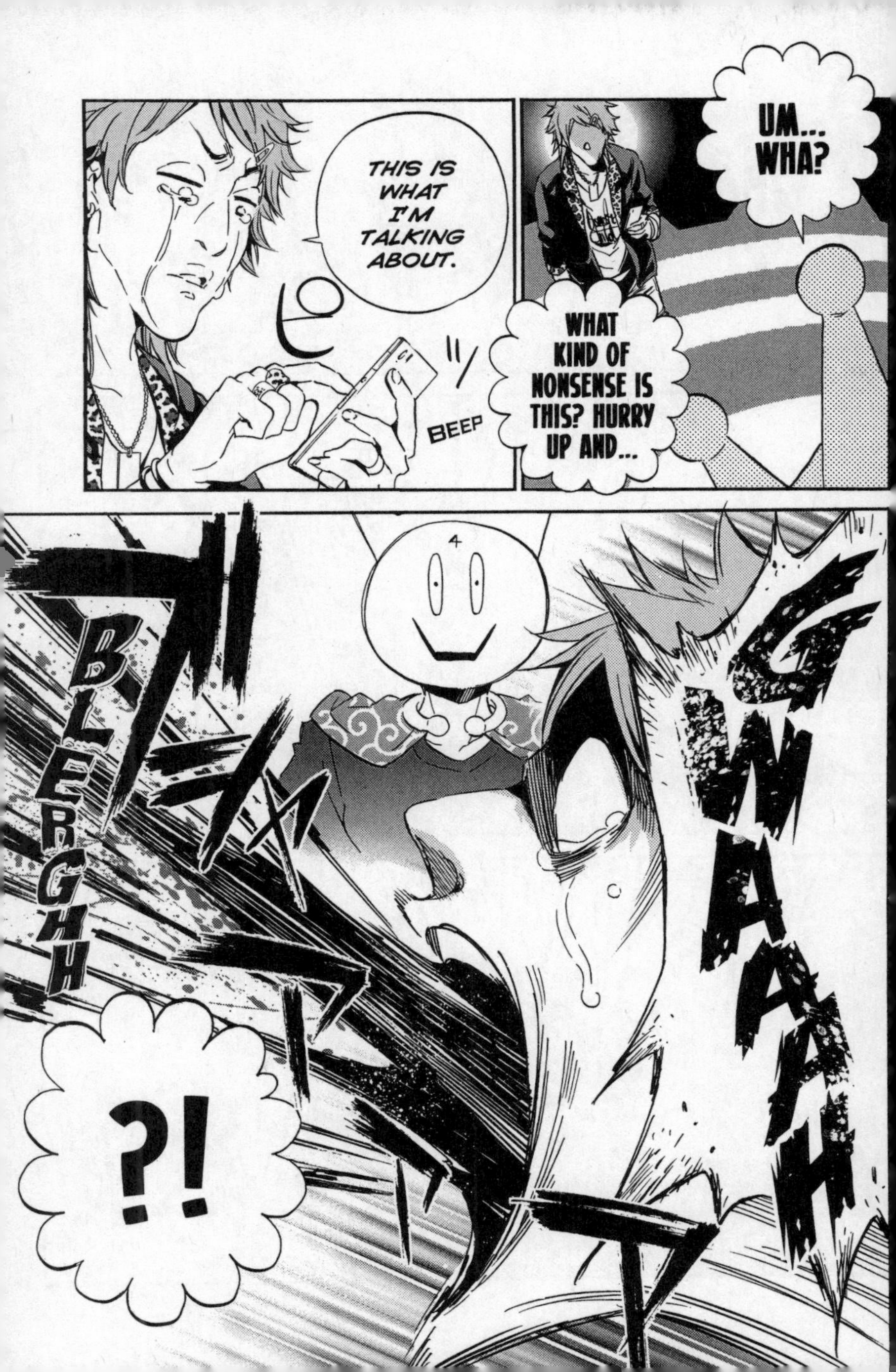
UM... WHA?
WHAT KIND OF NONSENSE IS THIS? HURRY UP AND...
THIS IS WHAT I'M TALKING ABOUT.
BEEP
GWAAAH
BLERGHH
?!

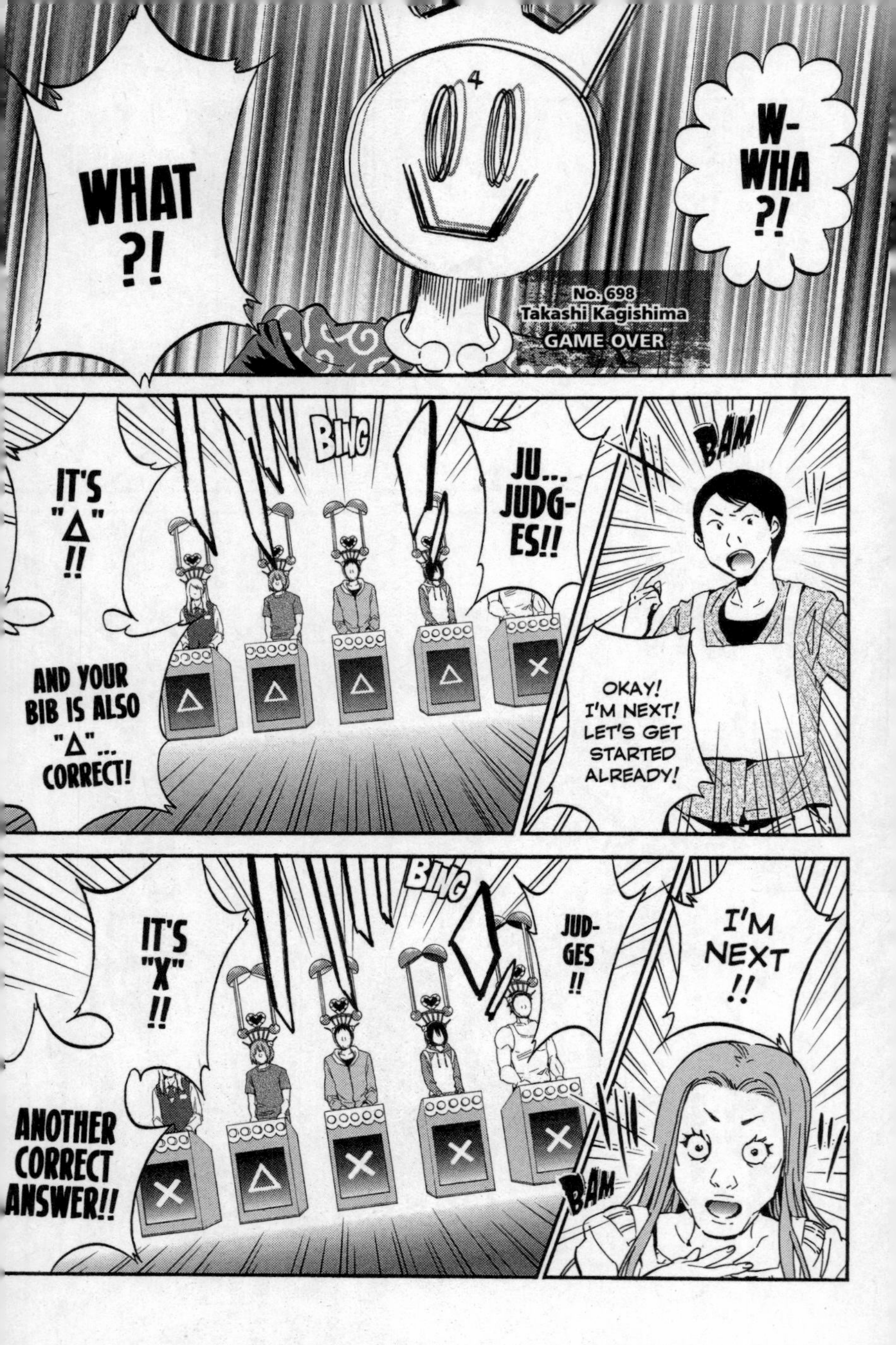
W-WHA?!
No. 698
Takashi Kagishima
GAME OVER
WHAT?!
BAM
OKAY! I'M NEXT! LET'S GET STARTED ALREADY!
JU... JUDGES!!
BING
IT'S "△"!!
AND YOUR BIB IS ALSO "△"... CORRECT!
I'M NEXT!!
BAM
JUDGES!!
BING
IT'S "X"!!
ANOTHER CORRECT ANSWER!!

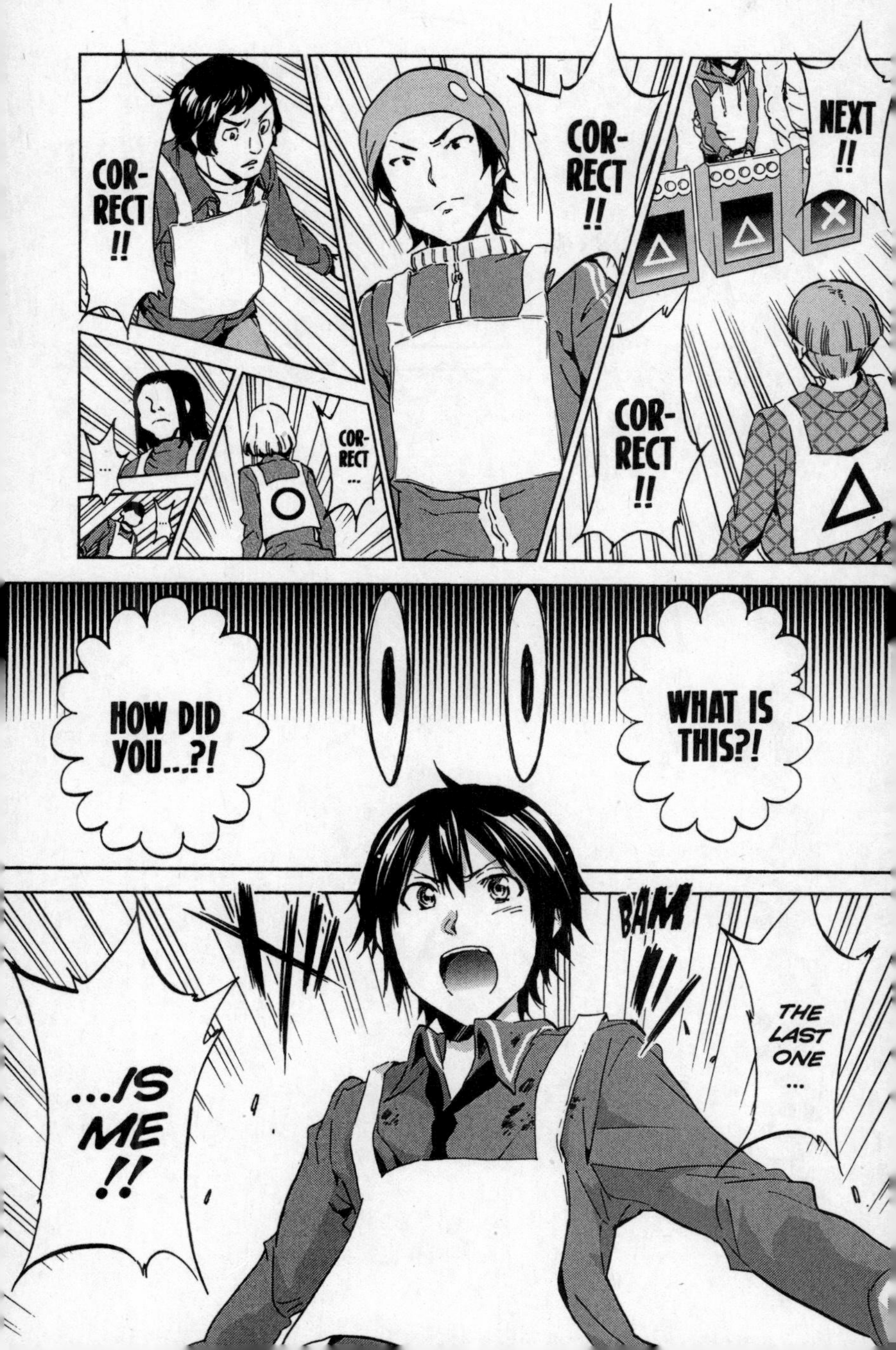
NEXT!!
CORRECT!!
CORRECT!!
CORRECT!!
CORRECT...
...
...
WHAT IS THIS?!
HOW DID YOU...?!
BAM!!
THE LAST ONE...
...IS ME!!

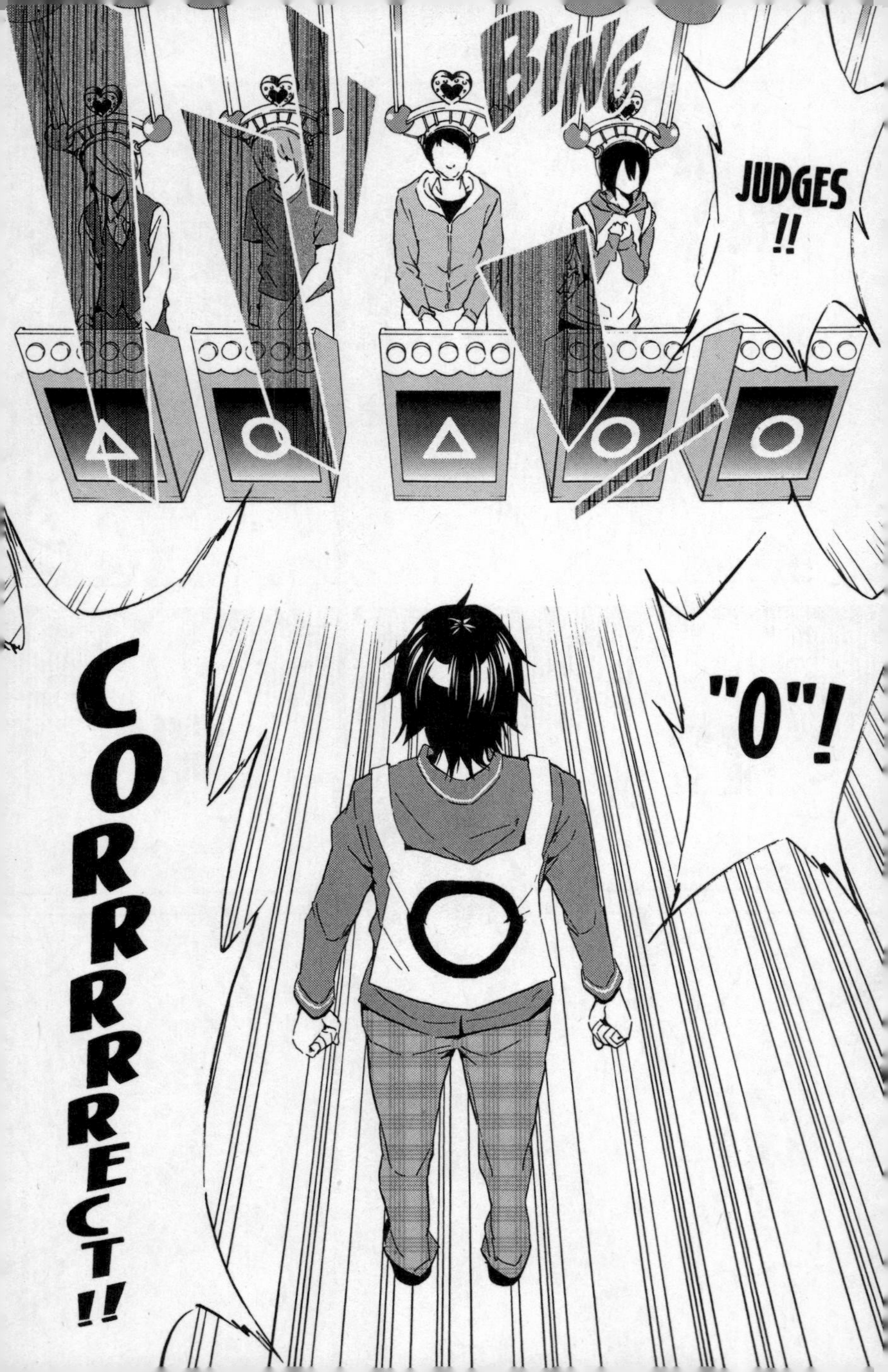
BING
JUDGES!!
"O"!
CORRRRECT!!

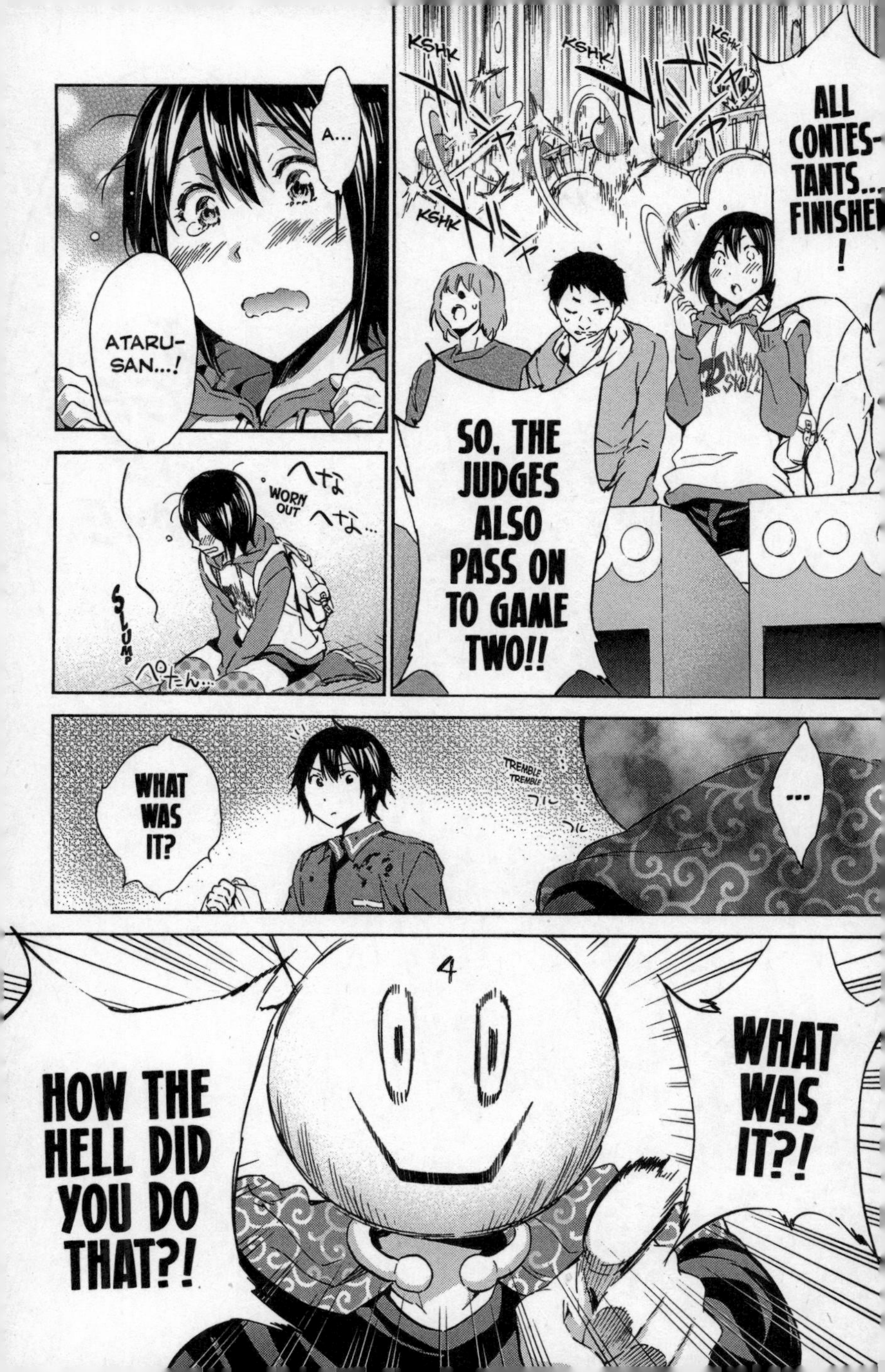
KSHK
KSHK
KSHK
KSHK
ALL CONTES-TANTS... FINISHE
!
SO, THE JUDGES ALSO PASS ON TO GAME TWO!!
A...
ATARU-SAN...!
へな
WORN OUT
へな...
SLUMP
ぺたん...
...
TREMBLE TREMBLE
WHAT WAS IT?
4
WHAT WAS IT?!
HOW THE HELL DID YOU DO THAT?!

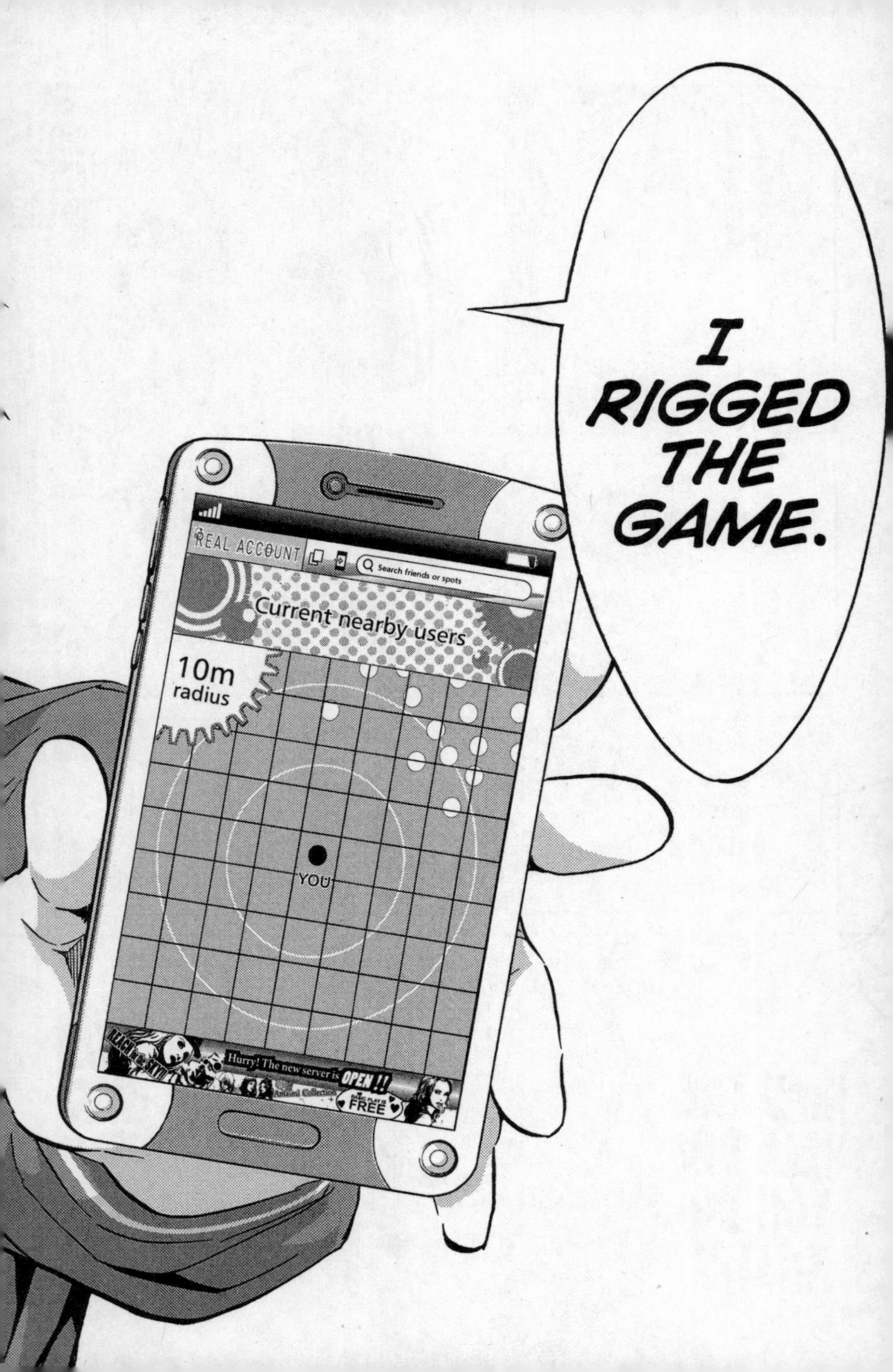
I RIGGED THE GAME.
REAL ACCOUNT
Search friends or spots
Current nearby users
10m radius
YOU
Hurry! The new server is OPEN!!
FREE

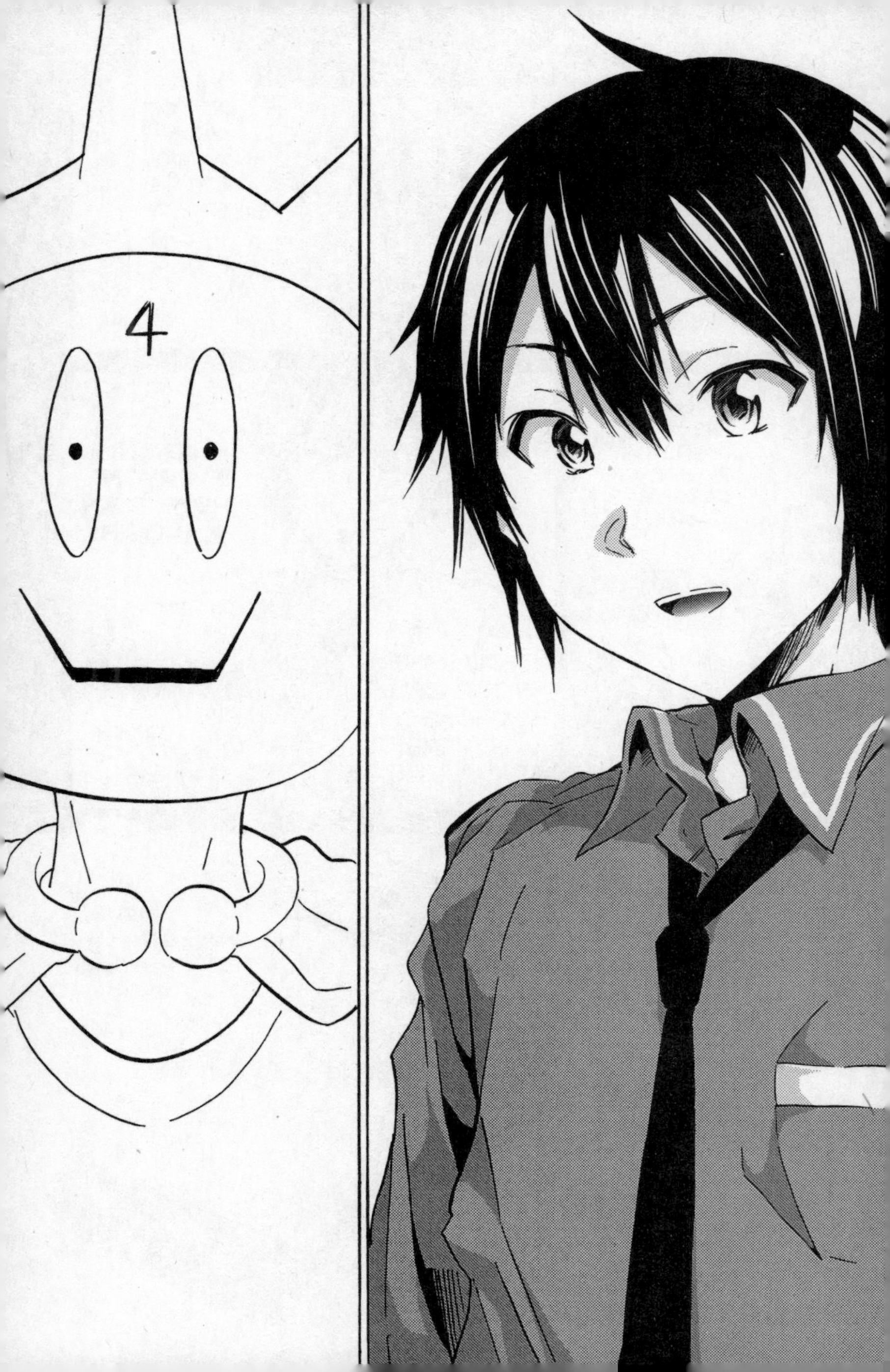
4

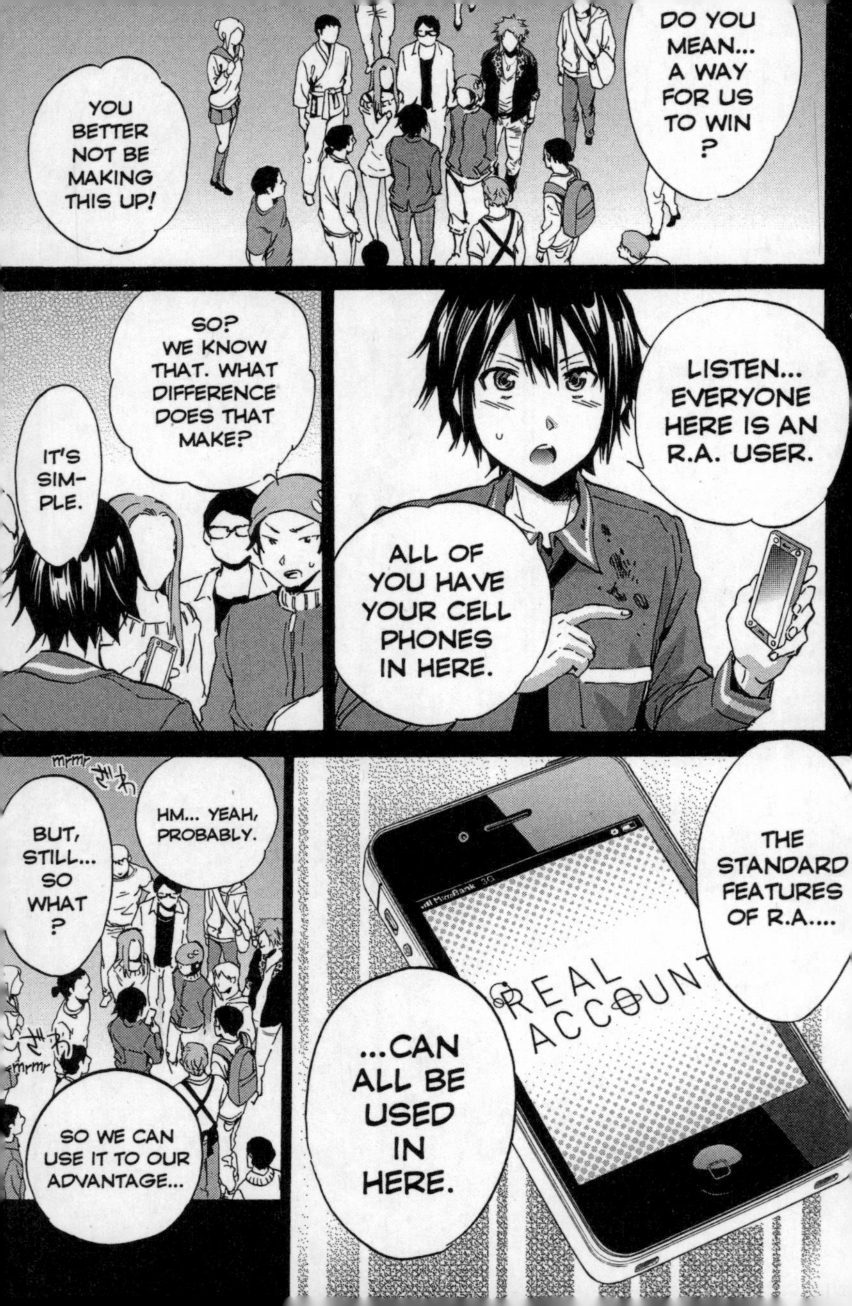
DO YOU MEAN... A WAY FOR US TO WIN ?
YOU BETTER NOT BE MAKING THIS UP!
LISTEN... EVERYONE HERE IS AN R.A. USER.
ALL OF YOU HAVE YOUR CELL PHONES IN HERE.
SO? WE KNOW THAT. WHAT DIFFERENCE DOES THAT MAKE?
IT'S SIMPLE.
THE STANDARD FEATURES OF R.A....
REAL ACCOUNT
...CAN ALL BE USED IN HERE.
mrmr
HM... YEAH, PROBABLY.
BUT, STILL... SO WHAT ?
mrmr
SO WE CAN USE IT TO OUR ADVANTAGE...

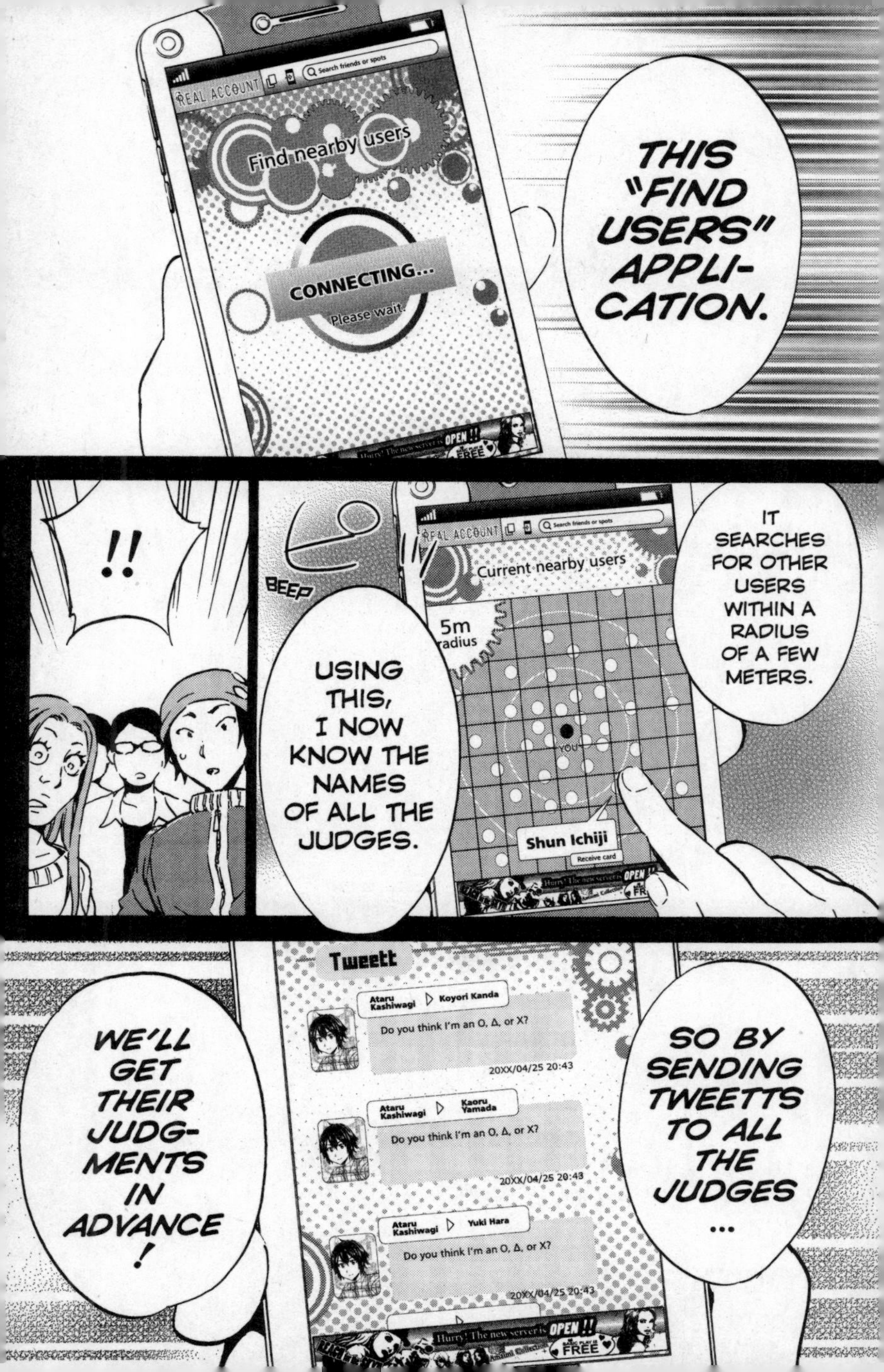
REAL ACCOUNT
Search friends or spots
Find nearby users
CONNECTING...
Please wait.
Hurry! The new server is OPEN!!
FREE
THIS "FIND USERS" APPLI-CATION.
IT SEARCHES FOR OTHER USERS WITHIN A RADIUS OF A FEW METERS.
REAL ACCOUNT
Search friends or spots
Current nearby users
5m radius
YOU
Shun Ichiji
Receive card
BEEP
USING THIS, I NOW KNOW THE NAMES OF ALL THE JUDGES.
!!
SO BY SENDING TWEETTS TO ALL THE JUDGES ...
Tweett
Ataru Kashiwagi ▷ Koyori Kanda
Do you think I'm an O, Δ, or X?
20XX/04/25 20:43
Ataru Kashiwagi ▷ Kaoru Yamada
Do you think I'm an O, Δ, or X?
20XX/04/25 20:43
Ataru Kashiwagi ▷ Yuki Hara
Do you think I'm an O, Δ, or X?
20XX/04/25 20:43
Hurry! The new server is OPEN!!
FREE
WE'LL GET THEIR JUDG-MENTS IN ADVANCE!

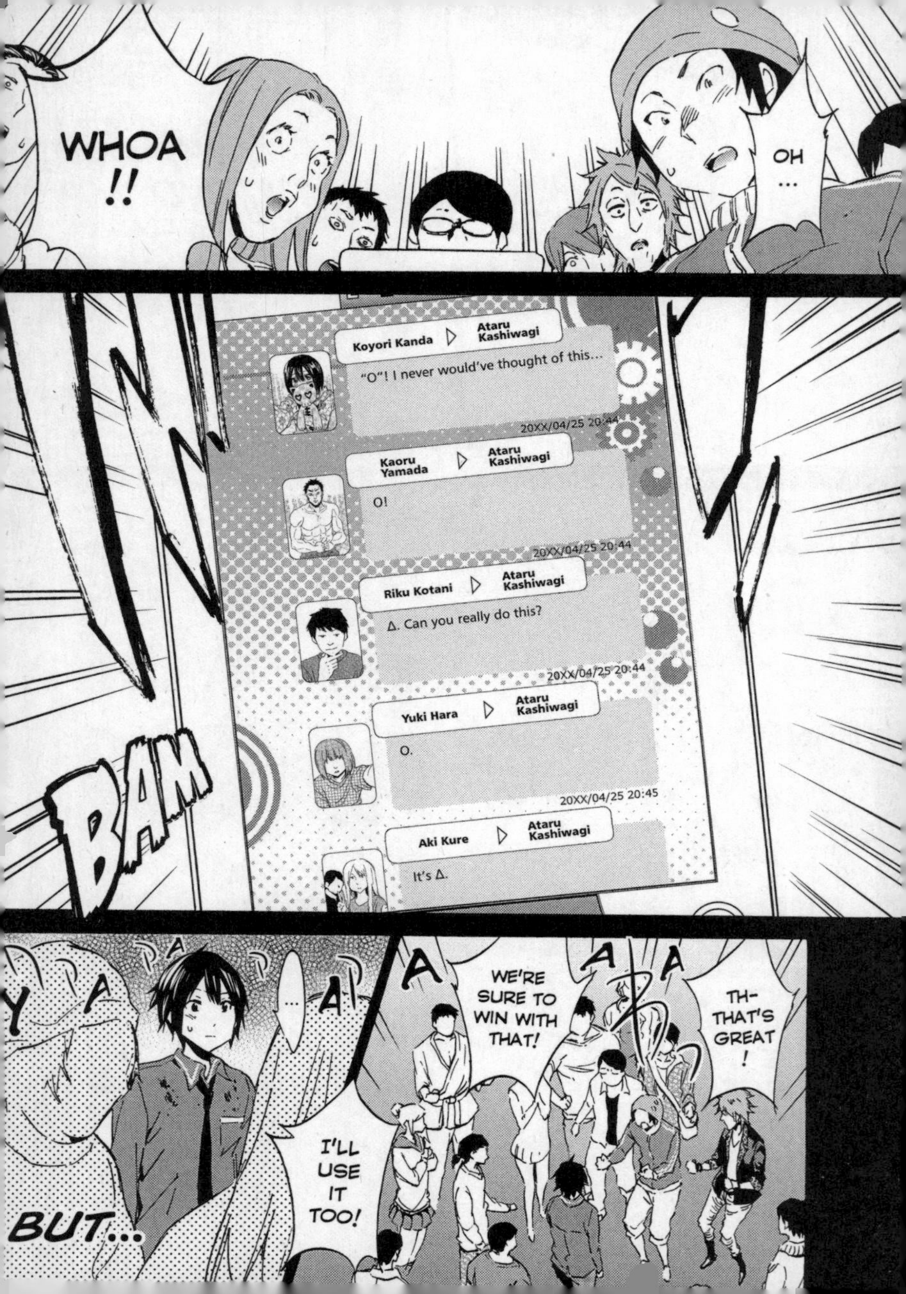
OH ...
WHOA !!
Koyori Kanda ▷ Ataru Kashiwagi
"O"! I never would've thought of this...
20XX/04/25 20:44
Kaoru Yamada ▷ Ataru Kashiwagi
O!
20XX/04/25 20:44
Riku Kotani ▷ Ataru Kashiwagi
Δ. Can you really do this?
20XX/04/25 20:44
Yuki Hara ▷ Ataru Kashiwagi
O.
20XX/04/25 20:45
Aki Kure ▷ Ataru Kashiwagi
It's Δ.
BAM
TH- THAT'S GREAT !
WE'RE SURE TO WIN WITH THAT!
I'LL USE IT TOO!
...
BUT...

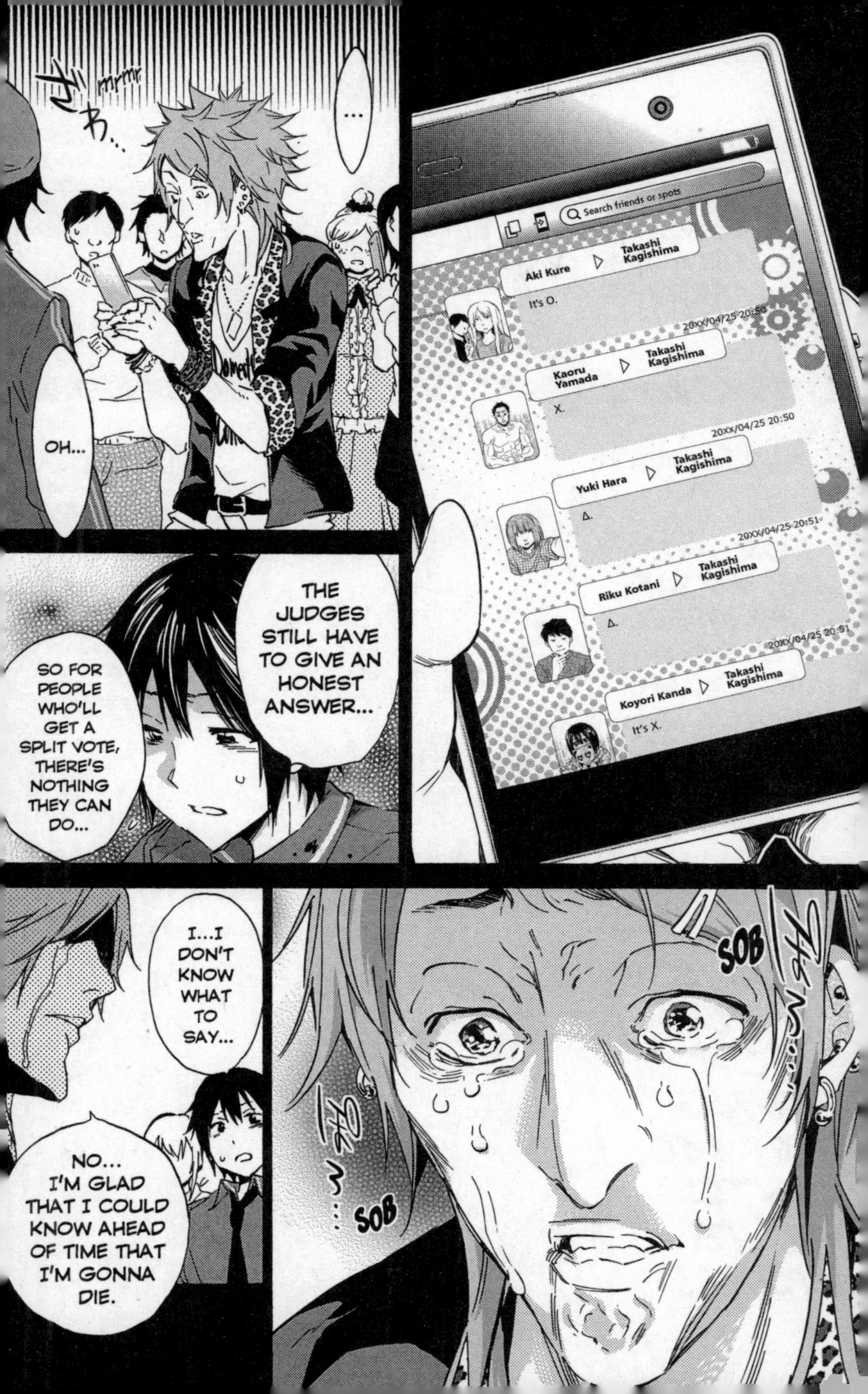

Search friends or spots
Aki Kure ▷ Takashi Kagishima
It's O.
20XX/04/25 20:50
Kaoru Yamada ▷ Takashi Kagishima
X.
20XX/04/25 20:50
Yuki Hara ▷ Takashi Kagishima
Δ.
20XX/04/25 20:51
Riku Kotani ▷ Takashi Kagishima
Δ.
20XX/04/25 20:51
Koyori Kanda ▷ Takashi Kagishima
It's X.
...
ざわ…
mrmr
OH...
THE JUDGES STILL HAVE TO GIVE AN HONEST ANSWER...
SO FOR PEOPLE WHO'LL GET A SPLIT VOTE, THERE'S NOTHING THEY CAN DO...
SOB
SOB
I...I DON'T KNOW WHAT TO SAY...
NO... I'M GLAD THAT I COULD KNOW AHEAD OF TIME THAT I'M GONNA DIE.

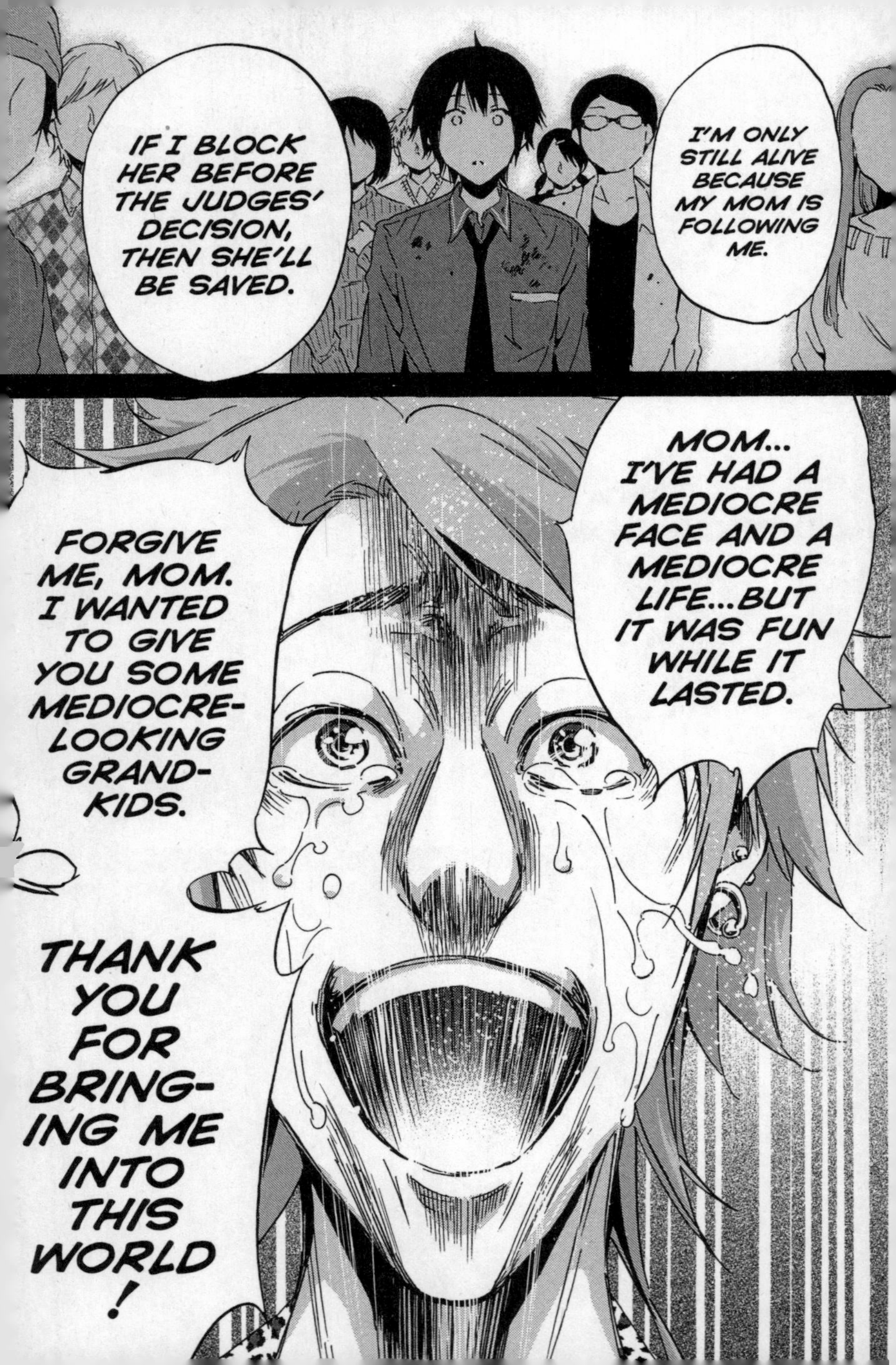
I'M ONLY STILL ALIVE BECAUSE MY MOM IS FOLLOWING ME.
IF I BLOCK HER BEFORE THE JUDGES' DECISION, THEN SHE'LL BE SAVED.
MOM... I'VE HAD A MEDIOCRE FACE AND A MEDIOCRE LIFE...BUT IT WAS FUN WHILE IT LASTED.
FORGIVE ME, MOM. I WANTED TO GIVE YOU SOME MEDIOCRE-LOOKING GRAND-KIDS.
THANK YOU FOR BRING-ING ME INTO THIS WORLD!

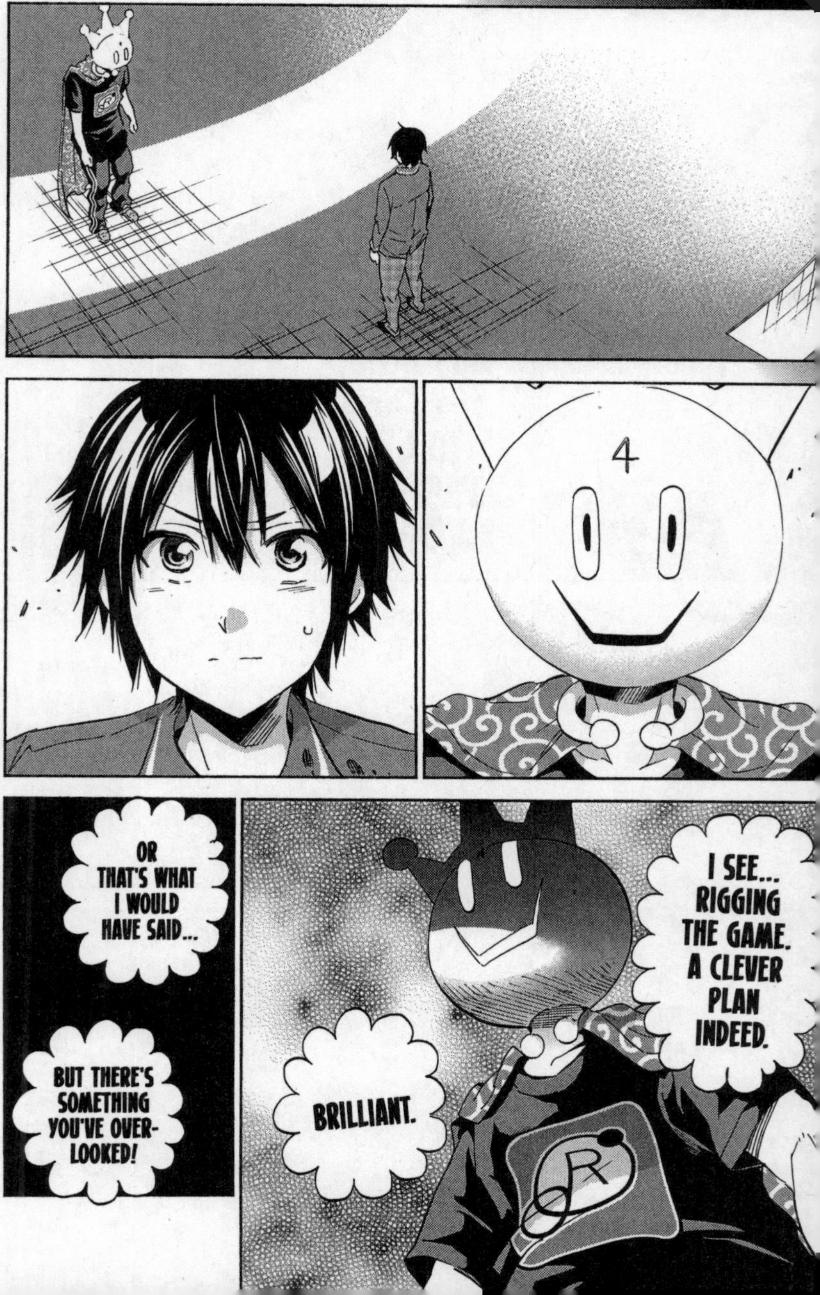
I SEE... RIGGING THE GAME. A CLEVER PLAN INDEED.
BRILLIANT.
OR THAT'S WHAT I WOULD HAVE SAID...
BUT THERE'S SOMETHING YOU'VE OVER-LOOKED!

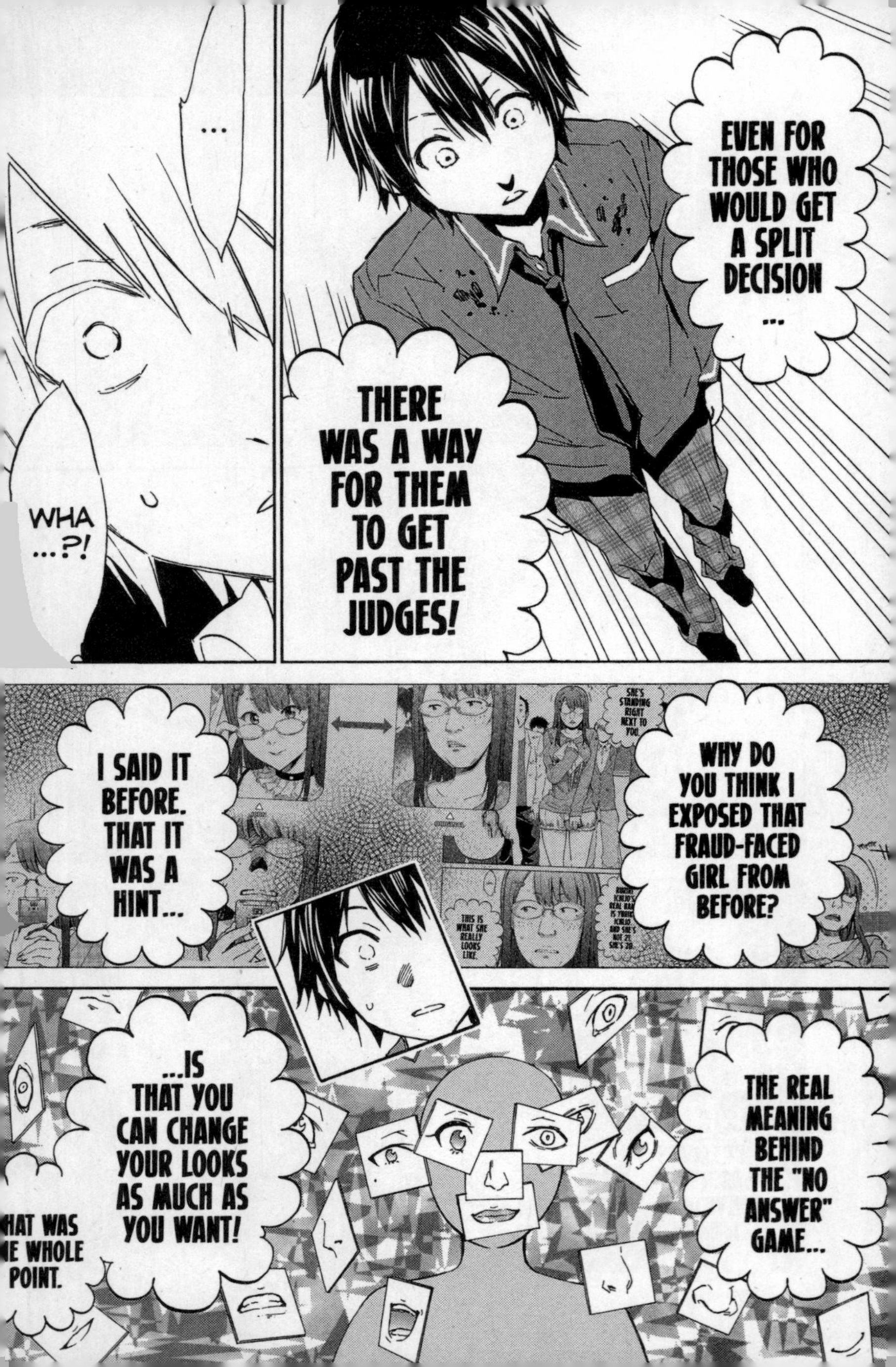
EVEN FOR THOSE WHO WOULD GET A SPLIT DECISION ...
THERE WAS A WAY FOR THEM TO GET PAST THE JUDGES!
...
WHA ...?!
SHE'S STANDING RIGHT NEXT TO YOU.
WHY DO YOU THINK I EXPOSED THAT FRAUD-FACED GIRL FROM BEFORE?
THIS IS WHAT SHE REALLY LOOKS LIKE.
I SAID IT BEFORE. THAT IT WAS A HINT...
THE REAL MEANING BEHIND THE "NO ANSWER" GAME...
...IS THAT YOU CAN CHANGE YOUR LOOKS AS MUCH AS YOU WANT!
HAT WAS IE WHOLE POINT.

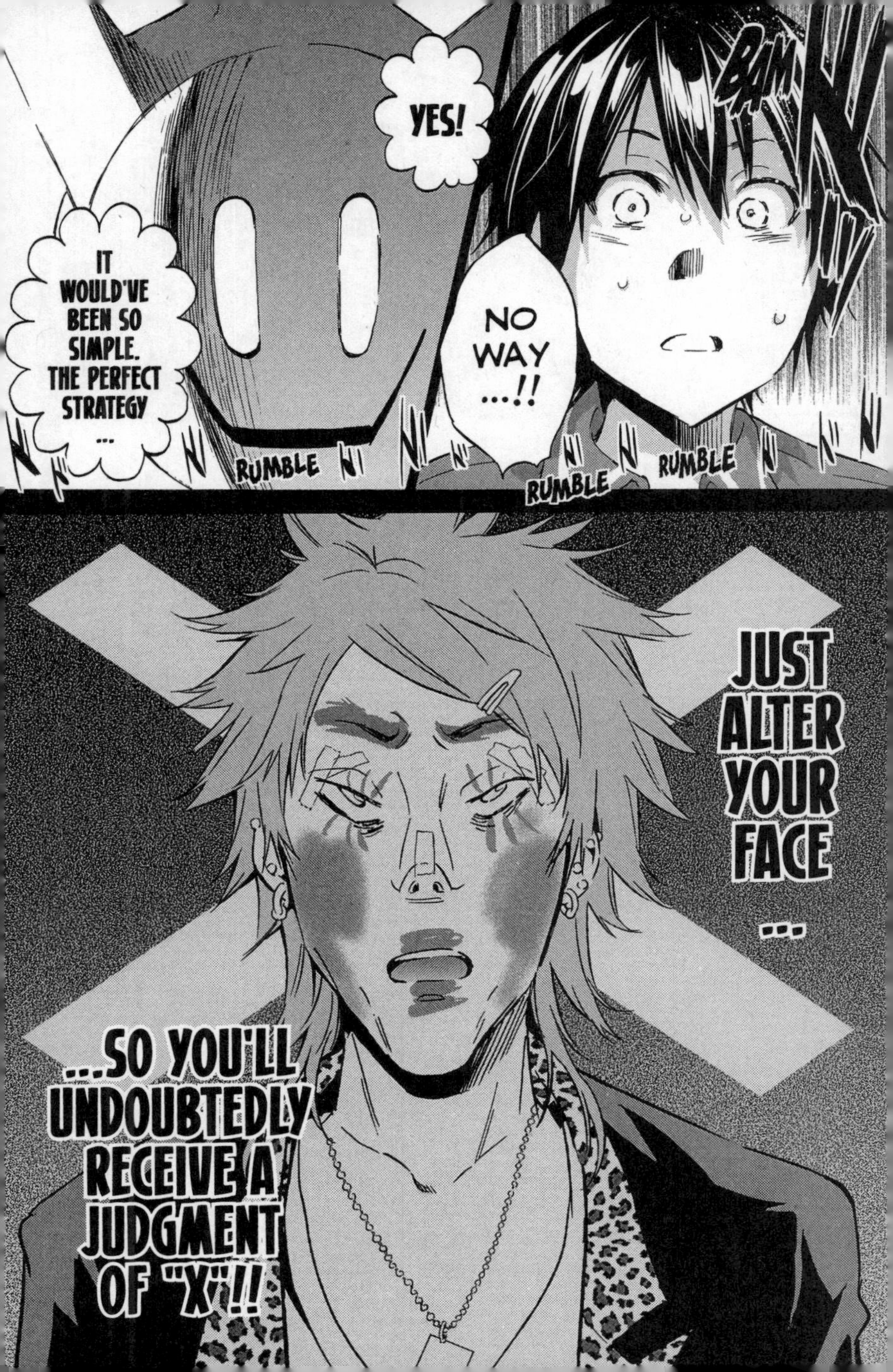
BAM
NO WAY ...!!
YES!
IT WOULD'VE BEEN SO SIMPLE. THE PERFECT STRATEGY ...
RUMBLE
RUMBLE
RUMBLE
JUST ALTER YOUR FACE ...
...SO YOU'LL UNDOUBTEDLY RECEIVE A JUDGMENT OF "X"!!

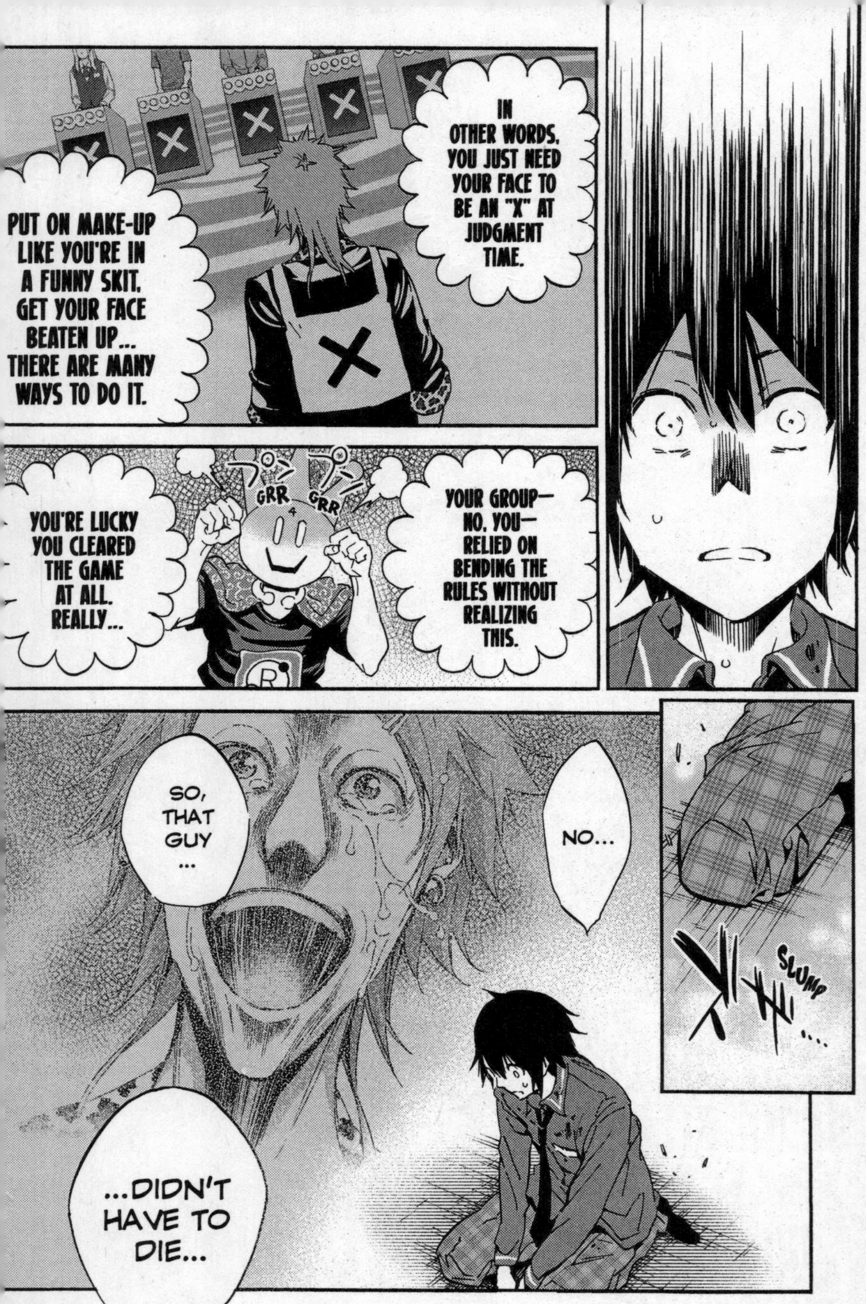
IN OTHER WORDS, YOU JUST NEED YOUR FACE TO BE AN "X" AT JUDGMENT TIME.
PUT ON MAKE-UP LIKE YOU'RE IN A FUNNY SKIT, GET YOUR FACE BEATEN UP... THERE ARE MANY WAYS TO DO IT.
YOUR GROUP— NO, YOU— RELIED ON BENDING THE RULES WITHOUT REALIZING THIS.
プンプン
GRR GRR
YOU'RE LUCKY YOU CLEARED THE GAME AT ALL. REALLY...
SLUMP...
NO...
SO, THAT GUY...
...DIDN'T HAVE TO DIE...

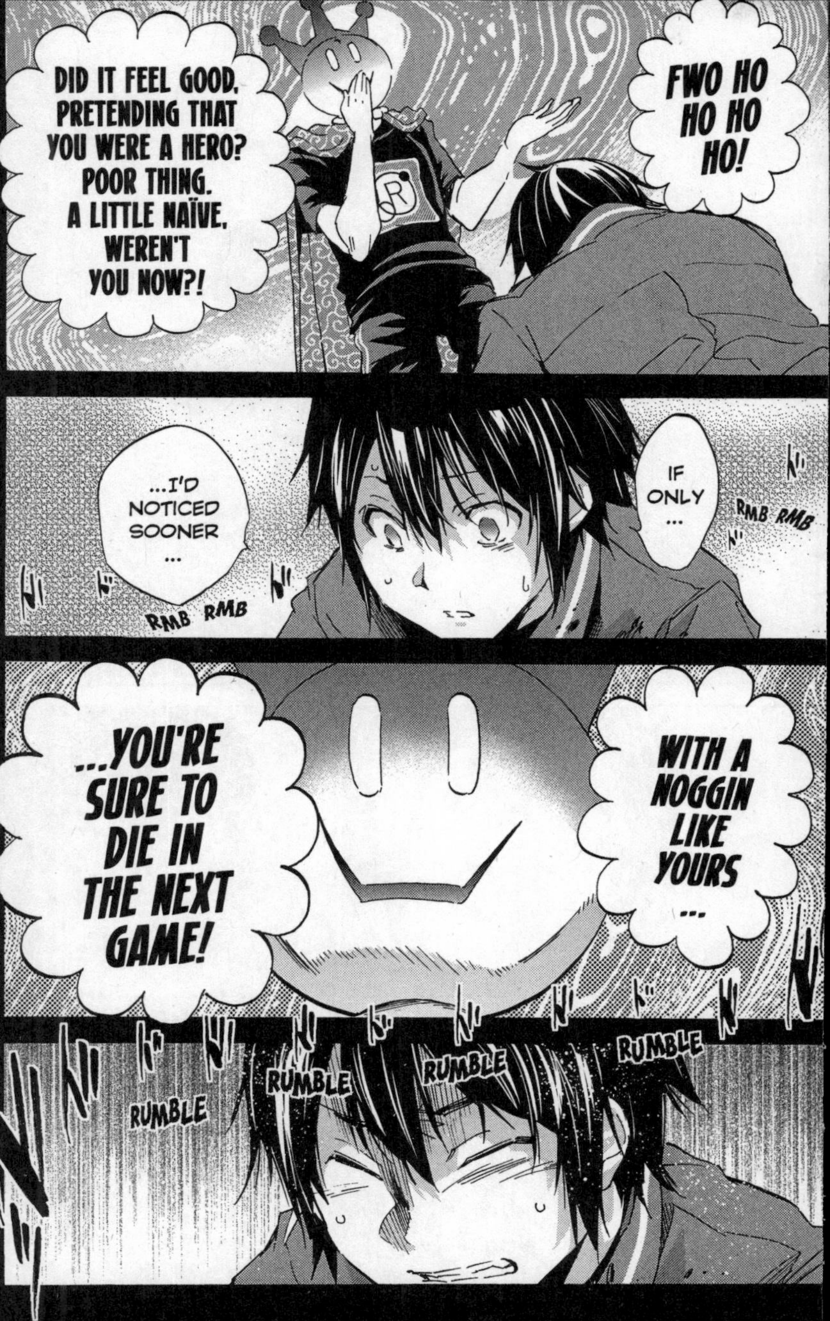
FWO HO HO HO HO!
DID IT FEEL GOOD, PRETENDING THAT YOU WERE A HERO? POOR THING. A LITTLE NAÏVE, WEREN'T YOU NOW?!
IF ONLY ...
RMB RMB
...I'D NOTICED SOONER ...
RMB RMB
WITH A NOGGIN LIKE YOURS ...
...YOU'RE SURE TO DIE IN THE NEXT GAME!
RUMBLE
RUMBLE
RUMBLE
RUMBLE

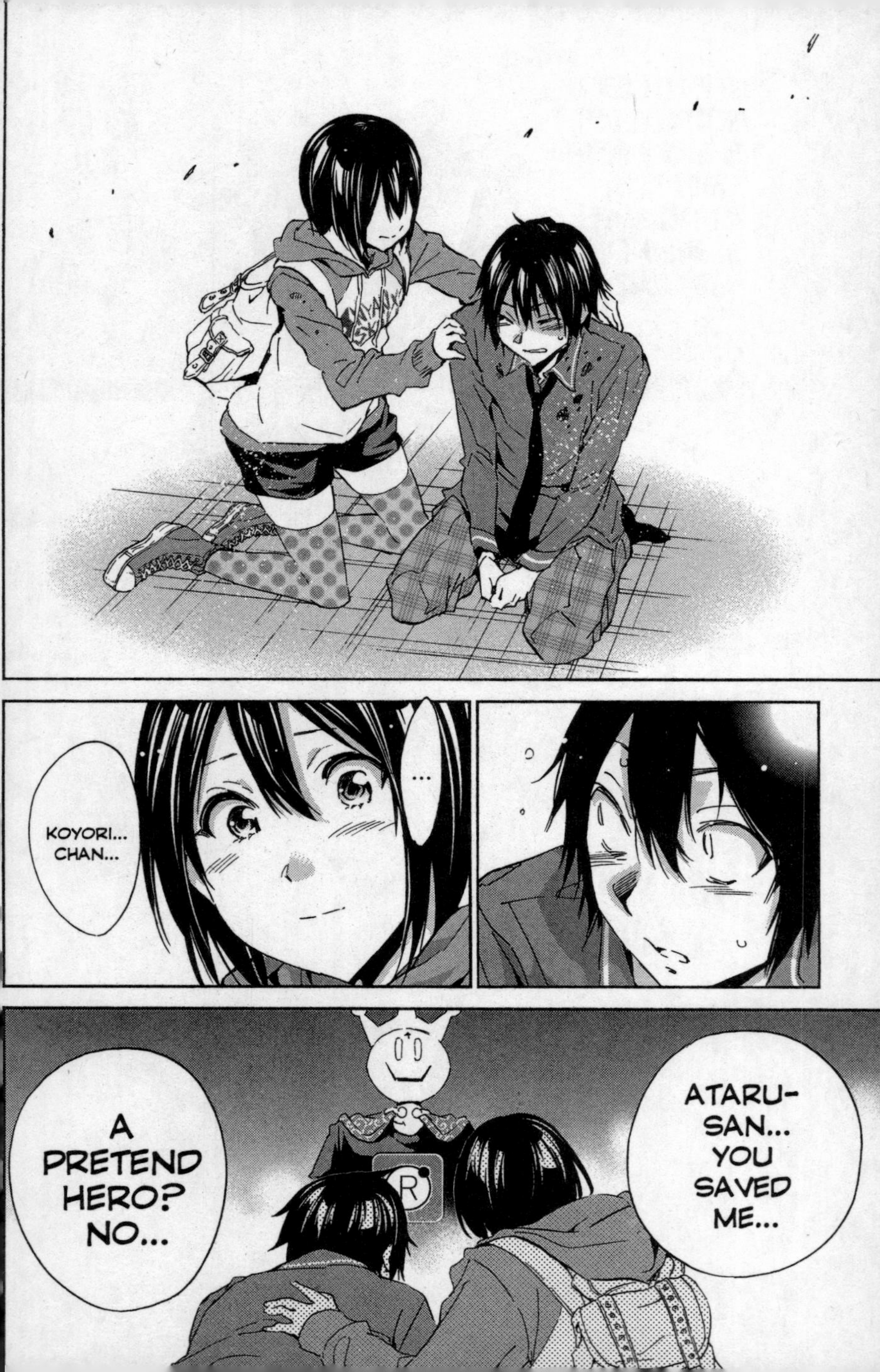
...
KOYORI... CHAN...
ATARU-SAN... YOU SAVED ME...
A PRETEND HERO? NO...

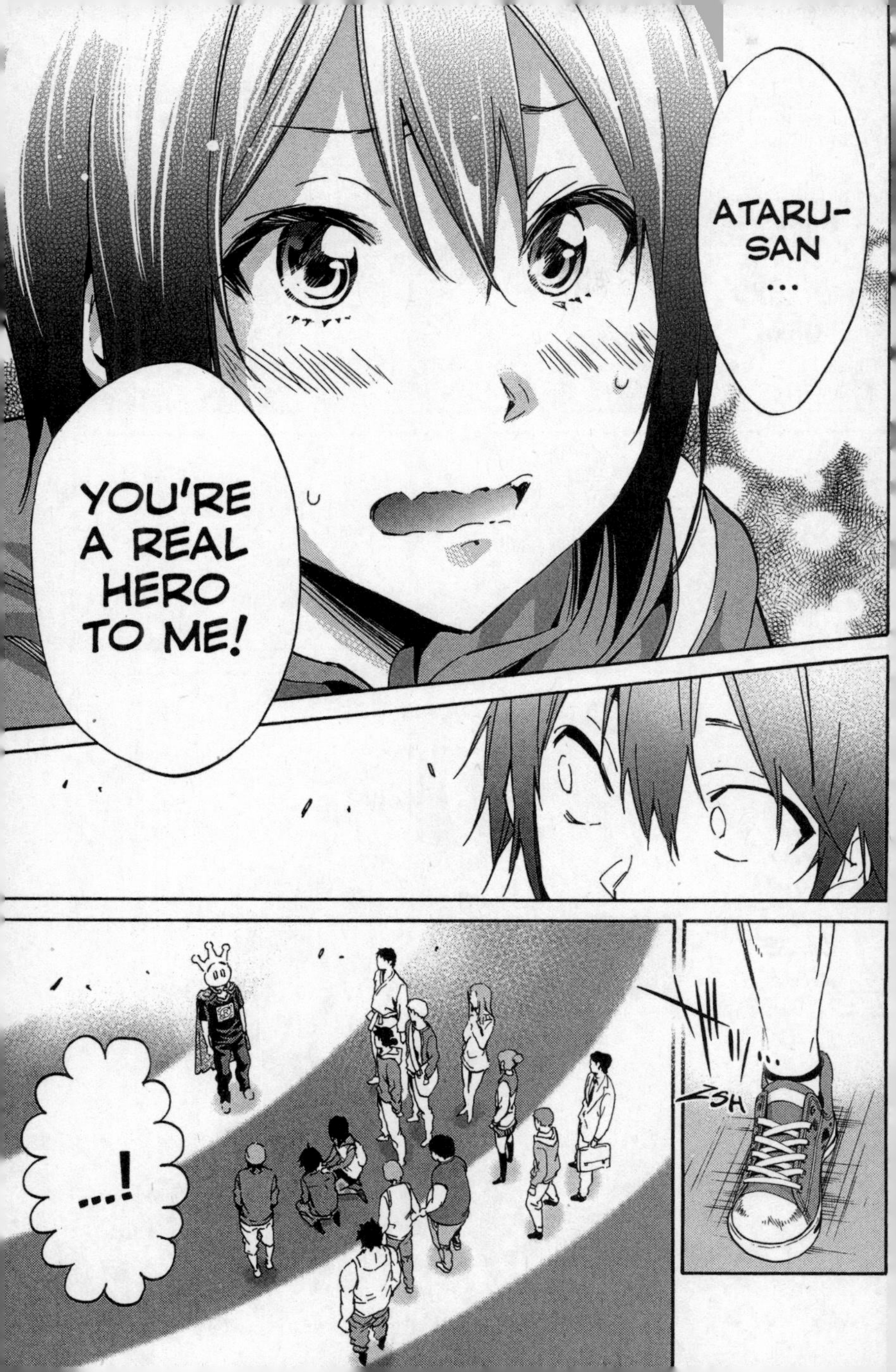
ATARU-SAN ...
YOU'RE A REAL HERO TO ME!
ZSH
...!

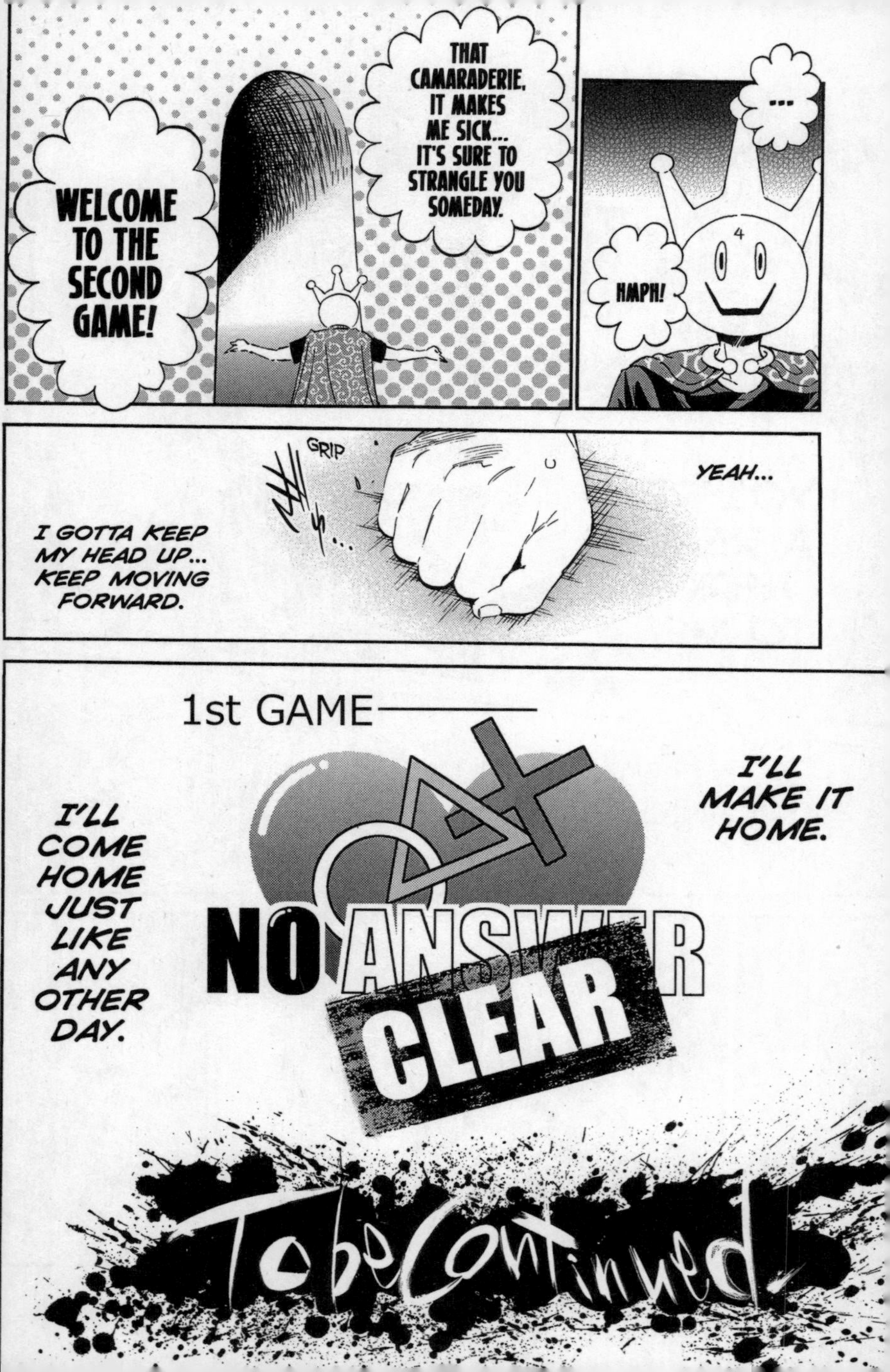
...
HMPH!
THAT CAMARADERIE, IT MAKES ME SICK... IT'S SURE TO STRANGLE YOU SOMEDAY.
WELCOME TO THE SECOND GAME!
YEAH...
GRIP
I GOTTA KEEP MY HEAD UP... KEEP MOVING FORWARD.
1st GAME
I'LL MAKE IT HOME.
I'LL COME HOME JUST LIKE ANY OTHER DAY.
NO ANSWER
CLEAR
To be Continued

CHAPTER 4
Please Share—RT Game

😺 PROFILE

NAME:	Koyori Kanda
SEX:	Female
DATE OF BIRTH:	May 6
AFFILIATION:	Junior High 3rd year
RELATIONSHIP STATUS:	Single

FOLLOWING:	**FOLLOWERS:**
82	2

ABOUT ME:

(=^・ω・^=) Meow! I love cats. I'm currently collecting NyanNyanSkull merchandise! Recently, I've started visiting cat cafes in my free time.

On RA, I mostly use the tweett feature. (I also collect cat pictures! LOL) If you like someone like me, please follow! ♪(ㅍ'ω'ㅍ)

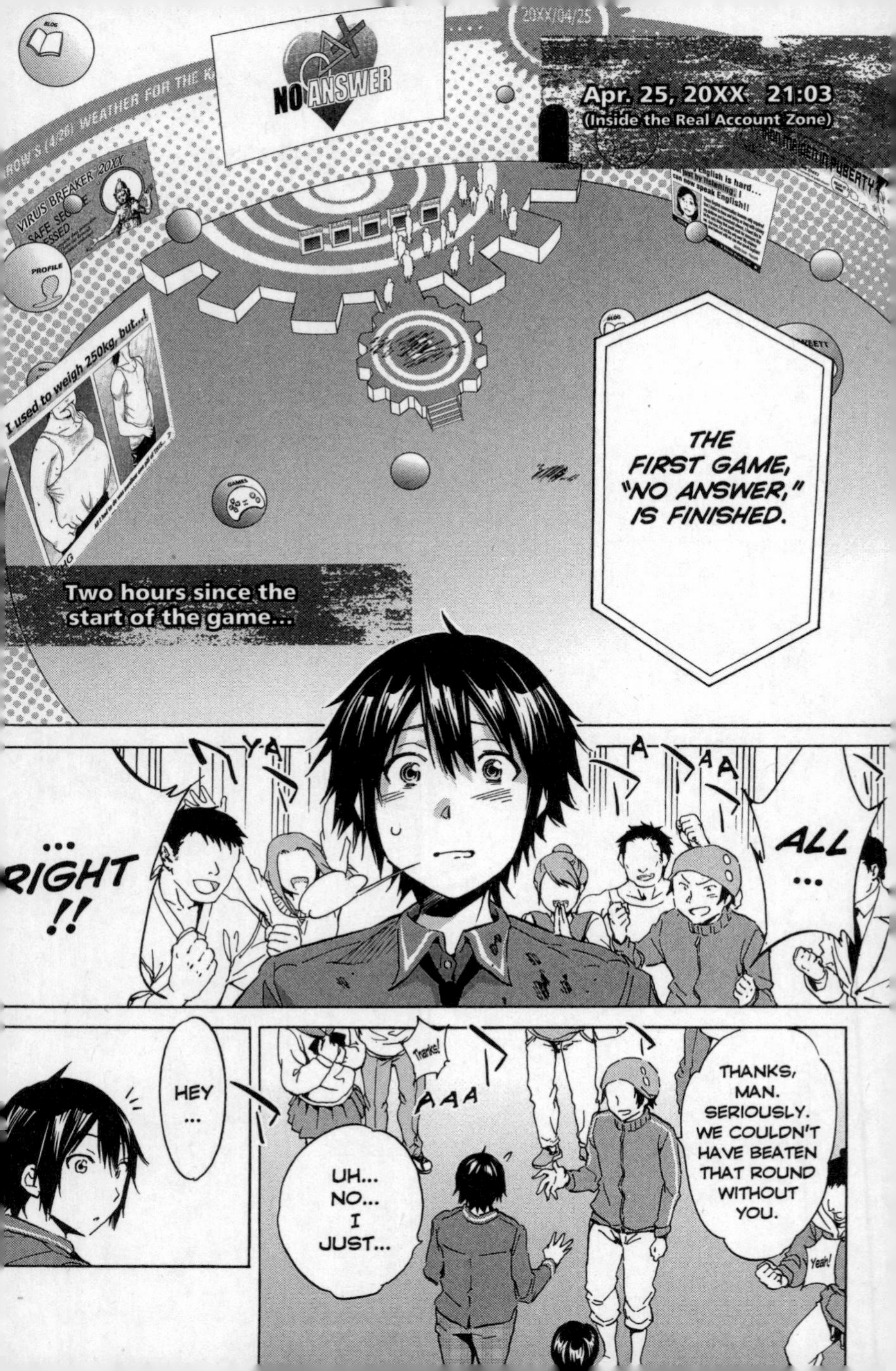
20XX/04/25
Apr. 25, 20XX 21:03
(Inside the Real Account Zone)
NO ANSWER
VIRUS BREAKER 20XX
PROFILE
BLOG
GAMES
I used to weigh 250kg, but...!
THE FIRST GAME, "NO ANSWER," IS FINISHED.
Two hours since the start of the game...
ALL ...
A
AA
YA
... RIGHT !!
THANKS, MAN. SERIOUSLY. WE COULDN'T HAVE BEATEN THAT ROUND WITHOUT YOU.
Yeah!
Thanks!
AAA
UH... NO... I JUST...
HEY ...

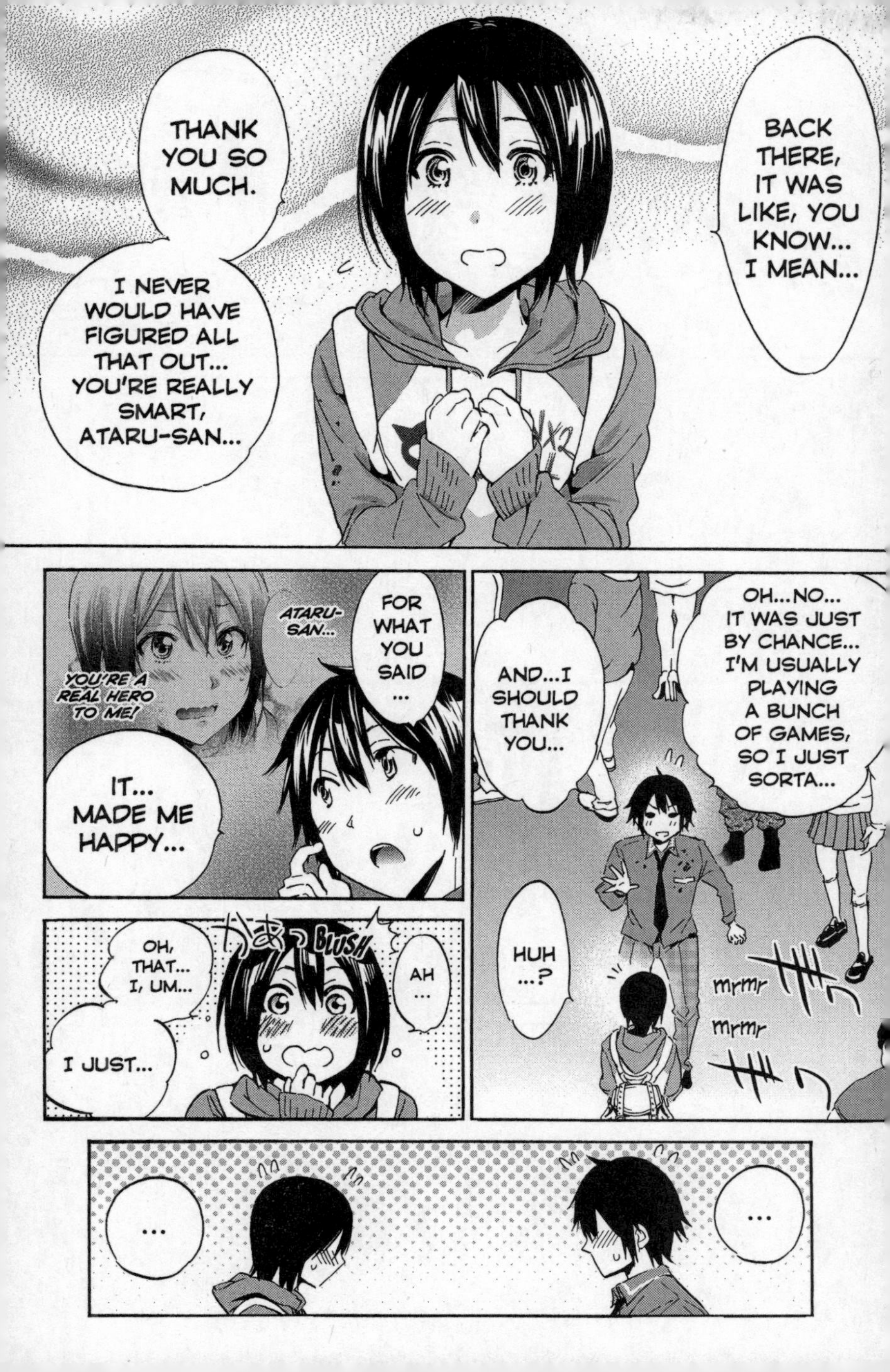
BACK THERE, IT WAS LIKE, YOU KNOW... I MEAN...
THANK YOU SO MUCH.
I NEVER WOULD HAVE FIGURED ALL THAT OUT... YOU'RE REALLY SMART, ATARU-SAN...
OH...NO... IT WAS JUST BY CHANCE... I'M USUALLY PLAYING A BUNCH OF GAMES, SO I JUST SORTA...
AND...I SHOULD THANK YOU...
HUH ...?
mrmr
mrmr
FOR WHAT YOU SAID ...
ATARU-SAN...
YOU'RE A REAL HERO TO ME!
IT... MADE ME HAPPY...
AH ...
BLUSH
OH, THAT... I, UM...
I JUST...
...
...

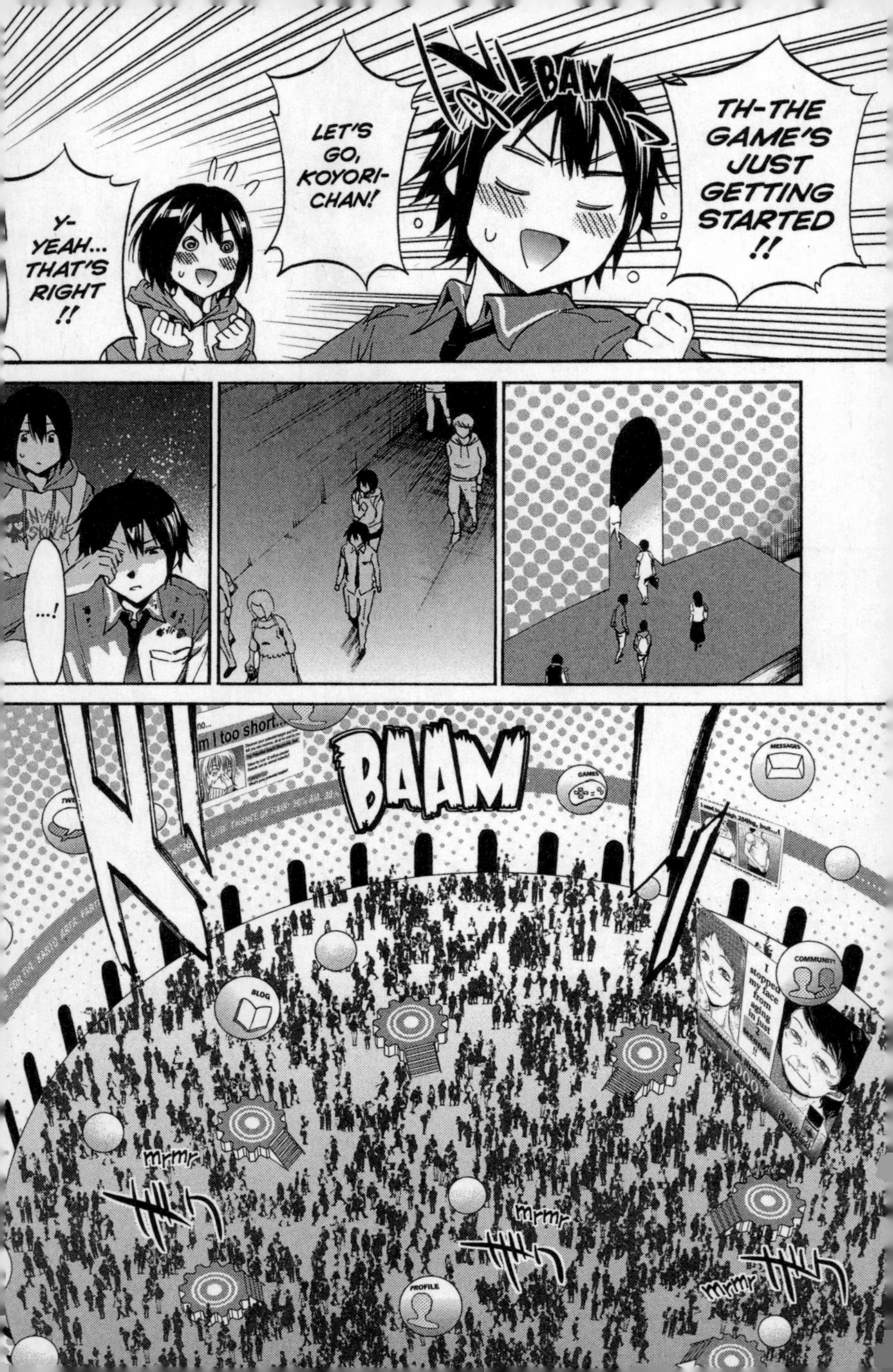
TH-THE GAME'S JUST GETTING STARTED!!
BAM
LET'S GO, KOYORI-CHAN!
Y-YEAH... THAT'S RIGHT!!
...!
BAAM
MESSAGES
GAMES
COMMUNITY
BLOG
PROFILE
mrmr
mrmr
mrmr

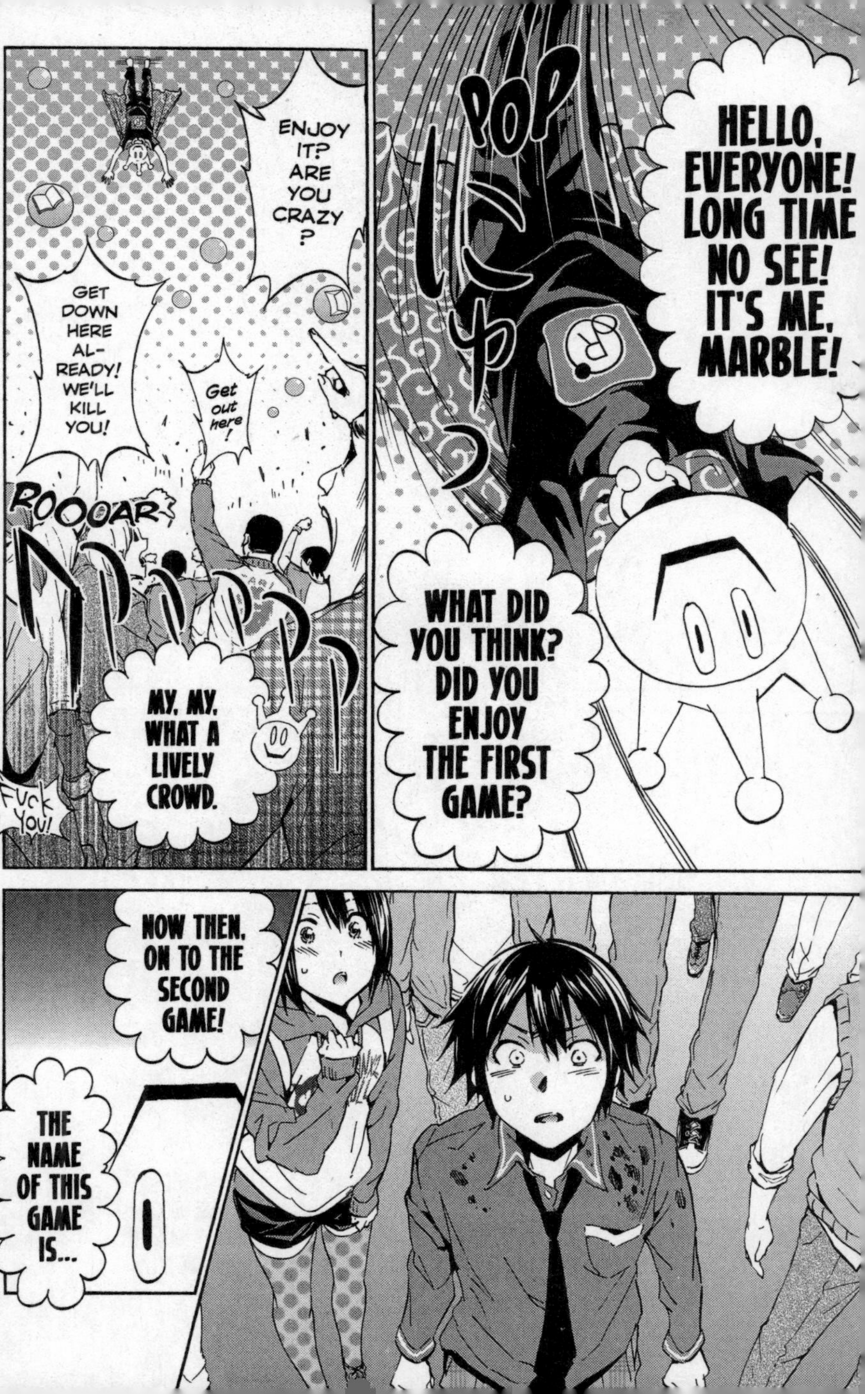
POP
HELLO, EVERYONE! LONG TIME NO SEE! IT'S ME, MARBLE!
WHAT DID YOU THINK? DID YOU ENJOY THE FIRST GAME?
ENJOY IT? ARE YOU CRAZY?
GET DOWN HERE AL-READY! WE'LL KILL YOU!
Get out here!
ROOOAR
MY, MY. WHAT A LIVELY CROWD.
Fuck You!
NOW THEN, ON TO THE SECOND GAME!
THE NAME OF THIS GAME IS...

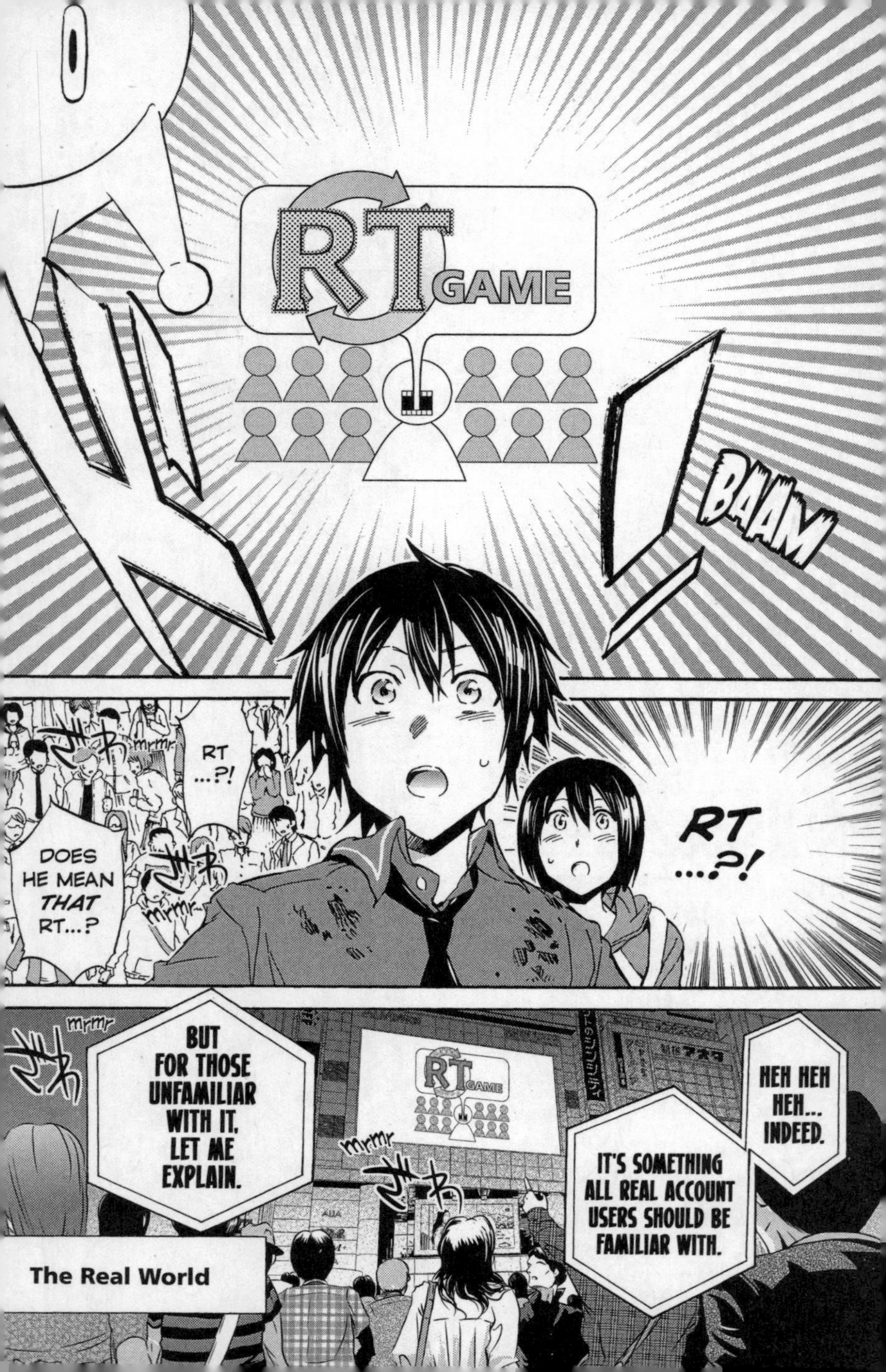

RT GAME
BAAM
RT ...?!
RT ...?!
mrmr
DOES HE MEAN THAT RT...?
mrmr
HEH HEH HEH... INDEED.
IT'S SOMETHING ALL REAL ACCOUNT USERS SHOULD BE FAMILIAR WITH.
mrmr
RT GAME
BUT FOR THOSE UNFAMILIAR WITH IT, LET ME EXPLAIN.
mrmr
The Real World

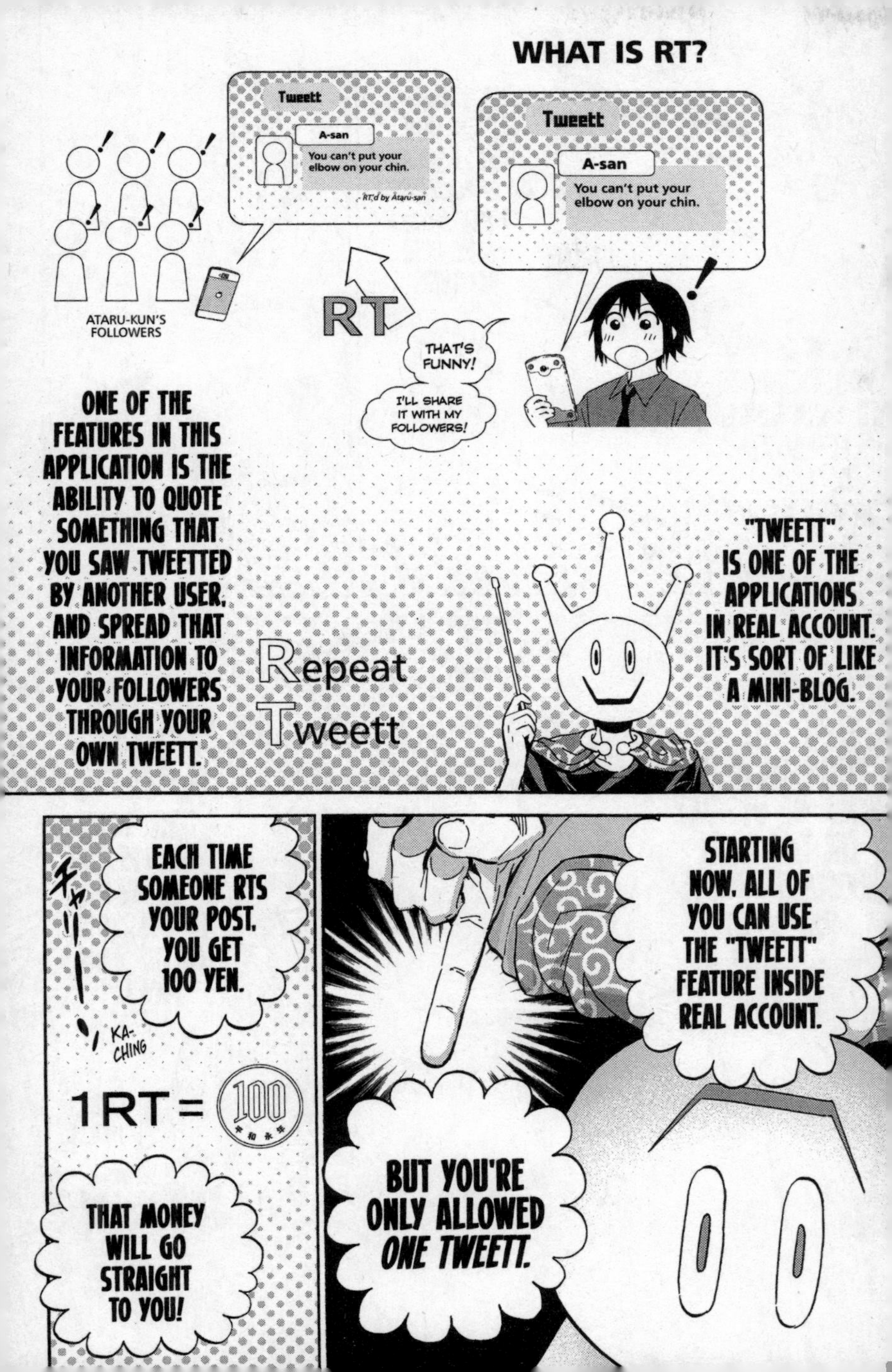
WHAT IS RT?
Tweett
A-san
You can't put your elbow on your chin.
THAT'S FUNNY!
I'LL SHARE IT WITH MY FOLLOWERS!
RT
Tweett
A-san
You can't put your elbow on your chin.
RT'd by Ataru-san
ATARU-KUN'S FOLLOWERS
"TWEETT" IS ONE OF THE APPLICATIONS IN REAL ACCOUNT. IT'S SORT OF LIKE A MINI-BLOG.
Repeat Tweett
ONE OF THE FEATURES IN THIS APPLICATION IS THE ABILITY TO QUOTE SOMETHING THAT YOU SAW TWEETTED BY ANOTHER USER, AND SPREAD THAT INFORMATION TO YOUR FOLLOWERS THROUGH YOUR OWN TWEETT.
STARTING NOW, ALL OF YOU CAN USE THE "TWEETT" FEATURE INSIDE REAL ACCOUNT.
BUT YOU'RE ONLY ALLOWED ONE TWEETT.
EACH TIME SOMEONE RTS YOUR POST, YOU GET 100 YEN.
KA-CHING
1RT = 100
THAT MONEY WILL GO STRAIGHT TO YOU!

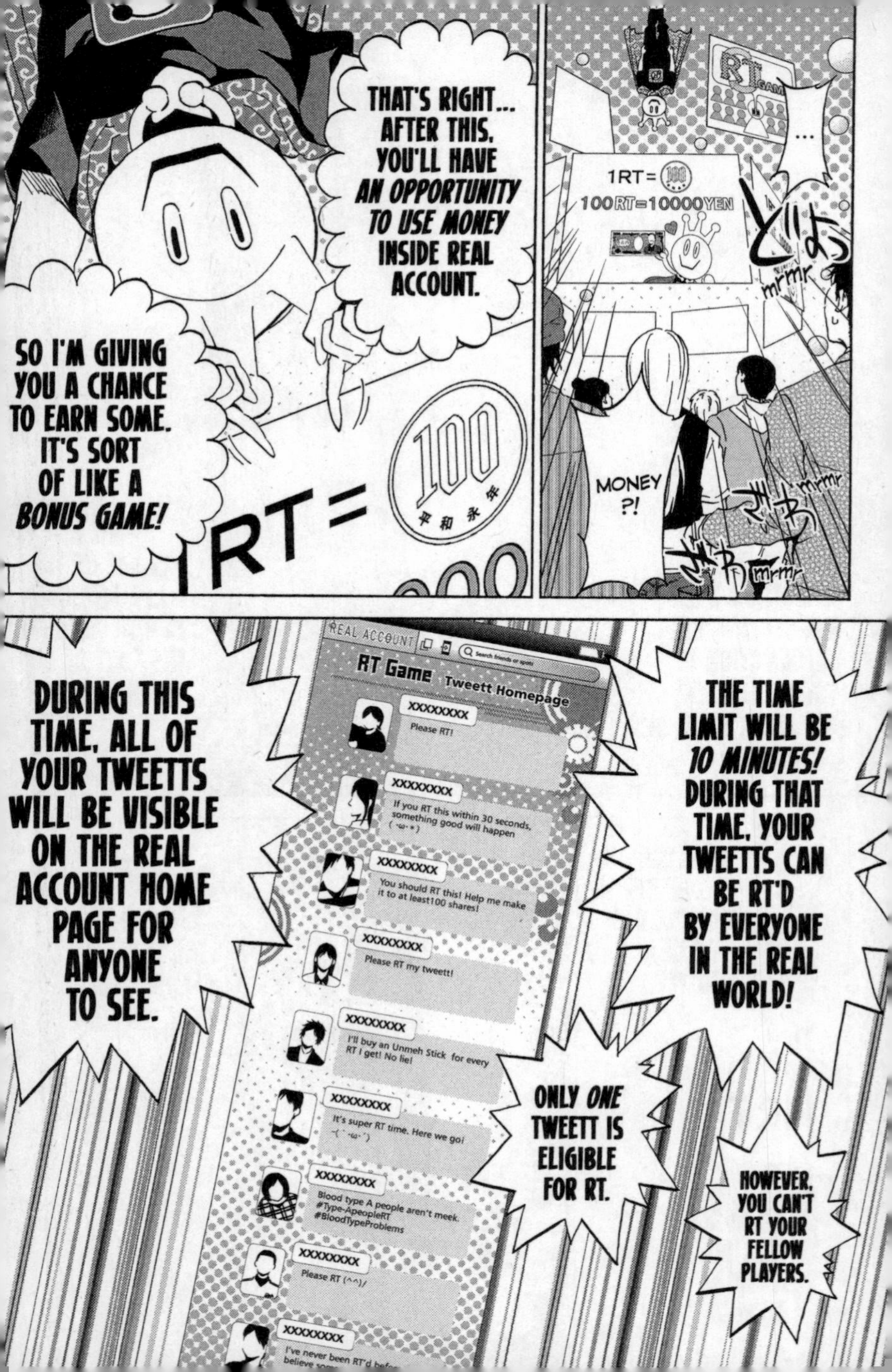
...
1RT = 100
100RT=10000YEN
mrmr
MONEY ?!
mrmr
mrmr
THAT'S RIGHT... AFTER THIS, YOU'LL HAVE AN OPPORTUNITY TO USE MONEY INSIDE REAL ACCOUNT.
SO I'M GIVING YOU A CHANCE TO EARN SOME. IT'S SORT OF LIKE A BONUS GAME!
1RT = 100
THE TIME LIMIT WILL BE 10 MINUTES! DURING THAT TIME, YOUR TWEETTS CAN BE RT'D BY EVERYONE IN THE REAL WORLD!
DURING THIS TIME, ALL OF YOUR TWEETTS WILL BE VISIBLE ON THE REAL ACCOUNT HOME PAGE FOR ANYONE TO SEE.
REAL ACCOUNT
RT Game
Tweett Homepage
XXXXXXXX
Please RT!
XXXXXXXX
If you RT this within 30 seconds, something good will happen
XXXXXXXX
You should RT this! Help me make it to at least100 shares!
XXXXXXXX
Please RT my tweett!
XXXXXXXX
I'll buy an Unmeh Stick for every RT I get! No lie!
XXXXXXXX
It's super RT time. Here we go!
XXXXXXXX
Blood type A people aren't meek. #Type-ApeopleRT #BloodTypeProblems
XXXXXXXX
Please RT (^^)/
XXXXXXXX
ONLY ONE TWEETT IS ELIGIBLE FOR RT.
HOWEVER, YOU CAN'T RT YOUR FELLOW PLAYERS.

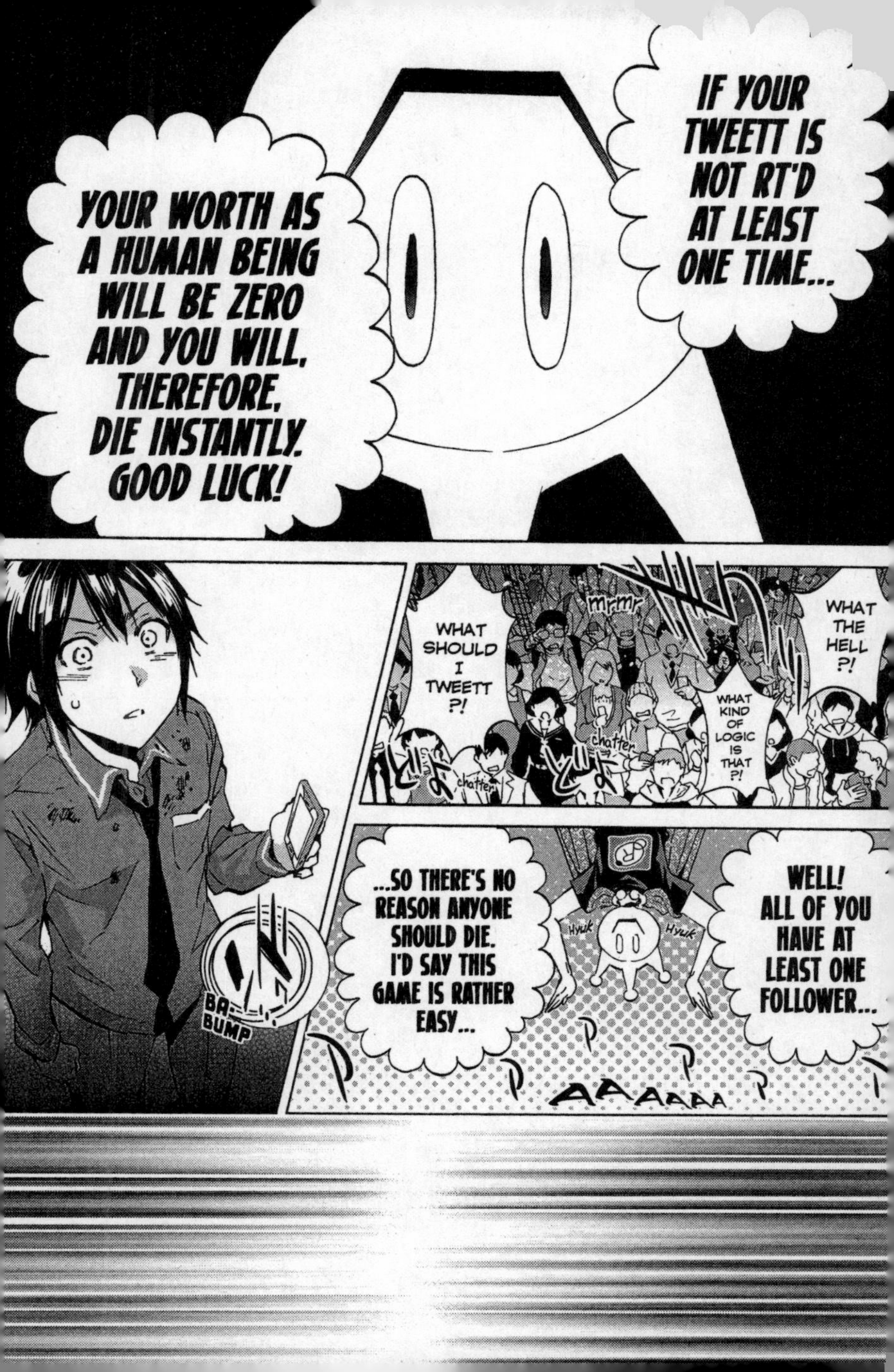
IF YOUR TWEETT IS NOT RT'D AT LEAST ONE TIME...
YOUR WORTH AS A HUMAN BEING WILL BE ZERO AND YOU WILL, THEREFORE, DIE INSTANTLY. GOOD LUCK!
mrmr
WHAT THE HELL?!
WHAT KIND OF LOGIC IS THAT?!
WHAT SHOULD I TWEETT?!
chatter
chatter
WELL! ALL OF YOU HAVE AT LEAST ONE FOLLOWER...
...SO THERE'S NO REASON ANYONE SHOULD DIE. I'D SAY THIS GAME IS RATHER EASY...
Hyuk
Hyuk
AAAAAA
BA-BUMP

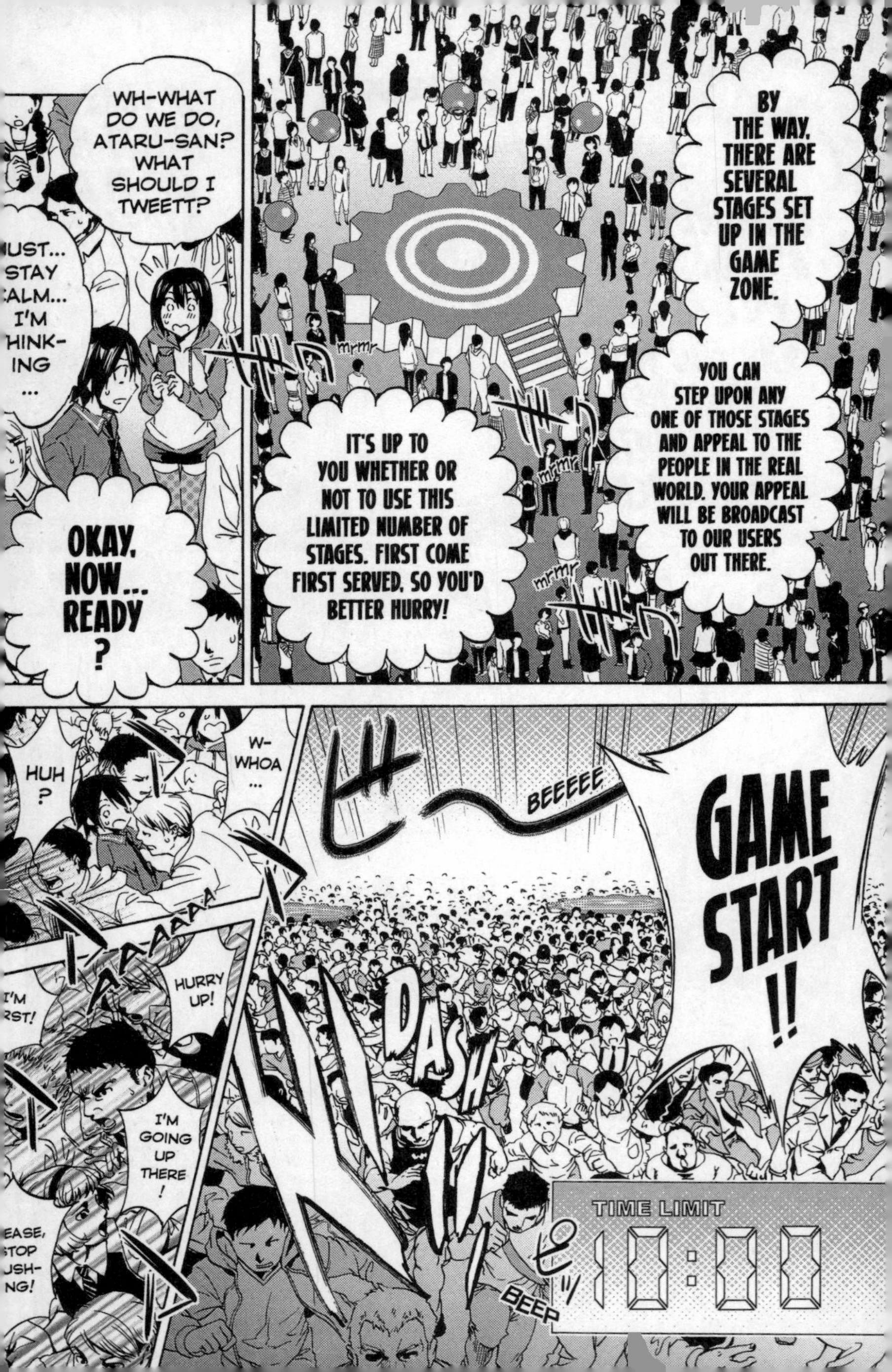
BY THE WAY, THERE ARE SEVERAL STAGES SET UP IN THE GAME ZONE.
YOU CAN STEP UPON ANY ONE OF THOSE STAGES AND APPEAL TO THE PEOPLE IN THE REAL WORLD. YOUR APPEAL WILL BE BROADCAST TO OUR USERS OUT THERE.
mrmr
mrmr
mrmr
IT'S UP TO YOU WHETHER OR NOT TO USE THIS LIMITED NUMBER OF STAGES. FIRST COME FIRST SERVED, SO YOU'D BETTER HURRY!
WH-WHAT DO WE DO, ATARU-SAN? WHAT SHOULD I TWEETT?
UST... STAY ALM... I'M HINK-ING ...
OKAY, NOW... READY ?
GAME START !!
BEEEEE
DASH
TIME LIMIT
10:00
BEEP
W-WHOA ...
HUH ?
HURRY UP!
I'M RST!
I'M GOING UP THERE !
EASE, STOP USH-NG!

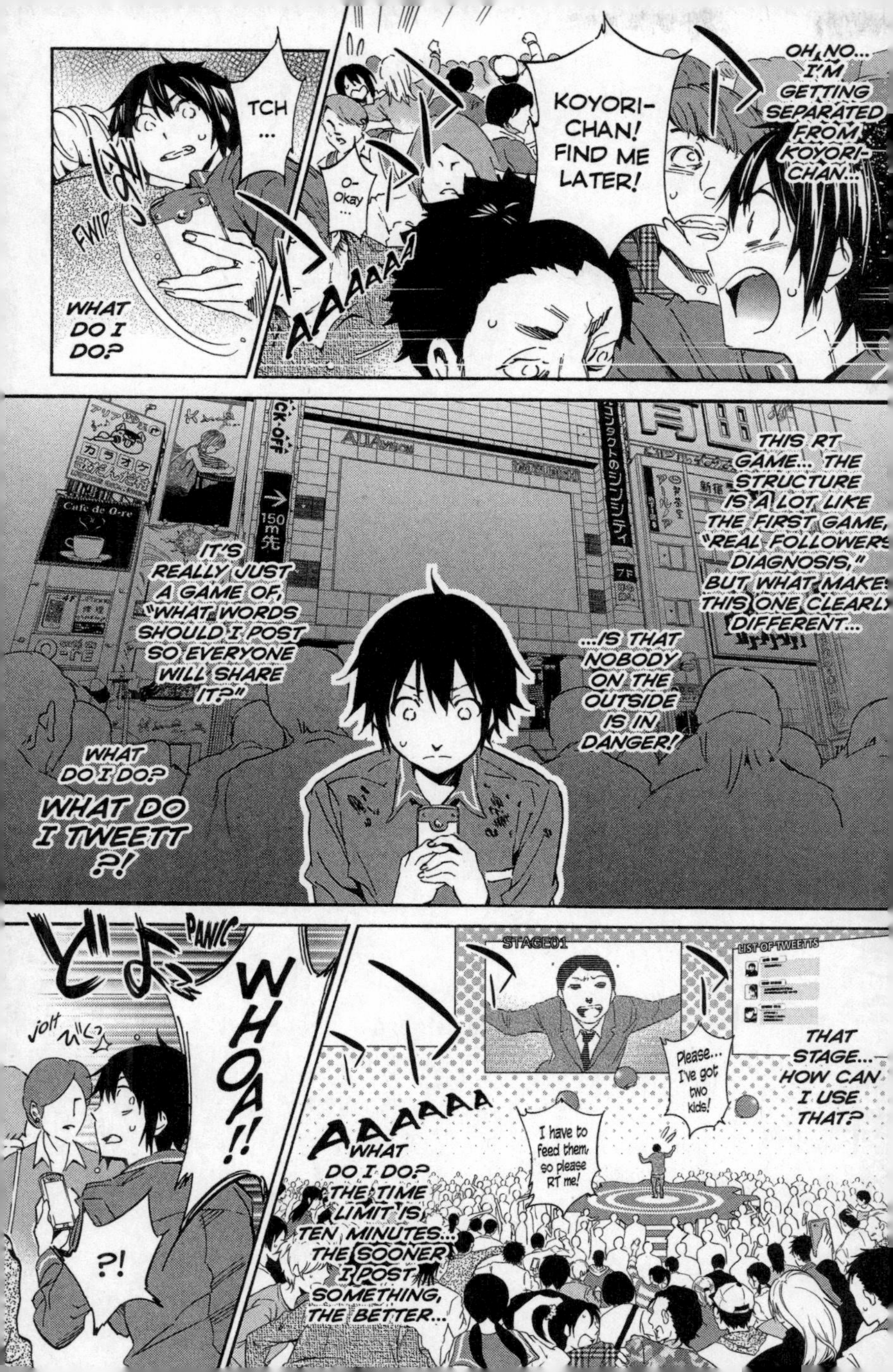
OH, NO... I'M GETTING SEPARATED FROM KOYORI-CHAN...
KOYORI-CHAN! FIND ME LATER!
O-Okay...
AAAAAAA
TCH ...
FWIP
WHAT DO I DO?
THIS RT GAME... THE STRUCTURE IS A LOT LIKE THE FIRST GAME, "REAL FOLLOWERS DIAGNOSIS," BUT WHAT MAKES THIS ONE CLEARLY DIFFERENT...
...IS THAT NOBODY ON THE OUTSIDE IS IN DANGER!
IT'S REALLY JUST A GAME OF, "WHAT WORDS SHOULD I POST SO EVERYONE WILL SHARE IT?"
WHAT DO I DO?
WHAT DO I TWEETT ?!
STAGE01
LIST OF TWEETTS
THAT STAGE... HOW CAN I USE THAT?
Please... I've got two kids!
I have to feed them, so please RT me!
AAAAAA
WHAT DO I DO? THE TIME LIMIT IS TEN MINUTES... THE SOONER I POST SOMETHING, THE BETTER...
どよっ
PANIC
WHOA!!
jolt
びくっ
?!

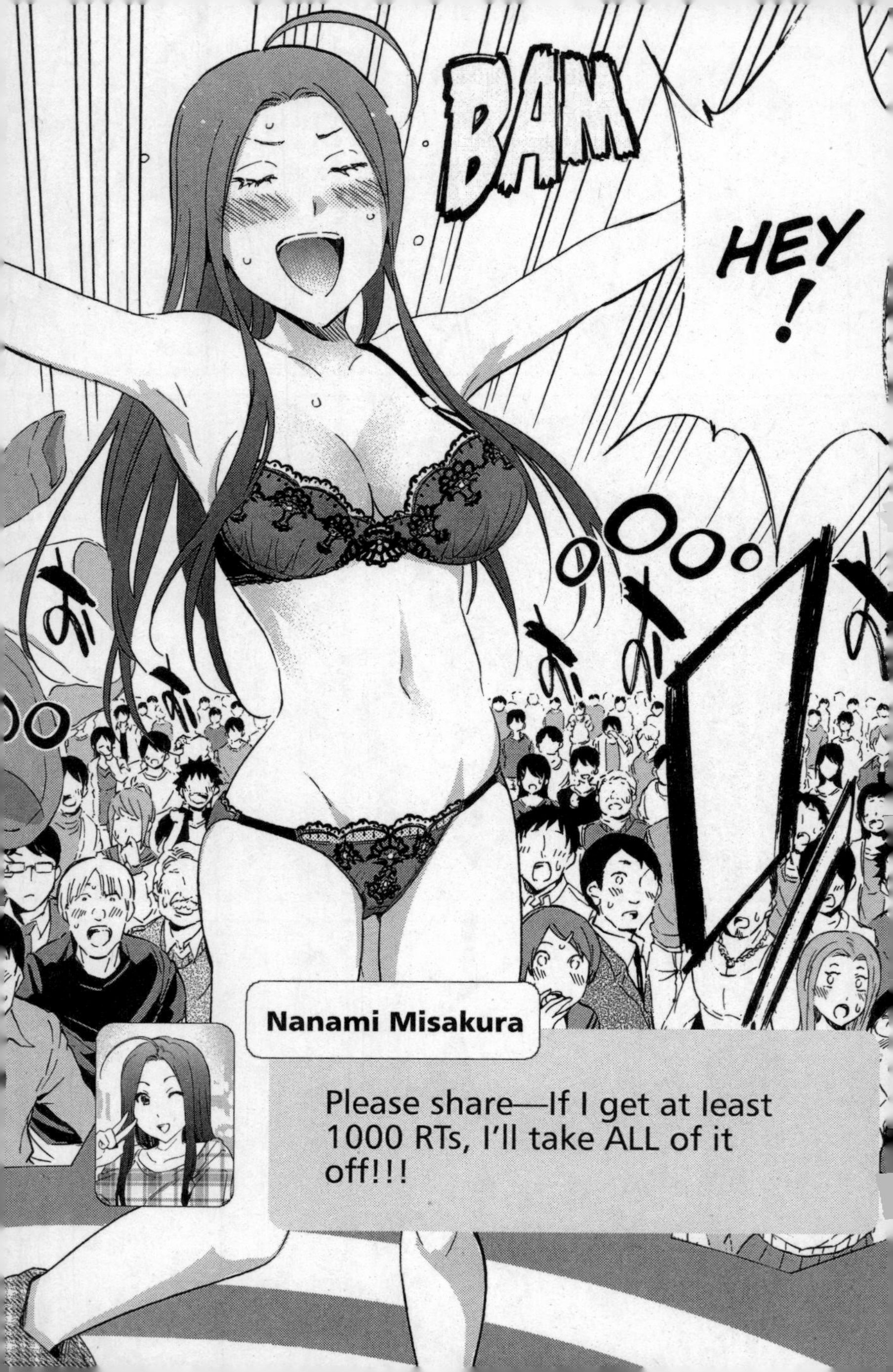
BAM
HEY!
OOOO
Nanami Misakura
Please share—If I get at least 1000 RTs, I'll take ALL of it off!!!

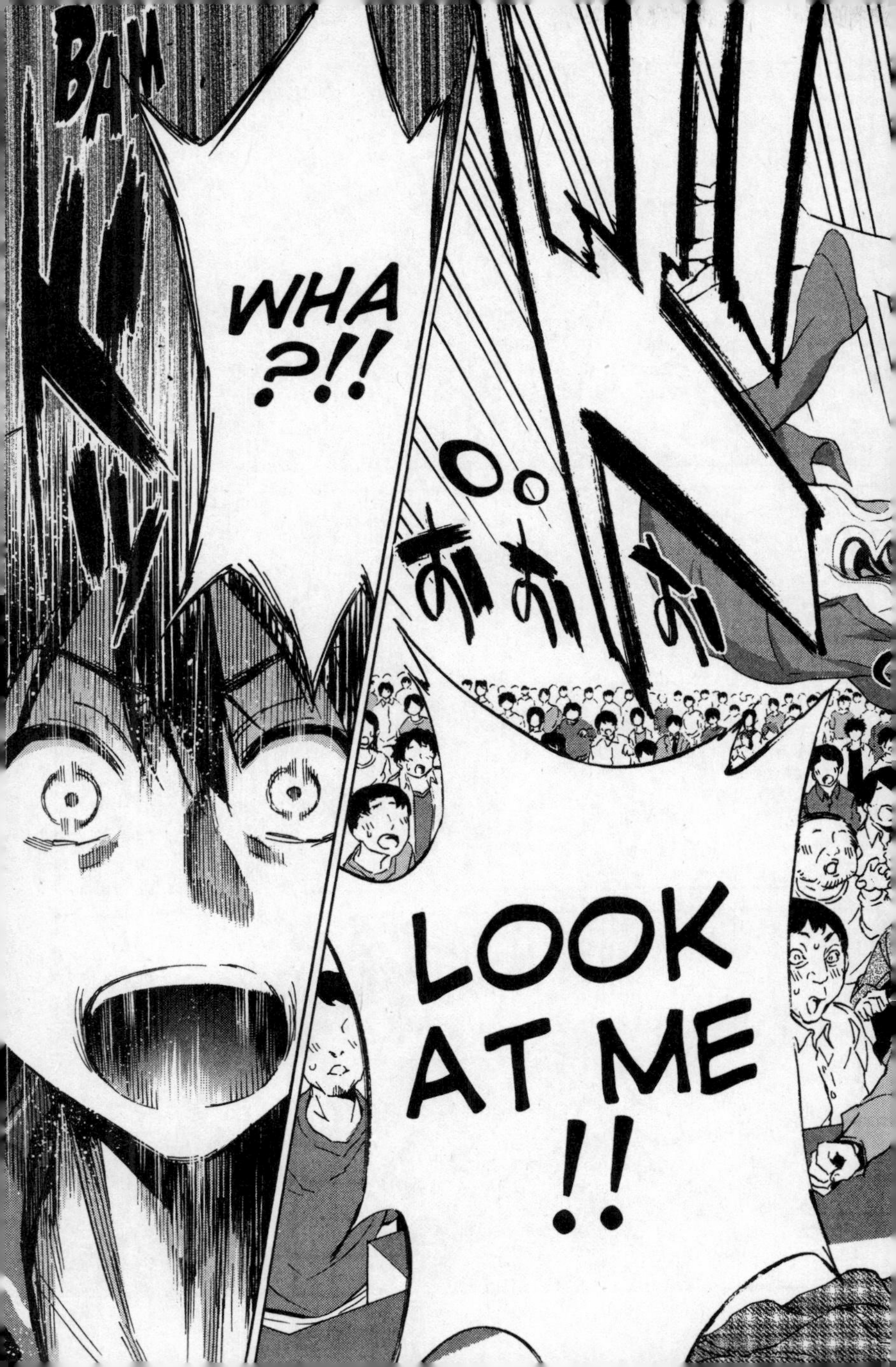
O。
おおお
LOOK AT ME!!
BAM
WHA?!!

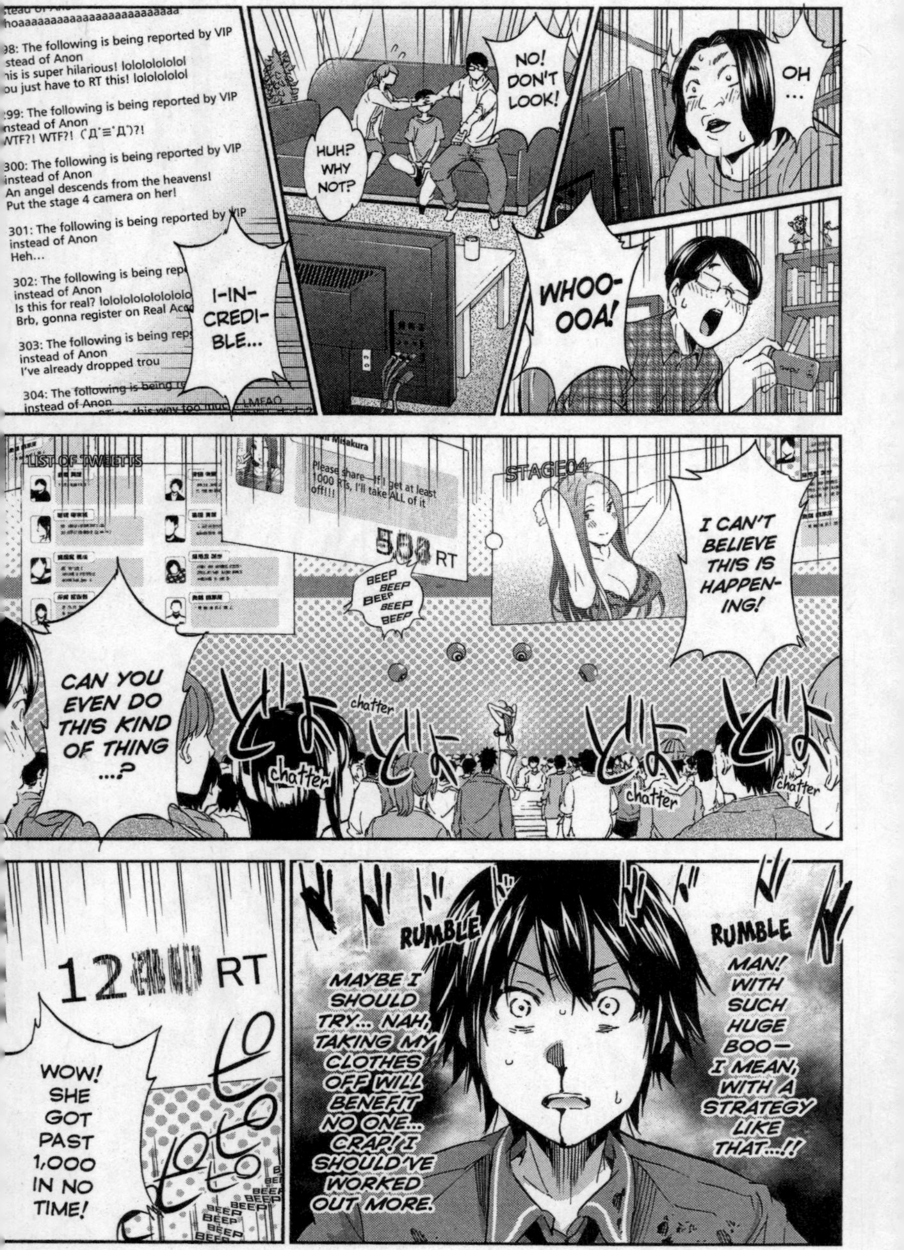
OH ...
WHOOO-OOA!
NO! DON'T LOOK!
HUH? WHY NOT?
hoaaaaaaaaaaaaaaaaaaaaaaaaaaa
98: The following is being reported by VIP
stead of Anon
his is super hilarious! lolololololol
ou just have to RT this! lolololololol
299: The following is being reported by VIP
nstead of Anon
WTF?! WTF?! (´Д`≡´Д`)?!
300: The following is being reported by VIP
instead of Anon
An angel descends from the heavens!
Put the stage 4 camera on her!
301: The following is being reported by VIP
instead of Anon
Heh...
302: The following is being repo
instead of Anon
Is this for real? lolololololololo
Brb, gonna register on Real Acc
303: The following is being rep
instead of Anon
I've already dropped trou
304: The following is being re
instead of Anon
I-IN-CREDI-BLE...
LIST OF TWEETTS
Please share—if I get at least 1000 RTs, I'll take ALL of it off!!!
RT
BEEP BEEP BEEP BEEP BEEP
STAGE04
I CAN'T BELIEVE THIS IS HAPPEN-ING!
CAN YOU EVEN DO THIS KIND OF THING ...?
chatter
chatter
chatter
chatter
RUMBLE
RUMBLE
MAN! WITH SUCH HUGE BOO— I MEAN, WITH A STRATEGY LIKE THAT...!?
MAYBE I SHOULD TRY... NAH, TAKING MY CLOTHES OFF WILL BENEFIT NO ONE... CRAP! I SHOULD'VE WORKED OUT MORE.
RT
WOW! SHE GOT PAST 1,000 IN NO TIME!
BEEP BEEP BEEP BEEP BEEP

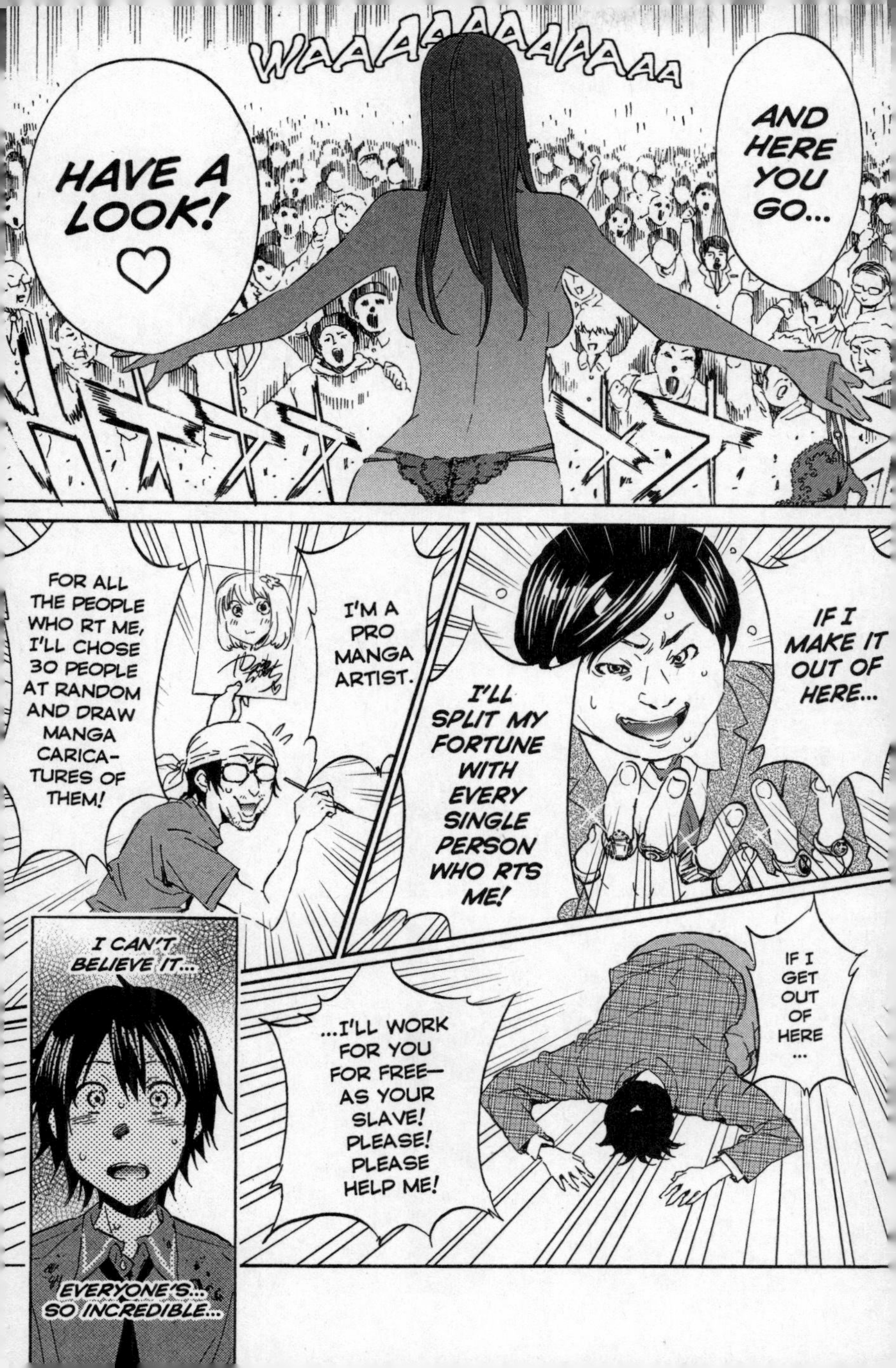
WAAAAAAAAAAAA
AND HERE YOU GO...
HAVE A LOOK! ♡
IF I MAKE IT OUT OF HERE...
I'LL SPLIT MY FORTUNE WITH EVERY SINGLE PERSON WHO RTS ME!
I'M A PRO MANGA ARTIST.
FOR ALL THE PEOPLE WHO RT ME, I'LL CHOSE 30 PEOPLE AT RANDOM AND DRAW MANGA CARICA-TURES OF THEM!
IF I GET OUT OF HERE ...
...I'LL WORK FOR YOU FOR FREE—AS YOUR SLAVE! PLEASE! PLEASE HELP ME!
I CAN'T BELIEVE IT...
EVERYONE'S... SO INCREDIBLE...

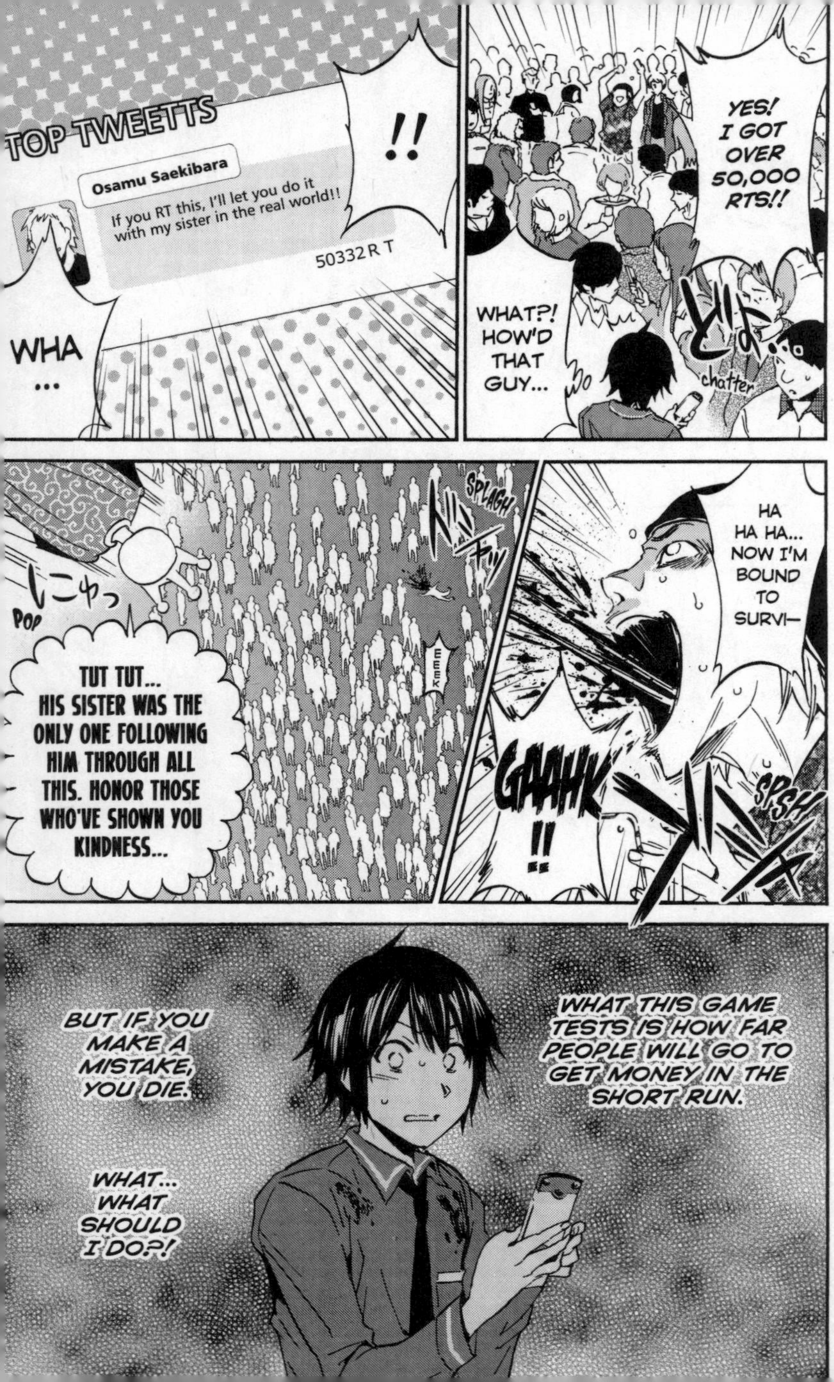

YES! I GOT OVER 50,000 RTS!!
WHAT?! HOW'D THAT GUY...
chatter
!!
TOP TWEETTS
Osamu Saekibara
If you RT this, I'll let you do it with my sister in the real world!!
50332 R T
WHA ...
HA HA HA... NOW I'M BOUND TO SURVI—
GAAHK!!
SPSH
SPLAGH
EEEK
POP
TUT TUT... HIS SISTER WAS THE ONLY ONE FOLLOWING HIM THROUGH ALL THIS. HONOR THOSE WHO'VE SHOWN YOU KINDNESS...
WHAT THIS GAME TESTS IS HOW FAR PEOPLE WILL GO TO GET MONEY IN THE SHORT RUN.
BUT IF YOU MAKE A MISTAKE, YOU DIE.
WHAT... WHAT SHOULD I DO?!

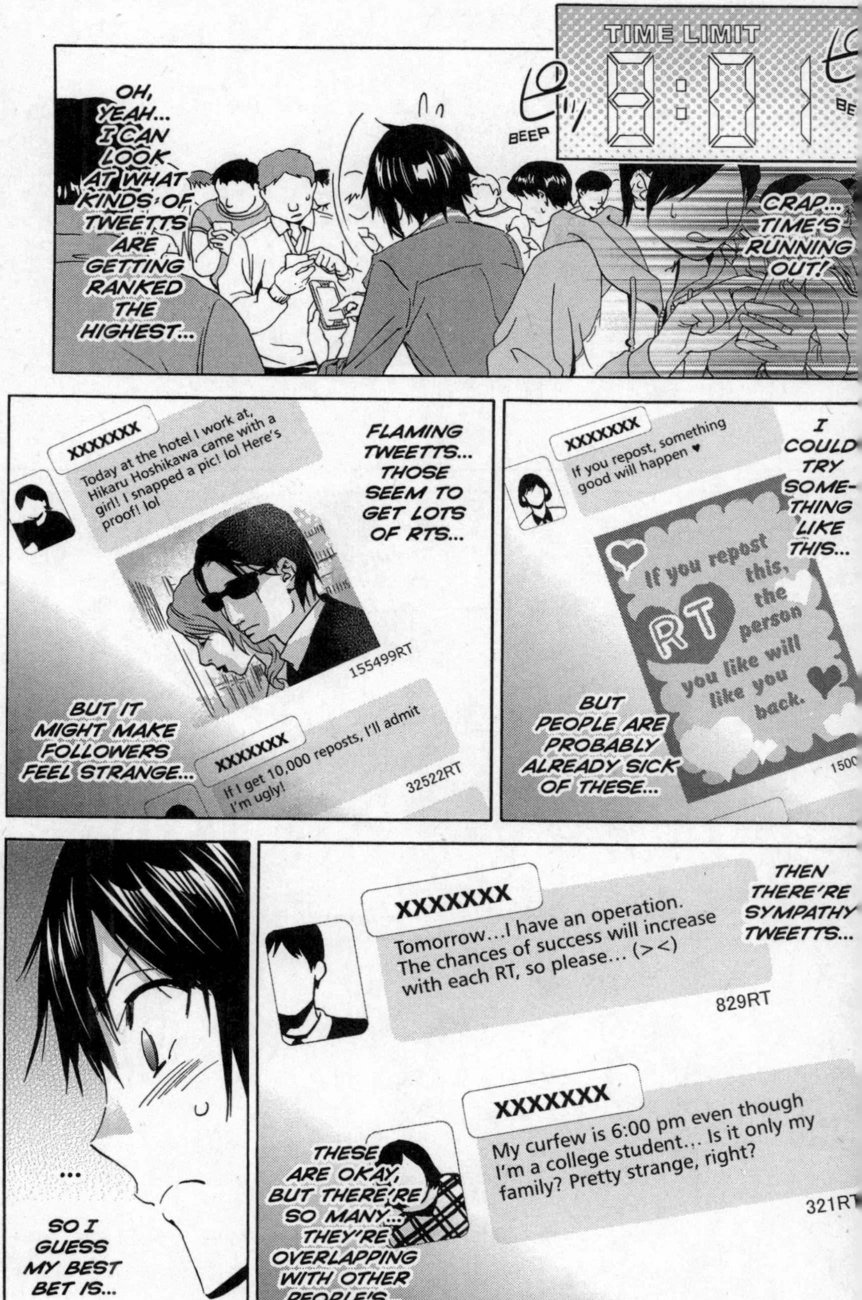
TIME LIMIT
8:01
BEEP
BEEP
CRAP... TIME'S RUNNING OUT!
OH, YEAH... I CAN LOOK AT WHAT KINDS OF TWEETTS ARE GETTING RANKED THE HIGHEST...
I COULD TRY SOMETHING LIKE THIS...
XXXXXXX
If you repost, something good will happen ♥
If you repost this, the person you like will like you back.
RT
BUT PEOPLE ARE PROBABLY ALREADY SICK OF THESE...
FLAMING TWEETTS... THOSE SEEM TO GET LOTS OF RTS...
XXXXXXX
Today at the hotel I work at, Hikaru Hoshikawa came with a girl! I snapped a pic! lol Here's proof! lol
155499RT
BUT IT MIGHT MAKE FOLLOWERS FEEL STRANGE...
XXXXXXX
If I get 10,000 reposts, I'll admit I'm ugly!
32522RT
THEN THERE'RE SYMPATHY TWEETTS...
XXXXXXX
Tomorrow...I have an operation. The chances of success will increase with each RT, so please... (><)
829RT
XXXXXXX
My curfew is 6:00 pm even though I'm a college student... Is it only my family? Pretty strange, right?
321RT
THESE ARE OKAY, BUT THERE'RE SO MANY... THEY'RE OVERLAPPING WITH OTHER PEOPLE'S...
...
SO I GUESS MY BEST BET IS...

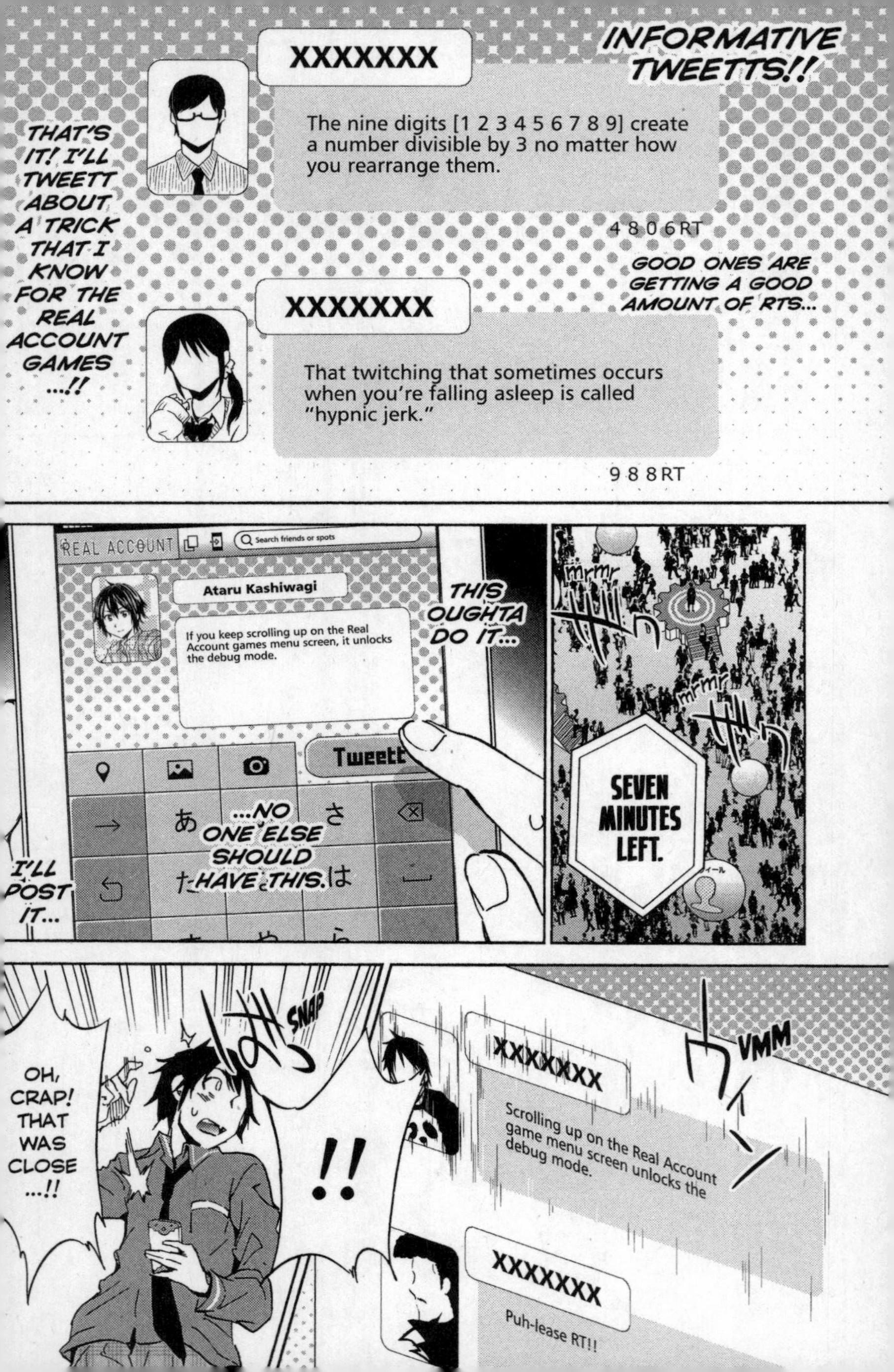
INFORMATIVE TWEETTS!!
XXXXXXX
The nine digits [1 2 3 4 5 6 7 8 9] create a number divisible by 3 no matter how you rearrange them.
4806RT
GOOD ONES ARE GETTING A GOOD AMOUNT OF RTS...
XXXXXXX
That twitching that sometimes occurs when you're falling asleep is called "hypnic jerk."
988RT
THAT'S IT! I'LL TWEETT ABOUT A TRICK THAT I KNOW FOR THE REAL ACCOUNT GAMES ...!!
mrmr
mrmr
SEVEN MINUTES LEFT.
REAL ACCOUNT
Search friends or spots
Ataru Kashiwagi
If you keep scrolling up on the Real Account games menu screen, it unlocks the debug mode.
Tweett
THIS OUGHTA DO IT...
...NO ONE ELSE SHOULD HAVE THIS.
I'LL POST IT...
VMM
XXXXXXX
Scrolling up on the Real Account game menu screen unlocks the debug mode.
XXXXXXX
Puh-lease RT!!
!!
SNAP
OH, CRAP! THAT WAS CLOSE ...!!

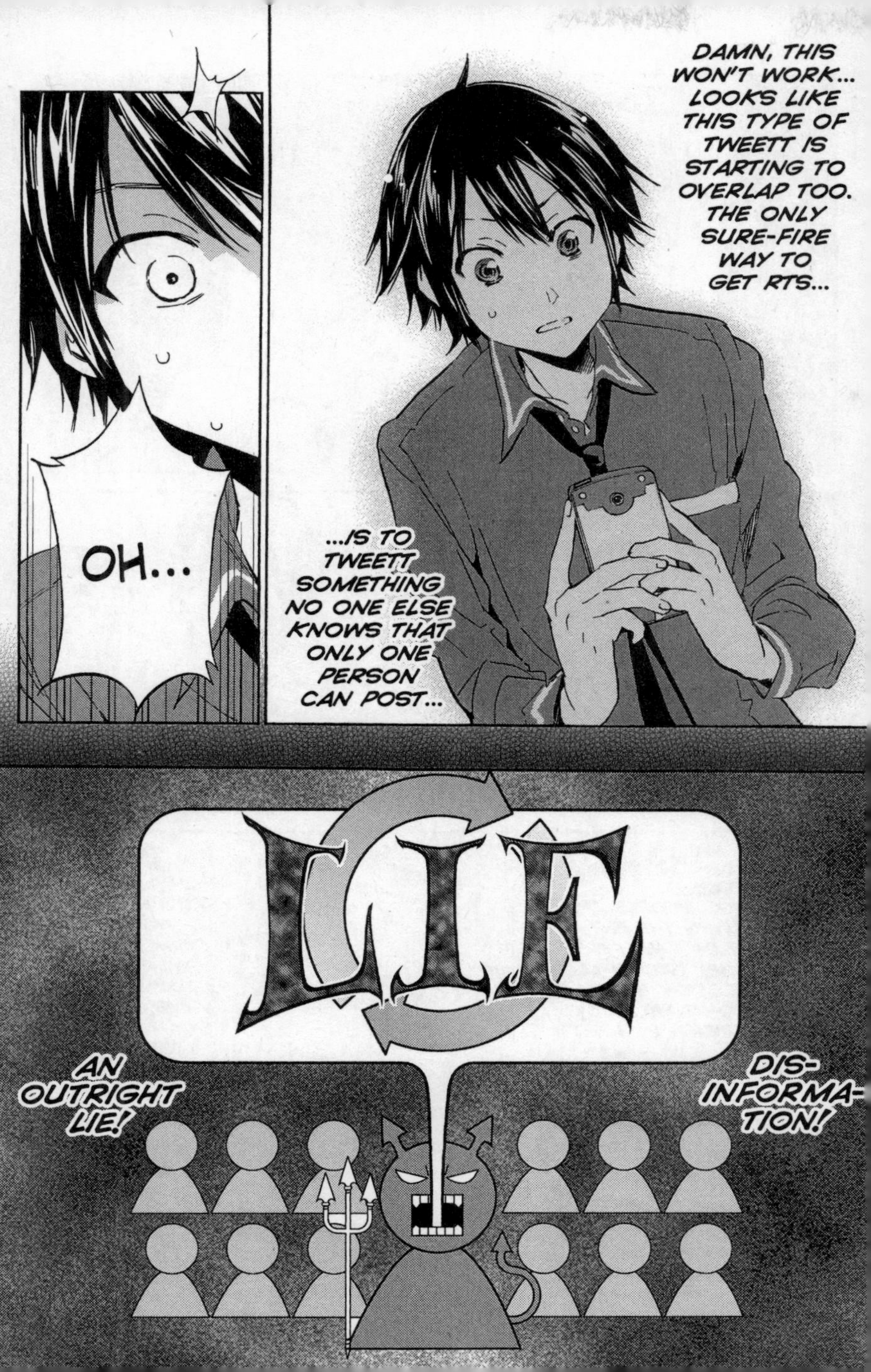
DAMN, THIS WON'T WORK... LOOKS LIKE THIS TYPE OF TWEETT IS STARTING TO OVERLAP TOO. THE ONLY SURE-FIRE WAY TO GET RTS...
...IS TO TWEETT SOMETHING NO ONE ELSE KNOWS THAT ONLY ONE PERSON CAN POST...
OH...
LIE
DIS-INFORMA-TION!
AN OUTRIGHT LIE!

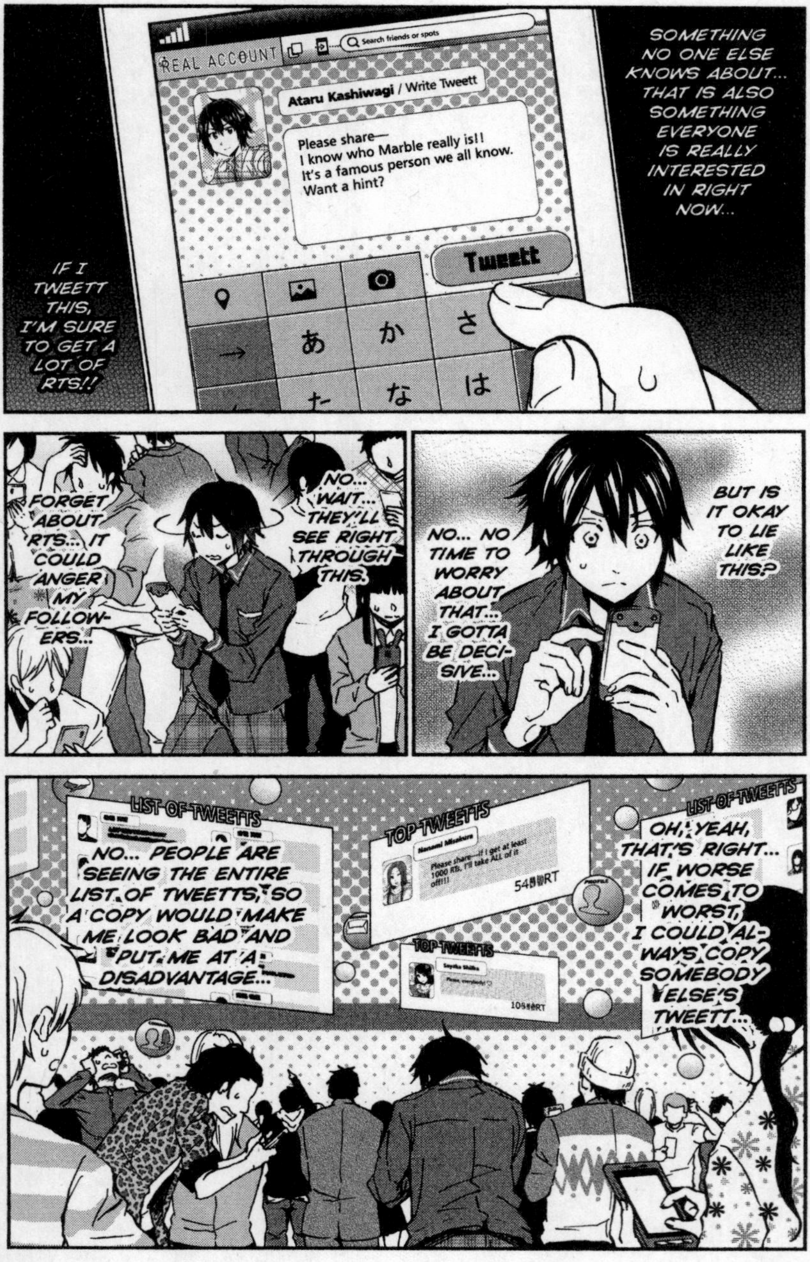
SOMETHING NO ONE ELSE KNOWS ABOUT... THAT IS ALSO SOMETHING EVERYONE IS REALLY INTERESTED IN RIGHT NOW...
REAL ACCOUNT
Search friends or spots
Ataru Kashiwagi / Write Tweett
Please share— I know who Marble really is!! It's a famous person we all know. Want a hint?
Tweett
あ か さ な は
IF I TWEETT THIS, I'M SURE TO GET A LOT OF RTS!!
BUT IS IT OKAY TO LIE LIKE THIS?
NO... NO TIME TO WORRY ABOUT THAT... I GOTTA BE DECISIVE...
NO... WAIT... THEY'LL SEE RIGHT THROUGH THIS.
FORGET ABOUT RTS... IT COULD ANGER MY FOLLOWERS...
LIST-OF-TWEETTS
OH, YEAH, THAT'S RIGHT... IF WORSE COMES TO WORST, I COULD ALWAYS COPY SOMEBODY ELSE'S TWEETT...
TOP-TWEETTS
Please share—If I get at least 1000 RTs, I'll take ALL of it off!!!
TOP-TWEETTS
LIST-OF-TWEETTS
NO... PEOPLE ARE SEEING THE ENTIRE LIST OF TWEETTS, SO A COPY WOULD MAKE ME LOOK BAD AND PUT ME AT A DISADVANTAGE...

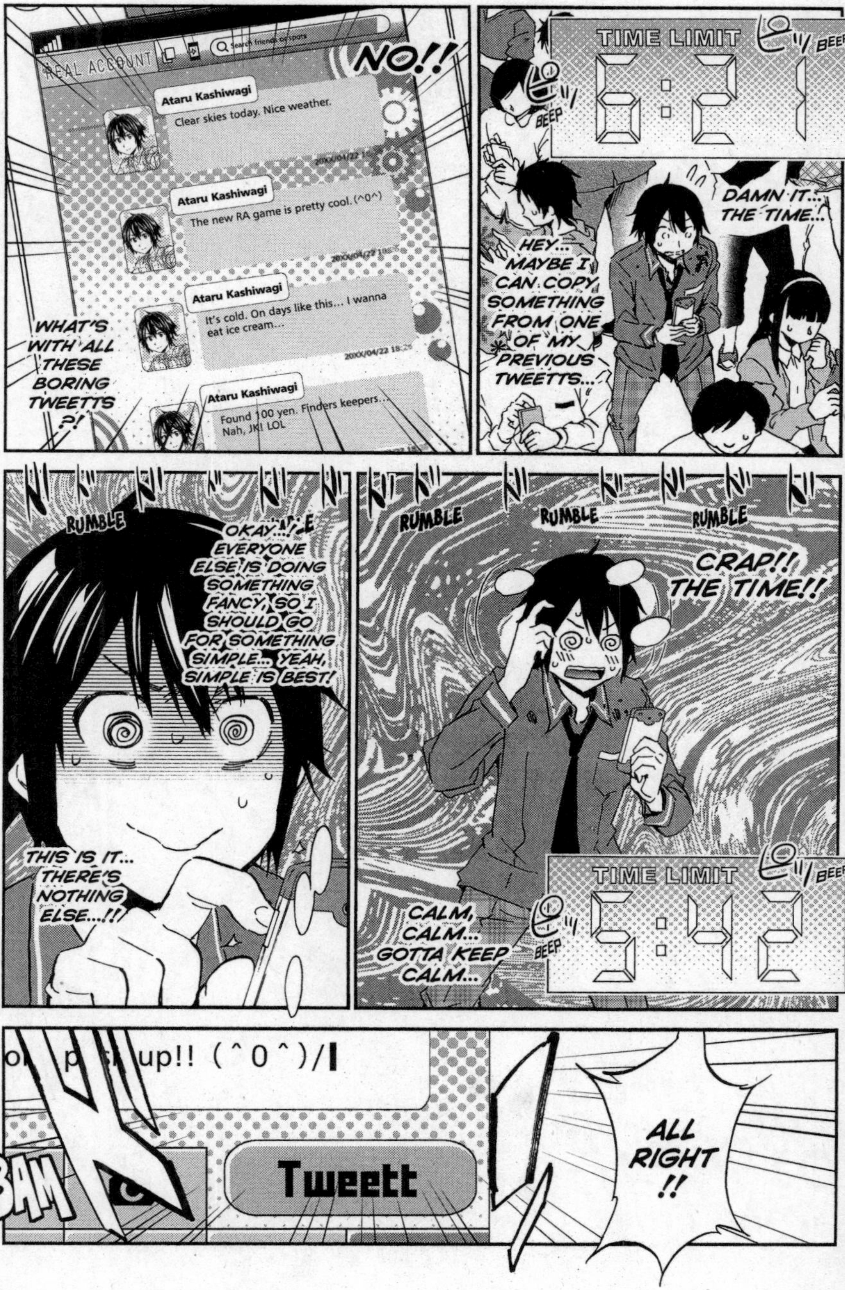
TIME LIMIT
6:21
BEEP
BEEP
DAMN IT... THE TIME...
HEY... MAYBE I CAN COPY SOMETHING FROM ONE OF MY PREVIOUS TWEETTS...
NO!!
REAL ACCOUNT
Ataru Kashiwagi
Clear skies today. Nice weather.
Ataru Kashiwagi
The new RA game is pretty cool. (^0^)
Ataru Kashiwagi
It's cold. On days like this... I wanna eat ice cream...
Ataru Kashiwagi
Found 100 yen. Finders keepers... Nah, JK! LOL
WHAT'S WITH ALL THESE BORING TWEETTS ?!
RUMBLE
RUMBLE
RUMBLE
CRAP!! THE TIME!!
CALM, CALM... GOTTA KEEP CALM...
TIME LIMIT
5:42
BEEP
BEEP
RUMBLE
OKAY...! EVERYONE ELSE IS DOING SOMETHING FANCY, SO I SHOULD GO FOR SOMETHING SIMPLE... YEAH, SIMPLE IS BEST!
THIS IS IT... THERE'S NOTHING ELSE...!!
ALL RIGHT !!
up!! (^0^)/
Tweett
BAM

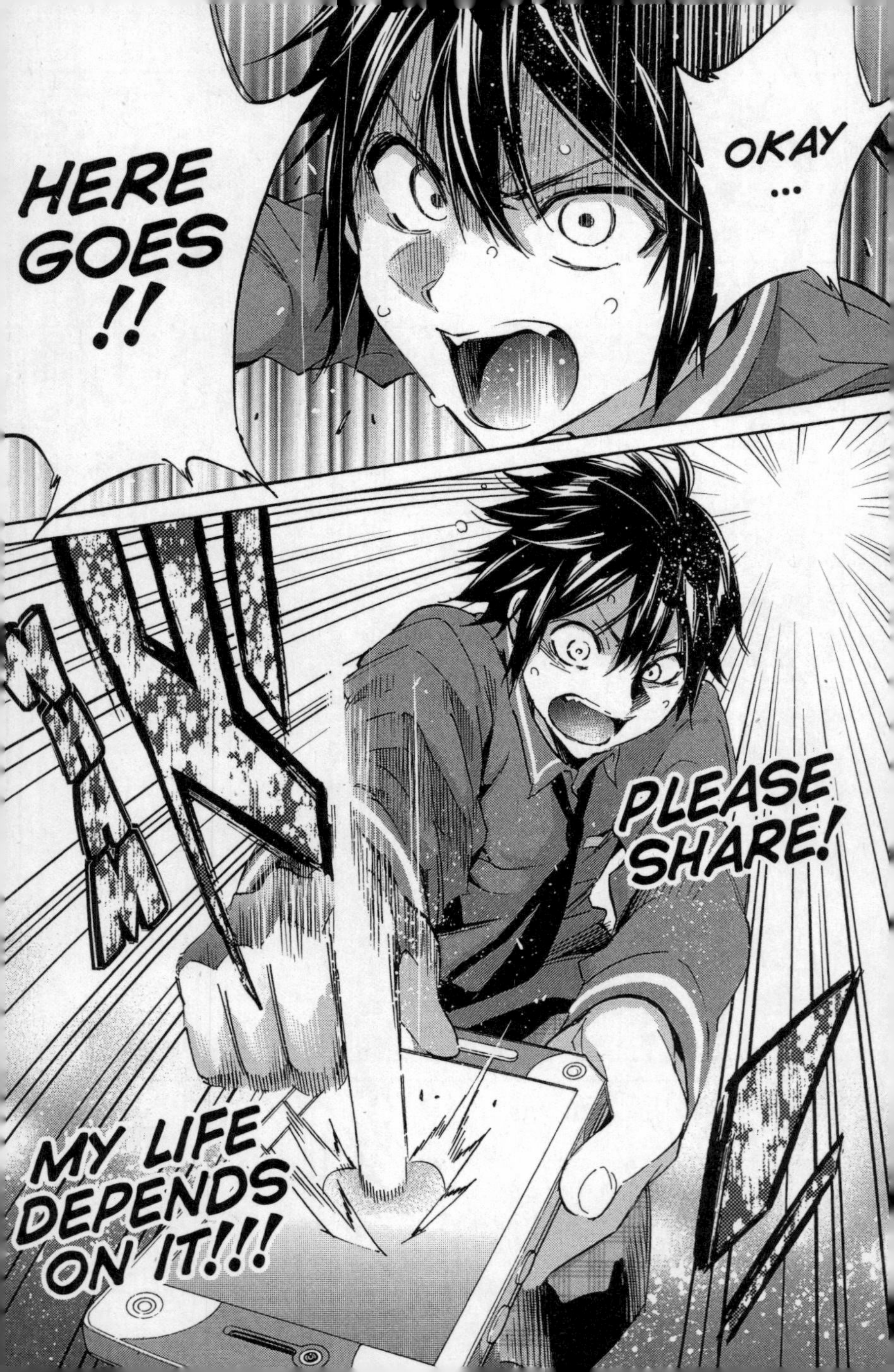
OKAY ...
HERE GOES !!
PLEASE SHARE!
MY LIFE DEPENDS ON IT!!!

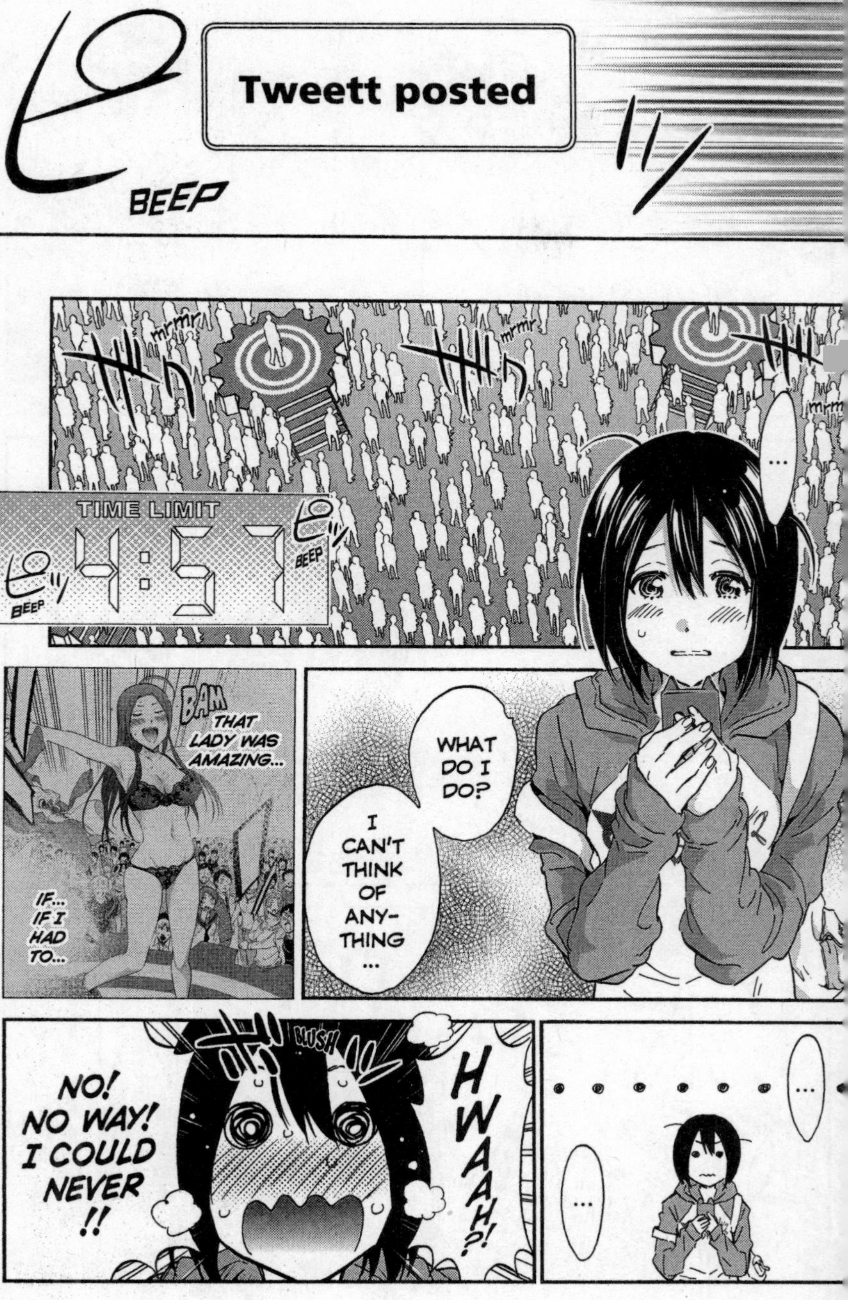

Tweett posted
BEEP
mrmr
mrmr
mrmr
...
TIME LIMIT
4:57
BEEP
BEEP
WHAT DO I DO?
I CAN'T THINK OF ANY-THING ...
BAM
THAT LADY WAS AMAZING...
IF... IF I HAD TO...
...
...
BLUSH
HWAAH?!
NO! NO WAY! I COULD NEVER !!

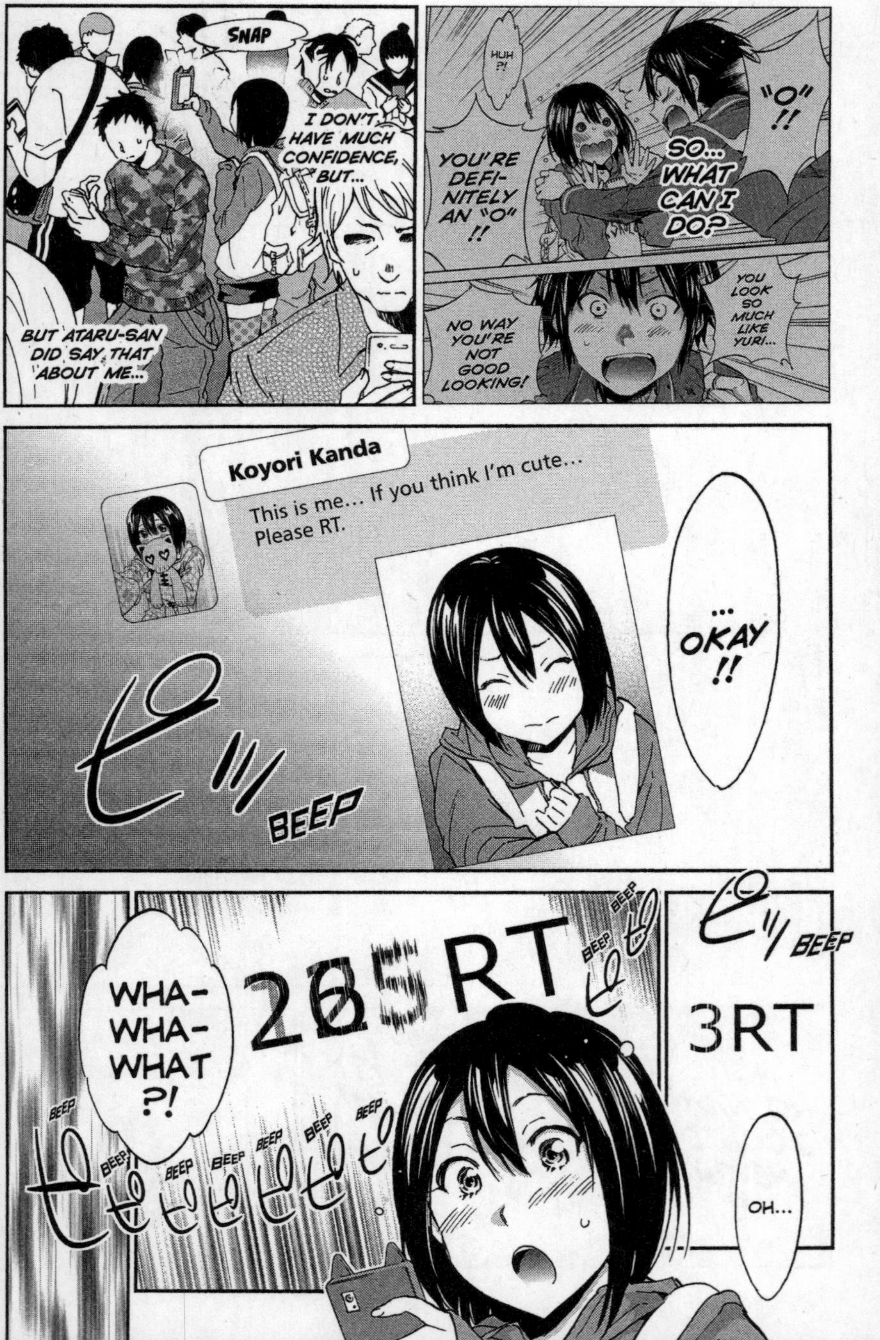
HUH ?!
"O" !!
SO... WHAT CAN I DO?
YOU'RE DEFINITELY AN "O" !!
YOU LOOK SO MUCH LIKE YURI...
NO WAY YOU'RE NOT GOOD LOOKING!
SNAP
I DON'T HAVE MUCH CONFIDENCE, BUT...
BUT ATARU-SAN DID SAY THAT ABOUT ME...
Koyori Kanda
This is me... If you think I'm cute... Please RT.
...OKAY !!
BEEP
BEEP
3RT
OH...
BEEP
RT
BEEP
BEEP
WHA- WHA- WHAT ?!
BEEP
BEEP
BEEP
BEEP
BEEP
BEEP
BEEP

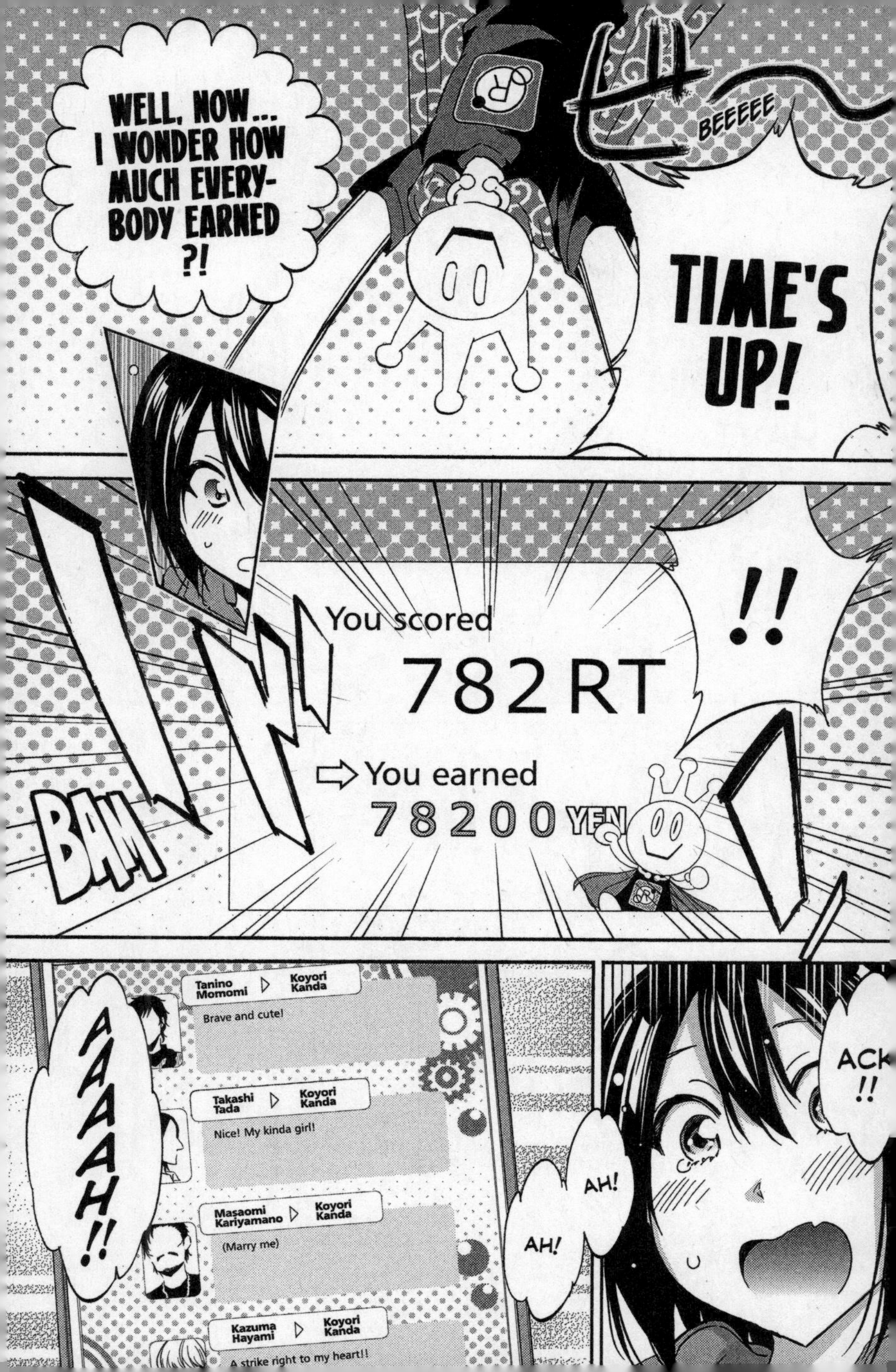
BEEEEE
TIME'S UP!
WELL, NOW... I WONDER HOW MUCH EVERY-BODY EARNED?!
!!
You scored
782 RT
You earned
78200 YEN
BAM
ACK!!
AH!
AH!
Tanino Momomi ▷ Koyori Kanda
Brave and cute!
Takashi Tada ▷ Koyori Kanda
Nice! My kinda girl!
Masaomi Kariyamano ▷ Koyori Kanda
(Marry me)
Kazuma Hayami ▷ Koyori Kanda
A strike right to my heart!!
AAAAH!!

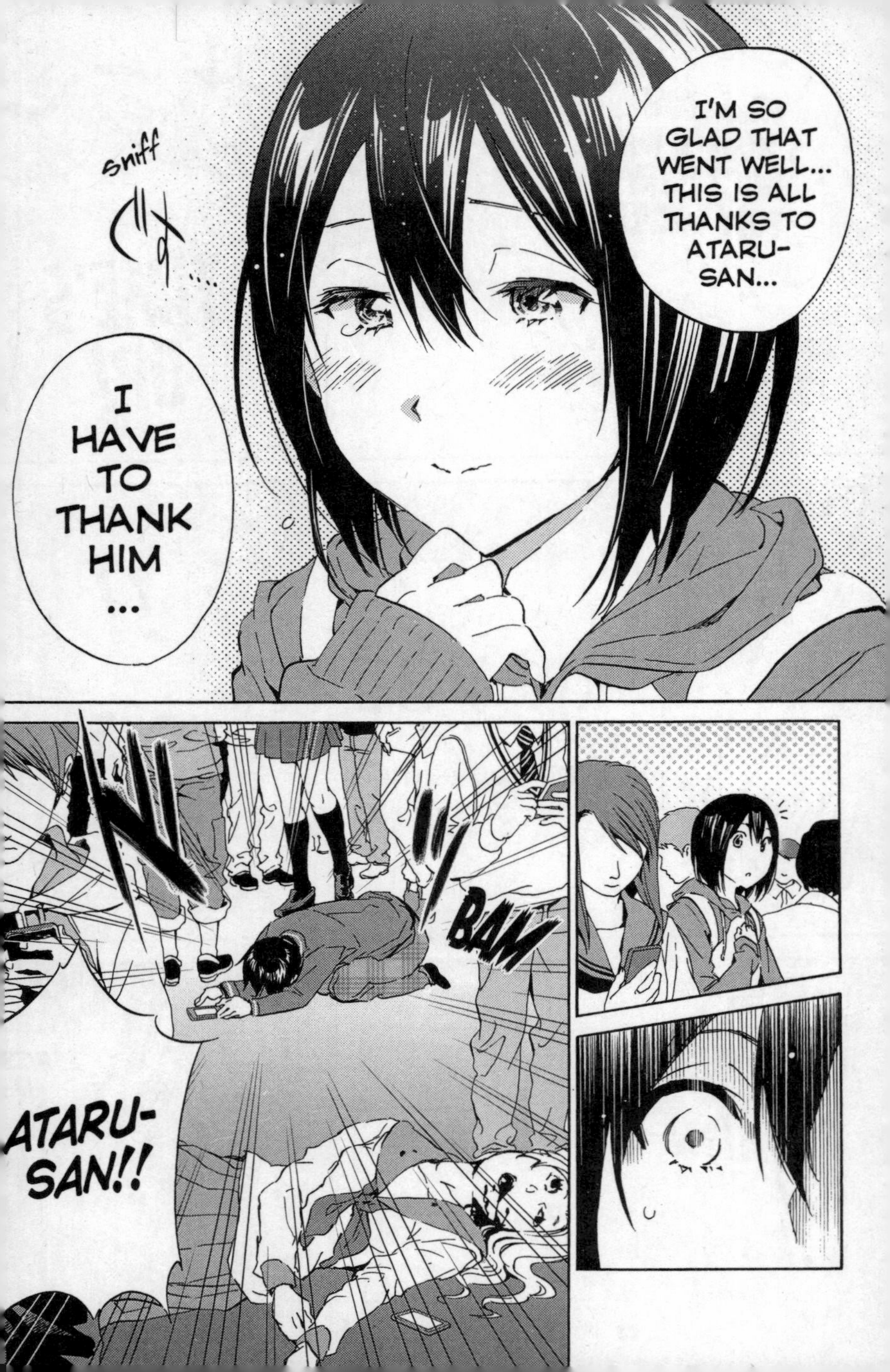
I'M SO GLAD THAT WENT WELL... THIS IS ALL THANKS TO ATARU-SAN...
sniff
...
I HAVE TO THANK HIM...
BAM
ATARU-SAN!!

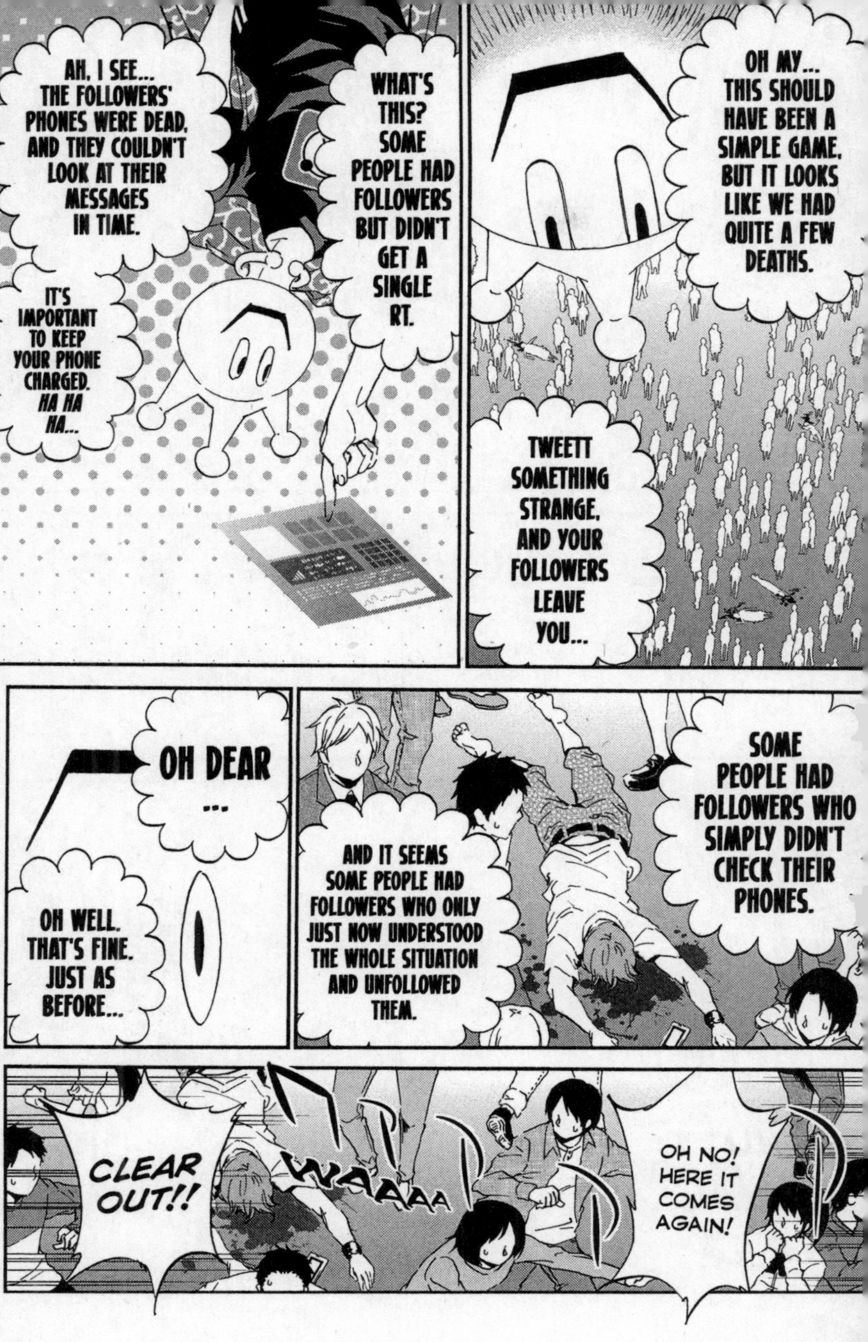
OH MY... THIS SHOULD HAVE BEEN A SIMPLE GAME, BUT IT LOOKS LIKE WE HAD QUITE A FEW DEATHS.
TWEETT SOMETHING STRANGE, AND YOUR FOLLOWERS LEAVE YOU...
WHAT'S THIS? SOME PEOPLE HAD FOLLOWERS BUT DIDN'T GET A SINGLE RT.
AH, I SEE... THE FOLLOWERS' PHONES WERE DEAD, AND THEY COULDN'T LOOK AT THEIR MESSAGES IN TIME.
IT'S IMPORTANT TO KEEP YOUR PHONE CHARGED. *HA HA HA...*
SOME PEOPLE HAD FOLLOWERS WHO SIMPLY DIDN'T CHECK THEIR PHONES.
AND IT SEEMS SOME PEOPLE HAD FOLLOWERS WHO ONLY JUST NOW UNDERSTOOD THE WHOLE SITUATION AND UNFOLLOWED THEM.
OH DEAR ...
OH WELL. THAT'S FINE. JUST AS BEFORE...
OH NO! HERE IT COMES AGAIN!
WAAAA
CLEAR OUT!!

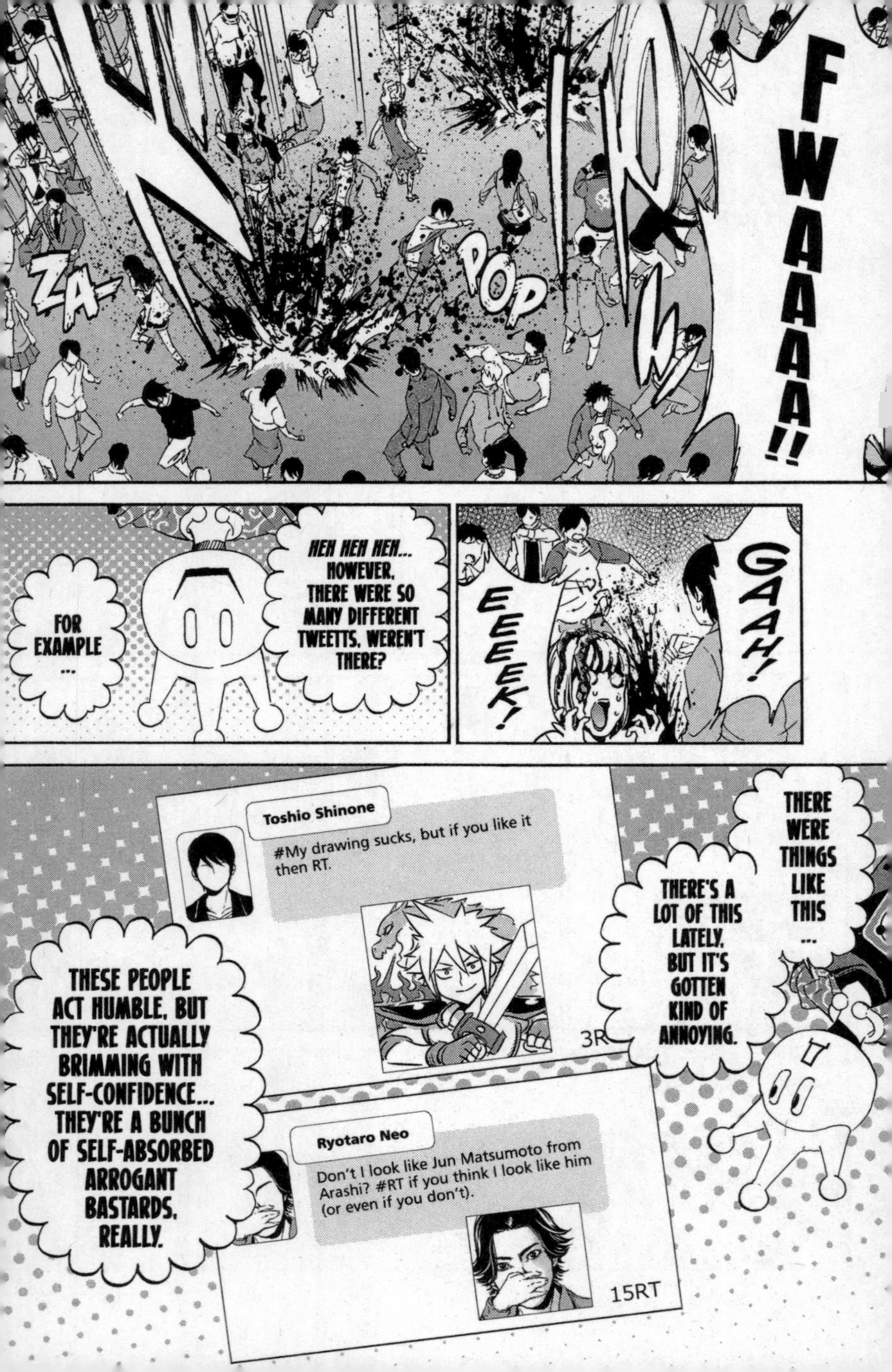
FWAAAA!!
POP
ZA
GAAH!
EEEEK!
HEH HEH HEH... HOWEVER, THERE WERE SO MANY DIFFERENT TWEETTS, WEREN'T THERE?
FOR EXAMPLE ...
THERE WERE THINGS LIKE THIS ...
THERE'S A LOT OF THIS LATELY, BUT IT'S GOTTEN KIND OF ANNOYING.
Toshio Shinone
#My drawing sucks, but if you like it then RT.
3R
Ryotaro Neo
Don't I look like Jun Matsumoto from Arashi? #RT if you think I look like him (or even if you don't).
15RT
THESE PEOPLE ACT HUMBLE, BUT THEY'RE ACTUALLY BRIMMING WITH SELF-CONFIDENCE... THEY'RE A BUNCH OF SELF-ABSORBED ARROGANT BASTARDS, REALLY.

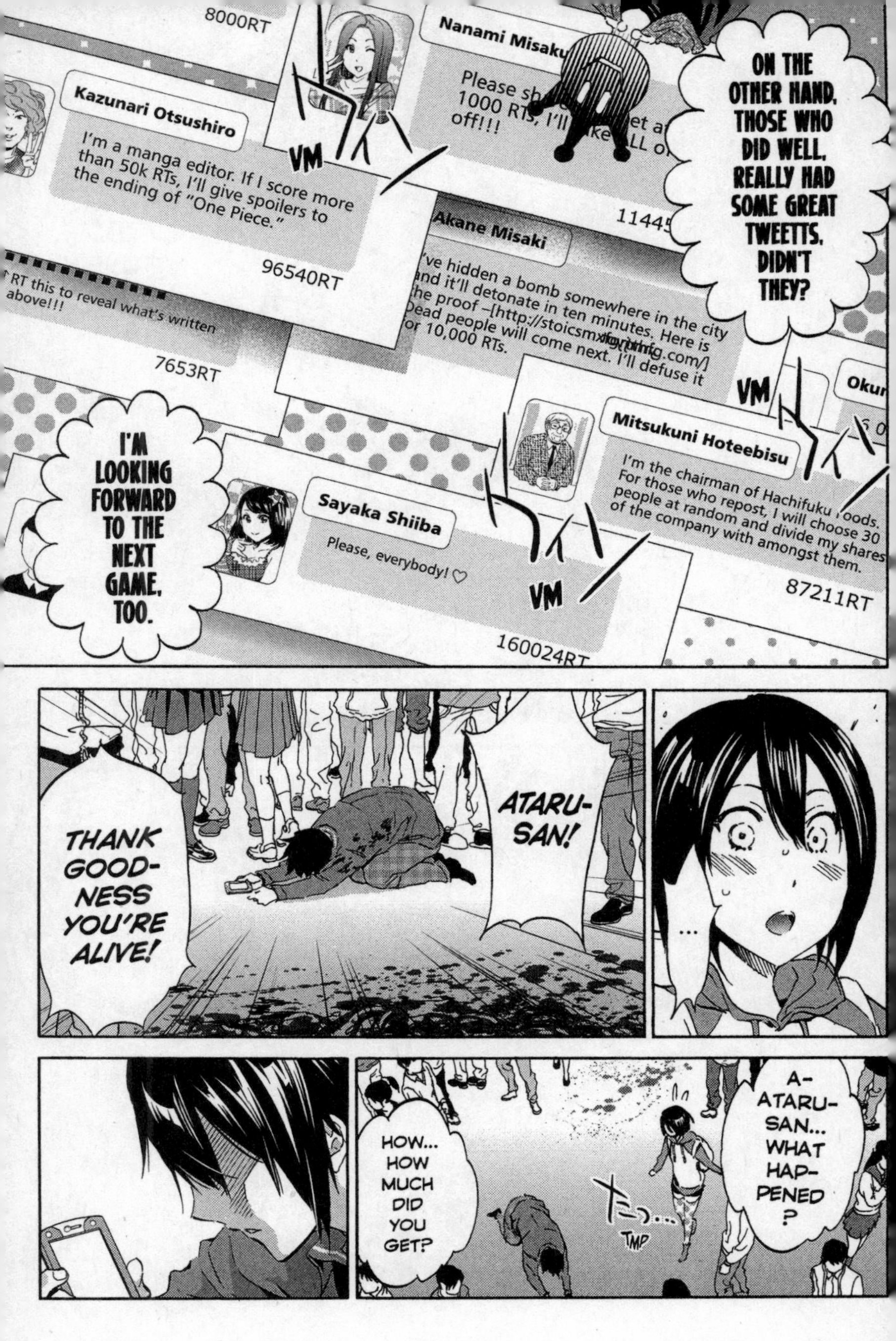

ON THE OTHER HAND, THOSE WHO DID WELL, REALLY HAD SOME GREAT TWEETTS, DIDN'T THEY?
Nanami Misaku
8000RT
VM
Kazunari Otsushiro
I'm a manga editor. If I score more than 50k RTs, I'll give spoilers to the ending of "One Piece."
96540RT
RT this to reveal what's written above!!!
7653RT
Akane Misaki
've hidden a bomb somewhere in the city and it'll detonate in ten minutes. Here is the proof –[http://stoicsmxforumfg.com/] Dead people will come next. I'll defuse it for 10,000 RTs.
VM
Mitsukuni Hoteebisu
I'm the chairman of Hachifuku Foods. For those who repost, I will choose 30 people at random and divide my shares of the company with amongst them.
87211RT
VM
Sayaka Shiiba
Please, everybody! ♡
160024RT
I'M LOOKING FORWARD TO THE NEXT GAME, TOO.
...
ATARU-SAN!
THANK GOODNESS YOU'RE ALIVE!
A-ATARU-SAN... WHAT HAPPENED?
TMP
HOW... HOW MUCH DID YOU GET?

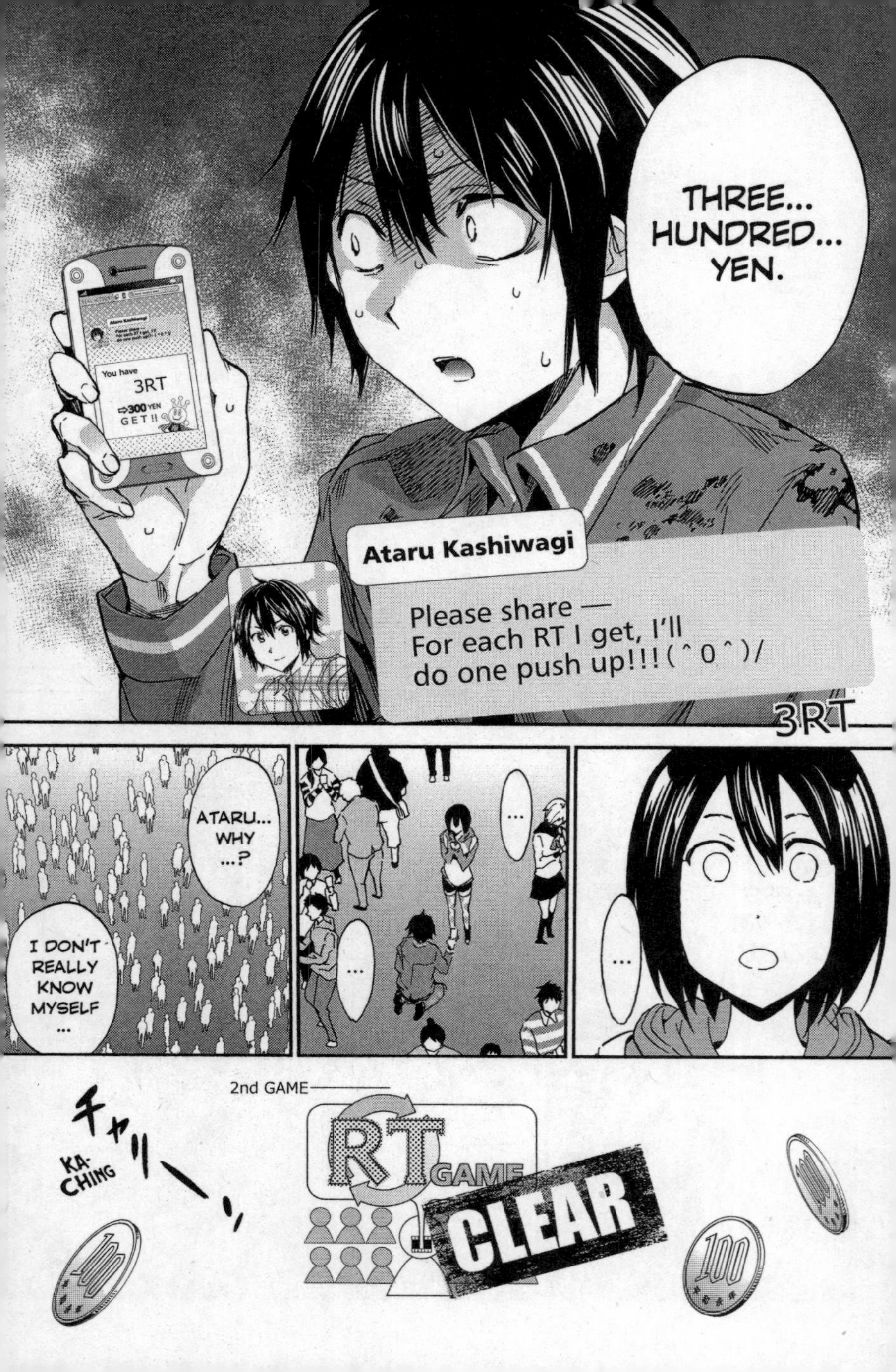
THREE... HUNDRED... YEN.
You have
3RT
⇨300 YEN
GET!!
Ataru Kashiwagi
Please share —
For each RT I get, I'll
do one push up!!!(^0^)/
3RT
...
...
...
ATARU... WHY ...?
I DON'T REALLY KNOW MYSELF ...
2nd GAME
RT GAME
CLEAR
チャリーン
KA-CHING

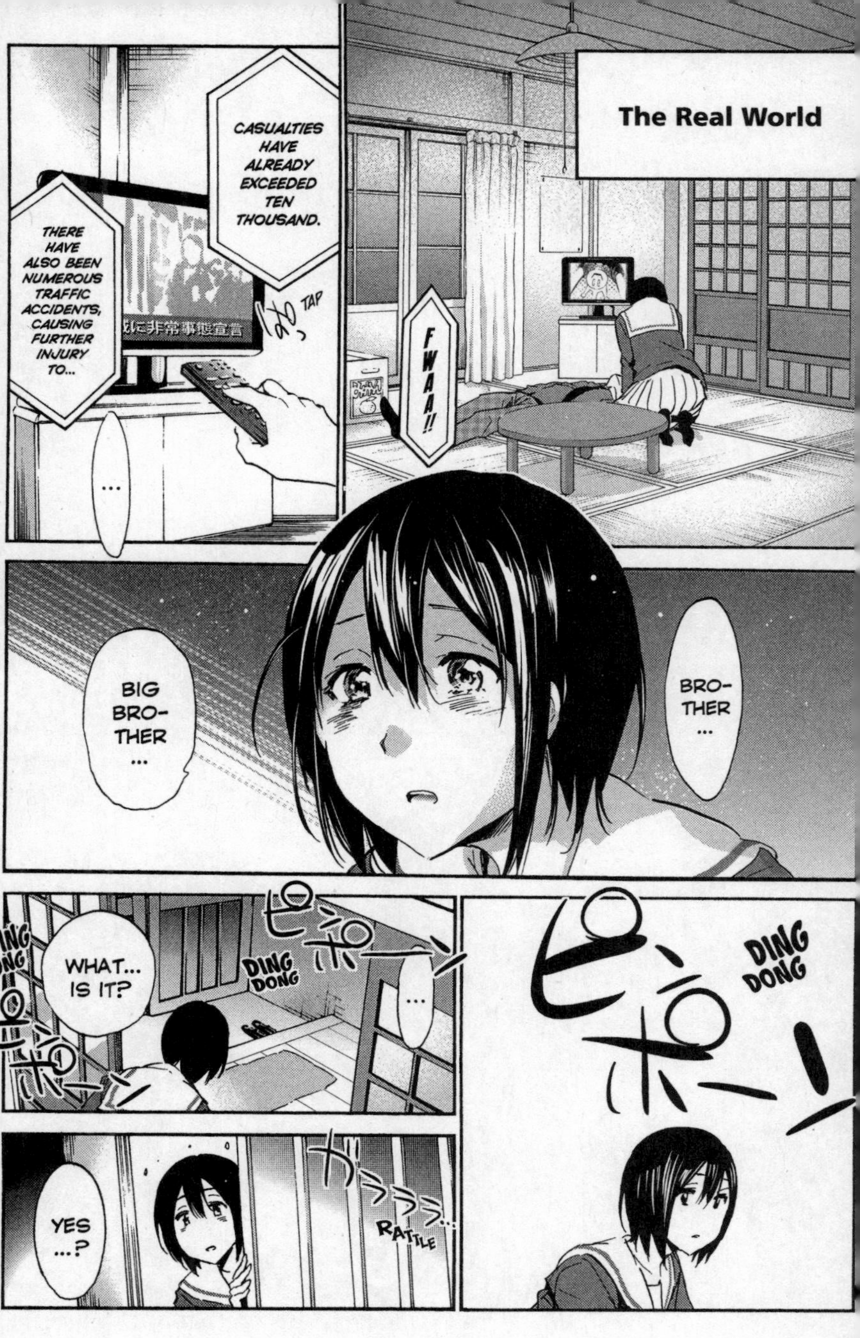
The Real World
FWAA!!
CASUALTIES HAVE ALREADY EXCEEDED TEN THOUSAND.
THERE HAVE ALSO BEEN NUMEROUS TRAFFIC ACCIDENTS, CAUSING FURTHER INJURY TO...
に非常事態宣言
TAP
...
BROTHER...
BIG BROTHER...
ピンポーン
DING DONG
ピンポーン
DING DONG
...
WHAT... IS IT?
DING DONG
ピンポーン
ガラララ...
RATTLE
YES...?

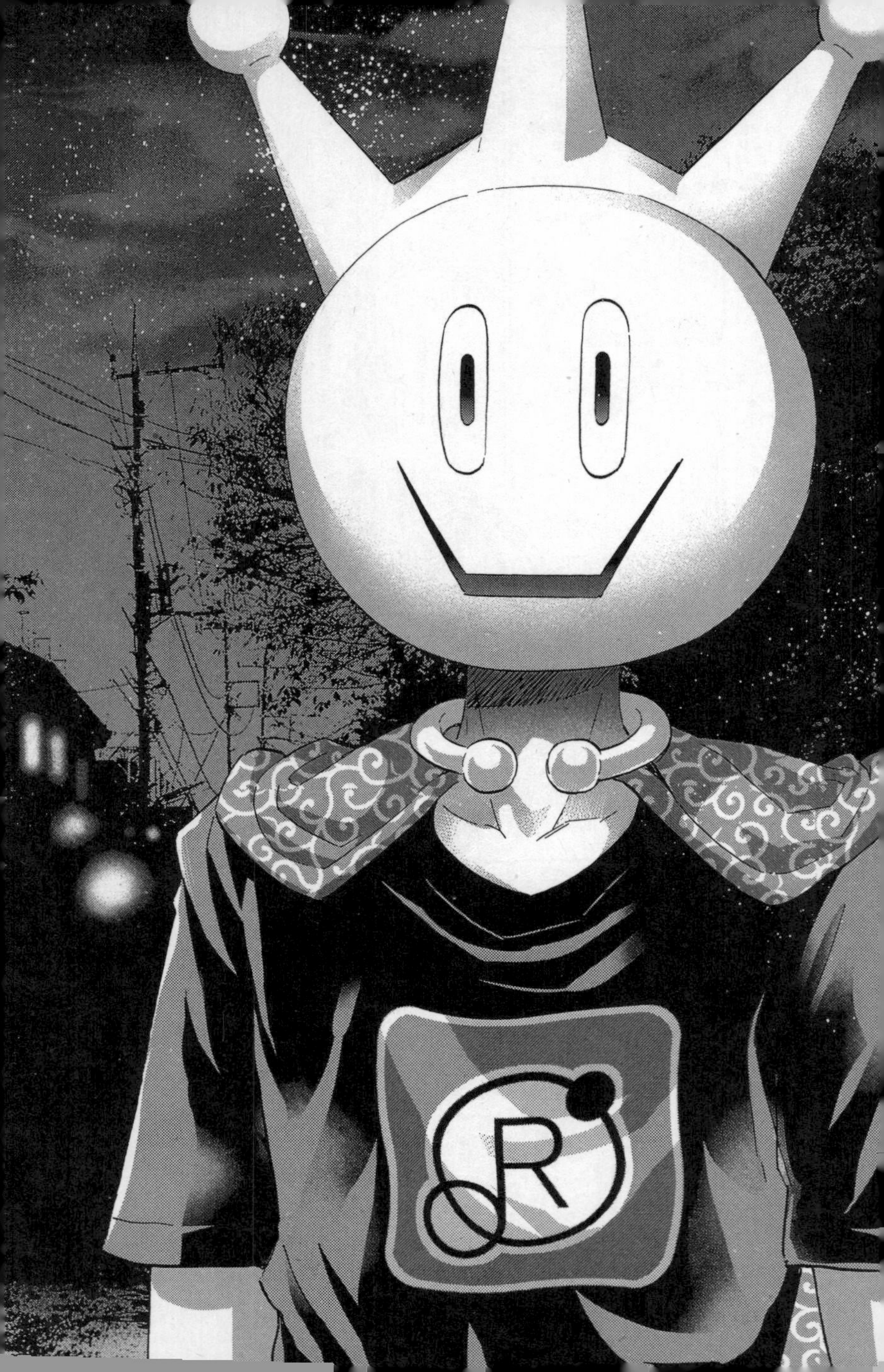

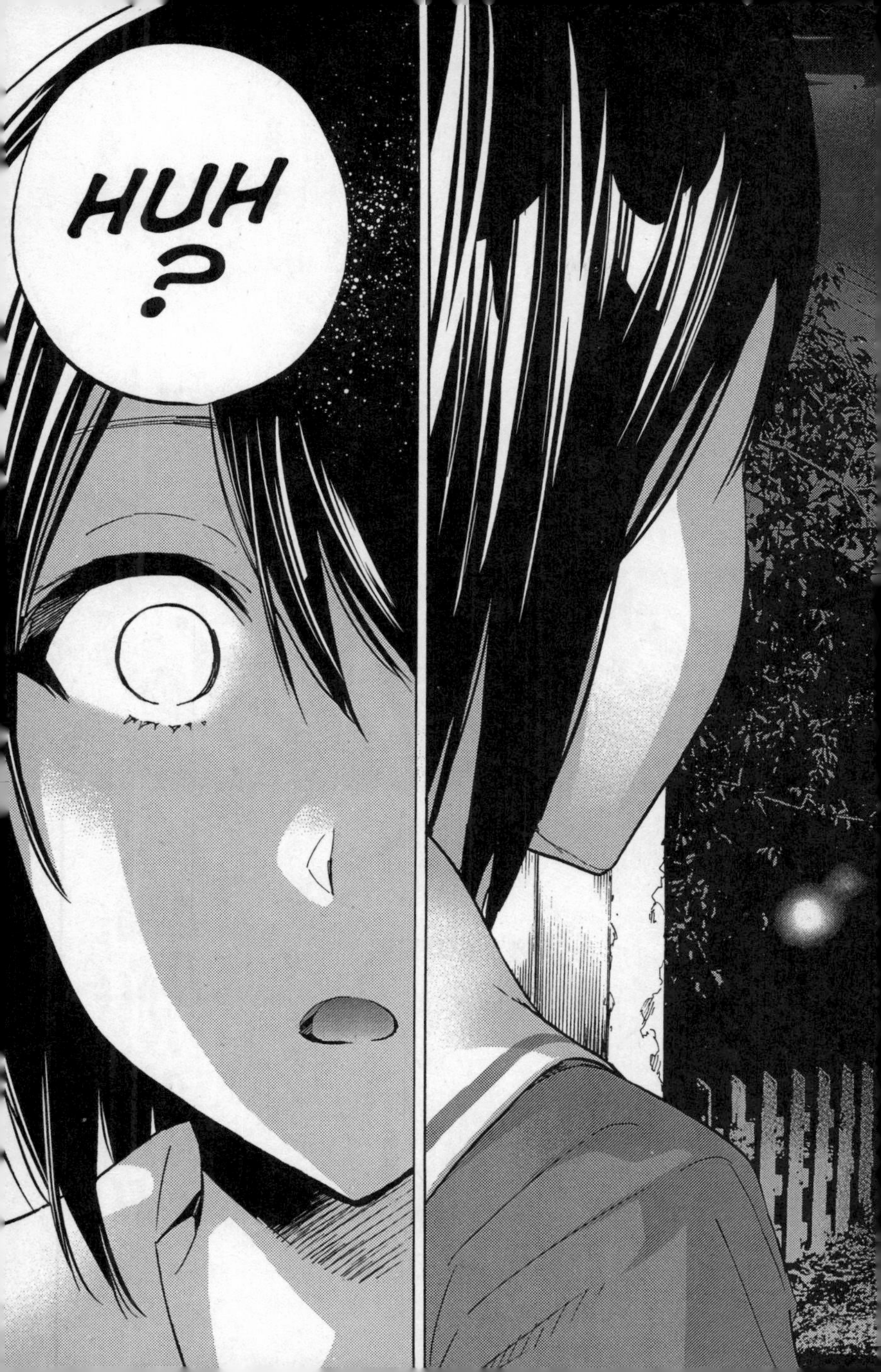
HUH?

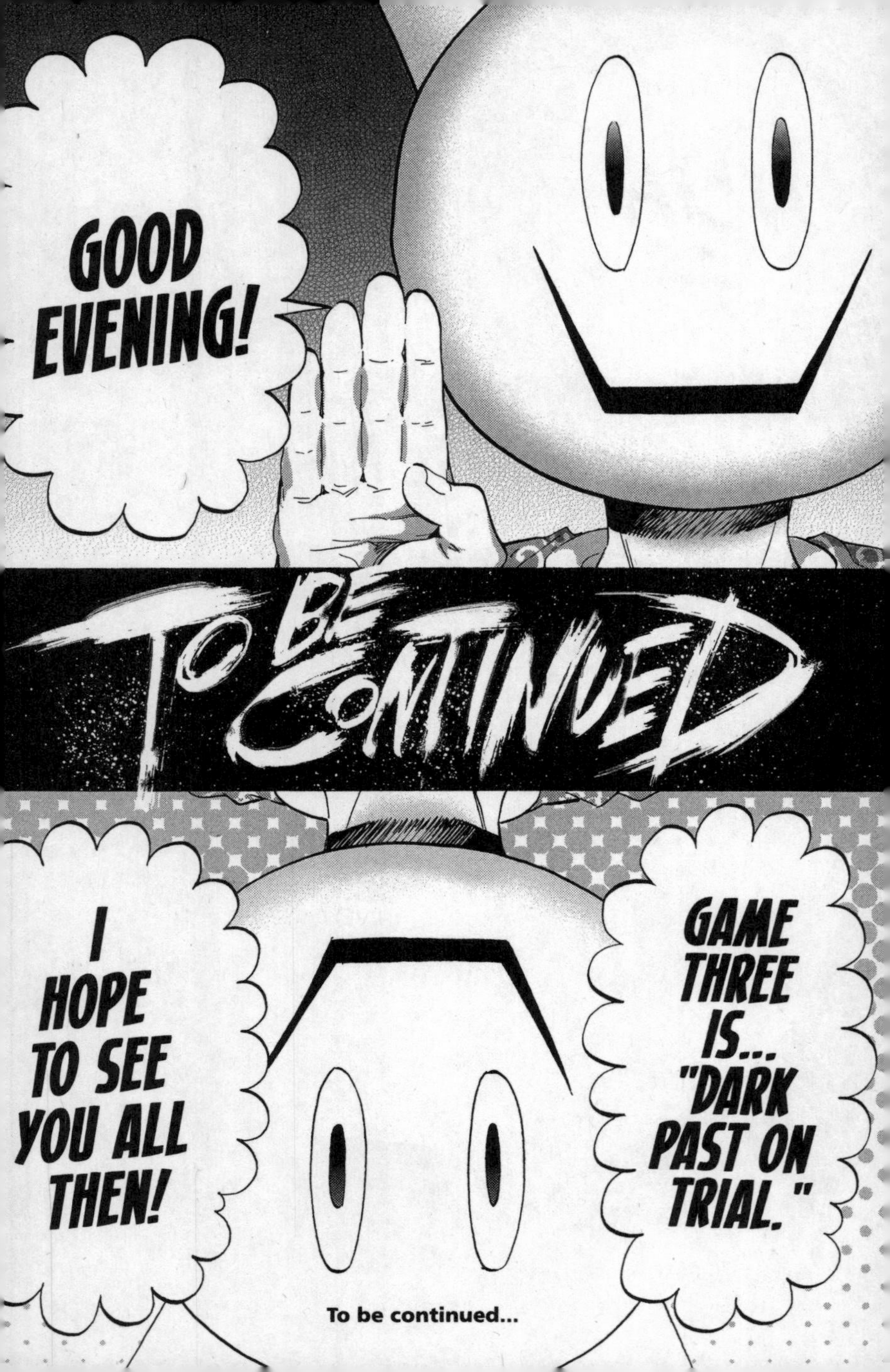
GOOD EVENING!
TO BE CONTINUED
GAME THREE IS... "DARK PAST ON TRIAL."
I HOPE TO SEE YOU ALL THEN!

To be continued...

REAL ACCOUNT

STAFF PAGE

STAFF
Naomi Sekiguchi
Mio Otsuka
Kimiko Kinkai
Shotaro Kunitomo
Tsuyoshi Yamamoto
Iyo Mori
Shotaro Edogawa

STAFF
Akoron
Yoneko Takemoto

EDITOR
Kzauhiko Otoguro

Hideki Morooka
(Japanese GN)

COVER DESIGN
Tadashi Hisamochi
(HIVE) (Japanese edition)

Artist:
Shizumu Watanabe
Twitter account: @shizumukun

This story had a strong impact on me. When I first read it, I thought, "What would I do if I were in this situation?" I think that's what makes this manga so appealing. "What would I do if I were in this situation?" It would make me happy if everybody read this with that question in their mind.

Author:
Okushou
Twitter account @okushou

This is my first ever compilation volume!! I've put so many different feelings into this work. I'm sure that depending on the reader, what you think and feel will be different, and you may agree or disagree with some things, but I'm happy as long as this manga leaves some kind of impression on the hearts of those who read it. I'm waiting to hear your thoughts on it.

BONUS PAGE

by Okushou

◎ Nice to meet you! I'm Okushou, the creator of Real Account. First, I would like to say thank you so much to everyone who bought this book. Also, I would like to say that I am indebted to the artist of this series, Watanabe-sensei, my editor, and so many other people for all your help— I am truly thankful for the fact that we somehow got this volume out... Please support us and cheer us on so that we may draw this manga perfectly until the "end." Yeah!

\\ "٩('ω')و"//

I WON'T LET YOU GO HOME TONIGHT.

☆ special thanks ☆ (in no particular order)

To all our readers, S.M.-sama, Maa-kun, Shimizu Yusuke-sama, Umiu-sama, Dad, Mom, my sibling, Grandpa, Grandma, my cousins, Y.Y.-sama, M.A.-sama, Ikoma-sama, etc...

To everyone, that helps me out on a daily basis.

etc ---.

Translation Notes

PAGE 83

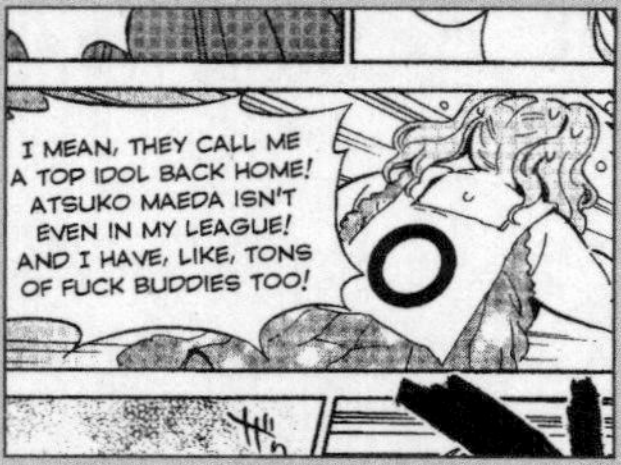
I MEAN, THEY CALL ME A TOP IDOL BACK HOME! ATSUKO MAEDA ISN'T EVEN IN MY LEAGUE! AND I HAVE, LIKE, TONS OF FUCK BUDDIES TOO!

Atsuko Maeda

The former top member of the 48-member idol group AKB 48. She graduated (retired) from the group in 2012 and currently continues her career as a solo singer and actress.

PAGE 7

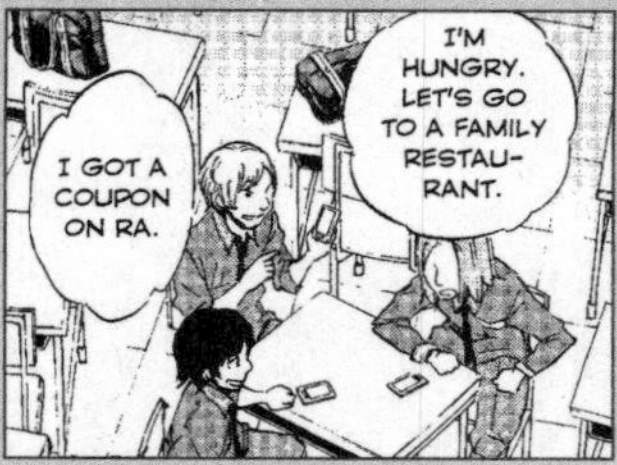
I'M HUNGRY. LET'S GO TO A FAMILY RESTAU-RANT.
I GOT A COUPON ON RA.

Family Restaurant

A family restaurant or *famiresu* is a chain restaurant that is inexpensive, but with food quality and service a step above fast food. Some famous Japanese family restaurants are Jonathan's, Saizeriya, and Royal Host.

PAGE 117

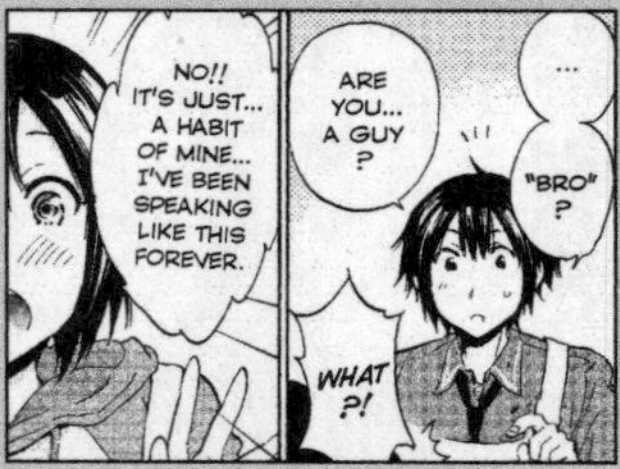
...
"BRO" ?
ARE YOU... A GUY ?
WHAT ?!
NO!! IT'S JUST... A HABIT OF MINE... I'VE BEEN SPEAKING LIKE THIS FOREVER.

Koyori's speech pattern

In the Japanese, Ataru wonders if Koyori is a guy after hearing her use *"boku." Boku* is a first-person pronoun primarily used by boys. It can be used by girls as well, but it's mostly used by sporty girls or tomboys.

PAGE 93

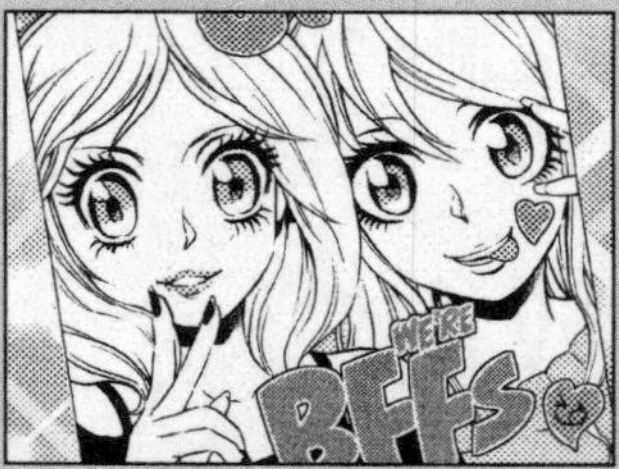
WE'RE BFFS

Purikura

Short for Print Club. *Purikura* are specialized photo booths that are a regular pastime for many teenage girls in Japan. They often include themes and various filters or effects to do things like make the participants' eyes look bigger or make their skin look paler.

PAGE 170

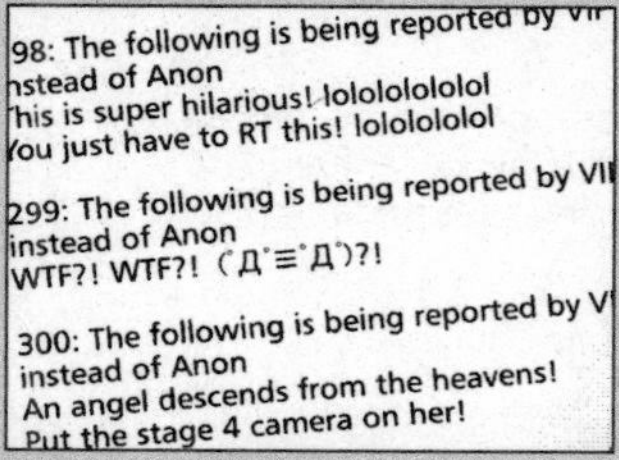
98: The following is being reported
nstead of Anon
his is super hilarious! lolololololol
ou just have to RT this! lololololol
299: The following is being reported by
instead of Anon
WTF?! WTF?! (ﾟДﾟ≡ﾟДﾟ)?!
300: The following is being reported by
instead of Anon
An angel descends from the heavens!
Put the stage 4 camera on her!

2chan and VIPPERS

2channel or 2chan is the most famous text-based message board in Japan. The majority of Japanese net-speak originates from 2ch users and the posts and culture of 2ch have often been at the center of controversy. VIPPERS are 2ch users who visit and primarily use a subsection of 2ch cal News4VIP. News4VIP is similar to 4chan's /b/ board and VIPPERS are equivalent to /b/tards.

PAGE 164

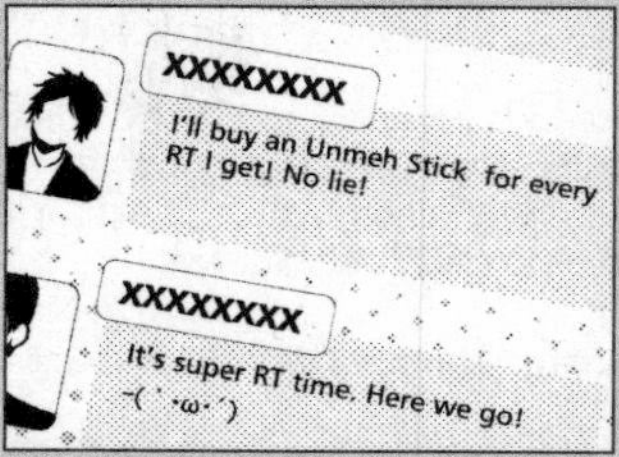
XXXXXXXX
I'll buy an Unmeh Stick for every RT I get! No lie!
XXXXXXXX
It's super RT time. Here we go!
~(´･ω･`)

Unmeh Stick

This is a parody of a real product called *Umaibou* (delicious stick). *Umaibou* are puffed-corn snacks that come in a variety of flavors from corn soup to salami and even beef tongue. They are popular with young children due to their cheap price at about ten cents per stick.

PAGE 185

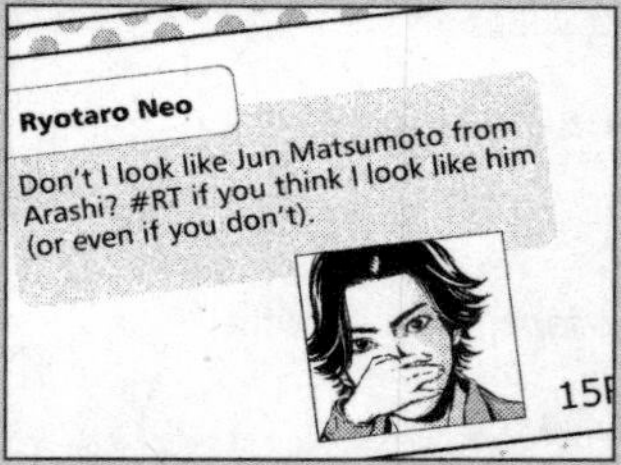
Ryotaro Neo
Don't I look like Jun Matsumoto from Arashi? #RT if you think I look like him (or even if you don't).

Jun Matsumoto & Arashi

Jun Matsumoto (nickname: MatsuJun) is a Japanese heartthrob and member of the boy band Arashi. Arashi is produced by Johnny & Associates, which is the most famous talent agency for boy bands, having created a multitude of successful acts including SMAP, KinKi Kids, and KAT-TUN.

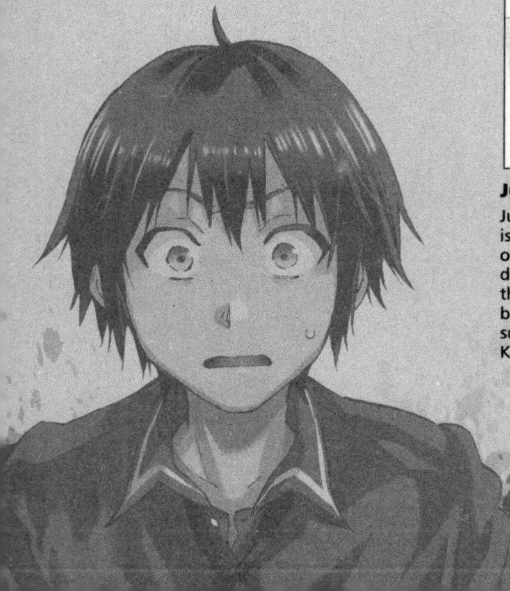

A Kodansha Comics Trade Paperback Original.

Real Account volume 1 copyright © 2014 Okushou/Shizumu Watanabe
English translation copyright © 2016 Okushou/Shizumu Watanabe

All rights reserved.

Published in the United States by Kodansha Comics,
an imprint of Kodansha USA Publishing, LLC, New York.

Publication rights for this English edition arranged through Kodansha Ltd., Tokyo.

First published in Japan in 2014 by Kodansha Ltd., Tokyo, as *Real Account* volume 1.

ISBN 978-1-63236-234-6

Printed in the United States of America.

www.kodanshacomics.com

9 8 7 6 5 4 3 2 1

Translation: Jonathan Tarbox & Kazuko Shimizu
Lettering: Evan Hayden
Editing: Ajani Oloye
Kodansha Comics Edition Cover Design: Phil Balsman